Ultralights

The Early British Classics

Ultralights

The Early British Classics
by Richard T Riding

PSL

Patrick Stephens
Wellingborough, Northamptonshire

First published in 1987

British Library Cataloguing in Publication Data

Riding, Richard T.
   Ultralights : the early British classics.
   1. Airplanes—History   2. Aeronautics—Great
Britain—History
   I. Title
   629.133'340426   TL685.1

ISBN 0-85059-748-X

*Patrick Stephens Limited is part of the
Thorsons Publishing Group*

Printed and bound in Great Britain

Contents

Foreword By A.R. Ward, co-designer of the Chilton DW 1.

I came to be interested in ultra-light aeroplanes at the end of 1935. My friend Andrew Dalrymple and I had been students at the de Havilland Technical School at Hatfield and we wondered to what use we could put our new aeronautical training. It occurred to us that by using all the latest know-how we could build an ultra-light that was something more like a real aeroplane, but in miniature. It would have a higher wing loading and, with a cruising speed of 100 mph, would have a better performance than existing ultra-lights. In addition we wanted to get away from the common practice of using converted motor cycle engines, which were very rough to fly behind and were generally of questionable reliability. These engines fitted to ultra-lights provoked C.G. Grey, *The Aeroplane*'s very outspoken editor, to label ultra-light aircraft as 'pop bottles'.

Our initial choice of engine was the Ford 10 car engine which Sir John Carden had converted for aero use. It ran very smoothly, was basically reliable but was very heavy for its power. The result of our efforts was the Chilton DW 1. Later we fitted a French Train engine which resulted in a more streamlined appearance and an increase in performance of nearly ten per cent more than we had calculated, though this may have been due to the highly-polished cellulose finish given to the wings in place of the standard silver.

Having designed an aeroplane that did all that we asked, our next task was to encourage other people to fly it and approve of it. At first people used to look at the Chilton and admit that they were wary of flying it because it was so small. I feel the same way about today's microlight aircraft, but then I am fifty years older! I imagine that most instructors breathe a sigh of relief when their pupils land safely after a first solo. Our problem was that every pilot's first flight in the Chilton was a first solo, as no dual could be given in a similar aircraft. This was further complicated by the fact that the majority of club pilots, and instructors, had been trained on biplanes and still flew them, and had never before flown a monoplane equipped with flaps. Nor were they used to the slightest rotation on take-off: they tended to proceed relentlessly across the field towards the far hedge without any attempt being made to take off. In addition, with the much lower drag characteristics of a monoplane, new pilots had difficulty in reducing speed sufficiently in order to use the flaps. It was also a problem judging landings, which were made some two or three feet lower than when flying a larger machine. Whilst this was not very good for one's nerves, it was nothing compared to watching a well-known Squadron Leader who once rolled a Chilton on its final approach over trees!

We saw the flying clubs as the main market for our single-seater. In it, club members would be able to put in solo cross-country hours towards their licences relatively cheaply and in a fully aerobatic aircraft that had a range of 500 miles cruising at 100 mph. We were in the process of negotiating a sizeable order for the Chilton when war put a stop to everything, including planned developments of the type.

Then, as now, the main obstacle to the impecunious potential private pilot was the high cost of putting in the necessary number of solo hours. The Chilton would have solved that particular problem, much as accumulating hours on today's microlights can be a cheap way of amassing hours towards achieving a Private Pilot's Licence. Today, I feel envious of the use of modern materials, double curvatures, bubble canopies, engines with wonderful power-to-weight ratios, etc. But fifty years ago we too were using the most modern methods available.

Of course Dalrymple and I were not the only people building ultra-light aircraft. Richard Riding's book covers a further ninety-odd types which were built and flown during that twenty-year inter-war period; an era in which British aviation was prolific in every area.

To

Nicholas Comper, creator of the Comper Swift, tragically killed in a Hythe street in June 1939.

Preface

It was in 1984 that Patrick Stephens Ltd approached me with the idea of producing a book around a series of articles first published in *Aeroplane Monthly*. Since 1976 this journal has been running an occasional series entitled *British pre-war ultra-light aircraft*, covering sixty types. Not all of them could strictly be termed ultralights, and the series was by no means exhaustive. Rather than publish an incomplete collection of articles, it needed little effort on my part to persuade the publishers to go the whole hog and produce a book covering most of the British ultra-light aircraft produced during the inter-war years. But first it was necessary to decide what constituted an ultra-light.

During the early years any aircraft that puttered around the skies on less than 40 hp was considered an ultra-light. The post-war Ultra-light Aircraft Association defined ultra-lights as aircraft with an all-up weight of no more than 1,000 lb, powered by engines of up to 75 hp and having a landing speed of no more than 40 mph. For the purpose of this book I have limited coverage to aircraft of no more than 1,000 lb all-up weight, give or take a few pounds. Though this effectively excludes such types as the DH 60 Moth, it embraces such lightplanes as the proto-type Blackburn Bluebird and Westland Widgeon, both of which fall just inside this weight limit.

This book describes some ninety types and variants, including most but not all of the ultra-light aircraft built in Britain between 1919 and 1939. Some, though, are foreign designs built in Britain in modified form under licence, such as the Aeronca C-3, Praga E 114, Mignet HM 14 and Tipsy B. Of the ninety, about sixty per cent were one-offs. Established aircraft manufacturers accounted for around 72 per cent of the designs whilst amateur groups and individuals make up the remaining 28 per cent. Although we are talking about ninety types, the total number of airframes built amounted to less than 500 units — including the Mignet Flying Flea, which accounted for about a sixth of that total.

Of the original sixty types covered in the *Aeroplane Monthly* articles only 25 appear here in the original published form; most of these cover the 1923-24 Lympne trials aircraft. Nineteen types have been excluded because they fall outside the weight limitation and twenty types have been re-written especially for this book. In addition a further 45 aircraft are described for the first time.

The aircraft are described in chronological order. Little attempt has been made to list every registration and construction number, or to record every individual aircraft built. Such information has been comprehensively assembled by the late A.J. Jackson in his three-volume masterpiece *British Civil Aircraft since 1919,* published by Putnam & Company Ltd; volumes that no serious student of the subject should be without. Many of the aircraft described are accompanied by three-view drawings previously published in *Flight, The Aeroplane* and *Aeroplane Monthly*, for which I gratefully acknowledge the co-operation of Business Press International Ltd.

The story of the British pre-war ultra-light is hardly a success story; nevertheless, I feel that the work of a dedicated band of professional and amateur enthusiasts should not be forgotten. The reader will come across certain names time and time again — names such as Frank Barnwell, L.F. Baynes, Sir John Carden, Flight Lieutenant Nicholas Comper, C.H. Latimer-Needham and A.R. Weyl. It is to the enthusiasm and devotion of men such as these that I have dedicated this book.

Richard Riding
Radlett,
June 1986

Acknowledgements

The author gratefully acknowledges the assistance of a number of individuals during the preparation of this book. Though it is not possible to name all of them special thanks are extended to the following:

Miss Elaine Jones, manager of the Quadrant Picture Library, which now houses the photographic collections of both *Flight* and *The Aeroplane*, from which many of the illustrations for this book were obtained. Prints from most of the photographs and drawings credited to *Flight, The Aeroplane* and *Aeroplane Monthly* can be obtained from The Quadrant Picture Library, Room 007, Quadrant House, The Quadrant, Sutton, Surrey SM2 5AS.

I am particularly indebted to Terry Heffernan who, some years ago, rescued the official Directorate of Research Reports on the 1923 and 1924 Lympne lightplane trials from certain destruction, and who allowed me to study them at leisure.

To Roger Jackson, for generous use of photographs from the collection of his late father, A.J. Jackson.

To A.R. Ward, for sparing the time to talk about the Chilton DW 1 which he co-designed with Andrew Dalrymple.

To Adrain Comper, brother of the late Flight Lieutenant Nicholas Comper, designer of the Swift and so many other brilliant light aircraft.

In addition I would like to thank the following who assisted in diverse ways: Don L. Brown, Squadron Leader Alan Curtis, Peter Green, Arthur Ord-Hume, Philip Jarrett and Michael Oakey.

Finally, my thanks to Lynette Richards, Susan Tyler and Jenny Wilson for their stenographic wizardry.

Introduction

The story of British ultra-light aviation of the inter-war years is a tale of enthusiasm, determination and not a little frustration. For twenty years professional and amateur aircraft constructors strove towards providing the man in the street with a really cheap, reliable means of powered flight; an aerial equivalent to the motor cycle. For a variety of reasons only a handful of these enthusiasts achieved even marginal success. The world had to wait until the 1970s before really cheap powered flight became a reality, in a form that very few had even considered. The recent introduction of microlight aircraft has once more focused attention on a branch of aviation which has simmered almost since aviation began. Only once before did it come to the boil, during the mid-1930s when the Pou du Ciel craze was at its height, and then it came from the inventive mind of a Frenchman. Modern microlights have, arguably, solved a problem that has challenged man since aviation's infancy.

The term ultra-light initially applied to aircraft powered by engines of 40 hp or less. This distinction between ultra-lights and lightplanes, however, would include many pre-First World War aircraft, a large proportion of which staggered around the skies on less than 40 hp. Indeed, the Wright brothers took to the air at Kitty Hawk in December 1903 on a mere 12 hp. Generally speaking, low-powered aircraft built before that war had negligible performance; one exception in England was A.V. Roe's 1910 triplane which, powered by a 35 hp Green engine, is considered to be the first British low-powered aeroplane to have a reasonable performance.

The world's first true ultra-light was the tiny Demoiselle, designed in 1908 by Alberto Santos Dumont, a Brazilian who is today better known for his series of airship designs. Having experimented too with normal-sized aeroplanes, Dumont decided that the future of aeronautics lay with light, inexpensive craft which could be handled with ease by the average person. Built mostly from bamboo, the 18 ft span Santos Dumont Demoiselle was powered by a 30 hp Darracq two-cylinder engine which drove a 6½ ft diameter two-bladed propeller. The pilot sat in a skeletal fuselage on a simple canvas seat almost at ground level. The wing and engine were positioned above and slightly in front of him. The aircraft weighed a mere 242 lb; the weight of the engine was 110 lb, and the Demoiselle could fly at 60 mph. It had remarkable short take-off capabilities, being able to take off in six seconds after a ground run of less than 80 yds — provided that the pilot was as light as the diminutive Santos Dumont himself. The Demoiselle could be constructed for around £200 and a number of examples were built. Though not technically outstanding, this little aircraft laid the foundations for its many successors to adapt. In its day the Demoiselle was the smallest aircraft in the world.

Ultra-light aircraft had no application for war and what little development there was ceased for the duration of World War One. During the immediate post-war years civil flying resumed and was sustained with an endless flood of ex-Service Avro 504Ks, which were snapped up by commercial operators and one or two flying schools. Many operators found lucrative business in pleasure flying, though the high number of people wanting to be flown was not reflected in the very low number that wished to fly themselves. The reason for this was the high cost of learning to fly in the early 1920s. The cost of acquiring an 'A' licence could cost anything from £100 to £150; equally, the cost of hiring a club aircraft ranged from £4 to £9 per hour, which was well beyond the pocket of all but the well-off.

The number of private owners during the immediate post-war period could be counted on the fingers of one hand. Although there was a glut of ex-Service pilots, many of whom hankered to get themselves back into the air, only a few were able to join the Avro 504 joyriding companies or join an endless queue for the limited number of commercial airline jobs available. The rest had to divert their eyes from the sky; aviating was beyond their pocket, and many of them were out of work anyway.

In 1919 several aircraft companies were quick off the mark in offering an alternative aircraft to the comparatively large Avros. The Austin Motor Company Ltd had gained valuable aeronautical know-how during the war when it produced a number of aircraft under contract to the War Office, in addition to building three indigenous designs. Intent on keeping some of its aviation department busy, the company introduced a fighter-like single-seat biplane hoping to attract the wealthy private owner. Named the Whippet, this promising aircraft was expensive — about £500 — and was ahead of its time. Only five were built. Another contender for the same market was Roy Chadwick's delightful Avro Baby, designed and built during the winter of 1918-19. Powered by the reliable but heavy 35 hp Green engine, the Baby was a first-class sporting aircraft and nine were built. Some were raced with some success and one was flown by H.J. 'Bert' Hinkler from Croydon to Turin in nine hours, thus proving that an ultra-light could be a practical form of transport.

Two manufacturers took a leaf out of Santos Dumont's book and produced aircraft based on the Demoiselle. The British Aerial Transport Company GB Ltd (BAT) produced the FK 28, which was almost a copy of the 1908 Demoiselle. It was truly a minimal aircraft, with the pilot suspended beneath the wings in a tiny nacelle resembling a motor cycle sidecar. Powered by a temperamental Gnat engine, the FK 28 Crow was a real handful to fly by any but an experienced pilot, and it came to nothing.

The Blackburn aircraft company took the idea a stage further and came up with a tiny side-by-side cabin monoplane powered by a 40 hp ABC Gnat. Called the Sidecar, an apt name for an aerial motor cycle, the aircraft probably never flew, though it was exhibited at Harrods in London and elsewhere priced at £450.

That same year two other sporting aircraft were put on the market. In an effort to catch the eye of the young ex-Service pilot, Bristol came up with the fighter-like Babe. Claude Grahame-White's Hendon-based company offered the racy GWE 6 Bantam and, though three examples of each were built none went into production. It was the same story: at 800 guineas the Bantam was just too expensive.

For those who could not afford to buy an aeroplane off the shelf there was an alternative — building their own. Though many budding designers stayed firmly on the ground, there was the odd exception. One young man not only taught himself to fly in an aircraft he designed himself but also designed and built a side-by-side ultra-light which had an impressive performance by any standards. F. Harold Lowe's Marl-

burian was one of the first true home-built aircraft to fly during the inter-war years and would have made an excellent mount for the sporting pilot.

It is often said that the British ultra-light aeroplane was conceived on Firle Beacon, near Itford Hill in Sussex in October 1922. In August that year that champion of early British aviation, the *Daily Mail*, offered a prize of £1,000 to anyone carrying out the longest glide exceeding half-an-hour in duration. The rules specified that flights must be made between sunrise and sunset on any day from 16-21 October. The use of any gas lighter than air was forbidden, thus eliminating balloon entries, and contestants were required to land within 800 yds of their launch point. Though automotive power was prohibited, man-powered flight was perfectly acceptable!

Contestants had but six weeks in which to design and build their entries. Because there were no entrance fees and complete absence of red tape, the number of entries was high at 35 on the competition closing date. Of that number many failed to materialize at Itford and, of those that did struggle to the top of that windy ridge, only about a dozen managed to fly at all. The only international participation was by Dutchman Anthony Fokker and the French. Although Germany led the world in sport gliding, that country had not yet been accepted back by the Federation Aeronautique Internationale (FAI) and thus was excluded from taking part. This exclusion was not total; a German Klemperer-designed glider was entered by a competitor from Nottingham.

Cynical 'experts' predicted that the *Daily Mail*'s generous prize would not be won, prophesying that even flights of ten minutes would be outside the capabilities of most of the motley collection of gliders that had assembled at Itford on the first day. How wrong the pundits proved to be. Since the wind blew persistently from the east, and was the wrong direction for gliding off Itford, the flying was carried out from nearby Firle Beacon. Of the gliders that actually flew at Itford, three are worth mentioning here in the light of forthcoming developments. The de Havilland company entered two 50 ft span DH 52 gliders. Of very light structure — too light as it turned out — they had high aspect ratio wings and had already been successfully tested before being taken to Itford. One was flown by Hubert Broad, the other by E.D.C. Herne. George Handasyde, Fred Sigrist and Sydney Camm had jointly designed the clean-lined Handasyde glider, built by the Air Navigation Company at Addlestone and flown by Fred Raynham. Then there was the Sayers S-C-W glider, designed by Captain W.H. Sayers, light aeroplane correspondent of *The Aeroplane*. This 42 ft 6 in-span glider was based on the German Hannover Vampyr but differed in construction. Legend has it that Sayers designed his glider in nineteen hours and built it in nineteen days. At Itford the flying was shared by Frank Courtney and Squadron Leader M.E.A. Wright.

On the second day of the contest Fred Raynham surprised everyone by staying aloft in the Handasyde for nearly two hours to achieve a British record for British gliders. This flight was all the more remarkable because the aileron controls were not properly linked up and the pilot had to operate them by holding on to the loose cable ends! Other consistently good performances came from the other two Fokker biplane gliders, one of which was a two-seater which set up a record flight for a passenger-carrying glider with a flight of 49 minutes. But the real surprise of the meeting took place on the last day of the event when the Frenchman Maneyrol took off in his 21 ft 8 in-span tandem-winged Peyret glider and stayed airborne for an incredible 3 hours 21 minutes. While he was still tacking back and forth along the slope the British Brokker glider was launched. This curious affair was a home-made glider consisting of a Bristol Fighter fuselage married to the upper wing from a Fokker D VII, which must have amused Anthony Fokker. Many watched in disbelief as this glider proved itself to be one of the most controllable present, remaining in the air for more than an hour. No-one could surpass Maneyrol's flight, though, and the *Daily Mail*'s £1,000 prize was won by the Frenchman.

The Itford meeting was the scene of many mishaps. The most spectacular occurred when one of the DH 52s suffered wing failure and broke up in mid-air, fortunately without injury to the pilot. Herne's DH 52 was originally designed with aileron control but for the purpose of Itford had been modified with warp control, for which the wing structure proved too flexible.

Though Itford was regarded as a success it did nothing to further British interest in gliding, despite a further prize of £1,000 being offered by Gordon Selfridge to the pilot who successfully flew a glider more than fifty miles in Britain during 1923. This prize was never won, nor seriously contested, and it was not for another eight years that gliding gained any popularity in England, due largely to German interest in the sport. Some of those experimenters at Itford who had spent much time and energy retrieving their gliders from the bottoms of nearby slopes, assisted by armies of helpers, looked at the possibility of fitting small motors to their aircraft. With an engine flights would not be restricted to hilltop sites, of which there were too few in England, and they would not have to rely on helpers to retrieve gliders weighing up to 200 lb. Already in France and

Germany there was immense interest in 'motor gliding', with competitions for designing such craft and cash prizes to be won for distance flights. Thus it was that several British designers turned their attention to very low-powered aircraft that were little more than powered gliders.

One of the first really low-powered aircraft with any kind of performance was the English Electric Wren, designed by W.O. Manning for trials by the Air Ministry for the purpose of finding a cheap-to-manufacture low-powered trainer. In designing the Wren, Manning concentrated on a very low structural weight coupled with the lowest possible engine power. Powered by a 398 cc ABC motor cycle engine, the Wren had an all-up weight of only 360 lb. It was first flown in April 1923 and performed well. It was delivered to the Air Ministry, complete with RAF serial number, but although it flew well the engine was unreliable. Conventional RAF training aircraft of the period cost around £1,200; the Wren put into production would have cost around £350 per unit, though the prototype cost a little more than £500.

One or two other aircraft companies were continuing experiments along similar lines. W.S. Shackleton embarked upon a design that closely resembled the German Komet. Rather than put his hopes in a converted motor cycle engine, Shackleton designed the ANEC I around the exciting new Bristol Cherub flat twin developed by Roy Fedden in 1922-23. At Shorts' factory at Rochester in Kent a curious bird-like twin propeller pusher was taking shape under the eagle eye of its designer Oscar Gnosspelius. This 36 ft span cantilever monoplane was powered by a 697 cc Blackburne motor cycle engine driving two propellers via chains at two-thirds crankshaft speed.

At Farnborough a more conventional design, based on the World War One FE 8 fighter, was taking shape. The RAE Zephyr was a twin-boomed biplane powered by a 500 cc Douglas engine built by a group of RAE personnel who in 1922 had formed a club to design, build and fly light aircraft.

In general there was little enthusiasm for such low-powered aircraft and some incentive was needed to change the situation. Such an incentive came with an exciting announcement in the pages of *Flight* and *The Aeroplane* in April 1923. The Duke of Sutherland, Under Secretary of State for Air, presented the Royal Aero Club with a £500 prize for a competition between low-powered aeroplanes. The money would be awarded to the competitor who 'Accomplished the longest distance in one flight, provided that such a flight is not less than fifty miles'. There were rules and conditions to be drawn up by the Royal Aero Club, but hardly had the announcement been made than the *Daily Mail* announced an identical contest but doubled the prize money, thus relegating the good Duke's prize to second place. After some natural hostility from the aviation press, the problem was neatly solved by running two separate competitions with identical rules. Whereas the *Daily Mail* prize was open to all-comers, the Duke of Sutherland's £500 was offered to British contestants only. The rules of Britain's first lightplane competition were as follows (from the official programme):

Organisation
The Competitions will be conducted by the Royal Aero Club.

Motor-Glider
The Competitions are open to any heavier-than-air machine with engine, the total piston displacement of which does not exceed 750 c.c. The Royal Aero Club reserves to itself the right to check the piston displacement of any engine taking part in the Competitions. Any additional motive power produced by the personal exertions of the occupants during flight is allowed. The machine must not be supported either wholly or in part by any gas which is lighter than air.

Competitors may use any launching device provided by themselves.

Fuel
The fuel is to be such as can be commercially obtainable in bulk.

Pilot
The weight of the pilot must be made up to a minimum of 168lb.

All pilots must be weighed prior to the start of the Competitions. Pilots under the minimum of 168lb must carry the additional weight necessary to make them up to this weight, and this will be checked before and after each flight.

Transport
Competitors must demonstrate to the Officials that the machine is capable of being transported on the ground a distance of one mile by not more than two persons without the use of any extraneous tackle, within a period not exceeding three hours. The selected course for this test will include the getting out of a field through an ordinary gateway, 10 feet wide, and proceeding along a 15-foot road, occupying not more than half the width of the road.

Machines may be presented to the Officials for the Transport Test from 10 a.m. on Saturday, 6th October, 1923.

Machines must be presented to the Officials fully erected.

Any time occupied in dismantling will be included in the three hours allowed for the Transport Test.

There is no restriction as to the number of persons engaged in any dismantling necessary for the Transport Test, but only two persons will be allowed for the purposes of Transport.

No special devices will be allowed for the Transport Test unless carried as part of the equipment of the machine in flight during the Competitions.

This test must be passed before any flight is made in any Competition.

Course
All flights will be made over a triangular course of approximately 12½ miles.

The Turning Points will be marked by White Crosses on the ground, which each Competitor must pass on his left at a height of not more than 1,000 feet, and at a sufficiently close range so that his number may be easily identified by the Official Observers.

Entries
The Royal Aero Club, in the interests of safety, reserves to itself the right to refuse any entries and/or prohibit the flight in the Competitions of any Competitor if it considers the flight would be dangerous.

Air Navigation Regulations
Competitors must comply with the Air Navigation Regulations in force, subject to any concessions which may be made by the Air Ministry for these Competitions.

Identification
Each machine will be allotted a number, which must be painted in black on a white surface on each side of the rudder and on the lower surface of each of the lower main planes. This number must be as large as the surface permits. Government Registration Marks are not necessary for these Competitions.

Flying Time
The Competitions will be open each day at 7 a.m. and will close at 5.30 p.m. Competitors will not be observed or timed after that hour. In all cases the number of circuit flights will be counted up to the last circuit completed at the closing hour.

Number of Flights
There is no restriction as to the number of attempts which may be made for the Prizes during the period of the Competitions.

Starting and Finishing Line
The same line will be used for starting and finishing for all the Competitions. Competitors will be at liberty to take off from any point on the Aerodrome, but will be timed from the first time they cross the starting line in flight, keeping the Aerodrome Turning Point on their left.

THE "DAILY MAIL" £1,000 PRIZE
To be awarded to the Entrant of the machine which accomplishes the longest distance in one flight with one gallon of fuel, providing such flight is not less than 50 miles.

This Prize is open to all nationalities.

Fuel
The distance covered by the use of one gallon of fuel only will be reckoned. Competitors, however, will be required to finish each flight at Lympne Aerodrome by crossing the finishing line in flight. No flight will count if the landing occurs outside the Aerodrome.

In order to enable this to be done Competitors will be served out with a measured quantity in excess of the one gallon as required by them. After the flight the amount remaining in the tank will be measured and the distance flown on the one gallon will be calculated *pro rata*, provided more than one gallon is consumed.

Competitors who consume less than one gallon will be treated as if they had consumed the whole of one gallon.

THE SUTHERLAND £500 PRIZE

To be awarded to the Entrant of the machine which accomplishes the longest distance in one flight with one gallon of fuel, providing such flight is not less than 50 miles.

The Entrant and Pilot must be British subjects, and the machine and engine must have been entirely constructed in the British Empire.

Fuel

The distance covered by the use of one gallon of fuel only will be reckoned. Competitors, however, will be required to finish each flight at Lympne Aerodrome by crossing the finishing line in flight. No flight will count if the landing occurs outside the Aerodrome.

In order to enable this to be done Competitors will be served out with a measured quantity in excess of the one gallon as required by them. After the flight the amount remaining in the tank will be measured and the distance flown on the one gallon will be calculated *pro rata*, provided more than one gallon is consumed.

Competitors who consume less than one gallon will be treated as if they had consumed the whole of one gallon.

THE ABDULLA £500 PRIZE

To be awarded to the entrant of the machine which covers two circuits of the course (approximately 25 miles) in the fastest time.

The prize is open to all nationalities.

The fuel allowance is not limited.

The starting and finishing line must be crossed in flight.

The Society of Motor Manufacturers and Traders £150 prize, and the British Cycle and Motor Cycle Manufacturers' and Traders' Union £150 prize.

To be awarded to the entrant of the machine which flies the largest number of completed circuits of the course during the period of the Competitions, with a minimum of 400 miles. Circuits flown in the other Competitions will count towards the prizes.

The Entrant and Pilot must be British Subjects, and the machine and engine must have been entirely constructed in the British Empire.

The same machine and engine must be used throughout, and parts will be marked to ensure this, but special tanks will be permitted, the fuel allowance not being limited.

The 'motor glider competition' took place at Lympne aerodrome in Kent during the week of 8-13 October 1923. The competition attracted seven major British aircraft manufacturing companies and by 1 October, the closing date for the competition, 28 entries had been received, four of which were French aircraft. For the period of the competitions the Air Ministry waived the requirements of Certificates of Airworthiness, which was just as well; some of the entrants were incapable of flight and others were somewhat dubious structures. Three entrants were not ready in time and on the day there were 23 British aircraft in contention. The aircraft, the competition numbers and the pilots are listed below (those that did not fly are omitted):

No 2	Gnosspelius Gull	J. Lankester Parker
No 3	English Electric Wren	Sqn Leader M.E.A. Wright
No 4	English Electric Wren	Flt Lt W.H. Longton
No 5	Avro 558	H.J.L. Hinkler
No 6	Avro 560	H.J.L. Hinkler
No 7	Gloucestershire Gannet	L.L. Carter
No 8	de Havilland DH 53	Capt G. de Havilland Capt H. Broad
No 9	Parnall Pixie I	Capt N. Macmillan
No 10	Vickers Viget	Capt S.F. Cockerell
No 11	Avro 558	Flg Off H. A. Hamersley
No 12	de Havilland DH 53	Maj H. Hemming
No 13	Handasyde	F.P. Raynham
No 14	RAE Hurricane	Flt Lt P.W.S. Bulman
No 17	ANEC I	J.H. James
No 18	ANEC I	M.W. Piercey
No 19	Gnosspelius Gull	Capt R.H. Stocken
No 24	Parnall Pixie II	Capt N. Macmillan
No 25	Handley Page-Sayers	G.P. Olley

Three aircraft entered owed their origins to gliders that took part in the previous year's Itford gliding meeting; namely the de Havilland DH 53, derived from the DH 52, the Handasyde monoplane and the Handley Page-Sayers, which was reminiscent of the S-C-W glider. All the British aircraft were powered by motor cycle engines variously adapted for aviation use and were mainly the products of ABC, Blackburne and Douglas, ranging from 350 cc to 750 cc. All the British entrants are described under their various headings in the main chapters of this book.

The rules and the very nature of the competitions encouraged freak aircraft, designed to compete for just one cash prize, though most hoped to succeed in the fuel economy trials, which had the largest cash incentive. Interestingly, in an age when the biplane prevailed, thirteen of the eighteen British aircraft that flew at Lympne were monoplanes.

Despite the poor weather some very creditable performances were put up by those aircraft that were not plagued with engine troubles. The Duke of Sutherland's £500 prize and the *Daily Mail*'s £1,000, offered for the greatest distance flown on one gallon of petrol, were jointly won by Flight Lieutenant Longton flying one of the Wrens and 'Jimmy' James on one of the ANEC I s. Both pilots managed to achieve 87.5 mpg, a truly staggering performance that even one of today's mopeds would find hard to better. Captain Norman Macmillan, flying a Parnall Pixie, won the £500 Abdulla Prize for achieving the highest average speed of 76.1 mph and Mauric Piercey coaxed the same ANEC I to a height of 14,400 ft to clinch the Wakefield prize of £200 for achieving the greatest height. Bert Hinkler covered eighty laps of the 12½-mile Lympne course, accumulating a total distance of 1,000 miles to win the combined £300 put up by the SMMT and BCMCMTU for the greatest distance flown. Because the weather was so gusty it was not possible to fly off the take-off and landing trials and the Duke of Sutherland's landing competition prize money of £100 was awarded to Captain Hamersley who narrowly missed bettering Piercey's height record (by 550 ft) in the Avro 558.

The meeting was regarded as a great success but it was plain that motor cycle engines, though efficient for the use for which they were designed, were unreliable when required to run at high loads in an aeroplane. The Blackburne engines had fared best of all. It was evident too that most of the competing aircraft were fair weather machines, having no turn of speed in gusty or windy conditions. The 'freak' aircraft had taken the prizes and ironically the best all-round performer, the DH 53, though not amongst the prize winners, was the only competing type to go into production. It was ordered by the RAF and was destined to fulfil its civil role several years later.

The Air Ministry, which in the early days was responsible for both civil and military aviation matters, showed particular interest in the Lympne competitions and the Directorate of Research produced a lengthy and detailed report, analysing airframes and engines, based on reports submitted by nine D of R staff. Their report considered that the light plane could prove very useful in the initial training of pilots, the cost of which could be reduced considerably. Such an aircraft would obviously have to be a two-seater. The Ministry stressed the importance of developing suitable engines specifically for aircraft use. Though the motor cycle engines had served a purpose for which they were not designed, the necessity to run them at high loads for long periods had caused failures and unreliability. It

was suggested that three sizes of engine were needed: a 750 cc motor for single-seaters, engines of 1,100 cc for either single-seaters or two-seat trainers and a 1,500 cc engine for a two-seat general service type. In order to obtain a suitable low-cost two-seat trainer the Air Ministry subsequently sponsored a second light aircraft competition. The limiting factor was again the engine size which was increased to 1,100 cc. The Air Council put up a generous £3,000 and this was supplemented by further cash prizes bringing the total to £3,900, which was to provide a lucrative incentive to aircraft manufacturers and amateurs alike. The cost of building an ultra-light was still its greatest stumbling block. Though the cost of making aircraft components was not high it was the time-consuming business of putting them together that ran up the bills. Experts at the time considered that £250 would have been an acceptable price to pay for a light-plane; the cost of producing many of the 1923 Lympe aircraft was considerably more than this sum. With the accent on light structures, the process of lightening was also time-consuming and thus expensive.

Learning from the limitations imposed by the rules for the 1923 trials, the organizers changed them in an effort to discourage freak aircraft. What was wanted was a good all-rounder, something along the lines of a two-seat DH 53. As it happened the de Havilland company did not take part in the two-seater competitions, having taken the decision — wisely, as it happened — not to bother with low-powered engines but to concentrate on producing a two-seater powered by a tried and trusted 60-70 hp engine.

The 1924 two-seater competition was based on a simple criterion of efficiency calculated from the ratio between an aircraft's maximum and minimum speeds. It began with a percentage figure obtained from the following formula:

$$\text{Percentage figure} = \frac{V_{max} - V_{min}}{V_{min}} - 0.333$$

V_{max} was the maximum speed, V_{min} the stalling speed and the factor 0.333 represented the minimum percentage which could be accepted as qualifying a machine to be awarded marks in the competition.

For each per cent in excess of 33.3, eight marks were awarded. Thus, if $V_{max} = 80$ mph and $V_{min} = 30$ mph, the percentage figure on which the marks were awarded would be:

$$\frac{80 - 30}{30} - 0.333 = \frac{50}{30} - 0.333 = 1.334,$$

or 133.4 per cent. When multiplied by eight the number of marks awarded totalled 1,067.2.

In addition to determining speed range the trials also included transport tests, take-off and landing trials. Above all, aircraft had to be reliable, and to this end no aircraft was eligible for any prize until it had completed at least ten hours' flying. Fuel economy was a less important factor and probably accounted for the fact that a higher proportion of biplanes than monoplanes took part, reversing the previous year's trend. One interesting compromise was the Parnall Pixie III, which could be flown in either configuration.

The 1924 Lympne trials were held from 29 September—4 October, though eliminations were staged the previous weekend, on 27-28 September. All competitors managed to pass the transport test, during which each aircraft had to manoeuvre through a 10 ft-wide gap, for which wings were folded or dismantled. But when it came to the flying eliminations half of the sixteen entrants failed to qualify, many of them unable to perform satisfactorily with full load.

Thus it was that on Monday, 29 September, only the following aircraft were ready to take part in the gruelling trials:

No 1	Bristol Brownie I	C.F. Uwins/T.W. Campbell
No 3	Cranwell CLA 2	Flt Lt N. Comper/R.P. Mackay
No 4	Beardmore Wee Bee I	M.W. Piercey
No 5	Westland Woodpigeon	A.J. Winstanley/S.H. Gaskell
No 14	Hawker Cygnet I	Flt Lt W.H. Longton
No 15	Hawker Cygnet II	F.P. Raynham
No 17	Parnall Pixie IIIA	W. Sholto Douglas/R.A. de H. Haig

Significantly, four of the remaining types were powered by the new Bristol Cherub engine, developed specifically for aircraft use by Roy Fedden.

Though the weather at Lympne was unkind during the first part of the week, the final two days were calm and good performances were put up by the survivors. Though the biplanes had outnumbered the monoplanes most of the prize money went to the latter. First place and the Air Ministry prize of £2,000 went to Maurice Piercey flying the Wee Bee I. His speed range had been measured as 39.6 mph to 70.1 mph. His measured take-off distance to clear a 50 ft tape was 235 yds and the landing run was 124 yds. During the week the Wee Bee had flown a distance of 737.5 miles and amassed a total of 588.52 marks. The Air Ministry's second prize, of £1,000, was won by Cyril Uwins flying the Brownie I, whose performance almost matched that of the winner's. His performance figures were: top speed 65.2 mph, low speed 38.7 mph, total distance flown 562.3 miles, landing run 102.6 yds, take-off run 215 yds; the total marks scored being 562.3. F.P. Raynham, flying the Cygnet II, won the £100 prize for take-off and landing performance and the amateur-built Cranwell

CLA 2 won the £300 prize money for flying the greatest distance, covering 762.5 miles in just less than eighteen hours' flying time. Though crude in appearance, the CLA 2 had sensible side-by-side seating and had been designed by Flight Lieutenant Nicholas Comper, whose name appears regularly throughout this book. Unfortunately, many promising aircraft were eliminated from the trials proper, either because of misbehaving engines or because of over-zealous officials.

The Air Ministry, having sponsored the trials, had followed events very closely, producing another detailed report on all competing aircraft and engines. It was again clear that engines were a weak link. Engines of 1,100 cc were not suitable for loaded two-seater aircraft and it was necessary to run them at maximum power to lift anything approaching full load. The impression often given is that engines were still unreliable in 1924. This was not the case, and in its report the Ministry commented: '. . . the true fact of the case was that the engines were putting up a wonderful performance, and instead of the engine builders being blamed, they were worthy of congratulation on the sporting manner in which they allowed their engines to be installed. Without exception they were aware that to obtain any performance they had to sacrifice reliability and it was only by resorting to freak compression ratios and running at excessive speeds that some of the aircraft were able to take off, whereas if they had played for safety it is doubtful if any of the aircraft would have been able to take off with the power available.'

For future competitions the Air Ministry recommended that: the minimum bhp required at normal rpm should be 34 hp; geared engines were not necessary, satisfactory results being more easily obtainable by using engines of larger capacity which would not increase the weight or overall size of the engine; carburettors required redesigning, and magnetos needed a greater range between advance and retard — one of the main shortcomings of many aircraft was that engines simply would not start. The exception was the Bristol Cherub, which was fitted with an impulse starter. The Air Ministry also recommended that engines should be fitted with dual ignition and advised that engines should be subject to type testing for at least fifty hours before being used in competition.

Because most of the two-seaters at Lympne were under-powered it was difficult to assess them for suitability for *ab initio* training. Both the Wee Bee I and the CLA 2 were evaluated by the Air Ministry. The CLA 2 was crashed by the Ministry pilot and the Wee Bee was rejected. The Ministry considered that no suitable *ab initio* training type had resulted from the trials and that if a further competition was to be staged the only way of producing a more workable formula was by accepting larger engines, perhaps with a weight restriction. The Ministry report had divided the 1924 two-seaters into three classes. Class One included types such as the Westland Widgeon, CLA 2 and Supermarine Sparrow; aircraft of conventional design, built purely for training purposes, but in order to perform properly they required engines of around 45 hp. This indeed happened with the Widgeon, which was produced in numbers in modified form. Class Two included such types as the Cygnet, which was designed with a very low structural weight in order to gain maximum efficiency from its engine. Because of the method of construction the airframe was considered insufficiently robust for rigorous training use. Class Three embraced such types as the Wee Bee I, Short Satellite and Pixie III. These were suited to training roles provided that the loaded weight could be kept below 900 lb; their aerodynamically efficient lines gave engines of 32 hp sufficient power reserve, only half that horsepower being required to sustain level flight.

The Air Ministry agreed to support a second competition for two-seaters and, after consultation with the Royal Aero Club and manufacturers, the competition rules were announced in April 1925. The good news was that rather than engines being restricted by capacity and horsepower, a weight limit of 170 lb was imposed. An engine of this weight would develop around 60 hp, probably a lot more if it was 'tweaked up', worked out on the assumption that the specific weight was in the region of 3 lb/hp. Because the rules had been published less than six months from the trials date there was obviously insufficient time for engine manufacturers to produce new engines to the limitations specified. The competition was postponed until 1926 to enable new engines to be tried and tested. In the meantime a meeting was staged at Lympne during the first week in August 1925, but it was restricted to racing and to establishing certified performances of both single-seat and two-seat entrants, many of which had attended previous Lympne meetings. The only brand new type present was the Cranwell Light Aeroplane Club's Comper-designed CLA 3.

Significantly, two of the new DH 60 Cirrus Moths took part, powered by 65 hp Cirrus engines which, by way of engine weight, precluded these aircraft from taking part in the performance trials. Many observers must have realized that the introduction of a suitable lighter engine would make the Moth eligible for the 1926 competitions. Having first flown in February 1925, the Moth was rapidly gaining popularity with private owners. The DH 60 was a scaled-down version of the DH 51 and was powered by a proven and reliable engine ingeniously designed by Major F.B. Halford, using one half of a 120 hp Airdisco eight-cylinder Vee engine mounted on a new crankcase. The Cirrus engine weighed 290 lb, some 120 lb above the weight limit for the forthcoming two-seater trials. By the time of the trials Armstrong Siddeley had produced the lightweight 75 hp Genet I and hardly surprisingly de Havilland installed a Genet into a specially lightened Moth and entered it for the 1926 two-seater competitions.

Since the announcement of the competition, and with the introduction of the Moth, the Air Ministry had lost interest in the contest. The Moth filled nicely the Air Ministry's brief for a cheap trainer and there was little point in pursuing the matter. Fortunately the *Daily Mail* had already offered £5,000 on top of any other official prize money and the trials were able to go ahead as planned.

Though a large number of types was entered for the 1926 Lympne two-seater trials (held on 12-17 September) mechanical failures and cussedness on the part of some officials resulted in a disappointing contest. Of the sixteen aircraft originally entered, four failed even to arrive at Lympne. They were the beautiful ANEC IV Missel Thrush, the RAE Aero Club's Sirocco, the Halton Aero Club's HAC 1 and one of the Cranwell Light Aeroplane Club's CLA 4s, which had been designed for the Pobjoy P engine which was not ready in time. Of those that did arrive at Lympne two more were knocked out during the preliminaries, which left only ten aircraft in the running. These were:

No 2	de Havilland DH 60 Genet Moth	H.S. Broad
No 3	Bristol Brownie	C.F. Uwins
No 4	Hawker Cygnet	Flt Lt J.A. Gray/ Flg Off. R.L. Ragg
No 6	Hawker Cygnet II	Flt Lt P.W.S. Bulman
No 7	Supermarine Sparrow II	H.C. Biard
No 9	Avro Avian	H.J.L. Hinkler
No 10	Avro Avis	Wg Cdr W. Sholto Douglas
No 12	CLA 3	Flt Lt N. Comper
No 14	Parnall Pixie III	F.T. Courtney
No 16	Westland Woodpigeon	Flt Lt A.P. Ritchie

The only new professionally-built entrant was the Avro Avian, a direct competitor with the DH 60 Moth, powered by the new Genet I designed specifically for use in the competition. The majority of aircraft, though, were powered by the much improved Bristol Cherub III and it was evident that the competition was very much a sparring match between this and the Genet.

The 1926 competition was run on the basis of a Figure of Merit which took into account fuel economy, load carried and the distance flown. Competitors were required to fly a distance of 1,994 miles in the six days, following a course that took in many seaside resorts along the Kent and Sussex coastline. Entrants were subject to a minimum average speed of 50 mph and were required to carry a load of 340 lb, equivalent to the weight of two people. The Figure of Merit was computed to the following formula:

$$\frac{(\text{pounds of useful load carried}) \times (\text{miles flown})}{(\text{pounds of fuel consumed})}$$

With the non-arrival of the four aircraft mentioned, only twelve aircraft embarked upon the preliminary eliminations. Early casualties were the Blackburn Bluebird, CLA 4, Westland Woodpigeon and the Supermarine Sparrow. In the event only four stalwarts completed the gruelling 2,000 miles. The winner, with the highest Figure of Merit, was Flight Lieutenant P.W.S. Bulman, with a figure of 2,203 lb miles/lb, flying one of the Cherub-powered Cygnets. Second was another Cygnet flown by the RAE Aero Club which achieved a Figure of Merit of 1,808 lb miles/lb. Uwins' Cherub-powered Bristol Brownie achieved 1,687 lb miles/lb. At one point it looked as though Hinkler on the Avian would run away with the prize but he was forced to retire at which point his Figure of Merit was 2,092.

Though the competition was generally disappointing it had, as *Flight* commented, 'produced one remarkable aeroplane and one very promising engine'. The aircraft referred to was the Avro Avian and the engine was the Cherub III which powered eight of the original sixteen entrants including the four aircraft that completed the 2,000 mile course. In any case the 1926 competitions had failed to take into consideration the all-important question of cost. Paradoxically the aircraft that succeeded in 1926 were to fade into obscurity, whereas some of those that had been eliminated or had retired from the running were later put into production, albeit in modified form; types such as the Avian, Moth and Bluebird. In fact, the 1926 trials paved the way for the standard lightplane and the motor cycle of the air was no nearer; it was to take another decade before such a craft was put on the market.

The lean years

The 1926 Lympne meeting was the last of its kind and consequently the interest in low-powered aircraft waned, though amateur enthusiasts kept the idea alive. Aviation was very much in the hands of the wealthy and hope began to fade for the impecunious aviator. Then, in 1929, interest gathered momentum with the introduction of several low-powered cheap-to-run flying machines. Most promising was the Glenny and Henderson Gadfly, a simple, no-frills, slab-winged monoplane single-seater powered by an ABC Scorpion. The ABC company even designed a

single-seat cabin monoplane around its own engine. Called the Robin, this promising aircraft could well have gone into production had it been a two-seater. An RAF Flying Officer produced an efficient little sesquiplane comprising components from a DH 53 and the Halton HAC 1 Mayfly, named the Clarke Cheetah after its brilliant young designer John Clarke. Following his tragic death in a flying accident the Cheetah was flown first as a parasol and was then incorporated into a new design, after which it became known as the Martin Monoplane, the mortal remains of which survive at the time of writing. Another commendable amateur effort was that of two Nottinghamshire brothers, who produced an unorthodox tailless swept-wing single-seater powered by a 32 hp Bristol Cherub engine. Called the Granger Archaeopteryx, it flew with some success and is still airworthy at the time of writing.

The year 1929 also saw the birth of the Hendy Hobo, a low-cost single-seater powered by an ABC Scorpion and incorporating a wing of novel construction. After it was re-engined with a 90 hp Pobjoy Cataract the Hobo enjoyed limited success as a racer, but only the one example was built. F.G. Miles' Southern Aircraft company redesigned the 1919 Avro Baby to produce a fast little single-seater of which a handful were produced. At about the same time pilot H.J. Hinkler completed an unusual twin-engined ultra-light named the Ibis which was originally designed as an amphibian for touring purposes. Limited finance prevented the Ibis from being amphibious and, despite its good flying qualities, no-one could be persuaded to put the twin into production.

As 1929 came to a close Flight Lieutenant Comper, now established at Hooton Park Aerodrome in Cheshire with his newly formed Comper Aircraft Company, made the first flight of an aeroplane that was destined to become one of ultra-light aviation's few success stories. Having designed a series of excellent light aircraft for the Cranwell Light Aeroplane Club — the CLA series — he left the RAF to set up his own company to produce the CLA 7, better known as the Comper Swift. The first prototype, powered by a 35 hp ABC Scorpion engine, displayed an incredible performance for such a low-powered aeroplane. The type was put into production at about the time Captain D. Pobjoy had perfected his remarkable seven-cylinder Pobjoy R radial engine. Pobjoy had served as an education officer in the RAF and had been experimenting with his tiny radial engine since the mid-1920s. The original Pobjoy P engine should have powered Comper's CLA 4 at the 1926 Lympne trials, but it was not ready in time. When Pobjoy left the Service he set up Pobjoy Air-motors at Hooton and the prototype Pobjoy R engine was installed in an early production Swift. It was the ideal marriage. The high-revving Pobjoy produced very little vibration and the 75 hp engine weighed only 135 lb, making it an ideal powerplant for ultra-light aircraft. All subsequent Swifts were sold with the Pobjoy R and this combination of engine and airframe produced some stunning record flights. The last three Swifts were powered by DH Gipsy engines of three times the power of the Scorpion installed in the prototype aircraft. A total of 41 Swifts were built and it is a tribute to the design integrity that a handful are still flying in the 1980s.

The year 1930 produced just one more ultra-light design. Wealthy young A.L. Angus produced an unusual chunky low-wing single-seater powered by a 40 hp Salmson. Named the Angus Aquila, the little aeroplane was a handful in the air and Angus' flying experience was limited. On 21 March 1931 the aircraft spun-in shortly after take-off, killing its designer. In 1932 the ever-enthusiastic and active RAE Club at Farnborough had not been idle. By utilizing DH 53 parts they produced a nice-looking parasol called the Scarab; the airframe survived until 1945. In August 1932 the Miles brothers were ready to test the Miles M 1 Satyr, a pretty biplane powered by a 75 hp Pobjoy R and built for aerobatics, the first of many Miles-designed aeroplanes. On the island of Guernsey in the Channel Islands a group of enthusiasts built and flew the Wee Mite, an unlovely parasol powered initially by a 30 hp ABC Scorpion. Despite plans for production only the prototype was built.

It was during 1932 that ultra-light history repeated itself. As some of the 1922 Itford gliders lent themselves to auxiliary power units so, ten years later, an established glider was fitted with a low-powered engine in an attempt to introduce cheap flying. A revival of interest in gliding in the early 1930s prompted C.H. Lowe Wylde to produce a series of gliders to combat the influx of German gliders — there being very little to choose from in Britain. The British Aircraft Company at Maidstone in Kent had built several gliders to Lowe Wylde's design, one of which, the BAC VII, was fitted with a pylon-mounted 600 cc Douglas flat twin engine above the wing and given a conventional undercarriage. This combination flew well and after modification the type became known as the Planette. After Wylde's death in May 1933 the Planette was further improved when Robert Kronfeld took over BAC. Renamed the Drone, it was produced in limited numbers before the company, renamed Kronfeld Ltd in 1936, went out of business.

An interesting experimental aircraft was completed in 1933 by Captain K.N. Pearson, who had designed the HSF II Gadfly. Pearson was obsessed with the idea of rotary ailerons, which he tried out with limited success on one of the Gadflys. He then set about designing a single-seat pusher which he called the KP 2. It had no rudder but had Pearson Rotary ailerons on the wing tips. There is no record of it ever having flown.

A couple of ultra-light autogyros were built in 1934, both emanating from north of the border. The Kay Gyroplane had variable incidence rotor blades and was powered by the Pobjoy R. The Weir series of Autogiros was based entirely on Cierva principles and powered by Weir engines. Comper was also experimenting with the C 25, an ultra-light Cierva Autogiro which embodied a Swift fuselage. None of these rotary ultra-lights went into production.

During the early 1930s the public was becoming increasingly air-minded once more. There were the incredibly popular Hendon Air Pageants each year and Sir Alan Cobham's National Aviation Day Displays were introducing thousands of people to the joys of flight. The skies were black with Moths and the new generation of monoplanes for the private owner were coming off the production lines of Miles, de Havilland and Percival. But flying was still the sport of the rich and well out of reach for the wide-eyed five-bob joy riders who were filling Sir Alan Cobham's fleet to capacity. In 1935 there were 3,000 'A' licence holders in Great Britain and only around 500 privately registered aircraft.

While it looked as though the search for that elusive motor cycle of the air had petered out in Britain, the reverse was happening across the English Channel. For more than ten years Frenchman Henri Mignet had been experimenting with unorthodox aircraft of his own design. Convinced that conventional aircraft controls were too numerous and over-complicated, he concentrated on designing an aeroplane that did away with ailerons and foot controls. At the same time he was looking towards a cheap, easy-to-fly runabout that any 'Tom, Dick or Harry' could build and fly themselves. After a great deal of experimentation, failures and frustration, Mignet arrived at a diminutive tandem-winged single-seater which relied on a pivoting wing for longitudinal control and which had neither ailerons nor foot controls. The definitive version of Mignet's brainchild was the HM 14 Pou du Ciel (Sky Louse). In 1935 it was exhibited at the Paris Aero Show where it attracted enormous interest. Mignet had no intention of manufacturing the HM 14; instead it was designed to be built by enthusiasts in their own homes. Two years earlier Mignet had published his classic best-seller *Le Sport de l'Air*, in which he described the aircraft and the sequence of events leading up to the first successful flights. The story of how his little aeroplane took the Continent by storm is told in the relevant chapter of this book. Around 120 home-built and professionally built HM 14s were constructed in Britain from 1935-36 and had it not been for an inherent design fault and subsequent fatalities the Flea (as the aircraft was also known in Britain) would doubtless have filled a need that many had doubted even existed — the need for a low-powered cheap aeroplane.

Though the HM 14 was banned from Britain and elsewhere, its existence benefited the ultra-light movement in the area of airworthiness requirements for this class of aircraft. Before the Pou epidemic there was no legislation to cover homebuilt aircraft; they fell outside the requirements of the standard Certificate of Airworthiness, the issuing of which was the responsibility of the Air Ministry. With the assistance of the Air League, who supported the Pou and even reprinted Mignet's book in English, a special flight certificate was created for homebuilts known as the Permit to Fly; the system worked well until the 1970s when it was superseded by the restricted category Certificate of Airworthiness. The first Permit to Fly was issued to a Pou.

The popularity of the Flea also confirmed without any shadow of doubt that there was indeed a ready market for a cheap low-powered aeroplane. One or two companies tried to emulate the Flea, such as E.G. Perman Ltd who produced the somewhat similar-looking Perman Parasol, ready made. But the Flea affair had left a nasty taste in the mouths of the potential buyer and it was left to designers such as C.H. Latimer-Needham and the industrious duo Zander and Weyl to produce more orthodox aircraft. Even Latimer-Needham experimented with a tandem-winged ultra-light but this aircraft graduated into the Luton Minor.

Latimer-Needham's newly formed Luton Aircraft company produced two outstanding designs during 1936. The Luton Buzzard was more or less a powered low-wing glider with a pylon-mounted pusher Anzani engine of which only one example was built. His Luton Minor was designed specifically for the homebuilder and, following two intermediate designs of which one was the tandem-wing aircraft, the Minor can be regarded as a direct successor to the designer's Halton HAC 2 Minus of ten years earlier. A number of Luton Minors were under construction on the outbreak of war. So outstanding was the basic design that improved Minors are still being constructed by homebuilders in the 1980s all over the world.

The Mignet HM 14 was not the only foreign ultra-light to be built in Britain during the 1930s. In 1930 a single-seat open cockpit Aeronca C-2 was imported from America by Colonel M.O. Darby. Such was the interest in this aircraft that a batch of American-built C-3s was imported and sold to a ready market. In 1935 Light Aircraft Ltd acquired a licence to build Aeronca C-3s and J.A. Prestwich took out a licence to build the aircraft's Aeronca E-113C engine. Eventually production was carried out by the Aeronautical Corporation of Great Britain Ltd but after six months of production the demand for the type ceased and the company was left with many unsold aircraft.

At about the same period the woodworking firm of F. Hills and Sons Ltd of Trafford Park in Manchester was laying down a production line of Czechoslovakian Praga E 14s, following the visit to Britain of the second prototype in August 1935. Like the Aeronca, the Praga offered side-by-side seating in cabin comfort and was eventually powered by the same Aeronca engine. The Praga was particularly popular with flying clubs.

Meanwhile, the Dunstable-based Dart Aircraft Company was turning out three widely differing ultra-light types. Messrs Zander and Weyl were both German and in 1934 formed a company to build gliders and ultra-light aircraft. Weyl's first Dart design was the pretty little Pup high-wing pusher which owed much to the Zogling-type glider. At the same time the Dart Flittermouse emerged, looking for all the world like a powered primary glider. The third Dart design, the Kitten, was a very promising low-wing single-seater but only three were built.

During 1936 another attempt was made to produce an ultra-light twin designed by L.E. Baynes, more noted for his series of Scud sailplanes, one of which was fitted with a 250 cc auxiliary pylon-mounted engine. In 1937 he designed and had built an unorthodox twin pusher monoplane powered by a couple of 50 hp Carden Ford engines. Named the Bee, it had its mainplane mounted on a turntable in order that it could be turned to lie along the top of the fuselage for storage.

On 16 April 1937 one of the finest British ultra-lights took to the air for the first time, from Witney. Two ex-de Havilland Technical School students had teamed together to produce what amounted to a miniature racing aircraft of very pleasing line and very low structural weight. A.R. Ward and the Hon Andrew Dalrymple's 24 ft span Chilton DW 1 was an essay in miniaturization. It was powered by the 30 hp Carden Ford water-cooled engine which Sir John Carden had converted from a Ford 10 car engine for use in British-built HM 14 Poux. Coupled with the Chilton's aerodynamically clean airframe, a top speed of 112 mph was possible with a cruising speed of 100 mph, a very marketable figure.

If the Chilton resembled a scaled-down racer, the Currie Wot of the same vintage resembled a scaled-down biplane from another era. Designed by J.R. Currie and built at Lympne, the Wot was a simple, no-frills fun aeroplane with a reasonable performance. After the war it was to receive a new lease of life when, in the 1950s, V.H. Bellamy and John Isaacs (of scale Fury and Spitfire fame) acquired the original drawings and built two further Wots. The type was ideal for homebuilders and examples are still being built in the 1980s.

The year 1937 also marked the arrival of another foreign ultra-light, this time from Belgium. E.O. Tips of Avions Fairey had designed the pretty Tipsy S1, powered by a 28 hp Douglas Sprite. Following a flying visit in May 1936, an improved version was put into limited production by Aero Engines Ltd at Kingsdown near Bristol, though only half a dozen were built. An almost identical aeroplane was being built by Premier Aircraft Constructions at Romford in Essex. The Gordon Dove, as it was called, was also powered by a Douglas Sprite and though production of nine Doves was planned, only three materialized.

Whereas the single-seat Tipsy S1 and S2 had failed to sell in numbers, a successor, the side-by-side two-seat Tipsy B, fared much better. The prototype was brought over from Belgium and demonstrated at Heathrow in May 1937. As a result, Tipsy Aircraft Ltd was formed to build the larger Tipsy under licence at the London Air Park at Hanworth. A total of nineteen aircraft had been built when war put a stop to further production.

Even in 1937 the amateur designer was still in evidence. One such person was Errol Shapley who designed and built an unusual-looking side-by-side two-seat, gull-winged open-cockpit monoplane in a disused storeroom in a Torquay iron foundry. His barrel-fuselaged design flew very well and was powered by a 40 hp radial Continental. Shapley produced a successor with enclosed cockpit and powered by a 50 hp Continental known as the Kittiwake Mk II. Plans were well advanced to put the Mk II into production after the war, but when the prototype crashed in December 1946 these plans came to nil.

One of the most respected and prolific of British aircraft designers was Frank Barnwell, chief designer of Bristol. Known for such military aircraft as the Bristol Fighter, Bulldog and Blenheim, he also designed the Bristol Brownie back in the Lympne days. During the late 1930s he designed a single-seat ultra-light for his own use. The Barnwell BSW Mk 1 was powered by a 28 hp Scott Squirrel and was built for the designer at Whitchurch. During an early test flight in August 1938, however, the BSW 1 crashed shortly after take-off and killed its designer.

Messrs Ward and Dalrymple were not the only DH Technical students to make their mark in the ultra-light aircraft field. During 1938 E.T. Watkinson and C.W. Taylor designed and built a 28-ft span single-seater powered, like the Chilton, by a 30 hp Carden Ford. Also like the Chilton, the Watkinson Dingbat was test flown by Ranald Porteous, another ex-D.H. Technical School student. It was put on the market at £300 but only the prototype was built.

With war only months away the prolific C.H. Latimer-Needham was busy building a successor to the open-cockpit Luton Minor. A cabin version emerged from the Gerrards Cross Phoenix Works and was first flown in March 1939. The Luton Major performed exceptionally well, though the war put paid to any further pre-war development. In 1958 the design rights were acquired by Phoenix Aircraft Ltd and the plans were marketed to homebuilders. The Major is likely to remain a firm favourite with amateur builders well into the 1990s.

The Luton Major was the last ultra-light to appear before war was declared in September 1939. It was to be six years before enthusiasts resumed the eternal search for cheap flying. During the immediate post-war period a number of pre-war types came out of hibernation. Most of them had been unsuitable for impressment into service with the RAF for taxi or hack work and had been shut away in barns and garages all over the land. Many had just mouldered away but some, such as the Chilton, Aeronca 100 and Drone, were put back into the air to provide their owners with cheap flying. The first post-war attempt at something new was Wren Aircraft's single-seat Goldcrest. Powered by a 28 hp Scott Squirrel, this promising aircraft was scheduled for production. Unavailability of materials brought such plans to an end, though.

Such was the enthusiasm for the ultra-light movement that the Ultra-Light Aircraft Association was formed in order to keep like-minded enthusiasts in touch. The Ministry of Civil Aviation's Informal Light Aeroplane Committee produced a report which included a specification for a single-seat ultra-light. The ULAA produced a more detailed specification and it recommended that such an aircraft should have a span of 20-25 ft; length, 15-20 ft; wing area, 100 ft^2; loaded weight 500-700 lb; cruising speed 70-88 mph; landing speed 30-35 mph; range, 200-300 miles and a price of £300. Except for the landing speed and the cruising speed the Chilton would have fitted the bill. But the Hon Andrew Dalrymple had been killed at the end of the war and A.R. Ward was no longer in the aircraft business.

Though there were one or two attempts to produce a cheap low-powered aeroplane, the only indigenous designs were post-war aircraft revamped and marketed for construction by homebuilders, examples being the Luton Minor and Major, the Tipsy Belfair, a cabin version of the Tipsy B and the Currie Wot. Two foreign aircraft, however, were licence-built in quantity, namely the French-designed Druine Turbulent, built by Rollasons at Croydon, and the Tipsy Nipper initially built by Avions Fairey in Belgium and much later produced by the sailplane manufacturers Slingsby.

Cheap flying was not really to arrive until the late 1970s and early '80s and it came from a completely unexpected quarter. During the 1960s the sport of hang gliding gave gliding a completely new dimension. By utilizing new methods of construction and modern materials, simple gliders could be made with steel alloy tubing and sailcloth to produce a robust and light glider. At first, hang gliders followed the old Rogallo wing shape, but were soon joined by more conventional wings. It was but a short, logical step to affix a low-powered engine to a slightly beefed-up structure. These early microlight aircraft were really powered hang gliders, with the pilot's legs providing the undercarriage. It was only another simple step, though, to provide a seat, and then a tricycle undercarriage, a bigger engine — and the answer to the sixty-year-old problem was there. Real flying was, at last, within reach of almost everybody. The flying motor cycle had arrived and one could fly in a simple machine costing one-tenth the price of a conventional light aircraft, with negligible running costs.

At the time of writing there are an estimated 50,000 microlights flying worldwide with 2,000 registered in Great Britain alone, a figure that accounts for a large proportion of all the private and club aircraft registered. Apart from cost, the reason for the sport's popularity is its comparative freedom from the many restrictions that apply to the microlight's bigger brethren. But there is currently a real threat that over-legislation and increasing regulations could greatly reduce the freedom, and thus the appeal, of this form of aviating. Allowed reasonable flexibility, the potential of microlight aviation is enormous. One

trend at the time of writing is towards producing scaled-down replicas of all types of full-size aircraft, particularly World War One biplanes. Microlights also provide an inexpensive method of research and development into new materials and new construction methods, a use to which several ultra-light aircraft were put between the wars. The de Havilland DH 71 was built to test the original DH Gipsy engine; the De Bruyne Ladybird was used to test plastic materials in aircraft construction; the Boulton and Paul P 41 Phoenix was an aerodynamic test aircraft. In addition the Dart Pup and Flittermouse introduced the use of synthetic-resin glues in aircraft, the Dart Kitten introduced the application of cambered aerofoil section at the wingtips as an antidote to tip-stall with tapered wings, and the same aircraft had a single strut, cantilever undercarriage with rubber discs inside telescopic struts — which, incidentally, became a feature of the Mosquito. The cantilever undercarriage was introduced with the Parnall Pixie. Thus the ultra-light was also used as a useful device for experimentation.

Many may argue that the microlight has taken the place of the ultra-light. It certainly provides the cheapest method of flight and it has brought powered flying within reach of almost anyone who has the desire to fly. Many of today's microlights bear more than a passing resemblance to Santos Dumont's 1908 Demoiselle. His dream of skies blackened with aerial motor cycles is within an ace of becoming reality.

Ultralights: the early British classics

Austin Whippet

One of the first companies to make a serious attempt at producing a sporting single-seater aircraft after the First World War was the motor-car manufacturer Austin Motor Co Ltd of Northfield, Birmingham. Under the direction of John D. North, who had earlier designed aircraft for the Grahame-White company at Hendon and later went on to work with Boulton and Paul, Austin Motors first became involved with the aviation industry during the war, building Royal Aircraft Factory BE 2c, RE 7, RE 8 and SE 5a aircraft under contract to the War Office. In addition, the company produced three designs of its own. These were the AFB 1 single-seat fighter built to the design of Captain Albert Ball VC DSO MC, the AFT 3 Osprey triplane and a two-seat fighter-reconnaissance biplane named the Greyhound. None was put into production.

When war ceased in November 1918 lucrative war contracts quickly evaporated. Instead of turning its back on the aircraft industry the Austin company retained a small staff headed by John W. Kenworthy, who had designed the Greyhound and who, before joining the company, had worked on the design staff of the Royal Aircraft Establishment at Farnborough under Captain Geoffrey de Havilland. During the winter of 1918-19 the Austin design staff designed a diminutive 21 ft 6 in fighter-like biplane of metal and wood construction intended for the wealthy private owner who had limited maintenance capabilities. Named the Whippet, the prototype aircraft was completed during the early summer of 1919 and was given the temporary registration *K-158*; it was registered to the manufacturers on 14 July.

The immensely strong steel fuselage was built up in two sections, the dividing point being located immediately behind the cockpit. The diagonally-braced structure consisted of longitudinals, diagonals and crossmembers of circular-section steel tubing, all of which were easily replaceable. There were no bracing wires and the makers claimed that the structure would remain unaffected by changing climatic conditions.

The 45 hp six-cylinder air-cooled Anzani radial engine was mounted so that it overhung the front of the fuselage frame. Special shock-absorbing rubber buffers fitted between the engine and the fuselage absorbed much of the engine vibration. The engine was neatly cowled in aluminium.

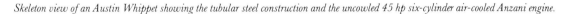
Skeleton view of an Austin Whippet showing the tubular steel construction and the uncowled 45 hp six-cylinder air-cooled Anzani engine.

The prototype Austin Whippet, K-158, in original paint scheme. This aircraft was later registered G-EAGS.

The foldable wings were of standard wood construction and had a very high factor of safety. Each wing was built up on hollow box-section spars with steel tubes acting as compression members and internally braced with piano wire. Streamline-section N-struts separated the top and bottom wings and lift bracing was via streamlined steel tube diagonal struts. The only wire bracing was used in the centre-section, which was carried on two pairs of vertical streamlined steel struts. The upper and lower

wings were hinged at the rear spar roots and, because the bracing tubes were anchored at their lower ends to the wings and not the fuselage, no de-rigging was necessary. The Whippet's wing incidence could be altered by adjustable rear lift struts. Ailerons were fitted to the top wings only, which had about 3 in of forward stagger and both wings had 3° of dihedral.

The tailplane was of similar construction to the wings and was of quite thick section, being braced with telescopic streamlined struts. In order to compensate for different pilot weights the tailplane incidence could be altered on the ground. Construction of the elevators and rudder was of steel tubing, though the ribs were wooden. The triangular fin had an additional ventral extension.

The undercarriage was of standard V-type with tubular tierods and a bungee-spring axle. The steerable tailskid was sprung by means of a compression spring working within telescopic tubes.

The flying controls were conventional, with engine control being via pushrods. Unusually for the time, the Anzani engine could be started from within the cockpit. Beneath the pilot's seat was sufficient space for a toolkit and luggage.

Initially the Austin was unregistered and it bore the Austin logo on the fuselage and rudder. Early *Flight* three-view drawings show the prototype fitted with a two-cylinder engine but it is unlikely that such an engine was ever installed. Advertised at between £400 and £500, the prototype remained unsold. It was granted a Certificate of Airworthiness on 4 December 1919 and given the permanent registration *G-EAGS*. Evidently engine cooling was a problem with this aircraft, for later photographs depict it with a different cowling, designed to expose the cylinder heads to the airflow. After the Austin company ceased its aviation interests the prototype passed to C.P.B. Ogilvie at Hendon. After the C of A had expired in November 1921 the aircraft was withdrawn from use.

A further four Whippets were built. The second and third aircraft, registered *G-EAPF* and *G-EAUZ*, were put on exhibition at Olympia at the Sixth International Aero Exhibition during July 1920. *G-EAUZ* was shown uncovered, its simple robust construction attracting much attention. This aircraft passed through several ownerships during the 1920s and during 1928 was re-engined with a 60 hp Anzani,

Above left *The prototype Whippet with uncowled Anzani, later registration and with the starboard wing folded. This aircraft remained unsold and after the Austin company turned its back on aviation the aircraft passed to C.P.B. Ogilvie.* **Left** *The second Whippet, G-EAPF, was originally registered in November 1919. Painted silver overall with black letters the aircraft survived until the early 1930s.* (P.T. Capon photograph)

before passing to F.G. Miles some time after the C of A had expired for the last time. The registration was finally cancelled in 1931. Whippet *G-EAUZ* was registered to A.J. Greenshields and was shipped to Argentina in July 1920, where it became *R-151* and was flown until withdrawn from use in 1929. The two final Whippets were exports to New Zealand where one was delivered to that country's first private owner, H.H. Shaw. One of the aircraft, registered *ZK-ACR*, was apparently still in existence at Kai-Iwi in the 1940s.

Unfortunately, the Whippet was ahead of its time. As someone once said, private flying was still regarded in official quarters as a secret vice. Had the aircraft been a two-seater and put on to the market at the same price the story may have ended differently. Perhaps the advent of private flying would have been brought forward by several years. The Whippet was a commercial failure, however, and the Austin company concentrated all its resources on the motor-car industry.

Austin Whippet data (45 hp Anzani)	
Span	21 ft 6 in
Length	16 ft 0 in
Wing area	134 ft^2
Empty weight	580-600 lb
All-up weight	810 lb
Maximum speed	95 mph
Cruising speed	not available
Stalling/landing speed	35 mph

Avro 534 Baby

One of the first contenders for what eventually transpired to be a non-existent single-seat sporting aircraft market during the immediate post-war years was Roy Chadwick's pretty, snub-nosed Avro 534 biplane, designed and built during the winter of 1918-19 at the company's Hamble works near Southampton.

There being a chronic shortage of small aircraft engines at the time, the Avro 534 was designed around the only suitable engine that could be found, in this case an ancient four-cylinder, inline, water-cooled 35 hp Green engine that had once propelled the Avro Type D biplane back in 1911. The engine was modernized by the Green company and installed in the unregistered prototype 534, which was originally referred to as the Popular but which was later christened Baby.

The prototype Baby was completed in the spring of 1919 and on 30 April Avro test pilot H.A. Hamersley took the Baby off for its one and only flight. The two-minute maiden flight ended when the Baby spun into the Hamble foreshore from low altitude after the ignition switch had been inadvertently turned off. Though Hamersley was flying again within days, only the engine of the prototype was salvaged and this was installed in the second aircraft. On 10 May this aircraft, differing in various respects from its short-lived predecessor and temporarily registered *K-131*, made its first flight, from Hamble.

The Avro Baby bore a very strong resemblance to previous members of the Avro family, both outwardly — even down to the Avro-style rudder, and internally. The Baby's fuselage was of rectangular section and had spruce longerons and struts of conventional wire-braced girder construction. The ridged fuselage decking was stringered and fabric-covered. The fabric fuselage covering could easily be removed for inspection purposes.

The 25 ft-span wings had built-up box-section spars with leading edges spindled out to a U-section. The trailing edges and wingtips were of steel tube and the ribs were of wooden girder construction. Box-girder ribs were located at compression points where loads were imposed by the internal drag bracing. Ailerons were fitted to the top and bottom wings and were interconnected by wires. The wing cells had one

The first, short-lived and unregistered Avro Baby prototype at Hamble in April 1919. The aircraft crashed on its first flight, on 30 April 1919, after the ignition switch was accidentally knocked off.

Top *The second Avro Baby, K-131, later G-EACQ, taking part in the Aerial Derby Handicap Race at Hendon on 2 June 1919. (Flight* photograph) **Middle** *The third Avro Baby, G-EAUG, had a plywood fuselage and is seen here leaving Hendon at the start of the Aerial Derby Handicap Race on 24 July 1920. The aircraft was destroyed at Ipswich a few days later. (Flight* photograph) **Above** *The two-seat Avro Baby, G-EAUM, had a longer nose, unlouvred cowlings and four engine exhaust stubs. G-EAUM survived until the mid-1930s.*

pair of wooden interplane struts on either side. The four centre-section struts were streamline steel tubes. The tailplane was of similar construction to that of the wings and there was no fixed vertical fin.

The Green engine was mounted on two wooden engine bearers on transverse supports bolted to robust struts. The honeycomb-type radiator was mounted car-fashion in the fuselage nose and gave the Baby its characteristic angular, snub-nosed appearance. The engine was gravity fed from an 8 gallon tank which gave a range of 200 miles at cruising speed. The engine was neatly cowled with a removeable aluminium cowling which had large inspection panels giving access to all vital engine parts. A large pipe located on the port side of the engine carried the exhaust well away from the fuselage. All engine controls were of the pushrod type.

The undercarriage was of simple V-type, with circular section steel tube struts, streamlined with fabric-covered three-ply fairings. The divided axle was sprung with rubber shock absorbers. The ash tailskid was sprung with rubber cord and tipped with a steel shoe.

For such a small aircraft the Baby's cockpit was quite roomy. The pilot was comfortably seated on an upholstered cushion beneath which was an aluminium bucket-type seat. Behind the padded headrest in the deck fairing was located a small luggage locker. A three-ply floor covered with aluminium sheet formed a heel rest for the pilot's feet. The decking in front of the folding-type windscreen was designed to deflect the slipstream from the pilot's face.

The Baby's cockpit controls operated the control surfaces via cables and pulleys. The Baby was fully aerobatic and had a very good short-field performance. It could be flown very economically, at half the maximum power of 1,500 rpm. The biplane was excellently finished and was put on the market at around £500.

The second Avro Baby, *K-131*, made its racing debut during the summer of 1919 in the hands of Hamersley. It won a trophy and £100 in the Hendon Aerial Derby held on 21 June. At the end of July the aircraft was repainted in a jazzy lozenge paint scheme and, again in the hands of Hamersley, proceeded to prove that it was no mere racing sprint freak by flying non-stop from Hounslow to Brussels in 2 hr 50 min on 14 August. It then proved its aerobatic prowess at Rotterdam on 31 August, flown by W.G.R. Hinchcliffe. On 13 January 1920 the Baby was wrecked in turbulent weather while being flown by its designer over Hamble. Once again the Green engine was salvaged and the aircraft was rebuilt, emerging a different aeroplane but still retaining the original registration markings. During the rebuild the chance was taken to incorporate various modifications. These included the fitting of tapered ailerons, raising the tailplane and extending the height of the rudder. In this form the Baby was purchased by H.J. 'Bert' Hinkler, who intended to fly it back home to his native Australia. Having taken off from Croydon on

31 May 1920 he had only reached Rome when he was forced to return to England because hostilities in Syria blocked his route. The non-stop flight from Croydon to Turin, a distance of 650 miles, was carried out in 9½ hrs, a feat which earned Hinkler the Brittania Trophy. *G-EACQ* subsequently made the journey to Australia by ship, arriving in Sydney on 18 March 1921. Shortly afterwards Hinkler sold the Baby to H.E. Broadsmith of the Australian Aircraft and Engineering Company Ltd, who put the aircraft on floats for film work. The Baby passed through several other ownerships, during which the cockpit was enlarged and it was turned into a two-seater. After being damaged in its hangar in December 1930 *G-EACQ* was grounded until 1936, when it was flown to Hamilton in Victoria. It subsequently disappeared into obscurity until it was rediscovered in a Melbourne garden in March 1970. It was restored to its original single-seat configuration by the Royal Queensland Aero Club and is currently on exhibition at the Queensland Museum at Brisbane, painted as *G-EACQ*.

Back in October 1919 a second Baby emerged from Hamble, fitted with twin-floats. Registered *G-EAPS* it was designated Avro 534A Water Baby. External differences from the original aircraft included the addition of a large fin and lower wings of less span, necessitating inward-sloping interplane struts. On 7 September 1921 the Water Baby crashed into Southampton Water.

In July 1920 a third Baby, with special plywood-covered fuselage and shorter span wings, was built and raced in that year's Hendon Aerial Derby Handicap. Flown by Hamersley, the Avro 534B, registered *G-EAUG*, came first, closely followed by Hinkler flying the Baby *G-EACQ*. The Avro 534B was lost in a crash at Bentley near Ipswich on 4 August 1920.

Built at the same time as *G-EAUG* was the two-seat Avro 543 *G-EAUM*, in which the cockpit had been enlarged to accommodate two occupants. The fuselage was lengthened by 2 ft to cope with the resulting change in the position of the centre of gravity. With two up the performance was marginal and, after several years of unsuccessful racing, *G-EAUM* was eventually acquired by F.G. Miles and Lionel Bellairs at Shoreham. There it was given more power in the form of a 60 hp ADC Cirrus I engine. How this aircraft led to the designing of the Southern Martlet is described in a later chapter. After Miles and Bellairs sold the Baby, it continued to soldier on until the mid-1930s, its ultimate fate being unrecorded.

Four further Avro Babies were built. A clipped wing Avro 534C was raced in the 1921 Aerial Derby but in the hands of Hinkler, who was by then Avro's chief test pilot, it forced-landed and was withdrawn from the race. On 6 September 1922, the same pilot

Top The Avro 534A Water Baby, pictured at Hamble in October 1919, crashed on 7 September 1921. **Middle** *The Green-engined Avro 534D Baby, G-EAYM, was flown in India for several years until withdrawn from use at Calcutta in 1929.* **Above** *The Russian pilot Gwaiter flew this Avro Baby from London to Moscow in May 1922 and is seen here enjoying a well-earned smoke on this arrival.*

was flying *G-EAXL* when the engine cut and he was forced to crash into Southampton Water.

There followed the Avro 534D Baby, *G-EAYM*, which featured steel engine bearers and other modifications to give better engine cooling for operation in the hot Indian climate where owner Captain E.

Villiers flew it on communications work for several years.

An unregistered experimental single mid-wing Baby was built to test multiple aerofoils, and then there was the Avro Baby *G-EBDA*, which was delivered to Moscow during mid-1922. A final Baby, designated Avro 554 Antarctic Baby and registered *G-EBFE*, was a two-seat seaplane modified for operation from a ship in sub-zero temperatures by unskilled operators. Modified to carry camera equipment, and fitted with an 80 hp le Rhone rotary engine, the Antarctic Baby left for the Antarctic aboard the Shackleton Expedition's ship *Quest* in September 1921, but returned a year later having been diverted to Rio de Janeiro through bad weather. Because the expedition's supplies had been left at Cape Town, the Baby was never used by the team. It had to wait until the following year before it could fly in the role for which it was designed, when it operated with the Aerial Survey Company, based in New-foundland from March 1924. It flew several seasons on the search for seals before it was replaced by an Avro Avian in 1927.

The Avro 554 Antarctic Baby, registered G-EBFE, was powered by an 80 hp Le Rhone rotary engine. Destined never to reach the Antarctic, for which it was designed, the Baby flew with the Newfoundland—based Aerial Survey Company during the mid-1920s.

the Blackburn Aeroplane and Motor Co Ltd. The First World War had hardly ended when the company came up with a design for a tiny, side-by-side mid-wing monoplane powered by a two-cylinder, horizontally opposed, air-cooled ABC Gnat of 40 hp. In true Blackburn tradition the Sidecar was the epitome of ugliness and is by far the least beautiful aeroplane covered in this book. Be that as it may, the Sidecar was a serious attempt to attract the private pilot — and his girlfriend — into the air as cheaply as possible. The sociable seating was in itself quite a departure from normal practice at the time, though Blackburn was to continue with the concept through its line of light aircraft and training aeroplanes for years to come.

The Sidecar's fuselage was of wood and had a tri-angular section. The three sides were built up with lattice girder and diagonal spruce struts, the whole

Avro 534 Baby data (35 hp Green)	
Span	25 ft 0 in
Length	17 ft 6 in
Height	7 ft 7 in
Wing area	180 ft²
Empty weight	616 lb
All-up weight	870 lb
Maximum speed	80 mph
Cruising speed	70 mph
Stalling/landing speed	32 mph

Blackburn Sidecar

Quick to pursue the motor cycle-of-the-air notion was

The one and only Blackburn Sidecar photographed in the factory shortly after completion. The two occupants lend scale to this 27 ft 3 in span mid-wing monoplane. (Via A.J. Jackson Collection)

The Blackburn Sidecar was originally engined with a 40 hp ABC Gnat, though it is doubtful if the aircraft flew at all. (Via A.J. Jackson Collection)

being fabric-covered. Added to the flat top of the main triangular structure was a light plywood framework which gave the occupants a modicum of protection. It came up to about shoulder height and converged towards the tail. The pilot and passenger sat atop this pyramidal structure in an open cockpit barely protected from the slipstream by two tiny windshields. Though there was provision for conversion to cabin comfort it is doubtful if this was ever carried out. Entry to the cockpit was via downward-hingeing doors.

The wooden wings were built with spruce and plywood ribs. The leading and trailing edges were of flattened steel tube and bracing wires ran from two-thirds out along the wing to a strengthened cross member located forward of the cockpit, which doubled as the instrument panel. Another pair of bracing wires ran from the same point on the wings to the keel-like bottom of the fuselage, on which was mounted the V-type undercarriage, the forward legs

The Blackburn Sidecar on exhibition at Harrods in April 1919. (*Flight* photograph)

of which were attached to the wingroot fittings. Each forward leg was made up of two steel tubes faired with wood veneer. The bungee-sprung half axles were hinged at the fuselage centre-line attachment points. The spoked wheels were faired with fabric and the tailskid was rubber-sprung.

The 14 gallon fuel tank was located beneath the seats and fuel was pumped by means of a wind-driven pump located on the starboard side of the cockpit; a hand-pump topped up the air pressure.

Construction of the Sidecar was completed at the company's factory at Brough early in 1919, some months before civil flying was officially resumed in Britain after World War One. In an effort to attract sales the Sidecar was exhibited briefly at Harrods department store in London in April 1919 and was later shown at a store in Reading, priced at £450. On 26 August the Sidecar was registered *G-EALN* to K.M. Smith, c/o Elder, Smith and Company of London and South Australia. In 1921 it was purchased by Blackburn's London manager B. Haydon-White, who re-engined the aircraft with a 100 hp ungeared Anzani air-cooled engine. The Gnat engine certainly never lifted the Sidecar off the ground and there are no reports of it flying with the Anzani. In any case the Sidecar was dismantled by the end of 1921.

Blackburn Sidecar data	
Span	27 ft 3 in
Length	20 ft 6 in
Height	6 ft 3 in
Wing area	123 ft^2
Empty weight	392 lb
All-up weight	850 lb
Maximum speed	83 mph
Cruising speed	not available
Stalling/landing speed	not available

The 15 ft span Crow was powered by a 35 hp ABC Gnat which was installed immediately above and forward of the pilot's head.

BAT FK 28 Crow

One of the most innovative aircraft designers of his day was Dutchman Frederick Koolhoven. His designs were numerous and varied from transport aircraft to fighters. The construction of Koolhoven's aircraft was contracted out to a number of companies, with each design prefixed FK and followed by a numerical designation. Sir W.G. Armstrong Whitworth Aircraft Ltd built or held the designations FK 1 to FK 17 and British Aerial Transport GB Ltd (BAT) built FK 22 to FK 28. BAT was formerly Youcques Aviation Company, formed in 1917; after December 1919 the works were taken over by General Aeronautical Contracts Ltd.

In 1919 Koolhoven became attracted to the idea of a motor cycle-of-the-air — a theme which recurs throughout the inter-war years like a hardy perennial. Koolhoven's FK 28 design was a truly minimal aircraft and in general layout was very similar to the pre-World War One Santos Dumont Demoiselle, often regarded as the world's first light aeroplane and developed by its Brazilian designer from 1907-9. The FK 28 Crow was powered by a 35-40 hp ABC Gnat two-cylinder horizontally opposed engine mounted on the leading edge of the wing. The pilot was suspended below the wing in a tiny streamlined nacelle, like a motor-cycle sidecar. Barely inches from the pilot's face was the propeller, the uncowled Gnat engine being located forward of and above him. Immediately above the pilot was the fuel tank and magneto and, as if this position was not already perilous enough, the pilot sat in a wicker-bound basket-type bucket seat, his backside only inches from the ground.

The wing had no bracing wires and the centre-section was a self-contained unit, carrying the engine and attendant fuel and oil tanks. The tailplane was supported on two booms and the tiny aircraft could be dismantled for road transport by removing twelve bolts.

The Crow was built at Willesden in north-west London and completed in 1919. In September it was shipped to Amsterdam for the ELTA exhibition, still unflown. It is uncertain when the first attempts were made to coax the Crow into the air but one of the few people to try was Major Christopher Draper, the 'Mad Major', who was BAT's test pilot. It is reported that the Crow handled well, though the Gnat engine was temperamental and rarely gave full power. On one flight from Hendon the Crow took five miles to reach a height of 500 ft! Another pilot who is reported to have flown the Crow was ex-RNAS Captain C.R. Vaughan. He apparently had a narrow escape in this machine when the bucket seat came adrift from its anchorage and he was unable to reach the rudder bar

The Crow's pilot sat in what amounted to a motor cycle side-car. Here the victim is seen clutching the control column with his right hand, whilst his other hand holds the throttle. (A.J. Jackson Collection)

as the Crow careered across Hendon's uneven grass surface. Vaughan eventually managed to get his act together, and the Crow was otherwise undamaged. Because of its proximity to the ground, landing and taking off would have presented a false impression of speed to the pilot. It was only too easy to attempt to take-off too soon, before flying speed had properly been reached. Similarly, approach and landing speeds would seem deceptively high and, unless the pilot was very experienced, the Crow would be stalled unintentionally.

In July 1920, by which time BAT has closed down, the Crow was exhibited at the Olympia show in London, where its small size attracted a great deal of interest particularly, as *Flight* reported, 'from the fair sex, and from the younger visitors of the "superior" sex'. However, the Crow was just too difficult to fly, it had a very poor gliding angle, and as a single seater it would have had little appeal as a social runabout to either sex — fair or 'superior'. Thus it was that the FK 28 Crow was scrapped, though its propeller survives in the hands of a Surrey connoisseur.

BAT FK 28 Crow data	
Span	15 ft 0 in
Length	14 ft 0 in
Height	4 ft 6 in
Wing area	76 ft^2
Empty weight	220 lb
All-up weight	400 lb
Maximum speed	75 mph
Cruising speed	not available
Stalling/landing speed	not available

The BAT Crow was similar in general layout to the Santos Dumont Demoiselle of 1908. Note pilot's wicker seat and the wheel/skid undercarriage arrangement. (A.J. Jackson Collection)

Bristol Type 30 and 46 Babe

At first glance the Bristol Babe looks more like a product of the mid-1920s rather than something produced a year after the ending of World War One. Bristol's designer, Frank Barnwell, guessed that with the glut of recently demobbed Service pilots there existed a market for a small, cheap-to-run aircraft with fighter-like lines that would appeal to private pilots who wanted a fun machine. The resulting design was a 19 ft 8 in span single-seat biplane of pleasing appearance.

The Bristol Type 30 had a fuselage built up of a light wooden framework covered with three-ply, which was fabric covered. To give better than adequate protection the fuselage was doped with three coats of red lead on the inside. In addition to the three-ply covering, the fuselage was braced with thin cross laths — there was no internal wire bracing.

The bottom wing was smaller in chord than the top wing and the streamlined V-type interplane struts were anchored to reinforced blocks on a strengthened rib on the lower wing. In effect the lower wing had three spars, the leading edge being particularly well built. Ailerons were fitted to the top wing only and were operated by cables passing over pulleys in the bottom wing. The wings had no dihedral and the bottom wing was sufficiently staggered for the pilot to have a good view forwards and downwards from his roomy cockpit. The fin and rudder were made of light steel tubing of flat section and were fabric covered.

The Babe had a simple V-type undercarriage of narrow track, the undercarriage struts being vertical when viewed from the front. The tailskid consisted of a simple small steel leaf-spring.

Close-up of the 40 hp Siddeley Ounce engine fitted to the third Bristol Babe, exhibited at the 1919 Paris Salon.

Immediately forward of the instrument panel and forming a streamlined continuation of the fuel tank and oil tanks, was a removable box or, as *Flight* described it on 7 January 1920, 'a portmanteau provided with a handle to facilitate its transport when removed from the machine' — in other words, a suitcase. Nick Comper was to use the idea in the Swift ten years later.

The finished Babe bore the unmistakable Barnwell lines, its designer having been responsible for the successful line of World War One fighters, including the Bristol F 2B Fighter.

It had been the intention to power the Babe, or Bobby as it was originally called, with a five-cylinder air-cooled ABC Gadfly radial, designed by Granville Bradshaw. However, by the time Bristol had reluctantly given the go-ahead for the production of two prototypes, ABC Motors Ltd had ceased production of aero engines to concentrate on motor cycle engines. The first Babe, construction number 5866, was fitted with an ancient 45 hp Viale radial engine which had earlier powered one of A.V. Roe's Avro biplanes. Later is was damaged after being fitted to an enclosed cockpit Avro monoplane and, as Barnwell had been involved with the fitting of this engine, he managed to retrieve it from Avro's Manchester works, refurbish it and fit it to the Babe.

The first flight of 5866 was made on 28 November 1919 by Bristol chief test pilot Uwins, albeit unintentionally. During fast taxi-ing trials he could only avoid a flock of sheep on Filton aerodrome by taking off over them. The Babe's flying characteristics were good and it was considered suitable for an experi-

Top left *Bristol Babe Mk 1 fitted with a 35 hp Viale, engine, originally used in an Avro biplane in 1911. (Via P.H. Green)*
Left *This view of the uncompleted Bristol Babe shows the plywood-covered fuselage and the structure of the uncovered wings and tail unit.*
Below *The fighter-like appearance of the Bristol Babe is apparent in this photograph. The engine is believed bo be an ABC Gadfly.*

enced pilot but a little unstable for the novice. In addition the engine would not run for more than ½ hr without overheating, which rather limited its flying.

In the meantime a third Babe, c.n. 5875, was built and fitted with a 40 hp Siddeley Ounce and exhibited at the Paris Salon in December 1919. The other two Babes meanwhile were without a suitable engine and it was not until they had been fitted with seven-cylinder 60 hp le Rhône rotaries that they were registered. Babe 5866 became *G-EAQD* on 18 December 1919 and 5865 was registered *G-EASQ* on 14 April the following year. Both were designated Mk III. The le Rhône engines were not really suitable because they vibrated badly when run above 45 hp. The Paris Salon machine, the Babe Mk II, was never flown and was not registered.

In May 1920 *G-EASQ* was modified to a monoplane. Barnwell had produced a thick-section cantilever wing which he wanted to test. Though it was fitted to the Babe, Barnwell was uncertain what affect the downwash from such a thick wing would have upon the elevators; the aircraft was not flown. Though the registration was cancelled in February 1921 the monoplane Babe, designated Type 46B, was still in existence in 1924 in company with *G-EAQD*. The latter never carried its registration letters, the registration being cancelled in December 1920.

The only surviving remnant of the Babe is the Viale engine, which can be seen today in the Science Museum in London. Had the Babe appeared at the 1923 *Daily Mail* Lympne trials its chances might well have been good, though the choice of engine would have been problematic. In addition, the empty weight of the Babe was 460 lb, which was equal to the all-up weight of some of the competitors. Barnwell did not forsake the ultra-light, for he designed the

Bristol Babe, G-EASQ, number 5865, was registered on 14 April 1914 and was fitted with a 60 hp Le Rhone radial engine.

Bristol Type 91 Brownie for the 1924 Lympne trials and later designed the BSW Mk 1, which was to be his undoing.

Bristol Type 30 and 46 Babe data	
Span	19 ft 8 in (upper wing) 18 ft 8 in (lower wing)
Length	14 ft 11 in
Height	5 ft 9 in
Wing area	108 ft²
Empty weight	460 lb
All-up weight	683 lb (Viale) 840 lb (le Rhône)
Maximum speed	85 mph (Viale) 107 mph (le Rhône)
Cruising speed	not available
Stalling/landing speed	not available

GWE 6 Bantam

On 1 May 1919, civil flying was officially resumed following the First World War. One of the first to make a bid for a share in the future of civil aviation was Claude Grahame-White, one-time owner of Hendon Aerodrome, whose aircraft manufacturing company had been lucratively employed on war contracts. After the Armistice a large percentage of the Grahame-White Company workforce had to be laid off or employed on non-aeronautical work. However, a skeleton design staff was retained to produce drawings of seven categories of aircraft designed to meet all the civil aviation requirements of the forseeable future. Of these, three reached prototype stage.

The first of the three was a single-engined two-seat trainer called the Instructional. The second was a large five-seat luxury passenger aircraft known as the GWE 7 Limousine and powered by two Rolls-Royce Eagle Vs, and the third was a diminutive sporting single-seat biplane called the Bantam.

The GWE 6 Bantam was designed for Grahame-White by Frenchman E. Boudot. Boudot had worked on the design staff of Boulton and Paul, where he had been involved with the P 7 Bourges, and he had also designed the little Nestler Scout, a Pup-like biplane powered by a 100 hp Gnome Monosoupape rotary engine. The Scout was completed in 1917 but was wrecked on 26 March the same year when being aerobatted in very windy conditions at Hendon. Fabric ripped away from the wings, causing one of them to collapse, and the aircraft crashed into the L & P hangar, killing the pilot J.B. Fitzsimmons.

Boudot's brief for the Bantam was simplicity and ease of construction and manufacture. The first two examples were built concurrently and were designated GWE 6 and GWE 6A. Their wings were of standard wooden construction with I-sectioned main spars and they employed a wing section designed for high lift rather than for speed. The top wing was of greater span and larger area than the bottom and had no dihedral. The rear spar was further forward than was customary, to allow for a larger cutout at the rear of the centre section to accommodate the pilot's head. The GWE 6A had the top wing attached to the top of the fuselage, below which a box-like structure contained the fuel tank. The lower wings, built in separate halves, were attached to the fuselage via two short spars integral with the fuselage. The front spar attachments were located between the front and rear undercarriage struts, whilst the rear spars joined the rear undercarriage strut.

The fuselage was of girder type with solid ash rectangular section longerons. The spacers aft of the cockpit were vertical and wire-braced but forward they were arranged in a series of rigid triangles. The

forward portion of the fuselage was covered with three-ply, the rear section being fabric covered. The nose section was circular, to accommodate the 80 hp le Rhône rotary engine, but thereafter the fuselage became less rounded to taper to an almost flat-sided section at the tail. The fuselage top was turtle-backed, and plywood-covered partway from the rear of the cockpit. Its underside was flat bottomed.

The neat and well laid out cockpit was well instrumented, the panel being mounted on to the rear spar of the centre-section just below eye level. The overhung le Rhône was mounted on pyramid-type engine bearers which were bolted on to a 14 gauge steel plate capping the front fuselage. The engine was tidily enclosed by an aluminium cowling. A small diameter wooden propeller had to be specially designed to allow adequate ground clearance without a stalky undercarriage. Even so, the clearance during take-off was minimal.

The other Bantam, GWE 6, differed from its sister aircraft in the top wing arrangement. Instead of being secured directly to the fuselage this machine had a small gap between wing and fuselage, thus giving the

Above *The GWE 6A Bantam, with the top wing attached to the top of the fuselage, was powered by an 80 hp Le Rhône rotary engine and had ailerons on the top wing only.*

Above right *Two Bantams, with K-153 in the background, lined up for the start of the Fourth Aerial Derby at Hendon on 21 June 1919. The Le Rhône rotary of the nearer Bantam seems to be chucking out a great deal of oil. (Flight photograph)*

Left *The GWE 6, G-EAFK, seen here with early K registration, was painted yellow with blue trim.*

Right *Bantam K-153 in the long grass at Hendon in 1919. The hangar in the background is now the site of the RAF Museum. (Flight photograph)*

pilot better forward vision. A larger, square cut-out in the centre-section enhanced the pilot's view. The fuel tank was carried in a hump in the top of the fuselage immediately forward of the cockpit.

The completed Bantams weighed 640 lb empty and tipped the scales fully laden at 995 lb, giving a disposable load of 200 lb less fuel. The wing span was 20 ft, the lower wing spanning 18 ft 4 in, and overall length was 16 ft 6 in. Total wing area was 130 sq ft, the top wing being 83 sq ft. The generously large tailplane was 9 ft across with 10 sq ft of elevator area. The aircraft had sufficient fuel capacity for 2-3 hr flying and a maximum speed of 100 mph.

Both Bantams were flying by April 1919, and were registered *K-150* (GWE 6) and *K-153* (GWE 6A). When the British system of registration changed in July 1919 they were re-registered *G-EAFK* and *G-EAFL*. Both were entered for the first British postwar air race meeting, the Fourth Aerial Derby, held on home ground at Hendon Aerodrome during the Whitsun Weekend, 21 June 1919. A dozen aircraft faced the starter's flag, and for the Bantams — which were not designed for racing — the field was formidable, competing aircraft having engines of four and five times the power. To confuse the layman the BAT company had also entered two aircraft called Bantams, though of totally different and earlier design. Bantam seems to have been a common term applied to small aircraft at the time. The racy BAT Bantams were powered by unreliable ABC engines but were much favoured to win. The rest of the field comprised a Bristol Monoplane, the second Avro Baby powered by a 35 hp Green engine and two Airco DH 4s, one a 4R with sawn-off wings and powered by a monster 450 hp Napier Lion. A Martinsyde F 4 and the fastest entrant, a Nieuport Nighthawk, completed the field.

Captain P.R.T. Chamberlayne flew *K-150* and Major R.H. Carr, a popular pre-war Hendon pilot, flew *K-153*. Since their early flights the Bantams' tails

had undergone modification. The original flat-topped rudders had been modified to follow the line of the top of the fin to a point. The aircraft was very sensitive longitudinally and not easy to fly.

In the event neither Bantam completed the course. Major Carr was forced down at Hounslow with engine trouble, and Chamberlayne completed only one lap before he was forced down at Epsom. The race was won by the Airco DH 4R, flown by Captain G. Gathergood. According to one observer this aircraft appeared to be dragged through the air rather than flown.

Both Bantams appeared at the Hendon Peace Meeting, held a couple of weeks later. This was an attempt to recapture the popularity of the pre-war pylon races, with four or five aircraft flying off heats towards a final. The Bantam did well, Chamberlayne taking first place and Major Carr third. But disaster awaited Chamberlayne.

Immediately after passing the post Chamberlayne decided to give an impromptu aerobatic display in *K-150*. He dived low and rounded one of the pylons and then appeared to lose control of the aircraft. The

Bantam G-EAFL seen at Shoreham after being acquired by F. G. Miles in 1926. Note the Gnat Aero Company's logo on the fin.

Bantam was notoriously difficult to handle, and one observer criticised Chamberlayne's handling of the Bantam as well as the design itself: 'He is a dashing pilot, but either the side surfaces of the machine need re-designing, or he has a curious way of handling it; it has an ugly habit of progressing cornerwise for an appreciable time before getting into a bank for a turn.'

At any rate Chamberlayne lost the Bantam at the pylon, and the aircraft careered towards a hangar, where it wedged itself into one of the metal supports. Soaked with fuel but uninjured, Chamberlayne carefully removed himself from the Bantam and descended to *terra firma*, none the worse for his spot landing. The Bantam was a write-off and never flew again. The other Bantam was raced extensively for the remainder of the 1919 season until put into storage.

Somewhat intrigued by some of the odd features of the Bantam's design, the author asked Arthur Ord-Hume to comment on the general arrangement of the aeroplane:

'An aspect ratio of only 4.4, directly overlapping sesquiplane-type wings a mere three feet apart (maximum) (ie a gap of only two-thirds that of the main wing chord), a super-imposition of the wings so arranged as to negate the stagger, and an angle of incidence far too insignificant for such a design all must have conspired most horribly to make the machine both unmanoeuvrable and unpredictable, particularly at any sort of speed.

'Sadly, the designer seems to have got very little right, for the massive tailplane area — the span was 45 per cent of the wing — was matched by a truly insignificant fin and rudder.

'The real fun must have occurred in aileron turns. With 8 sq ft on each side, almost ten per cent of the wing area, and before the days of differential aileron control, those barn doors must have been the cause of some moments of dubious control responses.

'If the gap had been increased to at least 4 ft 6 in, the lower wing moved back by about 6 in, both wings given around 3° nominal incidence, the tailplane area reduced to 12 sq ft and the rudder moved up to 7 sq ft it might have been a fair aeroplane. Of course, if we were doing it today, we would not start with that shape in the first place.'

Despite offering to sell the first ten Bantams at a reduced price of £500 each under the pretext of furthering sporting flying, only one other Bantam was built. This third aircraft was sold in South Africa and flown at agricultural shows by A.V. Everitt. In Britain there was little interest in single-seat aircraft, and there was no market for new aircraft when it was introduced.

Grahame-White GWE 6 Bantam data	
Span	20 ft 0 in
Length	16 ft 6 in
Wing area	130 ft²
Empty weight	640 lb
All-up weight	995 lb
Maximum speed	100 mph
Cruising speed	not available
Stalling/landing speed	40 mph

Lowe HL(M) 9 Marlburian

One of the first true homebuilt ultralight aircraft built in Britain was that built by twenty-year-old F. Harold Lowe of Heaton, Newcastle-upon-Tyne, in 1921. This enterprising young chap had already designed and built a series of aircraft and on one of them had taught himself to fly at the tender age of 16½. Lowe began building aeroplanes as a hobby in 1916 and the culmination of his several years' experience was a small monoplane that bore more than a passing resemblance to the Fokker E III. The H.L. Marlburian was a 28 ft 6 in span monoplane powered by a 60 hp Gnome engine. Design work on the aircraft took five months of spare time, while construction was completed in 840 hr. Apart from the engine, wheels, propeller and instruments the aircraft was built by Lowe from raw materials at his home at Heaton.

The Marlburian was an attractive little aeroplane of fairly orthodox lines. The fuselage taperered to a knife edge at the stern, after the style of those neat pre-war Morane-Saulnier aeroplanes. The fuselage was wide in order to accommodate a pilot and passenger side-by-side and was built on four longerons, with spruce struts and cross members, braced with steel wire. The front three bays were covered with plywood. At the undercarriage attachment points the lower longerons were built into a girder section to provide greater strength. The undercarriage was of normal V-type with solid spruce struts of streamline section, bound with tape. The Palmer Aero wheels were sprung from the chassis by rubber cord shock absorbers and the steerable tailskid was built of steel.

The wings has solid spruce spars, the front spar being located almost on the wing leading edge. They were of thin section and had considerable camber, the tips being raked with rounded edges. Alternate ribs were of box section and served as compression struts. There were four bays of internal bracing. The other ribs were of normal I-section. Great attention was paid to the wing bracing, which was in the form of a steel wire. Eight lift wires were attached to the bottom fuselage longerons and four landing wires were attached to two inverted-V cabanes, rather like the system used on the Deperdussin monoplanes. In addition there was one external drag wire attached to each wing. Because the only shed available to Lowe was small, the Marlburian had to have its wings removed frequently and for this purpose all wire attachments were of the quick-release type — the wings could be removed in about 20 min. The ailerons had channel-section spruce leading edges, with streamline steel tubing trailing edges. The controls were differential and all springs and control rods were underneath or inside the wing, thus allowing an unencumbered top wing surface.

The tailplane was made of spruce box spars, the

Top *F. Harold Lowe's Marlburian monoplane seen during an early stage of construction. Note the side-by-side seating and the windmill-type pump mounted on the forward right-hand undercarriage strut.* **Above** *In this view of the uncompleted Marlburian the uncovered port wing has been temporarily fitted. Note the wide fuselage and tiny vertical tail surfaces.*

Below *The completed Marlburian photographed in 1921. The likeness to pre-war Morane-Saulnier monoplanes is evident.*

Left *Another view of the completed Marlburian. Construction took 840 hours and apart from the engine, wheels, propeller and instruments the entire aircraft was built by Lowe from raw materials at his home.*

Right *The RAE Zephyr photographed at RAE Farnborough in 1923, where it was built by the Royal Aircraft Establishment Aero Club. Flight Lieutenant P. W. S. Bulman, who tested the aircraft, is seen sitting in the cockpit.* (*Flight* photograph) **Below right** *Only known photograph showing the RAE Zephyr in flight.* (Via A.J. Jackson Collection) **Bottom right** *Close-up of the 500 cc Douglas engine. Rated at 3 ½ hp this motorcycle engine developed closer to 17 hp at 4,000 rpm driving the 5 ft propeller at half engine speed.* (*Flight* photograph)

front spar being braced by tubes to the lower longerons while the rear spar was braced by wires to the top and bottom fins. The elevator was of the divided type. The original fin and rudder were too small, as can be seen in the photographs, and were later enlarged to give better control on the ground.

The 60 hp Gnome engine was mounted on a steel plate in the nose, the shaft being supported on a transverse channel steel bearer designed to take the thrust. The cowling and side panels were made of aluminium, the latter being hinged like the car bonnets of the time. The petrol tank was located beneath the seats and fuel was supplied by means of a windmill-type pump mounted on the forward right-hand undercarriage strut. The gravity-fed oil tank was situated just in front of the instrument panel.

The Marlburian made its first flight during the early part of 1921. The initial flight of nearly half an hour was followed by many more flights and, on 7 October 1922, the aircraft was registered to the designer, who was trading as the Northern Aerial Transport Company, as *G-EBEX*. Sadly, the Marlburian crashed on 25 November 1922.

Lowe HL(M) 9 Marlburian data

Span	28 ft 6 in
Length	17 ft 0 in
Height	8 ft 4 in
Wing area	107 ft²
Empty weight	450 lb
All-up weight	not available
Maximum speed	100 mph
Cruising speed	85 mph
Stalling/landing speed	33 mph

RAE Zephyr

In October 1922 a group of Royal Aircraft Establishment personnel formed a club to design, build and fly light aircraft and gliders. The group's chairman and test pilot was Flight Lieutenant P.W.S. 'George' Bulman, who was later to achieve fame as Hawker's chief test pilot. The RAE Club's designer was S. Child and the first design to progress beyond his drawing board was the Zephyr, a pusher-engined biplane that bore more than a passing resemblance to the World War One FE 8 fighter. The Club may well have been influenced by its choice of design by an article that appeared in *Flight* magazine some months earlier in which the advantages of the pusher concept were extolled; a far better view for the pilot and the absence of slipstream being two of them.

The single-seat, twin-boom Zephyr was built at RAE Farnborough during 1922-23 and was completed by the end of August 1923. The 29 ft span aircraft was powered by a 500 cc Douglas motor cycle engine rated at 3 ½ hp, though at 4,000 rpm it developed more like 17 hp. The two-bladed 5 ft diameter propeller was chain driven at half the engine speed.

Though originally intended to take part in the 1923 Lympne trials for single-seat light planes, the Zephyr was not solely designed as a competition aeroplane. It was robustly built and consequently was considerably heavier than most of the competing machines: its loaded weight, with pilot and fuel, was 635 lb.

Bulman made the Zephyr's maiden flight on 6 September 1923 from Farnborough. The aircraft lifted off after a ground run of only 80 yds in nil wind, and Bulman really put the aircraft through its paces for 15 mins. On landing he stated that the Zephyr was 'wonderfully controllable' and that he had full lateral control right down to the stalling speed — due no doubt to the large rudder area and the efficient

ailerons.

By the time that the Zephyr had flown, the RAE Club had completed its second aircraft, the Hurricane monoplane, which took the Zephyr's place in the 1923 Lympne trials. The Hurricane is described in a later chapter. The Zephyr was registered *G-EBGW* and was scrapped in 1925.

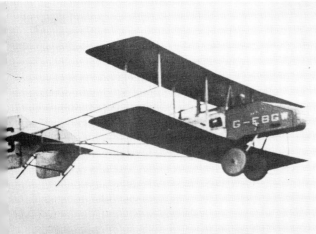

RAE Zephyr data	
Span	29 ft 0 in
Length	not available
Height	not available
Wing area	250 ft²
Empty weight	approx 435 lb
All-up weight	635 lb
Maximum speed	not available
Cruising speed	45 mph
Stalling/landing speed	not available

ANEC I

The Air Navigation and Engineering Co Ltd at Addlestone in Surrey was formed during the First World War, initially to build Blériots and later Spads for the RFC/RAF under the management of Norbert Chereau.

One of the most significant events in 1923 was the arrival of the Bristol Cherub engine, a flat twin of 1,070 cc capacity which could produce around 18 hp at 2,500 rpm. Work on the Cherub had begun in 1922, under the leadership of Roy (later Sir Roy) Fedden. During exhaustive tests the engine had successfully run non-stop for 10 hrs. Two versions were made available. One had a 2:1 reduction gear, and the other had a driving boss run at crankshaft speed for use with a chain-driven propeller. The engine weighed 85 lb. At that time the only engines available

Above *One of the two Lympne ANEC Is under construction at the Addlestone works of the Air Navigation and Engineering Company Ltd in mid-1923. (Flight photograph)* **Below** *ANEC 1, Number 17, seen at Lympne during the trials in October 1923. It was in this machine that Maurice Piercey climbed to 14,400 ft and clinched the £200 prize for the greatest height attained during the trials.* (Via Terry Heffernan) **Bottom** *Piercey's ANEC I being pushed out for further flying at the Lympne trials, October 1923. (Flight photograph)*

to the embryo lightplane movement were an assortment of unreliable motor cycle conversions. With the arrival of the Cherub, ANEC immediately set out to build an ultra-light aircraft around it.

ANEC's designer was an Australian, W.S. 'Bill' Shackleton, whose name crops up again in subsequent chapters. He was later to co-design the Shackleton-Murray SM 1 and a host of other aircraft, mainly for the Beardmore company, including the Wee Bee, covered in a later chapter. The shape of the ANEC I closely resembled that of the Dornier Komet, though on a reduced scale, and there were various design similarities.

The ANEC I was a high-wing, single-seat, single-engined wooden monoplane, designed to be as small as possible. It was one of the earliest ultra-lights in this country — and one of the most remarkable in terms of overall performance. The high engine position, the parallel semi-cantilever wing, the short cantilever beams projecting from the floor of the fuselage and carrying the shock absorbers were all reminiscent of the Komet. One of the more novel ideas in the design was the spar structure. The custom at the time had been for two spars spaced some distance apart, but in

Germany designers were having great success with a single spar strengthened by a plywood leading edge. This D-box arrangement gave great strength and good resistance to torsion. Shackleton was also impressed with the Junkers method of multi-spar construction, and in designing the ANEC wing he combined both methods. The spar consisted of three thin booms, running from wingtip to wingtip, covered with three-ply. The apex of the triangle formed by them was on the heavily cambered top surface of the wing, and the base was flush with the wing's flat lower surface. As it happened the flat-bottomed spar formed a convenient base for attaching the wing to the fuselage. Together with the three-ply leading edge the wing successfully withstood stresses of 6,200 lb/in^2 under bending tests.

The fuselage consisted of four spruce longerons covered with three-ply. The skeletal bulkheads were strengthened where necessary by covering them front and back with ply, thus forming boxes. At the rear of the fuselage the bulkheads were built up to form an integral fin.

The undercarriage consisted of two wheels mounted on a cantilever structure of steel tubes projecting from each side of the fuselage, between which the axles were rubber-sprung with cord shock absorbers. The wheels followed a German practice of the time and were quite ingenious. A rim of ash strip was wound spirally around a mould, the ends being tapered down and the wheel turned on a lathe to make it perfectly true. Five spokes supported the rim, and were secured to the rim and hardwood hub by triangular fillets. The whole was then covered with plywood. The tyre was simply a leather strip; the wheel weighed 5 lb and could sustain a weight of 1,000 lb.

Above *Close up view of the ANEC I's inverted 696 cc inverted Blackburne Tomtit Vee twin, a modified motorcycle engine built by Burney and Blackburne Engines Ltd of Bookham, Surrey.* (Via Terry Heffernan) **Below** *The clipped wing ANEC IA, G-EBIL, numbered 15, taking part in the Grosvenor Trophy Race at Lympne on 3 August 1925.* (*Flight* photograph)

The pilot sat in a low hammock seat; access to the cockpit was via a small hole in the middle of the wing. Initially the view from the cockpit was fairly good, but later modifications changed all that.

The thick, untapered, high aspect ratio wing was built in one piece and was attached to the fuselage by steel stirrup strips that passed over the triangular spar. The wing was externally braced by two struts either side of the fuselage.

The reduction-gear version of the Cherub engine was to have been mounted high in the nose of the ANEC to give sufficient ground clearance for the two-bladed propeller. At the same time it kept the aircraft very low to the ground, allowing the pilot to step from the cockpit straight on to the ground. Owing to the high position of the engine and because the carburettor was placed above it, gravity fuel feed was impossible.

The completed ANEC was an incredibly strong structure; the factor of safety was high, and with a projected wing loading of 3 lb/ft^2 and with a landing speed of 30 mph it would have been possible to put the ANEC down in almost any small field. The tailskid, located almost midway along the fuselage, made an effective brake.

When the *Daily Mail* Lympne trials were announced early in 1923 the rules stated that engines were limited to 750 cc or less. Shackleton nonetheless decided to enter the ANEC I and redesigned the front end of the aeroplane to take an inverted Blackburne Tomtit Vee twin of 696 cc. The ANEC thus became the first aeroplane to fly with an inverted engine in the UK. The engine was installed upside-down to enable the cylinders to lie snugly alongside the sloping sides of the upper part of the fuselage. The crankcase was covered by an easily removable front cowling, giving the new engine a much cleaner arrangement. There were differences too with the undercarriage, which was now hinged at its centre and protruded nine inches either side of the fuselage, giving slightly greater track. In addition a Cellon trapdoor covered the upper surface of the wing above the pilot's head, restricting the poor chap's upward view.

Two ANEC Is were initially built concurrently at the large Addlestone works and they were ready to fly in August. The first aircraft made its first flight on 21 August from Brooklands in the hands of Jimmy James. During the 15 min flight the pilot took the ANEC to 1,000 ft and landed at Brooklands satisfied with the machine's handling, though the rudder was

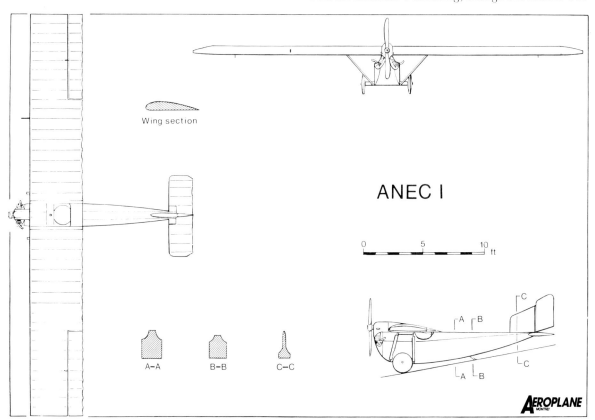

Wing section

ANEC I

0   5   10
ft

A-A   B-B   C-C

AEROPLANE
MONTHLY

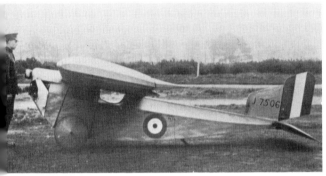

Top *ANEC I* G-EBHR *during an engine run at Brooklands in August 1923. The aircraft was sold to A. G. Simpson in Perth, Western Australia in 1924.* (Leonard Bridgman photograph) **Above** *In August 1924 the Air Ministry purchased ANEC I* G-EBIL *for evaluation at RAF Martlesham Heath. Fitted with an 1,100 cc Anzani engine the aircraft was given the RAF serial number J7506.* (A.J. Jackson Collection)

not effective on the ground, making it difficult to taxi. Shackleton had anticipated this; a larger rudder had already been built and this was fitted immediately. James flew the ANEC again on 24 August and, though the weather was stormy, managed to climb to 1,600 ft for further tests; flight-calibrated Smiths instruments had been fitted since the maiden flight. A speed of 75 mph was reached and a landing speed of about 27 mph recorded. A further flight was made on 8 September when James flew from Brooklands to Croydon and back. By the time the ANEC had received its Certificate of Airworthiness and the registration letters *G-EBHR* the second aircraft, *G-EBIL*, had also flown. Both aircraft arrived at Lympne in time for the trials to begin on 8 October.

The two machines had been entered with Jimmy James and Maurice Piercey listed as joint pilots, thus allowing both pilots to fly either aircraft — a shrewd move as other competitors learnt to their cost. The aircraft were numbered 17 and 18 and passed the initial ground manoeuvering tests without difficulty. The speed, height and fuel consumption tests were

flown over the entire week and the ANECs performed head and shoulders above most of the other competitors. One of the ANECs narrowly missed winning the speed prize, its speed of 75 mph being less than 2 mph slower than the winning clipped-wing Pixie flown by Norman Macmillan. However the £1,800 and £500 prizes for the best distance flown on one gallon of petrol were shared by Jimmy James and the pilot of the English Electric Wren, both covering 87.5 miles. Victory came again when Maurice Piercey climbed to a staggering 14,400 ft in Number 17, taking 2½ hrs to do so, thus clinching the £200 prize for the greatest height attained during the trials.

Throughout the week the only problems to affect the ANECs were when one of the Tomtit engines cracked a cylinder and another needed a change of plugs, having to forced-land when they sooted up. Piercey borrowed a spanner from a passing motorist, got him to swing the prop and keep the cows at bay, and then took off, none the worse for the incident.

Another incident could have been disastrous. After climbing to 14,400 ft, Piercey, numbed with cold and with the Tomtit stopped, landed late and rolled at a great rate of knots towards the railed enclosures. With commendable presence of mind the BP rep ran out and hurled himself at one of the wings, swinging the ANEC around at the last moment, though it clipped Hubert Broad's DH 53 in the process.

After Lympne, *G-EBIL* was entered for the Tour de France reliability trial at Buc near Paris, qualifying for the event purely on the strength of the ANEC company's French ancestry. On the first day the French pilot was eliminated after a forced landing.

In August 1924 the Air Ministry purchased *G-EBIL* for evaluation, as it did various other lightplanes of the period. Fitted with a 1,100 cc Anzani engine the ANEC was repainted as *J7506*. No orders were forthcoming and the ANEC returned to Addlestone where further modifications were made.

With a shorter wing the ANEC IA, as it became, was entered for the Royal Aero Club August Meeting held at Lympne from 31 July — 3 August 1925. A larger, brass petrol tank, first installed for the Tour de France, was mounted on top of the wing. It was difficult to find a suitable propeller for the Anzani, and the engine was unable to develop full power for the races. It was also considered that the cutting down of the wings did little to improve the performance. The take-offs were very long, and valuable time was lost getting onto course. In the racing Jimmy James was hopelessly outclassed. To cap it all he stood the aircraft on its nose after landing in a rut, and the inadequate prop was broken, but not before the ANEC had won the speed prize for averaging 83.7 mph over the 50 km course.

Meanwhile the other ANEC I, *G-EBHR*, had been sold in Australia as *G-AUEQ* to A.G. Simpson of Perth. A third and final ANEC I also went to Australia. In May 1925 *G-AUET* arrived at Rockhamton, where it was flown until withdrawn from use in May the following year.

ANEC I data (696 cc Tomtit)	
Span	32 ft 0 in
Length	15 ft 7 in
Height	4 ft 0 in
Wing area	145 ft²
Empty weight	290 lb
All-up weight	470 lb
Maximum speed	74 mph
Cruising speed	not available
Stalling/landing speed	32 mph

Avro 558

Quick to respond to the 1923 competition was the Avro company, which entered three aircraft: two biplanes to the same design, the Avro 558, and a monoplane, the Avro 560, subject of the next chapter. The unnamed Avro 558 biplane was designed by the company's chief designer, Roy Chadwick, whose later designs included the Lancaster and the Vulcan. The 558 bore the unmistakable Avro stamp and was built at the company's Hamble premises at the edge of Southampton Water. The aircraft's notable features included a marked stagger of the high aspect ratio wings, single I-shaped interplane struts and the proximity of the lower wings to the ground.

The wings, which had an aspect ratio of 10:1, were of standard construction with spruce spars of box section, ribs with spruce flanges and three-ply webs,

and leading and trailing edges of small diameter steel tubing. The wings were fabric-covered and the top wings were attached to a wide span centre-section. Interplane struts were made of solid spruce of streamline section and were slotted into V-shaped Duralumin plates which were bolted to fittings in the wings spars.

The fuselage consisted of four longerons braced with diagonal struts forming a Warren girder, the struts being attached to the longerons by three-ply plates. The top longerons formed a straight horizontal line and the main structure of the fuselage was fairly shallow, being made up to the required depth by a deep deck fairing consisting of spruce stringers supported on three-ply formers. The sides of the fuselage were not quite flat, as stringers were added to keep the fabric clear of the formers.

The tailplane was of the cantilever type to which was hinged the divided elevator. The fairly large rudder was balanced and hinged to the fuselage sternpost. There was no vertical fin.

The undercarriage was simply two 22 in diameter bicycle wheels carried on a steel axle and sprung by rubber cord. They were so mounted that about half their diameter projected through the fuselage floor, thus presenting little drag. The disadvantage was that the undercarriage track was necessarily narrow, but to compensate for this tip skids were added to the lower wings.

The two Avro 558s were powered by different engines. The first aircraft, which was unregistered but numbered 5 in the competition, was powered by a Grigg B and H engine of undisclosed power. It was a direct drive, twin cylinder, air-cooled Vee-type motor. The second Avro 558, registered *G-EBHW* and bearing competition Number 11, was powered by a 500 cc twin-cylinder, horizontally-opposed Douglas motor cycle engine. It had an external flywheel driving the propeller through a 12½:1 chain

reduction gear. Theoretically the engine would produce 18 hp at 5,400 rpm. The engines were mounted on Duralumin plates that projected forward from the fuselage sides. Petrol and oil were carried in a twin tank mounted on the top fuselage longerons immediately behind the engine. Such an arrangement gave sufficient height for direct gravity feed.

The aircraft's controls were standard but the rudder was controlled by pedals and not by the customary footbar of the period. The pilot sat on the floor and the decking over the cockpit was hinged to allow only his head to poke through. The view from the cockpit was very good, with the narrow fuselage and pronounced wing stagger giving particularly good vision vertically down over each side of the fuselage.

The first Avro 558, Number 5, had been entered for the competition by the A.V. Roe company, with the diminutive Bert Hinkler as pilot. The second aircraft, *G-EBHW*, had been built for G.E. Bush and H.A. Hamersley, the latter being the pilot. Right from the start of the competition the Grigg-engined machine ran into trouble. There were problems with both the propeller and the engine. This did not particularly worry Bert Hinkler because he was also the pilot of the Avro 560 monoplane and was able to concentrate on notching up miles for the distance prize in this aircraft.

The aircraft flown by Hamersley fared much better. It gained second prize of £100 for the height tests, reaching 13,850 ft on 13 October. The descent was so slow that some wag on *The Aeroplane* penned the following ode:

'Hamersley, Hamersley, where have you been?
I've been to the sky in my Avro machine.
Hamersley, Hamersley, what did you there?
The ruddy thing stopped so I came down by air.'

The Avro 558 was also very stable and Hamersley amused the crowd by flying up and down their ranks with his arms held up in the air.

When eventually the first Avro was coaxed into the air, by a Lieutenant Barrett, high winds forced it down suddenly and it was damaged. It did not complete any laps of the circuit and no official figures were recorded. After the competition it was returned to Hamble where it was modified to take the more powerful 698 cc Blackburne Tomtit engine. In addition both aircraft had their undercarriages changed to allow more clearance for the lower wings from the ground. Aircraft Number 5 was fitted with a more conventional, strutted undercarriage of wider track and the other aircraft was modified with an undercarriage that consisted of two wide vertical struts.

Two weeks after the Lympne meeting Number 11

Top *The first Avro 558, numbered 5 for the trials, seen at Lympne in October 1923. The hinged decking over the cockpit has been removed.* (Via Terry Heffernan) **Above** *The second Avro 558, G-EBHW, seen at Hendon after receiving a Blackburne Tomtit engine and revised undercarriage.* (A.J. Jackson Collection) **Left** *This front view of the second Avro 558 shows the wide wing span (30 ft) and the low frontal area.* **Below** *The modified second Avro 558 flying at Hendon on 27 October 1923, with Hamersley as pilot.* (*Flight* photograph)

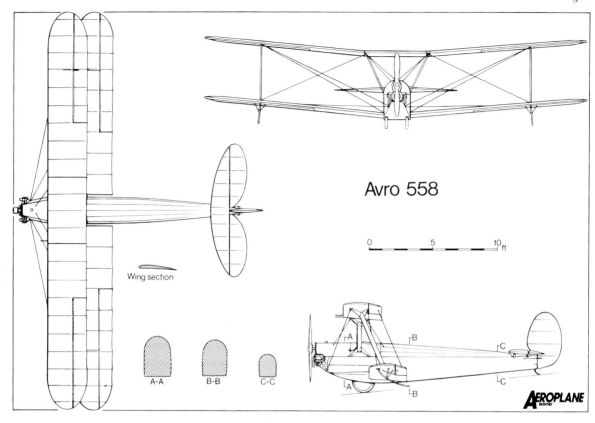

Avro 558

Wing section

A-A   B-B   C-C

Below *The first Avro 558 with 698 cc Tomtit engine and conventional strutted undercarriage, in which form it was raced at Hendon in October 1923.* (A.J. Jackson Collection)

took part in the Royal Aero Club Light Plane Demonstration at Hendon on 27 October 1923. Once again the pilot was Hamersley and, competing against some of the aircraft that had flown at Lympne two weeks earlier, he managed to come third in the main race with some pretty, low-level flying.

The ultimate fates of both Avro 558s are unknown, and there is no record of their colour schemes.

Avro 558 data (500 cc Douglas)	
Span	30 ft 0 in
Length	19 ft 6 in
Height	not available
Wing area	166 ft²
Empty weight	294 lb
All-up weight	480 lb
Maximum speed	60 mph
Cruising speed	not available
Stalling/landing speed	30 mph

Above *The Avro 560 photographed during construction at Hamble in mid-1923. Note the aerofoil shape of the fuselage. The 696 cc Tomtit engine was bolted to a Duralumin plate.* **Below** *The Avro 560 at Lympne in October 1923. Numbered 6 the aircraft was flown by H.J. 'Bert' Hinkler. (Via Terry Heffernan)* **Bottom** *In this view of the Avro 560 the narrow track undercarriage and the wide span (36 ft) are evident. (Via Terry Heffernan)*

Avro 560

In addition to entering the Avro 558 for the 1923 Lympne trials the company entered a 36 ft span monoplane, designed by Mr A.V. Roe himself. The existence of this aeroplane was announced in *Flight* in August 1923 and it was completed and test-flown shortly before the trials in October. It was a cantilever monoplane of conventional construction, powered initially by an upright 698 cc Vee-twin aircooled Blackburne Tomtit engine.

The fuselage of the Avro 560 was constructed in a similar manner to the 558 biplane, though the shape was totally different. It consisted of four spruce longerons with spruce struts placed diagonally to form a Warren girder and attached to the longerons with three-ply 'biscuits' glued and nailed into position. The fuselage was fabric covered throughout and longitudinal stringers kept the fabric clear of the struts. Though flat-sided, with flat decking and bottom, the aerofoil-shaped fuselage was well streamlined and offered little drag.

The wing had a pronounced taper, both in chord

and thickness, and was built in two halves. At the wing roots the spars projected in order to fit into openings, rather like a large model kit, and were then bolted together with joiner plates to form a continuous girder. The bi-convex wing section was an American idea, and had the disadvantage of producing a sudden stall. The spars were built-up box sections with flanges of solid spruce and webs of double diagonal spruce sheets which gave rigidity. The wing ribs had T-section spruce flanges joined by means of corrugated Duralumin struts and ties. The drag bracing consisted of spruce struts and ties arranged in the form of a Warren girder and attached to the spar by means of more three-ply 'biscuits'. The wings were covered with special lightweight linen fabric doped with Titanine glider dope. An alternative set of wings of reduced span was also built, though the dimensions are not recorded.

The tailplane was made in two parts which fitted into attachments inside the rear fuselage; the two halves of the tail were fastened together so as to form a continuous member. No external bracing was required. The unbalanced elevators were hinged to the rear spar of the fixed tailplane. The balanced

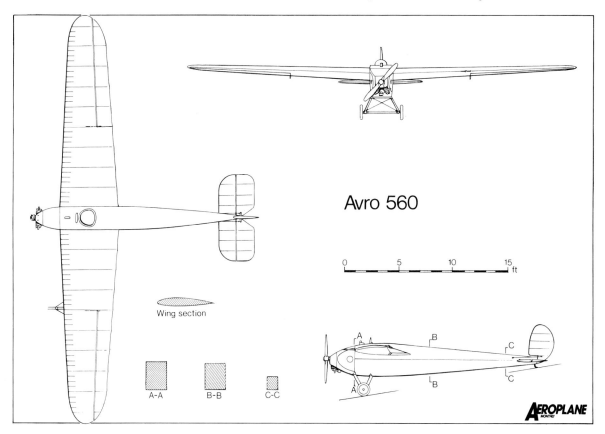

Avro 560

Wing section

A-A   B-B   C-C

rudder had a strong box-section main spar and spruce ribs. The ailerons were cable operated, though the elevators were activated by means of a long pushrod, and the rudder was operated by pedals.

The 698 cc Blackburne Tomtit engine was mounted onto a flat 8-gauge Duralumin plate by means of horizontal bolts through the crankcase lugs. The fuel tank was mounted under the deck of the fuselage immediately ahead of the front wing-spar. A special long induction pipe was fitted in order to give direct gravity feed to the carburettor.

The undercarriage was of simple design consisting of two light wooden wheels mounted on a steel tube axle supported from the fuselage by two struts on each side. The rubber shock absorbers were streamlined and the two struts were laterally braced by short tubes running diagonally to the centre of the fuselage.

The pilot's cockpit was located between the front and rear spars of the wing. The airspeed indicator was positioned in the wing root, thus allowing the mainplanes to be removed without disconnecting the instrument.

The empty weight of this 36 ft span aircraft was a mere 285 lb.

The unnamed Avro 560 arrived at Lympne in time for the first day of the trials on 8 October and was designated Number 6. H.J. 'Bert' Hinkler was the pilot. He was also the pilot of one of the Avro 558s, though in the event this aircraft was beset with engine problems and Hinkler was able to concentrate on the 560.

By the end of the first day's flying it was apparent that the 560 stood a good chance of winning the distance prize. The windy, dull weather prevented most competitors from doing any serious flying and all through the day Hinkler flew round the 12½-mile triangular course notching up the miles until 74 laps had been covered by the time dark fell. This was a distance of 925 miles and included ten laps, or 125 miles, in one non-stop flight. By the end of the trials Hinkler had covered 1,000 miles, or the equivalent distance of a flight from London to Rome, with fuel costs of only £1.

There was disappointment though for the Avro camp when the officials refused to allow the 560 to fly with the short wings. They argued that they would make it a different aeroplane. The Parnall team had solved this problem by entering two identical aircraft;

one with normal length wings, the other with them much shortened.

Over the four day period the Avro 560's fuel consumption had averaged 63 miles to the gallon, a figure that sounds good until one looks at the figures for both the Wren and the ANEC I, which both turned in a startling 87½ miles to the gallon!

A.V. Roe was well pleased with the company's performance at Lympne. The 560 had won two prizes from the Society of Motor Manufacturers and Traders and the British Cycle and Motorcycle Manufacturers' and Traders' Union, and one of the 558's had won £100 for reaching a height of 13,850 ft. A couple of weeks after Lympne, Hinkler took the 560 to the Lightplane Demonstrations held at Hendon aerodrome on 23 October. Some of the other Lympne contestants were also there and there was a race, for which the short wings were fitted to the Avro. Unfortunately there was a problem with the engine's inlet valve and Hinkler had to retire almost immediately.

The 560 was next seen at the Imperial Conference demonstration of British aircraft held at Croydon aerodrome on 10 November 1923. The six ultralights flew in company with their bigger brethren, providing a stark contrast with Vickers Virginia and Vulcan. Once more the Avro was flown with the short wings and in the hands of Hinkler was 'remarkably well handled'. The return journey to Hamble was made in 1 hr and 10 mins and the total fuel consumption for the double journey was just over two gallons.

In 1924 the Air Ministry had a requirement for a cheap light aircraft for use as a communications and general runabout. The Ministry assessed three aircraft; the Avro 560, the Parnall Pixie II and the DH 53 *Humming Bird*. By the time the 560 arrived at Martlesham Heath it had been fitted with a new inverted Blackburne Tomtit engine and a more conventional strutted undercarriage, with the wooden wheels replaced with those from one of the Avro 558s. For the assessment period the Avro bore the RAF serial number *J7322*. In the event the Ministry settled for the DH 53 *Humming Bird* and the Avro 560 never went into production.

Avro 560 data	
Span	36 ft 0 in
Length	21 ft 0 in
Height	not available
Wing area	138 ft²
Empty weight	285 lb
All-up weight	471 lb
Maximum speed	65 mph
Cruising speed	not available
Stalling/landing speed	34 mph

de Havilland DH 53

Bearing a strong resemblance to the DH 52 glider, built for the Itford gliding competition in 1922, the low-winged DH 53 was one of the first truly practical ultra-light aeroplanes and the first lightplane to be designed and built by the de Havilland Aircraft Co. Two were initially built for the 1923 *Daily Mail* trials; both were powered by 750 cc Douglas motor cycle engines.

The question of whether to produce a high-wing monoplane, as with the DH 52, or a low-wing design was carefully considered by de Havilland. The high-wing arrangement offered advantages of aerodynamic efficiency, and from the structural point of view wing struts worked in tension instead of in compression under flight loads, which meant that a

Above *The prototype DH 53 photographed at Stag Lane shortly after completion.* (*Flight* photograph) **Below** *The first two DH 63s photographed at Lympne in October 1923. Sylvia II, in the foreground, later became G-EBHZ and Number 8 was subsequently registered G-EBHX and is currently owned by the Shuttleworth Trust.* (Via Terry Heffernan)

certain amount of weight could be saved. A low wing, on the other hand, gave a good ground effect, and a narrower track undercarriage could be employed which, used in conjunction with wingtip skids, would help to prevent cartwheeling on landing — a manoeuvre that had been demonstrated by more than one ultra-light aeroplane. Another advantage of the low wing layout was that the position of the pilot could be moved around without having to meddle with the wing to allow access or adequate upward vision. A possible disadvantage was that, though the forward view was better with a low-wing configuration, a high wing offered better protection for the pilot's cranium in the event of the aircraft turning over.

A low-wing configuration was finally chosen and, although the DH 53 had been designed before the competition had been announced, construction was not started until shortly before the trials were held. The DH 53 was built along traditional de Havilland lines, to withstand the rigours of club-type mishandling, the wing structure having a safety factor of five. This show of strength was more than likely the result of a lesson learnt at Itford, when one of the DH 52s broke up in mid-air after the wing had warped uncontrollably. The aircraft was destroyed though fortunately the pilot, E.D.C. Herne, was unhurt in the accident.

The DH 53's fuselage was a light frame structure entirely covered with three-ply. There was no internal wire bracing and the four spruce longerons were connected at intervals by vertical and horizontal members which simply butted onto the longerons, unsecured except by way of the covering. The function of the members was more to prevent buckling of the ply than to tie the longerons together. However, by the end of the trials both aircraft were badly buckled by the damp conditions. The fuselage was rectangular in section and had a deep cambered deck. Steel tubing was employed in areas of greatest stress, such as where the wing bracing struts met the fuselage spars.

The wings were built up on two box-spars, with spruce flanges and three-ply walls. Very large ailerons were fitted. The spars were tapered, the

Above left *The wings of the DH 53 were originally intended to fold. Instead they could be detached by means of three quick-release pins and then attached to fittings on the fuselage sides. (Via Terry Heffernan)* **Above** *DH 53 Number 12 at Lympne in October 1923. Unusually for the time the Douglas engine wa silenced, short exhaust pipes being taken from each cylinder into a long collector pipe which can be seen curving beneath the fuselage. (Via Terry Heffernan)* **Below** *Almost the entire production run of DH 53s can be seen in this photograph taken at Stag Lane in early 1924. (Flight photograph)*

greatest depth being where the bracing struts were attached to the wings. The wings were not foldable, as had originally been intended, but could be detached by means of three quick-release pins and then attached to fittings on the fuselage sides. This, however, required more than one person to prepare the DH 53 for road transport. It had been intended to incorporate a universal joint at the rear spar so that wing folding could be a one-man operation.

The wing section used was RAF 15, though with varying thickness across the span. The ribs were spruce, and I-section compression struts were employed. The wing bracing struts were made of solid spruce, of streamline section, and they met at a point on the top fuselage longerons in an inverted V:

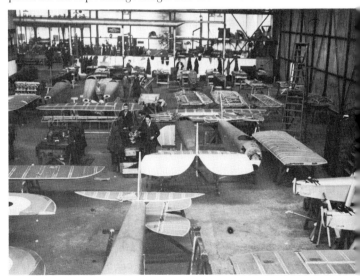

Six RAF DH 53s lined up at the 1925 RAF Pageant at Hendon. Powered by the Blackburne Tomtit, RAF DH 53s were used for light communications duties. (Flight photograph)

thus no wire bracing was necessary, the structure being triangulated.

The Douglas engine was simply fitted on a horizontal engine plate, the feet of which rested on the top longerons. With a small cowling fitting snugly over the top of the engine, the nose was uncluttered and neat. The ungeared Douglas engine drove a propeller of between 4 ft and 4 ft 9 ins in diameter. Unusually for the time, the engine was silenced, short exhaust pipes being taken from each cylinder into a long collector pipe which curved underneath the fuselage. This resulted in a pleasant purr instead of the earsplitting whine that accompanied motor cycle-engine-powered aeroplanes. The 2 gal fuel tank was located with the oil tank behind the engine bulkhead.

The DH 53's undercarriage was unlike those on most of the other competing aircraft. Many designers favoured partly enclosed wheels but the V-struts used on the DH 53 were both practical and well proven, being a miniature version of those used on standard-sized DH types.

The empennage of the DH 53 closely resembled that of the DH 52, being constructed in a similar manner with cable-operated rudder and elevators.

Though the DH 53 was designed early in 1923 the company's involvement with more commercial aircraft necessitated a late start on the first two aircraft. The first two DH 53s were completed in September 1923, with the second aircraft, construction number 99 (later to become *G-EBHZ*), making its first flight, according to Lloyd's, on 1 October 1923. The two aircraft were initially unregistered and were identified by names painted on their noses and competition numbers on their rudders. Thus the first aircraft, construction number 98, became *Humming Bird* and was numbered 8 and the second machine bore the name *Sylvia II* and the number 12. The de Havilland company had entered Number 8 with Hubert Broad as the pilot and A.S. Butler entered the second machine with Major H. Hemming as pilot. Before long Butler's machine had received the unofficial name *Hemming Bird*. Incidentally, it is

unclear whether the DH 53 was ever officially known as the Humming Bird — it is thought that the name given to the prototype came into use in favour of a type number.

After the two DH 53s arrived at Lympne on 6 October there was an anxious moment when it was discovered that neither aircraft would pass through the 10 ft gateway during the transport tests — the tailplane was just too wide. The problem was soon solved by clipping a few inches off each tip. Even before the trials proper began Hubert Broad was putting *Humming Bird* through its paces, carrying out evolutions that other competitors has no hope of emulating. But once again the common enemy — engine trouble — plagued both DH 53s through the meeting. Even though they were probably the best all-round performers at Lympne they won no prizes. They were not sufficiently powerful for the speed prizes, they were not clean enough for the consumption tests and they were not light enough for altitude competition. There was no prize for the best all-rounder, a state of affairs that was remedied at the following year's two-seater competitions, and only 'freaks' stood a chance of winning each class prize. The prize for the distance event, flown around a 12½ mile course, was almost within Hemming's grasp when a broken crankshaft put him out of the running.

During the consumption tests, Broad and Captain de Havilland had managed to cover 100 miles to average 50.8 mpg while Hemming, on Number 12, had averaged 59.3 mpg over a distance of 387 miles. Though the DH 53s had not taken away any prize money it was patently obvious to everyone present at Lympne that the type was the best performer. *The Aeroplane* commented, 'they will reap their reward in orders', and this was proved correct. After elimination from the trials Broad performed the whole gamut of aerobatics for the Lympne crowd.

The official report on the DH 53, compiled after Lympne, was full of praise for the aircraft. It gave high marks for the good take-off performance and drew attention to the good cushion effect of the low wing arrangement gave to landings. The large angle of wing incidence also greatly reduced the length of the landing run. The aircraft was regarded as a thoroughly good all-rounder in which spins could be carried out in complete safety. The DH 53 had excellent taxiing qualities and the pilot's view, except downwards, was good. The direct engine drive came in for some adverse criticism and was blamed as a contributory cause of the engine breaking up. It was felt too that, had the engine not been placed unnecessarily high up, the forward view would have been better still. The semi-monocoque construction was considered unsatisfactory, as the plywood had buckled and caused loss of strength.

After Lympne, *Humming Bird*, now registered *G-EBHX*, had its Douglas engine replaced with the more reliable 26 hp inverted, two-cylinder Blackburn Tomtit engine. The fuel capacity was increased by adding another fuel tank and disguising it in the form of a streamlined headrest, and the rather primitive bungee shock absorbers were replaced with little rubber compression units.

Now powered by a reliable motor, *G-EBHX* was flown from Lympne to Brussels on 8 December 1923, the 150 miles being covered in four hours! Slow as it undoubtedly was, the journey was made at a total fuel cost of just 10s. *G-EBHX*, renamed *L'Oiseau Mouche*, was raced extensively during the 1924 season with some success. Racing in the Grosvenor Trophy race that year *G-EBHX* came eighth, averaging 67 mph.

By this time the Air Ministry had taken notice of the Tomtit-engined DH 53 and ordered eight for light communications duties. As a result visitors to the 1925 RAF Pageant at Hendon were treated to the unique spectacle of six service DH 53s performing in the same piece of sky. These aircraft were numbered *J7268* to *J7273*. Two others, *J7325* and *J7326*, were successfully used in hook-on experiments with the airship *R33*. On 4 December 1926, Squadron Leader R.A. de Haga Haid, flying *J7325, successfully*

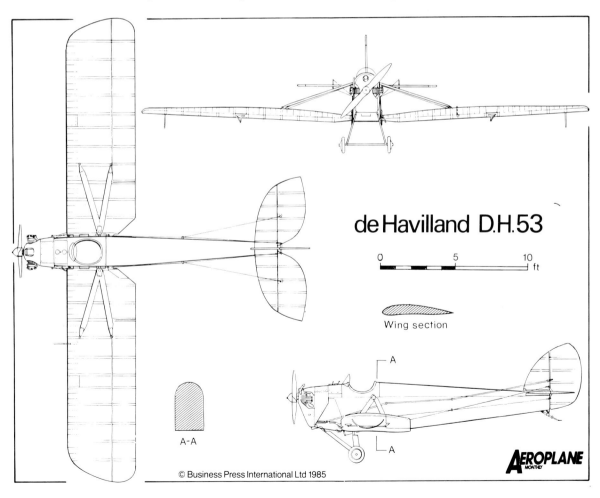

de Havilland D.H.53

Wing section

A-A

Aeroplane MONTHLY

The prototype DH53, G-EBHX, seen flying at its Old Warden base more than 50 years after it was built. (Air Portraits photograph)

dropped from a special rig attached to *R33* and returned, in flight.

Although no civil orders for the DH 53 were forthcoming, all eight RAF machines were disposed of to civil owners after they were struck off RAF charge. Several were made airworthy by the Royal Aircraft Establishment Aero Club at Farnborough, thus enabling most to fly on in private hands for many years. In addition five DH 53s were built for foreign buyers. *G-AUAC, G-AUAD* and one other went to Australia, and one each went to Czechoslovakia and Russia.

One British aircraft, *G-EBXN*, survived until destroyed in a hangar fire at Hooton Park Racecourse on 8 July 1940. Amazingly the prototype, *G-EBHX*, survives to this day and can be seen at the Shuttleworth Collection at Old Warden. In addition, a replica DH 53, powered by a 40 hp Continental A40, was built at Calgary in Canada. Registered *CF-OVE* to S.N. Green, the aircraft was first flown in May 1967.

In the not too distant future another 'DH 53' will be taking to the air in the UK. During the 1920s the

Clarke Cheetah Biplane was built utilising some DH53 parts. The mainplanes, Bristol Cherub III engine and other parts were then taken and used in the construction of the Martin Monoplane, *G-AEYY*, in 1937. This aircraft was acquired by Mike Russell recently and work is well advanced on producing two aircraft from the remains of the Martin. The intention is that one will be a DH 53, with many parts built from scratch; the other will be a new Martin Monoplane.

DH 53 data	
Span	30 ft 1 in
Length	19 ft 8 in
Height	4 ft 7 in
Wing area	125 ft²
Empty weight	326 lb (Douglas)
	326 lb (Tomtit)
All-up weight	524 lb (Douglas)
	565 lb (Tomtit)
Maximum speed	73 mph (Tomtit)
Cruising speed	50 mph (Blackburne)
Stalling/landing speed	33 mph (Tomtit)

English Electric Wren

Tucked away in a corner of one of the hangars at Old Warden, home of the Shuttleworth Collection of vintage aircraft, you will find a large, silver, single-seater monoplane that looks like a powered glider. A lucky few will have witnessed one of its rare excursions into the air, albeit at only treetop height. It is hard to believe that this 37 ft span aeroplane's empty weight is a mere 232 lb, that it is powered by a converted motor cycle engine of a mere 3 hp and that it comes from the same stable as the Canberra bomber, although 25 years separate the two designs.

In February 1923 the English Electric Co at Preston in Lancashire began work on a remarkable ultra-light designed by W.O. Manning in October 1922 for the Air Ministry. The Wren was an attempt at producing the lightest possible aircraft on the absolute minimum engine power. Manning designed

The first Wren was built for the Air Ministry and taken over during 1923 as J6973, having made its first flight on 8 April 1923.

what amounted to a powered glider of incredibly light structure powered by a 398 cc flat twin motor cycle engine.

The fuselage consisted of orthodox box girder structure reinforced at wing and main wheel attachment points. The longerons were made of ¾ in square section spruce, with crossmembers internally braced with 14 swg piano wire attached to plywood lugs or biscuits glued and screwed to the joints. Each bracing wire was adjustable by means of a 2½ in turnbuckle. There were no metal joints or brackets. The tubular undercarriage axle was fitted with two 300 × 60 mm wheels which were housed within the fuselage and protruded through the floor by just less than half their diameter. Springing was achieved by lashing the axle to the bottom longerons with elastic cord. A swivelling tailskid sprung with elastic cord gave excellent braking qualities.

The cantilever wings of 9.25:1 aspect ratio required no external bracing struts or wires and had a special high lift section. The spruce main spars were wire braced, and ribs were built up from ¼ in square spruce strips. The trailing edge was formed by a length of wire joining the ends of each rib, which gave an attractive scalloped appearance. The wings were built in two halves and joined together with steel plates and bolts fitted to the spar ends. Anchorage to the fuselage was by four U-bolts that passed around four cleats on the top longerons and were secured in position by butterfly nuts located on the top surface of the wings. The fuselage and wing leading edges were covered by three-ply on the upper surfaces. The rest of the airframe was fabric-covered and doped·with Titanine glider dope; the colour scheme was aluminium overall.

The 398 cc ABC engine, capable of producing between 7 and 8 hp, was mounted on light steel tubes and bolted to the top longerons in the nose. As a motor cycle engine the ABC would have been run at between 4,000 and 4,500 rpm but driving a 3 ft 9 in laminated Honduras mahogany propeller the engine produced a maximum of 2,700 rpm. Even at half throttle the Wren would sustain level flight.

The pilot sat in the nose of the aircraft immediately behind the engine with his head level with the wing leading edge. A portion of the wing was cut away to accommodate the pilot's head. From this position he had an excellent field of vision in all directions, especially over the downward-sloping front decking. The pilot's instruments panel was situated at the rear of the engine nacelle where it could be seen easily from the cockpit. The instruments consisted of an altimeter, engine rev-counter and airspeed indicator.

Initially one Wren was laid down, for the Air Ministry. Bearing the RAF serial number *J6973* it differed from the two following Wrens by having 4°

Top *Flight Lieutenant's Longton's Wren seen at the* Dail Mail *lightplane trials at Lympne in October 1923. (Flight photograph)* **Above** *Close-up of the prototype Wren's 3 hp ABC engine and the 3 ft 9 in laminated Honduras mahogany propeller. (Flight photograph)*

instead of 2° dihedral. First tentative hops of *J6973* took place at Ashton Park, Preston with the Air Ministry's pilot, Squadron Leader M.E.A. Wright, at the controls. Short hops of about 100 yds each and a few inches above the ground were satisfactory and a few days later, on 8 April, 1923, the Wren was taken to Lytham sands where Wright made a 7 min flight. The Wren took off in 50 yds and climbed to a height of 300 ft at 40 mph with the engine well throttled. Later a 68 min flight was made by the same pilot during which the Wren was flown for most of the time at full throttle. For the entire flight the Wren used less than a

gallon of petrol even though the carburettor was set too rich. The maximum level speed was measured as 52 mph and the Wren remained fully controllable right down to 26 mph, a little above the stalling speed.

The first Wren cost slightly more than £500 to build but it was thought that the type could be made available for around £350 — the cost of a contemporary training aeroplane was in the region of £1,200.

On 30 June, 1923 the Wren was displayed at the RAF Pageant at Hendon, for which it bore the number 11. C.G. Grey, editor of *The Aeroplane*, commented, 'She is intended for an RAF training machine, and as such ought to provide quite a lot of fun at RAF stations, though one imagines that before

Above left and above *Two further views of the first Wren,* J6973, *taken at the 1923 RAF Pageant at Hendon. This aircraft had 2° more wing dihedral than its successors.* (*Flight* photograph)

she is adopted for general use it will be necessary to fit a more powerful engine than the two-cylinder ABC. Perfectly tuned under Mr Manning's supervision, the ABC got the machine off the ground, and under the conditions of the Sutherland Prize (the Lympne trials) it will be worthwhile to fly the machine with such an engine, but for ordinary RAF training it would be unreasonable to expect RAF mechanics to keep these absurdly small engines up to competition pitch. She did at any rate show the crowd that it is

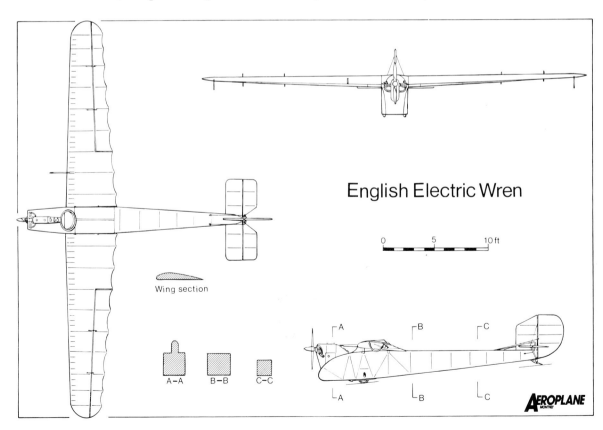

English Electric Wren

Wing section

A–A   B–B   C–C

AEROPLANE

After a long period of storage Wren Number 4 was restored to airworthy condition during 1956-57 and entrusted to the Shuttleworth Trust, where it remains today. (Air Portraits photograph)

possible to fly with ridiculously small power, but as she depends for her success on light loading, her wing span is quite as big as that of most higher-powered chasers, so that she did not give the impression of being a particularly small aeroplane.'

In fact the Wren's performance was not all that it should have been. During the 'parade' of New Types the ABC engine almost completely oiled up and it flew on virtually one cylinder.

The Wren remained at Hendon for a week while RAF pilots and others tried it out, including Squadron Leader Payn and Flight Lieutenant Longton. One pilot took the Wren up to 3,000 ft one evening and then had difficulty getting down before darkness fell. The gliding angle of the Wren was extremely flat and the pilot was anxious not to dive the machine too steeply.

Flight observed that with an empty-weight of 210 lb and allowing for a pilot of 140 lb, plus 10 lb of petrol and oil, the all-up weight of the Wren was 360 lb. At a speed of 40 mph it actually carried 100 lb per hp. Commercial aircraft of the period carried between 15 and 20 lb per hp and high-speed fighters around 61 lb per hp.

Two further Wrens were built and entered for the *Daily Mail* lightplane trials held at Lympne in Kent during the second week of October 1923. The Air Ministry pilot Wright flew the Wren numbered 3, and Number 4 was flown by Flight Lieutenant Longton. The two Wrens were identical.

As previously recorded the trials consisted of speed, height and fuel consumption tests. The big prize money was offered for the greatest distance flown on one gallon of petrol and it was this category that particularly interested the English Electric company.

Lots were drawn for the start of the flying order; Longton drew to fly off first and he set off just after 08:00 on 8 October. By the end of the afternoon he had recorded 85.9 mpg, though Jimmy James had already squeezed 87.5 mpg out of the ANEC I. Wright, on the other Wren, had managed nearly 72

mpg. On 11 October Longton equalled Jimmy James' figure and the Duke of Sutherland's £500 prize and the *Daily Mail*'s prize of £1,000 were shared jointly by the two pilots. On the last evening of the trials Longton performed his Hendon Pageant crazy flying routine on the Wren.

In April 1926 Wren Number 3 was registered *G-EBNV* to Alan Smith of Roundhay, Leeds, and the aircraft was stored at Bradford in 1929, later passing to R.H. Grant of Dumfries. Meanwhile Longton's Wren Number 4 was hanging up in the aeronautical section of the Science Museum in Kensington, next to Alcock and Brown's transatlantic Vickers Vimy, where it remained until returned for storage at Strand Road, Preston. In 1955 English Electric decided to rebuild the Wren and with the acquisition of the remains of Wren *G-EBNV* which were found on a farm in Dumfries, Wren Number 4 was restored to airworthy condition under the supervision of the aircraft's designer, W.O. Manning, then in his eightieth year. During the winter of 1956-57 the Wren took to the air once again. The English Electric company's experimental test pilot, Peter Hillwood, together with Roland Beamont, then flight operations manager and chief test pilot, did most of the flying. In 1957 the Wren was entrusted to the Shuttleworth Trust where it remains today, one of Britain's oldest airworthy civil aircraft.

English Electric Wren data	
Span	37 ft 0 in
Length	23 ft 0 in
Height	4 ft 9 in
Wing area	150 ft^2
Empty weight	232 lb
All-up weight	360 lb
Maximum speed	52 mph
Cruising speed	41 mph
Stalling/landing speed	25 mph

Gloucestershire Gannet

One of the prettiest, and unluckiest, aircraft designed and entered for the 1923 *Daily Mail* Lympne light aeroplane trials was the Gloucestershire Gannet, a diminutive biplane designed by the legendary fighter designer H.P. Folland around an experimental two-stroke engine. In November 1926 Folland had moved to Gloucestershire Aircraft Co Ltd, shortened to Gloster Aircraft, from the Nieuport and General Aircraft Co after it was closed down in 1920 and acquired by Glosters. Already responsible for the designing of the SE 5 and the Nieuport Nighthawk, Folland went on to design the Gamecock, Gladiator, Midge and Gnat fighters.

In 1923, while working on the Gloster Grebe and Grouse, he set to work to design a compact aeroplane that became an essay in miniaturization. The little biplane had a wingspan of just 18 ft and had an empty weight of only 283 lb.

The fuselage was flat-sided and covered with ply-wood. It had a deep top deck fairing which consisted of spruce stringers on light formers and covered with fabric. There was also a shallower fairing along the bottom of the fuselage. The lower wing centre section was attached to the lower fuselage longerons and the top centre-section, carried on four streamlined tubular struts, housed the fuel tank.

The wings were of standard construction and were of fairly thick section. The wing spars were I-section spruce beams; the ribs had spruce flanges and struts, with cut-out three-ply webs. Streamlined steel tube struts separated the unstaggered upper and lower wings and the wing bracing was in the form of stream-lined wires. The folding wings were hinged at the top and bottom of the spars and had quick-release pins in the front spar attachment points. In addition the top centre-section could be folded upwards to allow the pilot access into the cockpit.

The tail was of orthodox construction and consisted of a wire-braced fixed tailplane with divided unbalanced elevator, and a triangular fin on which was hinged the unbalanced rudder.

The pilot's cockpit was located immediately below the top wing centre-section and, once he was ensconced inside, the centre-section trailing edge could be folded down and locked.

The engine was somewhat unusual. It was designed by John (later Sir John) Carden specifically for the Gannet. It was a 750 cc two-cylinder, vertical, two-stroke, air-cooled engine mounted on an engine plate carried on tubular steel struts bolted to the fire-

This view of the nearly complete but uncovered Gannet shows the flat-sided ply-covered fuselage. The Carden engine and the undercarriage have yet to be added.

proof bulkhead. The engine had direct drive and was gravity fed by the fuel tank in the upper section.

The undercarriage was of the usual V type and had spruce struts carrying rubber shock absorbers for the axle.

The Gannet was completed shortly before the trials and was finished in the Gloster colours of blue fuselage and white wings, with the competition number 7 painted on the rudder. Right from the start the new Carden two-stroke proved troublesome and was probably the reason for the Gannet arriving late at Lympne for the trials — it was not present on 8 October, the first day of the competitions. Disappointingly, the Gannet made just the one flight at Lympne. On Wednesday, 10 October, pilot Larry Carter, recently recovered from a severe pneumonia attack, took off just after midday and headed for the cliffs and the sea. No sooner had he left than the mist, which had been hanging around all day, clamped right down. Ten minutes later Carter returned from the opposite direction and landed. The Carden engine had constant problems with the petrol system and with overheating and in addition there was persistent oil system failure. This combination successfully knocked the Gannet out of the competition.

Everyone at the meeting was impressed with the neatness of the Gannet and the excellent workmanship, always a hallmark of the Gloster company. *Flight* considered that Folland was on the right track with the two-stroke type of engine and that it would appeal to those private owners who did not want to dirty their hands. *Flight* commented that the fuel consumption of the two-stroke would be less than the converted motor cycle engines favoured by other ultra-light designers, though 50 mpg was not extraordinary. C.G. Grey remarked that the Gannet was a sad example of too much enterprise. True enough, it was a daring experiment to power it with a new and virtually untried engine, and had the Gloster/Carden team had a month or two more to get it right, the Gannet may well have been a success story.

As a postscript to the Lympne disappointment *The Aeroplane*'s resident wag wrote:

'Larry in a Gloster Gannet
Didn't fly as Follands plan it.
Engine feeling very blue
Fuselage same colour too.'

During the following year the Carden engine was replaced by a 650 cc 7 hp inverted Blackburne Tomtit V-twin, which gave the Gannet an improved maximum speed of 72 mph. Though kept airworthy the Gannet was rarely seen or flown after the 1923 trials. It did appear at the Olympia show in July 1929, though only as a decoration over the company's office, in company with the Gloster Survey, the Gnatsnapper and the Gloster IV Racer.

Top *Looking here like a king-sized model the Gannet is shown with original Carden two-stroke engine. With a wingspan of only 18 ft the Gannet was an essay in miniaturization.* **Above** *The Gannet was painted in the Gloster colours of blue fuselage and white wings. After the 1923 Lympne competitions the competition number 7, painted on the rudder, was replaced with the letter G.* **Below** *The Gannet's folding wings were hinged at the top and bottom of the rear spars and had quick-release pins in the front spar attachment points. The aircraft is seen at Lympne in October 1923.* (Via Terry Heffernan) **Bottom** *Pictured at Lympne with the propeller removed the Gannet's excellent finish is evident.* (Via Terry Heffernan)

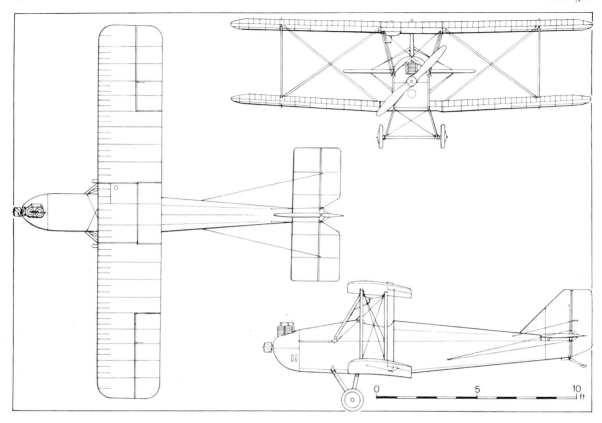

Gloucestershire Gannet data

Span	18 ft 0 in
Length	16 ft 6 in
Height	6 ft 0 in
Wing area	103 ft²
Empty weight	283 lb (Carden)
	330 lb (Tomtit)
All-up weight	410 lb (Carden)
	460 lb (Tomtit)
Maximum speed	65 mph (Carden)
	72 mph (Tomtit)
Cruising speed	not available
Stalling/landing speed	35 mph (Carden)
	36 mph (Tomtit)

Gnosspelius Gull

Oscar T. Gnosspelius had been dabbling in things aeronautical for a dozen or so years at the time of the 1923 *Daily Mail* lightplane trials. As early as 1910 he had experimented with hydroplane models and by 1912 had designed a successful full-size central-float monoplane which was followed by other designs until the outbreak of World War One. After service with the RNVR and RAF he was demobbed in 1919 and took up an appointment with Short at Rochester where he took over the new experimental department to concentrate on the development of Duralumin monocoque construction. He had also experimented with a man-powered ornithopter, though this came to nothing. Gnosspelius considered that the aeroplanes of the day were aerodynamically very inefficient. He believed that the average bird was a vastly more efficient glider than the normal aeroplane and he began making birdlike models, complete with pilot's head, landing wheels and tails. He discovered that the models showed a maximum ratio of Lift to Drag of 18:1, compared with an L/D ratio of 9:1 or so for the average biplane of the period. Gnosspelius took the experiments a stage further and built a full-sized glider. This design was finalized as a motor glider after the announcement of the *Daily Mail* competitions in an attempt to secure the £1,000 prize for the longest flight achieved on one gallon of petrol on an engine not exceeding 750 cc.

Named the Gull, the 36 ft span cantilever monoplane was built at Rochester in Kent by Short

Brothers. Power was provided by a 697 cc air-cooled, V-twin motor cycle engine made by Burney & Blackburne. It developed a peak of 24 bhp at 4,500 rpm which, though too fast for a direct-drive propeller, was quite suitable for driving two 4 ft diameter propellers via chains, at two-thirds crankshaft speed. The engine was otherwise unmodified. Construction of the Gull was of rock-elm hoops planked with spruce and reinforced where necessary with longerons and struts. The undercarriage consisted of a pair of 60 mm × 300 mm Palmer wheels attached to a cross axle slung in horn plates by rubber cords. The wheels protruded only through cutouts in the lower fuselage skin.

The wings were of heavily tapered planform and were in three sections. The two outer wing panels were attached to the 6 ft wide constant-chord centre-section by tapered vertical shear bolts, which ensured that the spar ends butted tightly together after assembly. The outer wing panels were of constant chord for two rib bays then tapered towards the tips, with leading edge sweepback of about 30°. The Gull was fitted with rectangular ailerons of 12 ft 2 in span. The wing section used was a modified RAF 19 but possessed a step on the upper surface at about 40 per cent of the chord; Gnosspelius claimed that this reduced drag and minimised the movement of the centre of pressure. The wings had four spars of box construction with spruce flanges and three-ply webs. The ribs were girder-built of spruce and the covering was lightweight doped linen fabric.

The tailplane was almost an equilateral triangle of flat section with a one-piece elevator. The triangular fin was fitted with a rectangular rudder and the whole tail unit was located on top of the rear fuselage.

The engine was positioned on the centre of gravity and the two pusher propellers were mounted on the

Top *The Gnosspelius Gull photographed at Lympne in October 1923 minus its wings. The thick Gottingen wing section and the long engine drive shafts are clearly evident. (Via Terry Heffernan)* **Above** *The Gnosspelius Gull's wing was built in one piece and was tapered over the outer half sections. The wing had no dihedral. (Via Terry Heffernan)* **Below** *The second Gull, number 19, returning after a flight at Lympne in October 1923, flown by Rex Stocken. (Flight photograph)*

The first Gull was later registered G-EBGN and is seen here competing in a Grosvenor Cup race at Lympne. (Flight photograph)

trailing edge of the centre-section. The drive chains passed through the wings in fibre tube guards. The propeller shafts were mounted in ball-bearings in the ends of large diameter tubes, the reduction drive allowing the propellers to turn at 2,200 rpm in the air. The total weight of the engine, including the flywheel, carburettor and single magneto, amounted to 73 lb.

The pilot was seated in front of the wing, from which position he had an excellent all-round view. The front of the fuselage was swept down and terminated in a conical aluminium nosecap. Behind the pilot's head was the streamlined petrol tank and behind that the engine.

On 26 May, 1923, the Gull was taken down to Lympne for its first flight. Registered *G-EBGN* and jointly owned by Gnosspelius and J. Lankester

Major Gnosspelius, on the left, watches as the Gull's two-cylinder Blackburne motor cycle engine is tweaked for even more performance. (Flight photograph)

Parker, the aircraft made its first flight in windless conditions in the hands of Parker. The Gull took off in less than 80 yds and, after a 12 min circuit, Parker rounded out a fraction early: the resulting heavy landing cracked one of the seat bearers. This was soon repaired and further flights were made. In order to achieve a higher ground angle larger wheels were fitted to the Gull and further flying continued in the following month.

A second Gull was laid down at Rochester in the hope that other aspiring competitors would order the type to try for the Duke of Sutherland's generous prize. No orders materialized and the unsold Gull was completed in August 1923. Except for its larger rudder it was identical to the first aircraft and both were entered for the *Daily Mail* trials. Lankester Parker flew *G-EBGN*, numbered 2 for the trials and Rex Stocken flew Number 19, the second unregistered Gull, which was tested by Parker on 8 October immediately before the trials were due to take place.

Frustratingly, both Gulls were beset with engine trouble, probably caused by the cold weather. The engines were mechanically trouble-free but, as one observer commented, 'they just softly faded away now and then'. The weather was also extremely gusty and onlookers noted with alarm the way that the bird-like wings of the Gulls flapped and twisted in the gusts. This of course was unintentional and was a result of the thin wing section, less rigid than the thick wings of other aircraft. The flapping was well within the limits of safe deflection of the spars, though severe gusts produced uncontrollable wing oscillations. Neither of the Gulls achieved the minimum aggregate distance of 400 miles to qualify for an award, though Stocken did complete three laps of the 12½ mile course at an average speed of 55 mph.

The official report on the Gulls, produced by the Directorate of Research, criticized the aircraft for

Top *The Handasyde Monoplane at Brooklands in September 1923. It was painted in the Handasyde house colours of yellow and grey. (Flight* photograph) **Above** *The thick Gottingen-section wing of the Handasyde was built in one piece and had no dihedral, though it was tapered over the outer half sections. (Flight* photograph)

poor lateral control, caused by the wing flexing. The Gulls were so close to the ground that the fuselage often touched it, making taxiing difficult. The report considered the wings insufficiently rigid, the undercarriage inadequate and the engine installation unduly complicated. The take-off run and climb was judged poor and because there was no engine-cooling the Blackburne could not be run for any length of time on the ground. In the aircraft's favour, the report praised the excellent view which the pilot had, and the cockpit accommodation.

After Lympne the second Gull was demonstrated at RAF Martlesham Heath by Parker and then both Gulls were put into storage. In January 1926 the second was sold to Messrs Baxter Ellis, Forsyth Heppell and Thompson and the aircraft was delivered to Cramlington, the home of the Newcastle upon Tyne Light Aeroplane Club. The club's chief instructor, Stanley Packman, was killed in the Gull in June that year when he undershot while landing. The fate of Gull *G-EBGN* is not recorded.

Gnosspelius Gull data	
Span	36 ft 4 in
Length	19 ft 6 in
Height	5 ft 10 in
Wing area	157 ft^2
Empty weight	360 lb
All-up weight	570 lb
Maximum speed	65 mph
Cruising speed	45 mph
Stalling/landing speed	38 mph

Handasyde Monoplane

One of the gliders that competed in the *Daily Mail* gliding competition, held at Itford near Lewes in Sussex in October 1922, was designed by George Handasyde with the assistance of Sydney Camm. The Handasyde glider was a 36 ft span, simple, square-cut craft that weighed only 160 lb empty and twice that weight fully loaded. It was built by the Air Navigation and Engineering Co (ANEC) at its works at Addlestone in Surrey.

Well known pre-war pilot and private owner Frederick P. Raynham flew the Handasyde in the competitions and managed to achieve the second longest flight, staying airborne for 1 hr 53 mins. This was no mean feat when one considers that the glider had been built so quickly that there was insufficient time to link the ailerons with the control column. Raynham controlled the glider by pulling on the cable with his left hand, a padded loop being supplied on which to pull!

After Itford a number of designers took the logical step of modifying their designs to take small converted motor cycle engines. Geoffrey de Havilland's glider, the DH 52, led to the successful little DH 53 *Humming Bird*, built for the 1923 *Daily Mail* light-plane trials; the Sayers glider led to the series of Handley Page Sayers motor gliders, one of which competed at Lympne in 1923; and George Handasyde entered the Handasyde monoplane, powered by a 750 cc Douglas motor cycle engine.

Though the monoplane differed in many respects from the glider the method of construction was the same. The fuselage was of rectangular section,

The Handasyde's fuselage was slab-sided and terminated at the stern in a horizontal knife-edge. (Flight photograph)

terminating at the stern in a horizontal knife-edge. It was entirely covered with plywood, though the wings and tail were fabric-covered. The semi-cantilever thick Göttingen-section wing was built in one piece and was attached to the top fuselage longerons by simple steel fittings. The wing was tapered over the outer half sections and the two wing spars were boxed in with three-ply which gave immense rigidity. The wing had no dihedral and was externally braced by a tube to the front spar and wire to the rear. This method of bracing was considered to be adequate with a Göttingen section, the centre of pressure being quite far back. Consequently the pilot's cockpit was

located further back than on many of the competing machines, being positioned between the spars with a cutout in the wing trailing edge to allow access.

The fuel tank was enclosed within a narrow fairing that ran from just aft of the engine to the pilot's cockpit. This was only a foot wide and allowed the pilot to see forward on either side of it. The view from the cramped cockpit was reasonable, though the wing obstructed vision downwards when the aircraft was climbing. The view during landing, however, was excellent. Some of the cockpit instruments were located below the cockpit coaming and were thus invisible to the pilot. Others were positioned on the

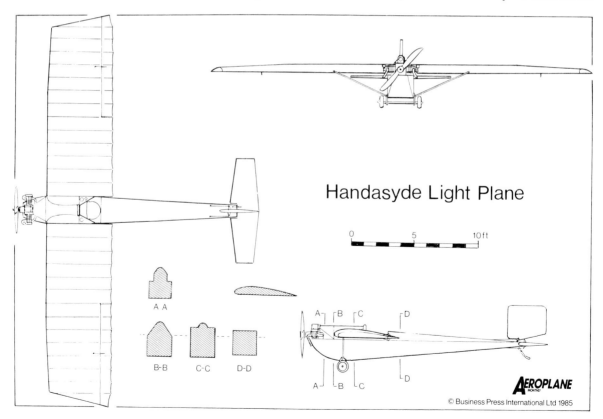

Handasyde Light Plane

0   5   10 ft

A A

B-B   C-C   D-D

top surface of the wings close to the cockpit.

The Handasyde had a partly-balanced all-moving type tailplane of truncated lozenge shape, and an unbalanced rudder without a fin.

The 750 cc Douglas flat-twin air-cooled engine was mounted on a very simple engine plate in the nose of the machine. With the engine mounted high and with the fuel tank being located only a little higher there was insufficient head to enable direct gravity feed. The engine was mounted on the top forward end of the longerons and could easily be removed. The drive to the propeller was direct; no flywheel was fitted to the engine, the propeller being sufficiently heavy to take its place. The Douglas engine developed about 15 hp at 2,500 rpm.

The Handasyde was taken to Brooklands for testing and on 9 September Raynham made a successful first flight, though difficulties were experienced with the carburation and there was undue elevator sensitivity because the gearing was too high. The speed range was found to be in the region of 30-65 mph. The monoplane was painted in the Handasyde racing colours of yellow and grey. The wings and tail were doped yellow and the fuselage dark grey. This colour scheme provoked comment from *The Aeroplane*'s editor, C.G. Grey, who thought that the Handasyde was something to do with the Wills cigarette company. From then on the monoplane was known as *Goldflake*.

On the first day of the 1923 Lympne lightplane competitions, Monday 8 October, the Handasyde flew well. It was soon lapping the 12½ mile circuit and averaging 65.6 mpg in the consumption trials. But the Douglas engine played up continually and only a couple of short flights were made after Monday. During the altitude test Raynham managed to reach 3,000 ft before the engine packed up again. As he glided down two other competitors, Hubert Broad on one of the DH 53s and Piercey on the ANEC I, were also making deadstick landings, and for a moment it looked like Itford all over again. The total mileage flown by the Handasyde during the trials amounted to 162, or thirteen laps of the circuit. Though the machine flew fairly well up until the chronic engine problems the Handasyde was not designed to win any particular prize—and consequently won nothing.

The official report on the Handasyde praised the construction but criticized it on a number of counts. It remarked on the poor visibility in the climb and the poor climbing performance; it also found it unstable fore and aft, with poor aileron control. The 300 mm wheels were regarded as being too small but praise was given for the take-off and landing performance. It was considered that the Handasyde was not a practical proposition for everyday use. As with the

ANEC I the Handasyde wing had three-ply covering over the leading edge. This tended to lose shape and it was suggested that additional former ribs were required.

The Handasyde was not given a civil registration and its ultimate fate is not known.

Handasyde monoplane data	
Span	30 ft 0 in
Length	19 ft 2 in
Height	not available
Wing area	135.5 ft^2
Empty weight	300 lb
All-up weight	500 lb
Maximum speed	65 mph
Cruising speed	not available
Stalling/landing speed	30 mph

Below *The instrument layout of the Handasyde was somewhat unusual and some of the instruments must have been difficult for the pilot to keep an eye on. (Flight photograph)* **Bottom** *Close-up of the Handasyde's 750 cc Douglas motor cycle engine, which developed 15 hp at 2,500 rpm. (Flight photograph)*

H.P. Sayers Monoplane

Like the DH 53 Humming Bird and the Handasyde monoplane, the Handley Page Sayers series of motor gliders stemmed from the gliders built for the 1922 Itford gliding contest. One entry, the S-C-W glider, had been entered by the technical editor of *The Aeroplane*, Captain W.H. Sayers. It is alleged that the glider was designed in 19 hrs, in collaboration with test pilot Frank Courtney and Martlesham test pilot Squadron Leader Maurice Wright.

The S-C-W glider closely resembled the German Hannover Vampyr glider, though it differed aerodynamically and by way of its construction. Built entirely of wood, the S-C-W had wings which tapered in thickness and chord towards the tips. It was built in nineteen days by Central Aircraft at Kilburn in North London. Unfortunately this promising glider was wrecked at Itford when its tent-type hangar collapsed on it in a gale before any official flights could be made.

After the announcement of the *Daily Mail* light-plane trials early in 1923 the Air Ministry offered to purchase the more successful aircraft taking part in the fuel consumption tests. Captain Sayers thereupon entered three similar aircraft, all based on the S-C-W glider. All three aircraft were built by Handley Page at Cricklewood, and because they were all different in detail they are described here separately.

The first aircraft, numbered 23 for the trials, was completed at Cricklewood in August 1923. It was powered by a 400 cc ABC engine and bore more resemblance to the S-C-W glider than did the other two. The engine was mounted on a pylon in the aircraft's nose immediately in front of the pilot. The wings were mounted on the top of the square section fuselage and the pilot sat immediately below the wing leading edge. The only problem with Number 23 was that it refused to fly. It fared no better with a 500 cc engine, and even with four people heaving on a rubber bungee the aircraft showed no signs of getting airborne.

Handley Page then called in ex-Bristol Aircraft Company draughtsman Harold Boultbee to sort out the design, and he recommended some pretty drastic changes. First the wing was lowered to the shoulder position and its incidence increased to 7°. Then the engine was faired into the nose in the normal manner and the whole design generally cleaned up, even to the point of covering the cockpit. Finally, the undercarriage was moved forward from its original position to just under the front wing spar and was mounted internally.

The Handley Page Sayers Number 25, as the improved design was called, was a fabric covered

Above *The H.P. Sayers Number 23 photographed during abortive bungee-assisted take-off attempts at Cricklewood early in 1923. (Flight photograph)* **Below** *Close-up of H.P. Sayers Number 23's pylon-mounted engine. The aircraft would not fly with either the ABC or Douglas engine and the design was abandoned. (Flight photograph)* **Bottom** *The H.P. Sayers Number 25, minus engine, at Cricklewood in 1923. The poor view from the cockpit portholes is apparent. (Flight photograph)* **Right** *Looking as though it is pilotless the H.P. Sayers Number 25 is in fact being flown by Gordon Olley at Lympne on 11 October 1923. (Flight photograph)*

cantilever monoplane powered by a 400 cc ABC engine which developed about 8 hp at 3,000 rpm. The propeller was direct-driven.

The fuselage was of approximately square cross-section with straight top longerons, and with the bottom set curved to meet them at the tail. The fuselage had spruce strut N-bracing on the sides and top, with three-ply covering the underside.

The wings were devoid of any external bracing and had high aspect ratio slotted ailerons. They were of the same thick section as was used on the Gloucestershire Gannet, but increased to 12 per cent camber. The wings could be attached to the fuselage sides for transport by road.

The pilot was seated just ahead of the front spar and was accommodated entirely within the fuselage, the cockpit being covered by a domed roof with two portholes which allowed the pilot a very restricted field of vision. The tailplane was of the all-moving type and the large rectangular rudder was located well above it. The undercarriage consisted of two small wheels mounted on the bottom fuselage longerons, within the fuselage.

While work proceeded on this second machine there was feverish activity on the third and final aircraft, Number 26. This had been entered for the speed trials at Lympne and it was similar in layout to Number 23 in that the engine, a more powerful 750 cc Blackburne, was mounted in the nose pylon. It also had larger wheels mounted on a wider track axle and larger, horn-balanced rudder. The wing-span was 10 ft less than on the two other aircraft, and the wing incorporated full leading edge slats, slotted ailerons and slotted flaps, in an effort to give this comparatively hot ship a slower landing speed.

Despite all this activity at Cricklewood only one aircraft, Number 25, was to make it to Lympne, and even that arrived late for the trials. Aircraft Number 23 was scratched before the competition began and Number 26, the speed machine, was not completed in time to compete.

Number 25 was flown by Gordon Olley, for whom the aircraft had been virtually tailor-made. The aircraft did not arrive at Lympne until 10 October, the third day of the trials. It passed its transport tests without fuss and on the fourth day was brought out of the hangar to commence fuel consumption tests, which consisted of continual lapping around a 12½ mile circuit around the aerodrome. It took a good hour to start the engine and then Olley was helped into the air by means of a bungee. After three-and-a-half laps engine rocker arm problems brought Olley down just outside the aerodrome boundary. Although the problem was cured, the aircraft had a wing damaged when it was blown to the ground in the gusty conditions and no further competition flying was carried out by Olley. This was a great pity because the three-and-a-half laps had been flown at an average time of 16 mins each. So the Handley Page team won no prizes, which did not please Olley because he would have pocketed a third of the prize money, had there been any.

Though not completed in time to compete in the trials, Number 26 was purchased by the Air Ministry for evaluation. It was given the RAF serial number *J7265* and delivered to RAF Martlesham Heath in 1924. Oddly enough it was never assembled and instead was left to rot on the hangar floor until, rain sodden and warped beyond repair, it was condemned as unsafe and dragged outside and burnt.

The official report on aircraft Number 25's performance at Lympne was not very flattering. The Handley Page Sayers was described as being 'practically a copy of the English Electric Wren, but seems to have lost some of the Wren's good qualities'. In fact the Sayers' flying qualities were reported as being extremely poor, due mainly to the inadequate rudder. The wings suffered from torsional deflection which rendered lateral control uncertain. The wheel track was considered to be too narrow, the fuselage ground clearance poor and the pilot's view non-existent. In addition the climb was poor and all control surfaces appeared to be insufficient. The only good points in the machine's favour were the very

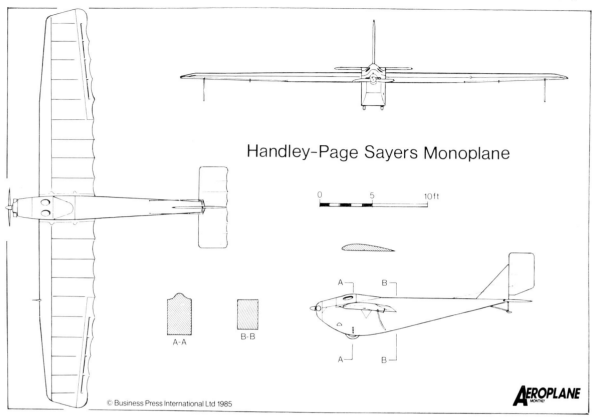

Handley-Page Sayers Monoplane

0   5   10 ft

A-A   B-B

© Business Press International Ltd 1985

AEROPLANE
MONTHLY

Below *The wings of the H. P. Sayers Number 25 could not be folded but were removed and then attached to the fuselage sides for transport by road.* (*Flight* photograph) **Above right** *Work on the H. P. Sayers Number 26 was still not completed in September 1923, when this picture was taken at Cricklewood, and it was not finished until after the Lympne competitions. Note the small slotted wing.* (*Flight* photograph)

short landing run and the method of engine installation.

Later the Handley Page Sayers monoplanes were given official Handley Page designations. Those with the larger 36 ft span wings, Numbers 23 and 25, became the HP 22, whilst Number 26 became the HP 23.

Handley Page, disenchanted with the ultra-light aircraft, did not bother to enter the following year's competition for two-seater aircraft, though Boultbee was to pursue the matter further. In 1928 he parted from Handley Page to form his own company, the sole product of which was the little Civilian Coupe.

Handley Page Sayers No 23 data	
Span	36 ft 0 in
Length	18 ft 6 in
Height	3 ft 8 in
Wing area	168 ft²
Empty weight	not available
All-up weight	480 lb
Maximum speed	not available
Cruising speed	not available
Stalling/landing speed	not available

Handley Page Sayers No 25 data	
Span	36 ft 0 in
Length	17 ft 0 in
Height	3 ft 2 in
Wing area	157 ft^2
Empty weight	250 lb
All-up weight	430 lb
Maximum speed	50 mph
Cruising speed	25 mph
Stalling/landing speed	not available

Handley Page Sayers No 26 data	
Span	20 ft 0 in
Length	17 ft 0 in
Height	4 ft 0 in
Wing area	62 ft^2
Empty weight	320 lb
All-up weight	500 lb
Maximum speed	not available
Cruising speed	not available
Stalling/landing speed	not available

Parnall Pixie I and II

The rules of the first *Daily Mail* trials for single seat lightplanes in 1923 were such that it was made virtually impossible for one single aeroplane to win all the prizes on offer. In effect the winners of each category —speed, height and fuel consumption—had to be freak aircraft, designed to win one category, with little or no value as transport for the non-wealthy. A good all-round performer stood little chance of winning anything, even though it could well be a far superior flying machine. The really limiting factor was the 750 cc limit on engine capacity, which was really too low for practical purposes.

One man who had an intelligent stab at the problem was Harold Bolas, the gifted chief designer of George Parnall & Co of Bristol. He came up with the idea of entering an aircraft with interchangeable components. By using a standard fuselage, tailplane and undercarriage, different sets of wings and engines could be fitted. Thus, the Pixie, as the aircraft was named, was designed in two forms. The Mk I was fitted with 28 ft 6 in wings and a 500 cc Douglas engine to compete in the fuel consumption tests. For the height tests the aircraft retained the same wings but would fly with the more powerful 750 cc Douglas engine. The Pixie Mk II was fitted with wings of 18 ft span and the 750 cc Douglas engine for participation in the speed trails.

Construction methods used in both Pixies were virtually identical. The fuselage was of rectangular section with spruce longerons. Diagonal spruce struts and vertical members were attached by plywood gussets except at the forward portion of the fuselage, where they were replaced with metal. There was no wire bracing and no trueing-up was necessary after construction. The forward part of the fuselage was covered with metal sheeting which acted as a shield between the engine and the front cockpit.

The wings were of standard construction with spruce spars of built-up I-section, with the web resting in grooves in the top and bottom flanges. The wing design was unusual in that the two wing spars ran parallel to the point of attachment of the bracing struts, at which point the rear spar sloped forward to meet the front spar at the tip. The ailerons were fitted on the rake, so that torsional loads were considerably reduced. Differential aileron controls were fitted and pushrods were used instead of cables. The wing

section used was from the family of R & M 322 propeller sections, similar to that used on the Westland Widgeon. The wings tapered in thickness, the maximum depth being at the strut attachment points, and the wings were braced to the top longerons with two streamline tubular steel struts adjustable in length. Though the wings were not foldable, they could easily be removed and clipped to the fuselage sides for transporting by road.

The clean undercarriage was of original design. The two struts formed an inverted V, the apex being located at the centre of one of the fuselage horizontal members between the top longerons. The struts sloped forwards and carried a tubular axle on which the wheels were mounted with about 10 in overhang from the strut attachment points. Such an arrangement not only gave a wider track than usual but provided the only shock absorption, by deflection of the axle. The tailskid was reinforced with a steel sleeve.

The tailplane was a fabric-covered steel frame of triangular shape, with the apex facing forward. The angle of incidence could be altered on the ground; the elevators extended the entire span. The fin and rudder were similarly constructed.

The Douglas engine was mounted on the bottom longerons and was braced by six steel tubes. The propeller was mounted with journal and thrust race on a built-up steel bracket bolted to the top of the crankcase. A chain drive gave a gear reduction of 2½:1. The 3½ gallon petrol tank was mounted in the faired decking over the front fuselage and the engine cowling could easily be removed with the aid of Parnall-designed toggle clips.

The Pixie was completed and ready for testing during September 1923 and Norman Macmillan MC, AFC tested it in Mk I form on 13 September. With only days to go before the start of the Lympne trials the aircraft was tested in Mk II form on 4 October.

The 1923 Lympne trials were held from 8-13 October and Macmillan was selected to fly the Pixie in both forms. For the consumption tests the Pixie, bearing Number 9, managed to achieve only 53 mpg, nowhere near the figure of 80 mpg plus being achieved by the English Electric Wren and the ANEC I. Three days into the event Macmillan did his quick change act. The 750 cc Douglas and the short-span

Above *Pixie Number 9 seen at Lympne in October 1923 fitted with the standard wings. The wings tapered in thickness, the maximum depth being at the strut attachment points.* (Via Terry Heffernan) **Below** *The Pixie II, with short span wings of only 60 ft² area. In this form the Pixie reached 100 mph in the hands of Captain Norman Macmillian.* (Via Terry Heffernan)

wings were fitted and the competition Number 24
applied. The experts doubted that the Pixie's 60 ft²
wing area was sufficient for flight and were thus very
surprised when Macmillan not only took off in a very
short distance but completed the speed circuits at an
average speed of 76 mph. In fact he was touching 100
mph on the straights. Later the Pixie returned to its
Number 9 configuration for further consumption
tests but it rained all day and it was hastily converted
back to take part in further speed tests the following
day. After making one timed circuit of 82 mph the
Douglas engine misbehaved on the second lap and
Macmillan had to forced-land in a field—so the previous speed of 76 mph stood. This was not bettered by
anyone else and so the £500 Abdulla speed prize was
Macmillan's.

The Air Ministry evaluation of the Pixie was
generally favourable. The basic design was considered sound and the fuselage very robust, though
the wings were regarded as flimsy. The flying
qualities were considered good and control and
stability of both versions were deemed satisfactory.
The engine trouble was attributed to the lightweight
nature of the steel pyramid-type mounting. In addition the clinging section of the chain on the driving
sprocket at high speeds also caused some problems.
The rudder area was criticized as being too small and
it was considered that the flat undersurface of the
varying wing section was insufficient compared to
other aircraft.

Shortly after the Lympne meeting Captain Macmillan competed in the Wakefield Prize event at
Hendon on 27 October 1923. Flying the Pixie II, with
the short wings, he won the pylon race with an
average speed of 81 mph. During the same month
Macmillan was demonstrating the Pixie before an
audience of Dominion prime ministers when one of
the Douglas engine's cylinders cut just as the aircraft
had become airborne. The pilot managed to coax the
machine around the Croydon hangars and then lob in
over the fence with just inches to spare.

Early in 1924 the Air Ministry ordered two Pixies
for evaluation at RAF Martlesham Heath for comparative trials with the ANEC I, Avro 560 and the

Top Parnall Pixie II G-EBKM *survived until it crashed in April
1939. It is pictured here at Maylands aerodrome, Romford in the late
1930s.* (E.J. Riding photograph) **Above** *The Pixie II at
Lympne in Ocotober 1923. The Douglas engine was unreliable yet
enabled Macmillan to win the 1923 Lympne speed trials with an
average speed of 76 mph.* (Via Terry Heffernan) **Below** *Parnall
Pixie II* J7323 *at the 1924 RAF Hendon Pageant, re-engined with
a Blackburne Tomtit engine.* (*Flight* Photograph)

DH 53. The two Pixies were given serial numbers *J7323* and *J7324*. They were powered by 696 cc Blackburne Tomtit engines and sported larger rudders. Pixie *J7323* was flown at the fifth RAF Pageant at Hendon in June 1924, numbered 13, in company with a DH 53. After the Ministry evaluation *J7323* was owned by a number of private individuals but was never registered. It passed through the hands of the Bedford Flying Club and was last reported to be part of C.P.B. Ogilvie's aircraft collection as late as 1935.

The second RAF Pixie, *J7324*, was later registered to the Parnall company, in December 1924 and appeared as *G-EBKM* at the August 1925 Lympne races, flown by Frank Courtney. Fitted with a 1,000 cc Blackburne engine and sporting the short-span wings the Pixie was doing well until heavy rain on the high-revving propeller caused the fabric covering the blades to come adrift. In another race Courtney managed to average 83.5 mph over a 3 km course.

Pixie *G-EBKM* passed through various private ownerships until it was crashed in April 1939 when owned by Ray Bullock of Fraddon, Cornwall.

Parnall Pixie I data

Span	28 ft 6 in
Length	18 ft 0 in
Height	not available
Wing area	100 ft^2
Empty weight	276 lb
All-up weight	457 lb
Maximum speed	65 mph (Douglas)
	90 mph (Blackburne)
Cruising speed	not available
Stalling/landing speed	36 mph (Douglas)
	33 mph (Blackburne)

Parnall Pixie II data (Douglas)

Span	17 ft 10 in
Length	18 ft 0 in
Height	not available
Wing area	60 ft^2
Empty weight	279 lb
All-up weight	460 lb
Maximum speed	105 mph
Cruising speed	not available
Stalling/landing speed	45 mph

RAE Hurricane

Not all the competing aircraft in the 1923 Lympne lightplane trials were designed, built and entered by established aircraft companies. In October 1922 some of the personnel of the Royal Aircraft Establishment at Farnborough formed a club to design, build and fly aircraft and gliders. The club's chairman and chief pilot was Flight Lieutenant P.W.S. 'George' Bulman and the designer was S. Child.

The club's first design was the Zephyr, described in an earlier chapter. While the Zephyr was making its initial flight the club's second aircraft design was being completed in a race against time for the Lympne trials, exactly a month away. The club had decided to have a go at the £500 Abdulla speed competition, open to aircraft of 750 cc or less. Child had designed an all-wood shoulder-wing monoplane of particularly racy design, far different in appearance to the Zephyr, called the Hurricane.

The Hurricane had a triangular section fuselage, with the base at the top, and only 16 ft long. The wingspan was 23 ft and the wing area a meagre 80 ft^2. The engine was the same Douglas unit as was used in the Zephyr. The wing section was a selection of Göttingen thick aerofoils which tapered in thickness and chord from root to tip.

The fuselage was very deep for its width and the pilot sat between the wing spars with his head positioned well above the shoulder-level wings. The cockpit was very confined and quite unsuitable for a large man. The 600 cc Douglas engine was mounted about two thirds of the way up the triangular nose so that practically the whole of both cylinders protruded each side. The undercarriage was a simple but very heavy affair, which consisted of a single leaf-spring, as an axle, attached to the lower fuselage longeron. The wheels were built-up motor cycle rims with heavy gauge spokes.

In order to carry out the all-important 'gate' test, in which every aircraft had to be manoeuvred through a 10 ft gap, the wings were detached and heaped on a trailer with other parts of the aircraft; the machine was then pushed through or carried through piece by piece. Removal of the wings from the fuselage was a fairly simple act — sixteen bolts covered by inspection doors connected the wing spars to the centre-section root spars.

Child estimated the Hurricane would have a top speed of around 100 mph and, on paper at least, the club's chances of winning the speed competition seemed good. The Hurricane was hurriedly completed and was barely ready for the start of the trials on 8 October 1923. Only one example was built, and this was registered *G-EBHS*. It carried the competition number 14 on its rudder and Bulman was to

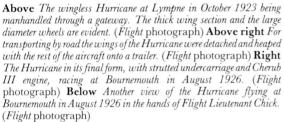

Above *The wingless Hurricane at Lympne in October 1923 being manhandled through a gateway. The thick wing section and the large diameter wheels are evident. (*Flight* photograph)* **Above right** *For transporting by road the wings of the Hurricane were detached and heaped with the rest of the aircraft onto a trailer. (*Flight* photograph)* **Right** *The Hurricane in its final form, with strutted undercarriage and Cherub III engine, racing at Bournemouth in August 1926. (*Flight* photograph)* **Below** *Another view of the Hurricane flying at Bournemouth in August 1926 in the hands of Flight Lieutenant Chick. (*Flight* photograph)*

undertake the flying trials.

Most of the competitors assembled at Lympne aerodrome on Sunday 7 October. However, the Hurricane, which had been taken there by road, was not erected until the Monday. Consequently it was not ready in time to fly for the Abdulla speed prize. In fact the Hurricane was not ready to fly until Thursday, when it was brought out of the hangar amidst great interest. The engine had already been tuned and, prior to starting, a tray was slipped beneath the engine to catch fuel overflowing from the carburettor. On starting, the engine backfired and ignited the fuel that had collected in the tray.

All hell was let loose. As Flight Lieutenant Bulman

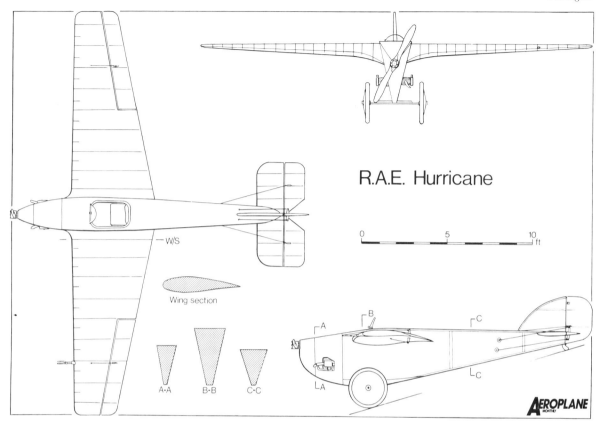

R.A.E. Hurricane

Wing section

A-A   B-B   C-C

0   5   10 ft

whipped the tray away the others tried to beat out the flames with their hats, much to the annoyance of the busy cine photographer who tried to push the fire-fighters out of the way to get a better picture. A fire extinguisher soon put out the flames and the little Hurricane was hurriedly withdrawn to its hangar where it was found to be unscathed. Shortly after-wards it was brought out again to fly. Such was the compression of the Douglas engine that *Flight* was moved to comment, 'the noise was like a battery of machine guns'.

Bulman took off for a short flight and it was soon apparent to everyone that the Hurricane was very underpowered. It flew in a pronounced tail-down attitude and its performance was less than exciting. *The Aeroplane* commented, 'though she looked quite fast on the ground there was not really very much hurry about her'. Their advice to the RAE Club was to enlist the services of a more experienced designer!

Above left *The Hurricane was 'absurdly heavy' and its empty weight of 375 lb was only 45 lb less than the all-up weight of the English Electric Wren. (Via Terry Heffernan)* **Left** *This photograph shows the Hurricane in its later form, with lengthened fin and rudder and the rounded fuselage top decking. (Oliver Tapper photograph)*

Child was later to achieve fame as the co-writer of the first official history of the Royal Aircraft Establishment.

The Hurricane was able to complete only two laps of the 12 mile circuit, and recorded an average speed of 58.5 mph, well below the speed of 76.1 mph recorded by Captain Norman Macmillan on the Parnall Pixie. Apart from being underpowered the Douglas engine suffered a broken rocker arm and Bulman made a trouble-free forced landing.

The Airworthiness Department of the RAE, which produced a report on the Lympne trials, criticized the Hurricane on several accounts. It was 'absurdly heavy' and it is interesting to note that although it had half the wingspan of the Wren its empty weight of 375 lb was only 45 lb less than the all-up weight of that remarkable aircraft. The undercarriage was considered to be far too heavy and observers had reckoned that the Hurricane flew most of the time just above the stall. The report also considered that the Hurricane was dangerous to all except experienced pilots and criticized it for being vastly underpowered.

After the trials the Hurricane was modified and re-engined with a 32 hp Bristol Cherub III engine. Other modifications included the fitting of a proper strutted undercarriage. This consisted of V-struts from the wing spar roots, incorporating tension rubber cord shock absorbers, supporting a divided axle which pivoted at the bottom of the fuselage. The tail unit was redesigned with a taller fin and rudder and a shallow rounded decking was added to the fuselage top, the portion around the pilot being hinged on the port side. With a more powerful engine, and considerably lightened, the Hurricane appeared at the 1924 Lympne two-seater light aeroplane trials but was not eligible to compete, though it did fly unsuccessfully in the Grosvenor Challenge Cup Race at the same meeting.

The following year was to see a change of fortune for the Hurricane. It appeared at the Royal Aero Club's August meeting at Lympne where it was successfully flown by Flight Lieutenant J.S. Chick, a Royal Aircraft Establishment test pilot. The combination won the Light Aeroplane Holiday Handicap race, covering the 50 km course at an average speed of 78.2 mph. In the International Handicap Race, flown over a distance of a 100 miles, the Hurricane dropped out after the first lap but in the Grosvenor Challenge Cup Handicap, also flown over 100 miles, the Hurricane flew to victory with an average speed of 81.2 mph. Chick also won the final race of the day, the Private Owner's Race, in which he completed the 50 mile course in a little over 36 mins. Throughout the meeting Chick had elected to fly higher than the other competitors and his tactics paid off handsomely — the haul in prize money amounted to £300.

During 1926 Chick raced the Hurricane at the Bournemouth Summer Aviation Race Meeting in August and in various races at Lympne in September. At Lympne the Hurricane was reaching average speeds of 85 mph. The ultimate fate of *G-EBHS* is unknown.

RAE Hurricane data	
Span	23 ft 0 in
Length	17 ft 7¾ in
	16 ft 0 in (Cherub)
Height	not available
Wing area	80 ft²
Empty weight	375 lb
All-up weight	565 lb
Maximum speed	58 mph (Douglas)
	85 mph (Cherub)
Cruising speed	not available
Stalling/landing speed	not available

Salmon Tandem

Of the 27 aircraft entered for the 1923 *Dail Mail* lightplane trials, three were not completed in time to participate. One of these three was the unorthodox Salmon Tandem, the brainchild of Percy Salmon, chief draughtsman of the Royal Aircraft Establishment Drawing Office at Farnborough. Very little is known about this aircraft although further information came to light in 1972 as a direct result of Philip Jarrett's 'Lost and Found' column in the Royal Aeronautical Society's journal, *Aerospace*. AVM Sir Cecil Bouchier KBE, CB, DFC recalled Salmon building his aeroplane in his bedroom at the Senior Officers' Staff Quarters of the RAE Mess at night after dinner. Apparently Salmon had asked Bouchier, who was then an RAE test pilot, if he would be willing to test his own aircraft on a purely private basis — to which suggestions Bouchier agreed.

The Salmon was powered by a 3½ hp Bradshaw engine and a description of the aircraft was given in

The Salmon Tandem nearing completion. Note the side-mounted Bradshaw engine. (Via Philip Jarrett)

Top *The Salmon Tandem completed, less engine covers.* (Via Philip Jarrett) **Above** *The Salmon Tandem photographed at RAE Farnborough. It was completed in September 1923 and registered G-EBHQ the following month.* (Via Philip Jarrett) **Below** *Another view of the Salmon taken at Farnborough late in 1923, showing the rudder arrangement.* (Via Philip Jarrett)

Bouchier's letter to *Aerospace,* following the journal's appeal for further information;

'After fifty years, my memory of it all is a little hazy, but I recall that the prototype was a really tiny light monoplane type of contraption, very low to the ground... Its main departure from normal construction design was that it had no elevator; the incidence of the whole tailplane, or rear wing, could be increased or decreased by an appropriate movement of the small control "stick" in the same way that a more normal aircraft's elevator is operated.

'Came the great day when dear old Percy Salmon proudly wheeled his brainchild out on to Farnborough aerodrome, and telephoned me that all was ready. After "contact" and warming the engine, I gently opened the throttle to increase my rather sluggish speed towards take-off, when suddenly "all Hell was let loose", the propeller having disintegrated into a thousand pieces before my face .'

Another letter published in *Aerospace* came from E.L. Chivers, who was twelve years old at the time of Salmon's first flight attempt. He recalled that the take-off site was Farnborough common, 'near the bottom slope of the track that used to lead from Farnborough road near the Queen's Hotel, over the hill where the present Farnborough Air Show Exhibition is sited.' Of the attempts to coax the Salmon Tandem into the air Chivers wrote, 'there were about ten attempts to fly the aircraft. It was taken to the top of a sandy, dusty track, where heather and grass grew on either side, and the slope was about one in fifteen. The engine was revved up and a few men helped it on its initial roll but it just ran down the track without gaining much momentum. It ended up after about 150 yds at the bottom of the slope and tipped sideways on to the front wing tip. After these

attempts it was abandoned; it never left the ground and never looked like taking off. I doubt if it ever reached a speed of more than 12-15 mph'.

No matter what happened to the Salmon Tandem, it did not materialize at Lympne. Work on the aircraft was completed during September 1923 and the aircraft was officially registered *G-EBHQ* on 24 November that year and issued with Registration Certificate Number 1019. Legend has it that the Salmon was cleared out of a shed at RAE Farnborough and burnt by RAE labourers. Salmon was reported to have been so angered by the fate of his aircraft that he sought compensation for its loss — and succeeded.

The only known data on the Salmon is that it had an all-up weight of 445 lb. Any further information would be most welcome.

Vickers Type 89 Viget

One of the more professional entries in the *Daily Mail* lightplane trials held at Lympne in October 1923 was the Vickers Viget, designed by Rex Pierson and built at Weybridge. Like the Gloucestershire Gannet, the Viget was an orthodox light aircraft scaled down to take a 750 cc Douglas motor cycle engine in accordance with the rules of the *Daily Mail* competition. One observer described the Viget as a normal aeroplane viewed through the wrong end of a telescope. The quality of construction and finish of the Viget, like that of the Gannet, was excellent.

Pierson had opted for a biplane configuration, believing that its lighter construction and smaller overall size offered more advantages than those possessed by the cantilever monoplane. The Viget's fuselage was a wooden, wire-braced girder structure with spruce longerons and struts. The longerons were of square section and the struts were spindled out to a cruciform section. The basic fuselage was rectangular in section but shallow fairings were added to the top and bottom. The one on top was deeper and ran from the pilot's head and shoulders to the tail. The fuselage sides were flat.

The pilot's cockpit was located under the trailing edge of the top wing and, in order to facilitate entry, a small door was located in the port side. The controls were of the usual type, the stick being a Duralumin tube mounted on a universal joint.

The Douglas flat-twin air-cooled engine was mounted in the nose and was neatly cowled. Immediately aft of the engine was a fireproof bulkhead, and from this the lines of the lower longerons were extended forward in the shape of two steel tubes. The top members of this portion were also tubes, sloping down at a sharp angle to meet the lower tubes. The forward ends of the structures thus formed were joined by cross-tubes which carried the engine.

The 6 ft 6 in diameter propeller was chain driven with a reduction gearing of $2\frac{1}{2}$: 1. The undercarriage was of normal V type and was built up of streamlined steel tubes. Rubber shock absorbers were used.

The wings used the RAF 15 aerofoil section and were of standard construction, made of wood and fabric-covered. Full span ailerons were fitted to all four wings. The top ailerons were hinged to the upper edge of the wing rear spar, while the lower ailerons

Test pilot Stan Cockerell comes in over the Brooklands banking during an early test flight in the Viget during the summer of 1923. (Flight photograph)

*Above In this rear view of the Viget the full span ailerons, fitted to all four wings, can be seen. (*Flight* photograph)* **Above right** *this full frontal view of the pristine Viget shows prominently the 2½/1 chain reduction gear of the Douglas flat twin engine. Only the bottom wing had dihedral and the wings were staggered. (*Flight* photograph)* **Below** *The Viget photographed at Lympne in October 1923, the competition Number 10 on the rudder and the pilot's personal logo on the fuselage! (*Flight* photograph)* **Bottom** *The Viget after re-engining with a 35 hp Blackburne Thrush and application of the registration letters G-EBHN. (Via Terry Heffernan)*

were hinged at the lower edge. Interplane wires connected the upper and lower ailerons. For folding the wings the top ailerons could be disconnected and folded upwards, and the lower set could be folded downwards. The wings were hinged at the rear spar root and, when folded back, would lie with the rear spars against the fuselage sides. This operation could be easily carried out by one person.

The tail of the Viget was of standard construction, externally braced with streamline wires. Provision was made for adjusting the tailplane while on the ground.

The Viget was registered *G-EBHN* and numbered 10 for the Lympne trials. Stan Cockerell, Vickers' test pilot, was to put the aircraft through its paces and he even had his own identification logo on the side of the aircraft.

On arrival at Lympne the Viget was the subject of great interest. In contrast with many of the machines entered, the Viget bore the hallmark of the professional aircraft builder. On Monday 8 October, Cockerell took off to notch up some mileage for the consumption tests. After only two laps of the 12½ mile circuit a broken rocker forced Cockerell to put down at the nearby village of Brabourne. On landing he folded the Viget's wings and set off to push the aircraft the six miles back to the aerodrome. On the way he paused at a pub and, on coming out to continue his journey, found the Viget surrounded by locals. 'When does the performance begin?' asked someone. They had assembled in the hope of watching a Punch and Judy show.

Later that day Cockerell amused the Lympne spectators with some pretty flying turning the Viget onto its back at one stage in a kind of half roll, something that few of the other competing machines could have achieved without ending up as matchwood.

Though the Viget performed well it did not shine sufficiently to win prizes. Perhaps if it had been cleaned up a little it might have fared better. At the end of the week *The Aeroplane*'s resident poet penned the following ode:

    'Cockerell, Cockerell, here's something fine:
    Thou shalt not fly Vulcans nor loop on a
      ''Nine'',
    But sit on a Viget and stunt it like H . . .
    On Anglo-American, BP or Shell.'

The Directorate of Research's report on the Viget, on completion of the trials, was full of praise. It declared that the pilot's view was good, except upwards as he was seated under the top wing. The aircraft taxied well, the wheels being of reasonable size. The take-off was good — the Viget needed a run of just 50 yds (the forced landing at Brabourne had taken place in a field 50 yds square and surrounded by trees). The flying qualities were good, there being ample control. One pilot reported that the controls were as responsive as those of a Camel. Praise was given to the wing folding, and the only adverse criticism was that the Viget was too heavy for its size and too large for its engine.

After Lympne the Viget was flown to Croydon and demonstrated on 10 November. Vickers had reduced the dihedral on the bottom wing in an effort to make the aeroplane more stable in gusty conditions. In the spring of 1924 the Viget had been re-engined with the more powerful 35 hp Blackburne Thrush engine. During extensive flying in the hands of Squadron Leader Payn, Pierson's technical assistant, the Viget was flown inverted for long periods.

The Viget was withdrawn from use in 1928 and its ultimate fate is not known.

Vickers Viget data	
Span	25 ft 0 in
Length	17 ft 3 in
Height	7 ft 3 in
Wing area	200 ft^2
Empty weight	395 lb
All-up weight	575 lb
	625 lb (Thrush)
Maximum speed	58 mph
Cruising speed	not available
Stalling/landing speed	not available

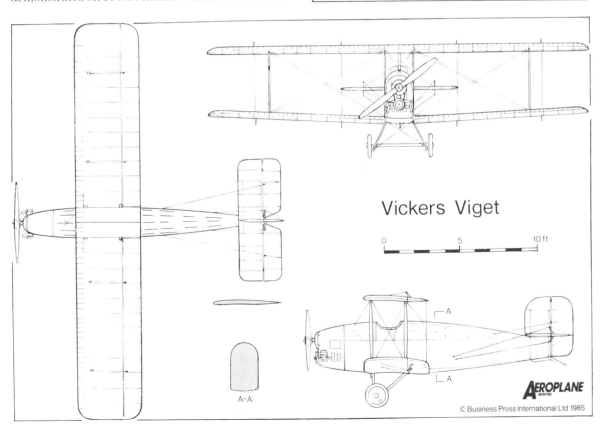

Vickers Viget

0   5   10 ft

ANEC II

When the Air Council announced its competition for all-British two-seater light aircraft early in 1924, a particularly enticing carrot dangled before prospective entrants was the possibility that the winner would be considered by the Air Ministry for use by flying clubs.

Naturally a number of designers who had already taken part in the previous year's *Daily Mail* competitions set to work creating two-seaters for the 1924 event. One such person was W.S. Shackleton, whose ANEC I had been particularly successful in 1923. Because the basic design was so efficient the ANEC II was more or less a larger version of the I. The wing span was increased by 5 ft and a second seat was added, positioned below the wing trailing edge. There were other differences which will be described later.

Shortly after designing the ANEC II Shackleton left for Scotland where he became designer to the Beardmore company at Dalmuir. His first task there was to produce a design for that company's entry to the same competition. Not surprisingly, the Beardmore Wee Bee bore more than a passing resemblance to the ANEC II!

Like its forebear, the ANEC II was built at the Addlestone, Surrey works of the Air Navigation and Engineering Co Ltd. By March 1924 the fuselage had been completed and it is believed that first flights took place in August, though the aircraft was seen engineless the following month, shortly before the trials were due to take place.

Construction of the ANEC II was similar to that of the earlier single-seater. The fuselage was much the same shape although changes were made to give the pilots a better forward view. This was achieved by making the fuselage decking narrower and by making the nose decking concave. The fuselage consisted of a slender framework of six spruce longerons and three plywood bulkheads. It was ply-covered to give adequate rigidity. The crew sat practically on the floor, their eye level just below the wing.

The wings were built on two spars of box section and were covered with three-ply back to the rear spar on the underside and the front spar on top. They were of parallel chord and in two halves, the roots being bolted to strong bulkheads in the fuselage, and they were braced by a pair of struts either side, one of each pair extendable to allow for incidence adjustment.

The tailplane was fixed and of narrow chord, with a much larger one-piece elevator hinged to it. Above this was mounted a tall, rectangular fin and an even larger almost rectangular rudder.

The simple undercarriage consisted of a bent steel tube axle that passed across the fuselage, projecting considerably on each side. The axle was anchored against torque and side loads at one point only, but was given full freedom to deflect under landing loads to form the only means of shock-absorbing.

The direct-drive two-cylinder Anzani engine was mounted inverted and was specially built for this and other competing machines by the British Anzani Engine Company. The fuel tank was mounted under the deck fairing aft of the fireproof bulkhead and gave the ANEC 3 ¼ hr endurance, fully loaded.

The two occupants were carried in tandem, one below the wing between the spars and the other behind the trailing edge. The front occupant sat with the top of his head inside the wing itself, his view upwards being via a transparent panel.

Jimmy James had been elected to fly the ANEC II in the trials and on arrival at Lympne in September 1924 the ANEC, numbered 7, passed its transport

test without problems, though the wings were not foldable but detachable. Trouble began, however, when it was time to fly the ANEC. It performed reasonably well with one person up but refused to leave the ground with two, which was the whole point of the competition. It was discovered that one cylinder had no compression and when it was dismantled a broken valve was found to be the culprit. Still the ANEC refused to take two up, even when the propeller was changed, and it was back to the hangar for more work. After a new carburettor was fitted the ANEC was dragged out for another try. After taking three hours to start, the Anzani finally performed, amid a deafening racket. But, alas, it was too late: the ANEC had already been eliminated because of the troublesome engine, despite the fact that James had even anchored a bunch of balloons to the back end in an effort to get the tail up! Interestingly enough all but seven of the competition's entrants were eliminated through some kind of engine trouble.

Official criticism of the ANEC II was, on the whole, favourable. So similar was the ANEC to the Wee Bee that the report bracketed the two together. The cockpits of the ANEC were deemed to be very cramped and 'quite inadequate for a pilot of average build'. The rear view from both cockpits was considered to be good, although the rear position was slightly restricted upwards. It was considered that there was insufficient ground clearance, which would cause problems on anything less than a smooth surface. The covered cockpits were frowned upon as they would be dangerous in the event of fire. The ANEC was regarded as a freak for service purposes though the flying qualities were praised — the average person could cope with the handling easily. The lack of wing folding was criticized and the integral tailplane and fin was marked down because of the difficulty and cost of replacement in the event of damage in this area.

In December the ANEC was certificated and registered *G-EBJO*, and was later purchased by G.L.P. Henderson. He fitted a 32 hp Bristol Cherub III and modified the undercarriage to strut-type

Left *The ANEC II, numbered 7 for the 1924 Lympne trials, in its original configuration with two-cylinder Anzani engine and simple bent-tube undercarriage, photographed at Brooklands. (Flight photograph)* **Top right** *Close-up of the installation of the direct drive Anzani which was mounted inverted and specially built for the ANEC II and other competing machines by the British Anzani Engine Company. (Flight photograph)* **Middle right** *Norman Jones flying the ANEC II during the 1927 King's Cup air race held on August Bank Holiday. (Flight photograph)* **Right** *Another view of the ANEC II, now registered G-EBJO, competing in the 1927 King's Cup race. Though first to take off the aircraft retired at Skegness after hitting a bird. (A.J. Jackson Collection)*

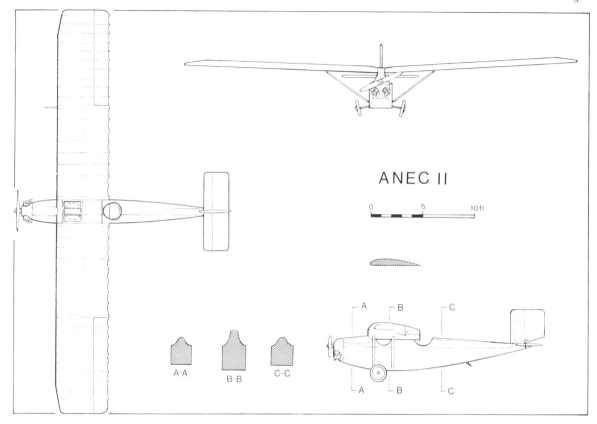

ANEC II

0   5   10 ft

A-A   B-B   C-C

before selling the aircraft to Norman Jones. He entered the ANEC in the 1926 Bournemouth Meetings and later raced it at the Hamble Air Pageant. It was not until 16 July 1927 that the little ANEC finally proved its worth when it won the air League Challenge Cup Race, flying the 116 miles from Castle Bromwich to Woodford and back at an average speed of 73½ mph. *G-EBJO* was entered for that year's King's Cup air race but had no more luck than it did in the 1925 event, when it was withdrawn before the

In this photograph of the ANEC II the revised strutted undercarriage is clearly seen. Though George Reynolds is ready to drop his flag at the start of this race the pilot seems to be otherwise engaged.

start. This time the ANEC hit a bird near Skegness
and had to retire. Later *G-EBJO* was sold to A.H.
Wheeler, later to become a Trustee of the Shuttleworth Collection at Old Warden. He flew the aircraft
extensively from Heston and elsewhere. Later the
ANEC was purchased by Jimmy Edmunds for the
princely sum of £8. The ANEC was at the time
hangared at RAF Henlow minus its engine, undercarriage and instruments and needed re-covering. It
took six months for Edmunds to rebuild *G-EBJO*,
assisted by Richard Shuttleworth who attended to
some welding, and the ANEC took to the air once
more on 22 June 1933, when it made a flight from
RAF Henlow to Leighton Buzzard. Thereafter the
aircraft was kept at Old Warden where it remained
until Edmunds disposed of it, with copious drawings,
to a South African. Edmunds' last flight in *G-EBJO*
was on 1 January 1935, when he took it to Heston.
The aircraft was subsequently owned by F.C.H.
Allen and E.J.D. Guild and the registration was
cancelled in 1937.

Today the ANEC II is stored in a barn near Old
Warden, awaiting restoration by the Shuttleworth
Collection.

ANEC II data	
Span	38 ft 0 in
Length	20 ft 8 in
Height	5 ft 8 in
Wing area	185 ft²
Empty weight	387 lb
All-up weight	730 lb
Maximum speed	85 mph
Cruising speed	not available
Stalling/landing speed	35 mph

Avro 562 Avis

One of the main criticisms of the early Lympne trials
was that the rules encouraged freak aircraft, tempting
entrants to put all their eggs in one basket and go for,
say, just the speed prize, or just the consumption
tests. There was thus very little chance of the prize
money going to good all-rounders, as was proved
with the delightful DH 53. In 1923 the Avro company
had tried to overcome this problem by entering a
single aircraft designed to fly with two sets of wing of
very different characteristics. This loop-hole was
soon plugged when the officials classed the Avro 560
as two separate aeroplanes and refused to let it fly in
more than one configuration. In order to safeguard
against this the following year, the Avro team
planned two machines for the two-seater trials —
though in fact only one airframe was entered, with
two different engines.

Top *The Avro Avis in its original form, with the Blackburne Thrush engine installed after the non-arrival of the Bristol Cherub. Photographed at Hamble the aircraft wears its Lympne competition number on the rudder. (A.J. Jackson Collection)* **Above** *The Avis photographed at the time of the 1926 Lympne trials, registered G-EBKP and painted in the colour scheme that earned it the nickname 'Flying Carrot'. (Flight photograph)* **Below** *The Avis seen at the 1926 Lympne meeting during the folding, housing and re-erecting trials. The ailerons on the top wing have been deleted. (Flight photograph)*

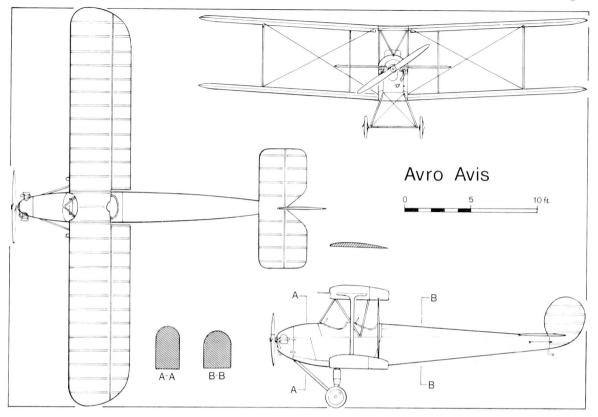

Avro Avis

0   5   10 ft

A-A   B-B

The Avro 562 biplane was of orthodox design and extremely clean in appearance. It owed much to the Avro 514 of 1914 and was very similar to the Avro 558, a competitor at the previous year's Lympne trials, though it was larger in order to accommodate two people.

Typically Avro in design, even down to the characteristic rounded rudder, the 562 incorporated some novel design features particularly in regard to the wings. The 562 was a single-bay biplane with wings of equal span and chord. The normal interplane struts were replaced with single I-struts of streamline sec tion with splayed ends, which embraced both spars, attached to special compression ribs. The interplane bracing picked up from the centres of these two special ribs, ie midway between the spars, and though the wires were duplicated the same anchorage was employed. The normal I-section spars were made of spruce and the Warren-girder-type ribs, also of spruce, had three-ply gussets. The thin aerofoil section used was Number 64.

The top centre-section had tubular spars and struts but ordinary wooden ribs. The centre-section spars were supported on two vees, one on each side, while the front spar was laterally braced by tubes converg-

ing on the centreline of the fuselage ahead of the cockpit. This allowed easy access to the front cockpit, located under the centre-section. In order to give maximum view from both cockpits both the leading and trailing edges of the centre-section were abbreviated as much as possible.

The full-span ailerons had large diameter steel tube leading edges, which formed torque tubes operated by cranks at the inner ends. Top and bottom ailerons were linked by means of a strut. The ailerons doubled as flaps, though the differential action of the ailerons could be retained when the flaps were lowered.

The top rear wing spars were hinged to the centre-section spars, and the bottom rear spar was hinged to a tubular cross strut in the fuselage. When the wings were folded a jury strut was placed between the top plane spars and a special anchorage on a strengthened rib at the inner end of the bottom plane.

The fuselage was constructed from square-section longerons with Warren-strut bracing and three-ply gussets. The sides and bottom of the fuselage were flat but a three-ply cambered deck was fitted onto normal formers and stringers.

The V-type undercarriage had an oleo shock absorber incorporated in the rear leg, which was attached below the front spar joint. The forward leg ran to the front fireproof fuselage bulkhead. The cantilever tailplane had divided elevators, and the rudder was partially balanced.

The engine mounting was designed to take a 32 hp Bristol Cherub or a 35 hp Blackburne Thrush engine. It was attached to the four corners of the fireproof bulkhead by a pyramidal steel tube affair which could be altered to accommodate either engine. The fuel tank was carried in the top fairing ahead of the front seat, which provided a short pipeline length and a good head for the gravity-fed tank.

The resulting aeroplane was exceptionally clean and the workmanship excellent — it was later agreed by officials that the Avro had the best doped finish of all the competing aircraft.

With only days to go before the start of the trials at Lympne, competitors were required to attend the eliminations on 27 September. The Bristol Cherub engine had still not arrived from the Bristol company and so the Thrush was installed for the first flights, which were carried out at Hamble by Bert Hinkler. The Avis was then sent by road to Lympne and on 28 and 29 September the Cherub was installed, tweaked, and generally readied for the flying competitions. The Avis was doped silver overall with black centre-section and interplane struts, radius rods and axle fairing. The trials number 10 was doped in black on the white rudder and the name Avis was painted in small black letters on both sides of the fuselage.

Right from the start the Cherub was troublesome. The engine vibrated seriously at anything more than idling speed and, by keeping the revs right down,

Above *At the 1924 Lympne trials the Avis was considered to be one of the few aircraft taking part that was suitable for Service training.* (A.J. Jackson Collection) **Below** *The Avis taking part in the 1926 Lympne trials for two-seater aeroplanes. It is fitted with a 1,500 cc Blackburne Thrush radial engine and is being flown by Sholto Douglas.* (*Flight* photograph)

Hinkler barely managed to keep airborne round the course. When the vibration threatened to shake the mountings apart the gearing was removed and a spare Bristol mounting, complete with multi-ply bulkhead was bolted to the front fuselage bulkhead. By the time the machine was ready to fly it had been eliminated. It could not be flown in the trials with the Thrush engine because Avro changed their minds about entering the Avis as two separate machines.

Ironically the Avis performed perfectly after the engine modifications, and so confident was Hinkler that he took up General Sir Sefton Brancker and Air Vice-Marshal Sir Geoffrey Salmond, carrying out beautiful aerobatics with each passenger in the aircraft.

All was not lost, though: the Avis won the Grosvenor Challenge Cup race (held at the end of the trials, for aircraft with engines of capacity not over 1,100 cc), with an average speed of 65 mph.

Although the Avis won no prizes during the trials, it won favourable comments from the scrutineers. They considered it one of the few aircraft present that would have made a practical training aeroplane, without modification and with the ungeared Cherub installed. They did not like the method of wing bracing, arguing that the decrease in resistance was outweighed by the weight of the wing spars. They considered the Avis ideal for mass production, and particularly favoured the use of wooden gussets in place of metal fittings in the fuselage. Minor criticism singled out the location of the centre-section splayed struts which, it was thought, interfered with the pilot's view. It was also felt that the positioning of the two cockpits made verbal communication somewhat difficult owing to the depth of the fuselage. The general handling was considered good, though the Avis was thought to be rather slow.

The Avis' career did not end with Lympne 1924. The following year it was flown at the Lympne August meeting, there being no trials that year, and it did quite well in two of the racing events. Since the previous year the Avis had acquired a Duralumin propeller and modified engine cowlings to accommodate the direct-drive Cherub. Registered *G-EBKP* and with Bert Hinkler as pilot, the Avis averaged 65 mph in the International Light Aeroplane Holiday Handicap and the Grosvenor Challenge Trophy Race, coming third and fifth respectively.

The Avis appeared at the 1926 Two-seater Light Aeroplane Trials at Lympne in September. By this time it was fitted with the 38 hp Blackburne Thrush and had ailerons on the lower wings only. It had been repainted and was flown with yellow-orange fuselage, gloss black cowling and centre-section struts and white rudder. All the flying surfaces were doped silver, as were the undercarriage, interplane and centre-section struts and wheels. The racing number 10 and the G on the rudder were also in black.

Flown by Wing Commander W. Sholto Douglas (later Lord Douglas of Kirtleside) the Avis was eliminated after the second day when the undercarriage was damaged after a forced landing en route for Hastings.

In 1927 the Avis reverted to the direct-drive Cherub in which state it was sold to E.L.O. Baddeley.

It was then sold to T.S. Baldwin of Totnes, Devon and in December 1931 the Avis was finally scrapped.

Avro 562 Avis data	
Span	30 ft 1 in
Length	24 ft 0 in
Height	9 ft 0 in
Wing area	255 ft^2
Empty weight	582 lb (Cherub I)
	565 lb (Cherub II)
All-up weight	950 lb
	995 lb (Thrush)
Maximum speed	75 mph
Cruising speed	not available
Stalling/landing speed	30 mph

Beardmore WB XXIV Wee Bee I

How W.S. Shackleton scaled up the successful ANEC I to a two-seat machine for competing in the 1924 Air Ministry two-seater lightplane trials has been covered in an earlier chapter. No sooner had Shackleton completed this design than he took up the position of chief designer to the Scottish-based William Beardmore & Co Ltd at Dalmuir in Dumbartonshire. This company had designed and built aircraft during World War One but the aviation section closed down in 1920 and it was not until the announcement of the 1924 Lympne trials that it returned to aircraft production.

Shackleton began work on a design that closely resembled the ANEC II. Though the latter was powered by a 1,100 cc Anzani, Shackleton selected the 1,096 cc Bristol Cherub for the Beardmore machine. Designated the WB XXIV Wee Bee I, the new aeroplane was built at Dalmuir during the Summer of 1924.

Below left and above *The Wee Bee in action at the 1924 Lympne trials for two-seater aeroplanes, piloted by Maurice Piercey.* (*Flight* photographs) **Below** *The Wee Bee at Lympne in 1926. The narrow chord tailplane had a one-piece elevator hinged to the top rear edge.*

The rectangular section fuselage was constructed on six spruce longerons with plywood bulkheads and covered with ¹/₁₆ in birch three-ply. The fuselage decking, instead of being domed in the normal way, was 'hollow-ground' in order to conform roughly to the shape of the pilot's head and shoulders. Thus the streamlining was retained, yet the pilot could easily see past the fairing. The two cockpits were situated one in front of the wing and the other aft of the rear spar, the rear cockpit being located below a square cutout in the wing which allowed easy access. During flight the cockpit was covered by a small celluloid window and entry to the front cockpit was via a small hinged portion of the wing leading edge which folded upwards. Once the pilot was inside, the leading edge was locked down into position.

The monoplane wing was of orthodox construction and consisted of two spars of box section with three-ply walls. Both the flanges and the walls tapered in thickness towards the tips. With three-ply covering the wings back to the front spar and back to the rear spar for half the span, there was no need for internal drag bracing. The high aspect ratio ailerons were hinged to false rear spars and were operated by crank levers through short pushrods — no control pulleys were used.

The tail unit was constructed in a similar manner to that of the ANEC II in that the tailplane's single spar was built integral with the rear portion of the fin. The front portion of the fin was integral with the fuselage. The elevator was activated by a short push-rod from cranks on a lay shaft.

The undercarriage was simplicity itself, consisting of a single bent tube which passed through the fuselage and was anchored to the sides. The nickel steel axle was supported on trunnions which allowed it to flex freely.

The weight of the direct-drive, two-cylinder horizontally opposed Cherub engine was taken by a pyramidal support of sheet Duralumin, the vertical position being maintained by two lower struts steadied by diagonal tubes running to the lower corners of the engine bulkhead. The engine could be removed easily by undoing four bolts and was gravity-fed from a wing tank located between the two spars.

The Wee Bee was completed in September 1924 and the trouble-free first flight was made shortly before the trials were due to begin. Maurice W. Piercey, who had flown one of the ANEC Is in the previous year's trials, was selected to fly the Wee Bee and, numbered 4, the aircraft arrived at Lympne in

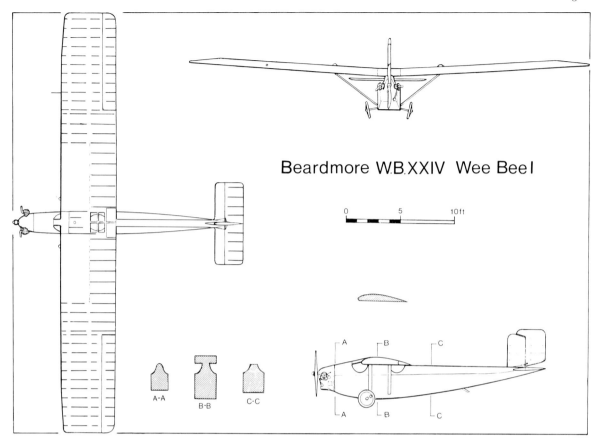

Beardmore W.B.XXIV Wee Bee I

time to pass the elimination events on Saturday 27 September. The Wee Bee was the sole competitor to pass the flying section of these eliminations on that day and, though others managed to scrape through the following day, eight were eliminated for one reason or another. The flying part of the elimination tests necessitated flying two laps of the 12½ mile course, which the Wee Bee undertook without difficulty.

The competitions proper began on the Monday and Piercey wisely decided to tackle the most difficult section first — the speed tests. By the end of the day he had turned in a speed of fractionally over 70 mph, having covered ten laps, or 125 miles. During the next couple of days Piercey built up the hours, consistently lapping the course. The engine behaved well though a valve spring had to be replaced at the end of Tuesday's flying. An overheating big end caused some anxiety as the rules forbade changing any components. By careful flying and by working overnight on the engine the Cherub kept running and Piercey was able to stay ahead of the field.

On the Wednesday, Piercey managed to keep the

Wee Bee down to 40.67 mph during the slow speed tests and in the take-off tests scored the highest marks by clearing the 25 ft barrier after a take-off of only 250 yds. This was shortened to 235 yds by the final day of the competitions, by which time he had also reduced the slow speed performance by a further 1 mph. On the last day Piercey improved his high speed performance to 79 mph, but at the expense of the big end. This overall performance was enough to win Piercey the £2,500 prize awarded by the Air Ministry.

The Aeroplane regarded the Wee Bee as 'one of the most astonishingly efficient aeroplanes yet produced', and stated that Shackleton had 'proved himself to be something of a genius among designers'. His other design, the ANEC II, would probably have performed equally well had it not been for its unsuitable propeller — the aircraft performed well when the propeller was changed after the trials had finished.

Despite all this fulsome praise from the aviation press, the Air Ministry observers, who were looking for a suitable two-seat trainer for mass production, levelled some criticism at the victorious Wee Bee. It

was considered that there was insufficient ground clearance, the bottom of the fuselage actually brushing the grass at times. The cockpits were too cramped and criticism was levelled at the covered cockpit because of the risk to the occupants in the event of fire, though removal of the covers would have been detrimental to the Wee Bee's performance. The aircraft was praised for its robustness and it was judged suitable for maintenance without the supervision of a ground engineer. The Wee Bee was, like many of the machines entered, regarded as a freak and unsuitable for Service training purposes. Because of the proximity of the fuselage to the ground the Wee Bee would have been difficult to operate from Service aerodromes, most of which were grass.

In the event none of the 1924 two-seat entrants were subsequently developed into practical two-seaters. Though exhibited at the Wembley exhibition and the Motor Cycle Show at Olympia, only the one Wee Bee was built.

The Wee Bee continued to be flown after Lympne and appeared at the Lympne meeting held in August 1925, by which time it had been registered *G-EBJJ*. Though it had been re-engined with an updated Cherub the little aeroplane was outclassed. Even so A.N. Kingwill put up a lively performance, and though unplaced in the Holiday Handicap heat he won the Scratch Speed Race for two-seaters with an average speed of 66.6 mph and attained 11,800 ft to achieve the greatest altitude.

Following evaluation by A&AEE at RAF Martlesham Heath the Wee Bee was registered to Lord Invernairn (Sir William Beardmore) in July 1928 and then passed to Arthur Vere Harvey (now Baron Harvey of Prestbury). The Wee Bee received its certificate of airworthiness on 4 March 1930, some six years after it was built, and passed through various private hands before being sold by Norman

Above *The Wee Bee photographed at Bristol Whitchurch, 1932-33, shortly before it was sold to Australia.* (A.J. Jackson Collection)
Below *In 1932 the Wee Bee was advertised for sale at £145. It had by this time been fitted with a Bristol Cherub Mk II engine.*

Edgar to R.T. Parker of Victoria via the Larkin Aircraft Company of Melbourne.

Registered *VH-URJ*, the Wee Bee remained with Parker until the mid-1930s, when it was sold to E.R. Betts. The Wee Bee was then stored during the war and emerged in 1949, still in good condition. After it was sold to Vincent Boyes, *VH-URJ*'s fate is unclear, though it is thought that after a crash it was used by children as a plaything.

Beardmore WB XXIV Wee Bee I data	
Span	38 ft 0 in
Length	22 ft 2 in
Height	not available
Wing area	187 ft^2
Empty weight	462 lb
All-up weight	837 lb
Maximum speed	86 mph
Cruising speed	not available
Stalling/landing speed	36 mph

Blackburn L 1 Bluebird

The Blackburn Aeroplane and Motor Co's entry for the 1924 Air Ministry trials for two-seater aircraft with engines of not more than 1,100 cc was one of the more promising and practical entrants. Unfortunately, it was not ready in time to compete and it was held over until the 1926 event. However, as we are currently covering the aircraft that competed in the 1924 trials, it will be dealt with here.

Some years earlier, in 1919, Robert Blackburn produced the tiny, unattractive Sidecar, designed for the non-existent motor cycle-of-the-air market. Although the Sidecar was unsuccessful, the idea of its side-by-side seating arrangement was certainly good from the social point of view and it was very practical for training purposes, particularly as one of the criticisms levelled at many of the 1924 contestants was that the separate cockpits were separated too widely for adequate communication between the occupants. Blackburn was to revive the idea in the Bluebird, the company's entry for the 1924 event.

Instead of designing a freak aircraft, with the intention of winning points for specific sections of the 1924 trials, designer A.C. Thornton, who later designed the Arrow Active, looked further ahead and concentrated on producing a robust trainer, suitable for touring, that could accommodate a bigger engine than the 1,100 cc powerplant specified for the Lympne trials.

Not surprisingly the Bluebird bore a strong resemblance to its bigger Blackburn brethren and was likened to a scaled-down Blackburn Dart torpedo bomber, which was in production at the time. The Bluebird was designed by a staff that had amassed considerable experience of producing aircraft capable of low landing and flying speeds for carrier operations — qualities for which points could be won at Lympne.

Naturally, the side-by-side seating necessitated a wide fuselage, with consequent increase in frontal area and drag. The fuselage was built in two separate sections, the forward portion being built up on two rigid box-frames of spruce, plywood and steel. Forward and aft of the cockpits was a combination of rigid triangulated and semi-monocoque construction. The rear section of the fuselage had four longerons, with strut joints reinforced with ply gussets and Duralumin plate. Doors were provided on each side of the cockpit and although seated side-by-side the two occupants were separated by a strip of decking at neck level.

The wings had spruce spars, Warren-girder ribs, Duralumin drag struts and swaged rod drag bracing. The wings had 6° dihedral and were rigged with slight stagger. The wing section T 64 was used, the same as that used on the Dart, and when on the ground the wings had considerable incidence. The interplane bracing was of the single bay type and the flying wires were of 2BA streamline section. The top wing centre-section was built on steel spars braced with tie-rods and supported on vertical steel tube struts which were taper-pinned into metal sockets. The wings folded about the rear spar roots, hinged ribs being fitted in the trailing edge, adjacent to the hinges.

The undercarriage was of the V-type with front vertical telescopic legs below the front spar joint, the rear legs running to below the rear spar hinges. The fuselage was sufficiently wide that there was no need for the undercarriage legs to be splayed outwards. The axle was faired in an aerofoil.

The ample adjustable tailplane was so arranged that the two elevators could be operated by independent control lines which, together with the rudder control pedals, were routed vertically upwards aft of the cockpit and ran via pulleys externally back down the fuselage.

The three-cylinder Blackburne radial engine was mounted on a triangular tube structure which in turn

was bolted to a fireproof bulkhead. A special small competition 4½ gal fuel tank was mounted above the top wing centre-section, though provision was made for a tank of larger capacity for use with larger engines. A Pyrene fire-extinguisher was fitted directly to the front cowling, close to the carburettor.

In accordance with the competition rules dual control was fitted. The single control column was placed centrally and lateral control was by two parallel-acting rudder bars. A small windscreen was located in front of each occupant.

Though the Bluebird was structurally complete in time for Lympne, problems with the Thrush engine forced Blackburn to withdraw the aircraft from the competitions. Despite continuing problems with the engine, which refused to develop full power, the Bluebird was successfully test flown during October 1924 and, as predicted, had excellent short take-off and landing qualities.

On 4 September 1926 the Bluebird was registered *G-EBKD*, by which time it had been modified to take part in the 1926 *Daily Mail*-sponsored Lympne trials, held from 10-17 September. The competition rules had been changed for the better. Instead of a restriction on engine capacity there was a weight limit of 170 lb, inclusive of accessories, which enabled aircraft fitted with engines of at least 60 hp to take part. In addition to the customary dismantling and erection tests, take-off and landing trials and demonstration of realistic dual control operation, the competition had taken the example set by the German Ründflug meeting and introduced long-distance out-and-home flights, totalling 1,994 miles.

Blackburn Bluebird *G-EBKD* was fitted with a 60 hp five-cylinder Armstrong Siddeley Genet I radial engine. In order to comply with seat width restrictions the decking strip between the occupants was removed and the left-hand seat was staggered behind that of the passenger. This arrangement necessitated substituting proper dual controls for the single

Below left *Though completed on time and numbered 12 for the 1924 Lympne two-seater aeroplane trials the Bluebird I was prevented from competing because of teething troubles with the 1,100 cc Blackburne Thrush engine.* **Above** *Another view of the Bluebird I in its original configuration. Note the entry door, the unstaggered wings and the broad fuselage.* **Below** *The Bluebird I in revised form with aerofoil shaped fuel tank in the wing centre-section and re-engined with a 60 hp Armstrong Siddeley Genet I engine.*

control column. In this form the Bluebird was first flown on 4 June 1926 by Flight Lieutenant N.H. Woodhead.

Doped silver and blue and wearing the competition number 1, the Bluebird was sent to Lympne with Squadron Leader W.H. Longton, of earlier Hendon RAF Pageant fame, as pilot. That year the competitions were marred by over-enthusiastic and exacting officials and stewards who did everything strictly by the rule-book. A number of very promising aircraft were eliminated or disqualified for petty rule infringements, one particular bone of contention being what constituted a major repair. Any aircraft that underwent any major repairs was immediately disqualified. The Bluebird was the first victim to fall foul of the stewards. Early on, Longton managed to bend the undercarriage axle during full load tests, twisting the unit and necessitating the replacement of a lug which attached the legs to the fuselage. The stewards refused to give permission for a new lug to

Above *the modified Bluebird I photographed shortly before participation in the 1926 Lympne trials.* **Below** *The Bluebird I, now registered G-EBKD, in the form in when it took part in the Bournemouth Easter Meeting in 1927.* (*Flight* photograph)

be fitted, suggesting that the bent one could be straightened and re-fitted. This would have weakened it and, in order to make the structure safer Blackburn asked if they could fit a new washer and auxiliary wiring plate. This, too, was refused on the grounds that it would make the aircraft's structure different from when it was presented for scrutiny. This was ridiculous in view of the fact that it was perfectly acceptable to replace a broken propeller or tailskid, providing the parts were of identical design.

Instead of packing up and returning home in disgust, Longton spent two entire days lapping one of the 12½ mile circuits, stopping only for food and fuel, covering 400 miles each day without any mechanical snags. The stewards were not allowed to forget his presence because Longton beat up their tent on every lap! On 18 September Longton won the

Grosvenor Trophy Race, held at the end of the trials, and covered the 75 mile course at an average speed of 85 mph. The Bluebird had demonstrated in spectacular fashion that it was a very practical two-seat touring aeroplane. This was further demonstrated in December that year when an RAF officer and his new bride made a return trip across the English Channel to France on their honeymoon.

The Bluebird was put into production as the Bluebird II. Production versions were similar to the prototype but were powered by the bigger 80 hp Genet II engine. Being somewhat heavier than 1,000 lb fully loaded, these and successive marks of the Bluebird fall outside the scope of this book.

Meanwhile the prototype Bluebird had been further modified for the 1927 racing season. The cockpit has been faired over, except for a small hole to accommodate the pilot's head — a streamlined fairing acting as a headrest. A Fairey-Reed metal propeller was fitted and the aerofoil section was deleted from the undercarriage axle. Longton flew the modified Bluebird at the Bournemouth Easter meeting held on 15-18 April. He raced with some success, averaging 83.5 mph during one of the heats of the Business Houses Handicap Race and came second in the final. While they were flying practice laps before the racing an irate local resident had taken pot-shots at the Bluebird and other competitors, hitting some of the aircraft but without causing injury.

Longton returned to Bournemouth race course with the Bluebird for the Whitsun race meeting during the first week of June. There, on 6 June, he collided with the prototype Westland Widgeon III, flown by Westland test pilot L.P. Openshaw. Both pilots were killed and the Bluebird was no more.

Close-up of Bluebird's Blackburne Thrush engine. Note the small diameter propeller. (Flight photograph)

Blackburn L 1 Bluebird 1 data	
Span	28 ft 3 in (upper wing)
	28 ft 0 in (lower wing)
	9 ft 8 in (folded)
Length	21 ft 8 in
Height	7 ft 11 in
Empty weight	495 lb (Thrush)
	705 lb (Genet)
All-up weight	875 lb (Thrush)
	1,150 lb (Genet)
Maximum speed	74 mph (Thrush)
	85 mph (Genet)
Cruising speed	60-65 mph (Thrush)
	70 mph (Genet)
Stalling/landing speed	33 mph

Bristol Type 91 Brownie

An aircraft which merited particular attention at the 1924 Lympne trails for two-seaters aircraft was a low-wing monoplane produced by a company noted more for its successful line of World War One fighters: the Bristol Aeroplane Co Ltd at Filton. The company had toyed with the idea of entering for the single-seater competitions sponsored by the *Daily Mail* the previous year. At that time the company had produced a small flat-twin engine of 1,095 cc and around 18 hp for use with portable generating plants. Roy Fedden produced a lighter version suitable for use in light aircraft and capable of producing 30 hp. One can imagine the disappointment at Bristol when it was learned that the trials were open to aircraft with engines of up to 750 cc only. Bristol's designer had already made tentative drawings of a tandem-winged

aircraft, loosely based on the Maneyrol tandem monoplane, winner of the 1922 Itford gliding trials.

For the 1924 two-seater trials the engine capacity limit was raised to 1,100 cc and Barnwell set to work to design an aircraft around the Cherub flat-twin. The tandem wing arrangement was dropped in favour of a straightforward monoplane configuration but the unusual decision was taken to build it of steel.

Originally, two Bristol Type 91 Brownies were ordered, but in May 1924 this number was increased to three, by which time the others were already being built at Filton.

The Brownie's fuselage was built entirely of steel tube and was wire-braced, except in the bays immediately behind the engine mounting, where swaged rod bracing was used. The strut joints were sleeves sweated to the longerons, the strut ends being fitted with screwed terminals which passed through the sleeves and also secured the necessary wiring plates. The fuselage had a fairly maximum cross-sectional area and was slab-sided and flat-topped.

Several wings were designed for the Brownie, two sets of metal and one of wood. The wooden wings were 16 ft long and the metal wings 14 ft and 17 ft - the smallest set being intended for the speed trials at Lympne. The metal wings had steel spars and Duralumin ribs, the spars consisting of top and bottom flanges uniform in section throughout the span. They were tied together by Warren bracing made from single lengths of large diameter steel tube, flattened at each joint and riveted to the flanges. The ribs were very simple Warren-girders built from

The yet-unregistered Bristol Brownie, G-EBJK, being flown during the 1924 Lympne trials by Uwins. (Flight photograph)

channel-section Duralumin. The ailerons extended over two-thirds of the wingspan, and tapered in chord from the tips inwards.

Though the wing section was thick, it was not a high-lift section. It bore some resemblance to certain American sections in use at the time but was in fact developed by Barnwell himself and had been properly tested in Bristol's own wind tunnel. In an effort to produce an automatic variable camber, the Brownie's ailerons were held down by rubber cord and pulled up by the stick. As the speed of the aircraft increased, and the pressure on the ailerons with it, both ailerons rose automatically. This method of control was later to cause problems.

The wings were very thick biconvex section at the roots, but tapered both in thickness and in chord towards the tips where the section was approximately RAF 15. They were set with marked dihedral. The metal and wooden wings were interchangeable and were secured by four bolts which were quickly removable for transport by road. They could then be

Above The simple box-like construction of the Brownie's fuselage is apparent in this photograph, taken during the Lympne trials in September 1924. (Via Terry Herffernan) Below Brownie G-EBJL with the fuselage covering removed for inspection following wing flutter during the 1924 Lympne trials. The wings and fuselage were discovered to be undamaged. (Via Terry Heffernan)

attached to the fuselage sides by brackets permanently fitted to the wing under-surfaces. The wing-securing arrangement also allowing for fine dihedral adjustment independently on each wing. Thus any tendency for a wing to drop could be remedied quite simply.

The undercarriage consisted of two steel tube legs attached to the front wing spar. The special Palmer Aero wheels were attached to an axle that had considerable overhang either side to provide the only method of shock absorption. The undercarriage was held in position by means of fore-and-aft wires to the fuselage.

The tailskid was of the leaf-spring variety, and the tailplane was of conventional design with spindled spars and steel tubular drag struts. The incidence of the tailplane could be adjusted on the ground. The fin and rudder were mounted on the last bay of the fuselage, the one-piece elevator extending without a break across the entire span of the tail. The rudder post was inclined forward at an angle to the fuselage centreline.

The Bristol Cherub engine was mounted on four stiff steel pillars projecting from the front bulkhead and screwed on to the projecting crankcase studs. The four supports were entirely unbraced and it was intended that the lack of rigidity of the structure would help to minimise engine vibration.

The 3.4 gal petrol tank was housed in the fuselage fairing over the front seat and gave about 80 mins duration at full power, or 1¾ hrs at cruising speed.

The tandem cockpits were comfortable and the view from both was good, except vertically downwards from the rear cockpit. The view from the front seat was particularly good though the cockpits were rather widely separated.

The three Bristol Brownies were registered on 14 July 1924, as *G-EBJK*, *G-EBJL* and *G-EBJM*, and were known as *Jack, Jill* and *Jim* by the Filton pilots that flew them. That same month the Bristol Cherub engine passed its 25 hr civil type tests and, on 6 August, Cyril Uwins took *G-EBJK* on its maiden flight. It handled well, particularly near the stall. On the same day Frank Barnwell flew it, and later that

day full-load tests were flown with both men aboard.

With three weeks to go before the date of the Lympne trials *G-EBJK* crashed at Filton on 5 September after hitting some telephone wires. The other two aircraft had not yet flown and it was not until 22 September that *G-EBJL* made its first flight, to be followed two days later by *G-EBJM*. The first two aircraft, *G-EBJK* and *G-EBJL*, had been entered for the trials and were numbered 1 and 2 respectively, with Uwins and Campbell as pilots. Both aircraft arrived at Lympne in time for the elimination tests, and, though Uwins' passed without problems, Campbell's aircraft, with the wooden wings, narrowly avoided disaster. During a preliminary flight and while turning above the hangars, wing flutter developed on the port wing and aileron. As the pilot reduced speed so the flutter died away, and Campbell was able to forced-land in a field adjacent to the aerodrome. The Brownie was folded, returned to its hangar by road and re-erected. The covering was removed from the port wing and the port side of the fuselage in order to assess any damage. There was none. Not a single part of the aircraft's structure had failed — not even the varnish had cracked. The cause of the flutter had been the unorthodox aileron control. The elastic return on the ailerons was doubled on Uwins' machine as a precaution and the Number 2 machine was eliminated. In its place went the third Brownie, which had been modified to a single seater and fitted with long range tanks in order to compete in the Grosvenor Cup race, held after the end of the trials at Lympne.

Uwins steadily built up points in the various trials and at the end of the week took second prize of £1,000 put up by the Air Ministry. He also won the Duke of Sutherland's £500 prize for the best take-off and landing performance. Throughout the trials the Brownie had achieved the following performance: high speed 65.2 mph; low speed 38.7 mph; take off 215 yds to clear a 25 ft barrier; landing run, after clearing a 6 ft barrier, 103 yds. During the trials the Brownie flew 512 miles in 10 hrs 23 mins.

Campbell came third in the Grosvenor Cup race. As it happened, all of the first four aircraft in the race

Top *Brownie* G-EBJK *photographed in its original form at Filton, before it crashed there on 5 September 1924.* **Above** *Brownie* G-EBJL *after conversion into a single-seater. In this form it was raced by the Bristol & Wessex Aeroplane Club.* **Below and bottom** *Brownie* G-EBJM *with curved fuselage decking and the front cockpit faired over for racing.* (A.J. Jackson Collection)

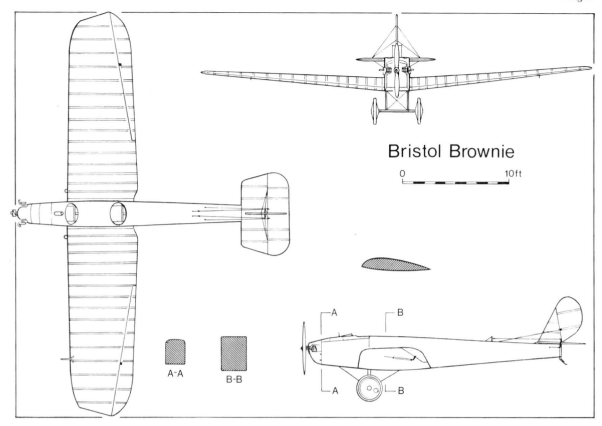

Bristol Brownie

0   10ft

A-A   B-B

were powered by the Cherub engine.

The Brownie received generally favourable reports from the Air Ministry officials at Lympne, though they thought that the metal structure was too light and likely to buckle in the hands of the hamfisted. The undercarriage was considered too light and, indeed, it had been buckled during the trials after not too heavy a landing. The rudder area was insufficient for turning on the ground and, naturally, the sytem of aileron control came under fire. The report questioned why the tailplane, unlike the rest of the airframe, was made of wood. It also drew attention to the fact that considerable drag was caused by the head and shoulders of the occupants, there being no fairing to minimise this.

After Lympne *G-EBJL* was sent to RAF Martlesham Heath for evaluation, but was rejected. Similarly, the wooden-winged *G-EBJK* was evaluated but, after some consideration, it was also returned to Bristol.

By December 1925 the more powerful 36 hp Bristol Cherub III had passed its tests and was installed in the much-modified *G-EBJK*. In an effort to streamline the nose the Cherub had been mounted lower and the top fuselage longerons consequently sloped down towards the nose. Fitted with steel wings and a larger fuel tank, *G-EBJK* was designated Type 91A and sent off once more to Martlesham Heath. Again it was refused, and once more it returned to Filton for further modification. A curved top decking was added, which gave the Brownie a far less angular appearance. In addition the undercarriage was modified to take compression shock absorbers and a large rudder was fitted. Designated Type 91B, the Brownie was entered for the 1926 Lympne trials and flown once more by Uwins. In addition to winning the third prize of £500 he also came second in the SMTT Handicap race with an average speed of 71.5 mph. During the *Daily Mail* competition Uwins had flown a total of 1,994 miles at an average speed of 59.7 mph during which had burned 402 lb of fuel, achieving a figure of merit of 1,587. This was computed by multiplying useful load by miles flown, and the lot was divided by pounds of fuel used.

Also competing in the air racing events at Lympne was Brownie *G-EBJM*, flown by C.T. Holmes. Fitted with metal wings, with the rear cockpit covered and with 28 lb of ballast added to the sternpost, it came third in the Lympne Handicap with an average speed of 76.4 mph. This aircraft was raced frequently and

Above *Brownie* G-EBJK *after considerable modification. The Cherub engine has been mounted lower and the top fuselage longerons have been sloped towards the nose to improve streamlining. In addition 'JK has a larger rudder, and a longer undercarriage. (*Flight* photograph)*
Right *Brownie Type 91B* G-EBJK *after Captain Frank Barnwell wrote it off at Farnborough in March 1927.*

in 1927 was hired by the London Aeroplane Club at Stag Lane as a hack. The aircraft's Certificate of Airworthiness expired in July 1928 and *G-EBJM* was finally scrapped in 1930. *G-EBJL* was flown by the local Bristol & Wessex Aeroplane Club and raced as a single-seater until withdrawn from use on expiry of its C of A in November 1932.

The Brownie Type 91B was passed to Frank Barnwell for his private use in 1927. On 21 March the following year he wrote off the aircraft at Farnborough after encountering turbulence over some trees while taking off.

Bristol Brownie data	
Span	34 ft 7 in (91 wood)
	36 ft 7 in (91 metal)
	30 ft 7 in (91 single-seat)
	37 ft 7 in (91A, 91B)
Length	26 ft 3 in
Height	6 ft 6 in
Wing area	204 ft² (91 wood)
	208 ft² (91 metal)
	172 ft² (91 single-seat)
	210 ft² (91A, 91B)
Empty weight	500 lb (91)
	690 lb (91A, 91B)
All-up weight	870 lb (91)
	720 lb (91 short span)
	1,011 lb (91A, 91B)
Maximum speed	70 mph (91, 91A)
	78 mph (91B)
Cruising speed	not available
Stalling/landing speed	36 mph (91 wood)

Cranwell CLA 2

During the latter part of 1923 the staff and apprentices of Number 4 Apprentices Wing of the RAF College of Cranwell formed the Cranwell Light Aeroplane Club. The Club's designer was 26 year-old Flight Lieutenant Nicholas Comper, the lecturer in charge of the engineering laboratory. His first design for the Club, the CLA 1, never progressed beyond the drawing board and it is not known what form this design took, though whatever it was Comper obviously thought better of it and came up with the CLA 2, which was designed for the Air Ministry's two-seater lightplane competitions held at Lympne in 1924. At the same time Comper considered that a market existed for a robust, low cost, low-powered trainer that was both cheap to build and economic to operate. With these criteria in mind he set to work to design such an aeroplane that could also be built by amateurs with limited facilities in their spare time, ie by members of the Cranwell Light Aeroplane Club.

The resulting design was a crude, boxy aeroplane with little aesthetic beauty. Nevertheless, a great deal of thought had gone into its design. For a start the

side-by-side seating arrangement was unusual for the time, but logical for a training aeroplane. However, by opting for this configuration Comper had made things difficult for himself. The width of the fuselage was dictated by the width of the rudder bars, which resulted in twice the normal frontal area and a consequent increase in drag. To offset this additional drag the forward fuselage longerons converged almost to a point at the engine mounting, which gave the machine its crude appearance. Such an arrangement reduced the body drag however, smoothed the airflow behind the propeller and provided clear access to the engine.

Comper also designed the control surfaces as large as possible in an effort to maintain flying control at low airspeeds. In order to simplify construction and keep costs to an absolute minimum, the wings and fuslage involved no pretty curves or streamlining.

The fuselage was of normal wire-braced wooden construction with ash longerons in the front section, which had fairly sharp curves and spruce longerons behind. The slab-sided fuselage had a flat bottom, but the top fuselage decking was cambered by means of formers and stringers. The roomy cockpit was located immediately beneath the wing centre-section and to facilitate access the top fuselage decking aft of the cockpit was hinged. All cockpit controls were interconnected, allowing the aircraft to be flown from either seat.

The unstaggered wings were built of I-section spruce spars with spruce lattice ribs and square spruce drag struts. The wing section was RAF 64, which, although not possessed of any startling performance features, gave a good compromise in lift/drag characteristics. The top wing was of greater span and of larger area than the bottom, its leading edge being slightly further forward than that of the lower wing. The interplane struts were of spruce and braced with streamlined wire. The wing centre-section was carried well clear of the fuselage by four slightly splayed spruce struts. Although the wings were not foldable they could be detached and stowed alongside the fuselage, retained in position by strategically placed clips.

It had been originally intended to install an Anzani engine into the CLA 2, but in the event a 32 hp Bristol

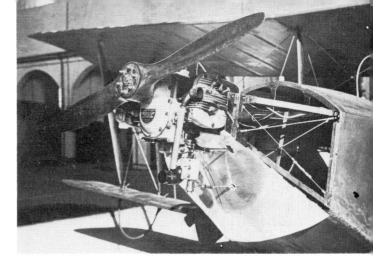

Cherub was used. This was mounted on a minute bulkhead which could be changed for a larger unit in the event of a bigger engine being fitted. The engine was fed by a 4½ gal tank mounted in the wing centre-section. The undercarriage was of the V-type with the legs cut in one piece from plywood. Shock absorbers were of the standard rubber cord type. The entire air-craft was fabric covered.

The CLA 2 was built at RAF Cranwell and was completed early in September 1924. Comper made the first flight, from Cranwell's south aerodrome, on 14 September. There was barely time for him or his second pilot, Flight Lieutenant E.P. Mackay, to familiarise themselves with the biplane before they flew it down to Lympne, via Croydon, for the trials.

The trials commenced on Saturday 27 September and it soon became evident that many of the competing aircraft were not capable of standing up to the rigours of the tests. Many were unable to take off with full loads — which was the whole point of the exercise. The Cranwell Club had prayed for light winds and in this respect they were unlucky. Before the flying, though, there was the transport test which involved pushing the aircraft through a 10 ft wide gateway and then re-erecting it for flight. Some competitors had sophisticated wing folding devices but the impecunious Cranwell team had to practically dismantle the CLA 2 and then drape everything around it like a Christmas tree. The team needed every second of the two hour time limit to complete these transport tests.

The CLA 2 handled well during the dual control tests but it was very apparent that it was too under-powered to make its mark in anything other than the Reliability Test Trial. This involved flogging around a set course throughout the trials, the winner being the aircraft that notched up the longest distance and the highest number of hours flown. By Thursday 2 October, Comper had passed the 10 hr test and he continued lapping and eventually won the SMMT reliability prize of £300, having flown a distance of 762.5 miles in 17 hrs 53 mins.

The Cranwell team had great difficulty with the slow speed flying tests, as *The Aeroplane*'s correspondent reported: 'Although excellent in many ways the Cranwell is quite naturally not so aero-dynamically efficient as the other machines designed with all the experience of old-established aircraft firms behind them. It made one dash down the course and from the rough timing of this one run it appeared that its slow speed was 2 mph faster than its high speed round the 12 mile odd course. This somewhat para-doxical result caused much amusement. On getting to the end of the course furthest from Lympne village, the machine had great difficulty in surmounting the fence at the bottom of the aerodrome, owing to the fact that it was almost on stalling speed and it was flying downwind and the wind had rather a down than up-lift about it, owing to the topography. It disappeared flying a few feet off the ground in Mr Baird's field, but it flew back later undamaged.'

The Directorate of Technical Development's report on the two-seater trials aircraft, produced during November 1924, criticised the CLA 2 on a number of points. The side-by-side seating arrange-ment, though advantageous for a training machine, necessitated a very large body, with consequently large drag, to an extent prohibitive in a lightplane — particularly with such a low-powered engine. The undercarriage was considered too low for use on the average grass aerodrome and the report criticised the lack of wing folding. The CLA 2, though, was regarded as one of the most interesting aircraft in the competition, from the point of view of Service use. It was praised for its cheapness of construction. Its suitability for Service use would have depended on the Service's policy regarding the use of side-by-side dual control. Because of the reduction of performance due to the increased width of the fuselage, it was felt that a compromise could be met whereby the seats could be staggered — something that was later carried out to good effect in the Tipsy Trainer. With these reservations the report considered the CLA 2 the only competing aircraft suitable for Service and training use. One advantage of the side-by-side seating arrangement was that it was not necessary to carry ballast during single pilot operation.

Had the ungeared Cherub engine been more efficient (it had only developed 55 per cent efficiency) as against the designed 30 hp at 3,000 rpm, the CLA 2 might have stood a better chance. Even so, the maximum speed of 60 mph was better than Comper envisaged. The CLA 2's stalling speed was 30 mph but more important was the fuel consumption, which was 30 mpg.

The CLA 2 survived for only a short while after the trials, for it was written off by an Air Ministry pilot during later evaluation. The money received by way of compensation, together with the £300 Lympne prize money, went towards building the CLA 3 for the 1925 Lympne event.

Though registered *G-EBKC*, the CLA 2 never carried these markings.

Cranwell CLA 2 data	
Span	29 ft 8 in
	(upper wing)
	23 ft 8 in
	(lower wing)
	9 ft 6 in
	(wings folded)
Length	23 ft 6 in
Wing area	223.5 ft²
Empty weight	510 lb
All-up weight	890 lb
Maximum speed	55 mph
Cruising speed	not available
Stalling/landing speed	30 mph

Hawker Cygnet

If the de Havilland DH 53 can be considered as one of the first truly practical British light monoplanes, the Hawker Cygnet certainly ranks as one of the first practical biplanes. The Cygnet was the Hawker concern's only venture into the lightplane market and it was the first powered aircraft to be designed by Sydney Camm. It could perhaps be described as the progenitor of the Fury biplane, which in turn led to the Hurricane. Sydney Camm joined the H.G.

Hawker Engineering Co Ltd at Kingston in 1923 and, although the little Cygnet was his baby, he had the company's chief designer Carter looking over his shoulder throughout.

When the Air Ministry announced on 10 January, 1924 that it was putting up a prize of £3,000 for a competition for two-seater lightplanes with engines of no more than 1,100 cc a number of aircraft companies suddenly became interested in the light aircraft market, though most would not otherwise have touched the 'pop-bottle' end of the industry with a bargepole.

In August 1924, just weeks before the trials were due to be held at Lympne, Hawker announced that they would be entering two Cygnets, both of which were nearing copmpletion. The old Sopwith firm, from which the Hawker company emerged after the former company closed in 1920, had a wealth of experience in designing fighters, where strength and lightness were key factors. This knowhow was put to good use in the Cygnet and the finished biplane weighed only 373 lb empty, a truly remarkable achievement with a 28 ft span biplane. Though the two Cygnets were identical they were powered by different engines. One was powered by a 1,100 cc British Anzani and the other was fitted with a 34 hp ABC Scorpion two-cylinder engine. The Hawker Cygnet was a staggered-wing biplane with large upper and small lower wings. The rear spars were so arranged that they were in the same vertical plane when the thrustline was horizontal.

The fuselage was constructed with four longerons, spindled where possible, and braced in the form of a Warren-girder by diagonal struts of cruciform section. The struts were attached to the longerons by three-ply gussets riveted and screwed into position. Though the top fuselage decking was cambered, the sides and bottom were flat. The aft fuselage decking consisted of formers and wedge section stringers with fabric covering. The nose decking and that between the cabanes was of three-ply. Between the wing attachment points the fuselage bays were braced with tie rods; crosswire bracing was embodied in the cross frames.

The wings had spars of normal box construction with spruce flanges and three-ply webs but were wrapped in fabric. To give additional strength the rear spars were stiffened for about 5 ft from the root with Duralumin channel-section, which was screwed and taped to the back of it. The spruce ribs were of Warren-girder construction with three-ply gussets. The compression ribs were of spruce box section and the single raked interplane struts, also of spruce, had a streamline section. They were hollow and constructed in two halves, then bolted to heavy compression members and reinforced with Duralumin side

plates. The full-span ailerons, fitted to all four wings, doubled as flaps. Top and bottom ailerons were connected by a wire.

The braced V-type undercarriage embodied rubber cord shock absorbing and the streamlined struts were made of spruce. The tail unit was of normal construction, consisting of box-section spars with spruce flanges and three-ply webs. The ribs were of similar construction to those of the wings. No fin was fitted and the partially balanced rudder had a box-section spar.

Two different engine mountings were used. The Anzani was originally fitted on a mounting built up of mild steel plate. Just prior to the competition the mounting was wrecked following engine failure and the Anzani was subsequently mounted on steel tube supports. The mounting for the Scorpion engine consisted of two steel brackets carrying the rear engine feet, with steel tubes, anchored to the bottom rails of the fuselage, supporting the front feet.

The Cygnet had folding wings. The trailing edge of the top wing centre-section was hinged to fold downwards. The bottom wing was mounted on small stub spars in line with the bottom longerons (just like a model aircraft) and the wings folded normally. A Duralumin jury strut, normally carried inside the fuselage, supported the top front spar at its inner end when wing folding was carried out.

The two cockpits were necessarily cramped and it was not easy to climb in and out without risking damage to the structure. The view from the front seat was very good, though restricted from the rear cockpit. The emphasis during construction was on weight saving. There were very few metal fittings and even fully loaded the Cygnet weighed only 730 lb.

The two Cygnets arrived at Lympne for the elimination trials. The Anzani-powered aircraft, numbered 14 for the trials, was flown by Fred

Above *The Scorpion-powered Hawker Cygnet, numbered 15 for the 1924 trials, photographed at Brooklands shortly after completion.* (*Flight* photograph) **Below** *Close up fo the ABC Scorpion fitted to Cygnet Number 15. The horizontally opposed air-cooled engine produced 30 hp at 3,000 rpm.* (*Flight* photograph) **Bottom** *Cygnet G-EBJH, numbered 4 and entered for the 1926 Lympne meeting by the RAE Aero Club, photographed during the folding, housing and erecting tests.* (*Flight* photograph)

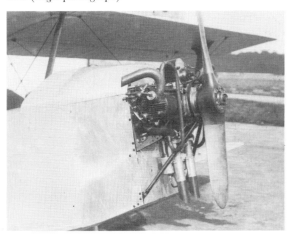

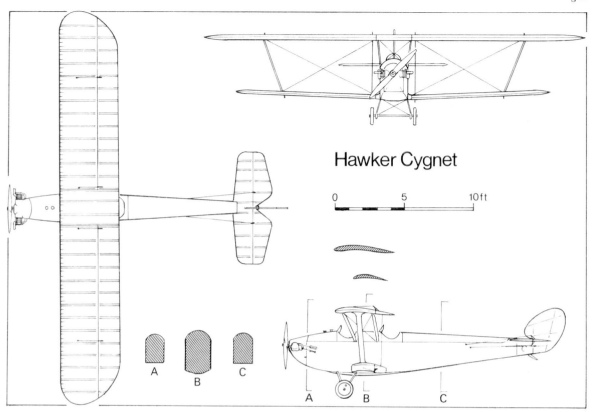

Hawker Cygnet

0   5   10 ft

A   B   C

A   B   C

Below *The RAE Club's Cygnet taking part in the 1926 Lympne meeting.* (*Flight* photograph) **Right** *Flight Lieutenant P. W. S. Bulman won the £3,000* Dail Mail *prize at the 1926 Lympne trials flying Cygnet G-EBMB.* (*Flight* photograph)

Raynham. The other Cygnet, numbered 15 and powered by the Scorpion, was entrusted to Squadron Leader Longton. Because the Anzani engine was new Longton began the tests cautiously. The aircraft performed well though at one point the fuel tank split, necessitating a forced landing at Monks Horton. A spare tank was despatched by car and Longton managed to fly out of the field and back to Lympne. Both engines played up during the speed tests, which was particularly frustrating in the case of Raynham because he was within an ace of winning the £2,000 prize when a thrust race began running hot. He was eventually forced to retire in order to replace the cylinder heads. His hopes were again dashed later on when he ran out of fuel, and Longton broke three valves in one lap. The valve problem persisted and Longton was put out of the running for the speed tests. During the slow flying tests, during which competing pilots took as long a time as possible to fly between two points, Longton raised a few smiles when he put his crazy flying expertise to good use — he did everything but fly backwards.

Engine trouble was to plague both Cygnets constantly and it was only through sheer determination that Raynham and Longton were placed third and fourth respectively. Raynham won a £100 prize for the best take-off and landing performance and the performance for both machines was as follows:

Hawker Cygnet Number 15 (F.P. Raynham): Low speed 34.42 mph; Take-off 250 yds; Landing run 72½ yds; Number of hours flown 10 hrs 29 mins; Miles flown 437.5.

Hawker Cygnet Number 14 (Squadron Leader Longton): Low speed 43.95 mph; Take-off distance 269 yds; Landing run 66.7 yds; Number of hours flown 8 hrs 24 mins; Miles flown 400.

After the competition-flying had finished and in between changing valves, Longton gave a dazzling display of aerobatics on the Cygnet. Observers noted that the biplane was, if anything, overpowered for its weight. Both Cygnets had been entered for the Grosvenor Challenge Race, held after the trials, but Raynham's aircraft was grounded with engine trouble and during the first lap of the race Longton was forced down with further valve trouble — it was rumoured that the pilot had shares in a valve-manufacturing company!

When it was all over the Directorate of Technical Development report came out in favour of Camm's little biplane. The design was described as excellent though they criticized the small, low undercarriage, which had the habit of collecting grass. It was thought that although the airframe was not exactly flimsy it was probably insufficiently robust for training purposes. The fuselage was considered insufficiently wide but the airframe was thought suitable for mass production. It was recommended that the single I interplane bracing struts be replaced by a normal twin strut arrangement.

Both Cygnets were registered shortly after the Lympne trials. Aircraft Number 14 became *G-EBJH* and Number 15 was registered *G-EBMB*. Despite the trouble experienced with the British Anzani inverted vee engine, the aircraft was entered for the 1925 August meeting at Lympne, where it was entered by T.O.M. Sopwith and Fred Sigrist and flown by P.W.S. Bulman, who won the International Handicap Race, run over 100 miles, at an average speed of 75.6 mph.

Both Cygnets took part in the 1926 Lympne light-plane meeting, held during September. *G-EBJH* had been acquired the previous year by the RAE Aero Club, producers of their own ultra-light aircraft described elsewhere in this book. Cygnet *G-EBMB*, numbered 6 for the event, was entered by Fred Sigrist with Bulman as pilot once again. Both Cygnets had been re-engined with the well-proven Bristol Cherub III.

In complete contrast to previous trials Bulman's Cygnet ran sweetly throughout the competition and required no attention whatsoever. After flying 1,994 miles in a total flying time of 30 hrs 41 mins, at an average speed of 64.9 mph, Bulman easily won the *Daily Mail* £3,000 prize. After the flying his engine was stripped down completely and examined in public. No repairs or replacement of parts was necessary. The RAE Cygnet too found success when pilot Flying Officer Ragg won the Lympne Open Handicap Race with an average speed of 78 mph. In the same race Bulman came sixth with a speed of 82 mph.

Cygnet *G-EBMB* continued to race until its Certificate of Airworthiness expired in March 1929, when it was put into storage at Brooklands and forgotten. During the late 1940s the aircraft was rediscovered

and restored by Hawker. It returned to the civil register in May 1950, its C of A being renewed at Langley. The Cygnet was flown frequently in company with the parent company's Hurricane *G-AMAU* and the famous Hart *G-ABMR*. In the 1970s both the Cygnet and the Hart were presented to the RAF Museum at Hendon where they can be seen in the Sydney Camm Memorial Hall today.

Hawker Cygnet *G-EBJH* was not so lucky. In November 1927 Flight Lieutenant R.L. Ragg tried to take off for a non-stop flight to Bucharest from Lympne. He crashed on the airfield during take-off and *'JH* was no more.

Hawker Cygnet data	
Span	28 ft 0 in
	8 ft 0 in
	(wings folded)
Length	20 ft 3 in
Height	5 ft 10 in
Wing area	165 ft²
Empty weight	373 lb (Cherub)
All-up weight	730 lb
Maximum speed	82 mph (Cherub)
Cruising speed	50 mph (Cherub)
Stalling/landing speed	30 mph (Cherub)

Parnall Pixie III and IIIA

With the announcement of the 1924 ·Air Ministry trials for two-seater lightplanes, two entrants to the previous year's competition for single-seat machines decided to enter suitably modified versions of their 1923 entries. W.S. Shackleton's ANEC II has already been covered in a previous chapter. By enlarging the wings of the ANEC I, and by fitting a larger engine and an additional cockpit, Shackleton was able to enter a proven design. Similarly, Harold Bolas, who had designed the Parnall Pixie I and II for the single-seater trials, modified the Pixie I to qualify for entry to the 1924 competitions.

Two airframes were built for the two-seater trials. The Pixie III doubled as a monoplane and a biplane; in its biplane configuration it was known as the Pixie IIIA. The Pixie IIIs were registered *G-EBJG* and *G-EBKK*. The first aircraft was powered by a 32 hp Bristol Cherub III flat-twin engine and *G-EBKK* was fitted with the slightly more powerful 35 hp Blackburne Thrush three-cylinder radial.

The fuselage construction of the Pixie III was similar to that of the Pixie I, described in an earlier chapter. It consisted of four spruce longerons, braced as Warren-girders, with spruce struts attached by three-ply gussets. The sides and bottom were flat but the top decking was cambered. The undercarriage legs incorporated oleo-pneumatic shock absorbers and a simple axle with overhang for the wheels was attached to the ends.

The monoplane wing was attached to the bottom longerons with strut bracing to the top longeron, the two sets of bracing struts being inverted vees. The wing spars were as on the Pixie I, the front spar being straight while the rear spar ran parallel for half the span before it raked forward to join the other spar at the tip. The wings had their maximum thickness at the strut attachment point and tapered towards both the tip and the centre-section. Differential aileron controls were fitted, the ailerons being mounted on the raked portions of the rear spar. The wing leading edges were plywood covered.

The mountings for both the Cherub and Thrush engines were separate structures attached to the fuselage, ahead of a sheet metal bulkhead. The precise form of the mounting depended on which particular engine was installed. The Cherub was carried from the four corners of the fireproof bulkhead by four steel tubes that converged to the four crankcase bolts. The lower pair of tubes was stiffened by diagonal tubes from the top corner fittings to a point as near the engine studs as could be reached without fouling the engine parts. The installation was well carried out and, for ease of maintenance, the engine cowlings were attached by means of spring studs.

The tailplane shape and its method of construction was similar to that of the 1923 Pixie. Basically triangular in form, it was built mostly of steel, though the mainspar was made of wood.

The Pixie IIIA biplane was of identical construction. The top wing was of less chord and span (25 ft 8 in) than the lower. It had a straight leading edge and straight taper but both spars had forward rake, each

The detachable top wing of the Pixie IIIA was strut braced and a little over 6 ft shorter in span than the lower wing. Pixie IIIA G-EBJG is seen here at the 1924 Lympne trials with Flight Lieutenant R.A. de Haga Haig flying from the rear cockpit. (Flight photograph)

maintaining a constant position proportionate to the wing chord. The wing was supported at mid-span on N-type interplane struts raked outwards from the strut anchorage on the bottom wing (from which the lower wing was braced to the top longeron). The two halves of the wing were joined above the fuselage centre-line; the junction was supported from the top longerons by an inverted V strut sloping back to the front spar and by a tripod arrangement sloping forward to the rear spar. The top wing spars were made of I-section spruce. For transporting by road the top wing could be removed completely, the two halves being stowed alongside the lower wings, the tips resting on the tailplane with the roots supported by the bottom wing struts. The 25 ft 8 in span top wing had no ailerons and was thinner in section than the lower wing.

The Parnall Pixie III was first flown on 5 September 1924 from Parnall's aerodrome at Yate, near Bristol. Squadron Leader W. Sholto Douglas and Flight Lieutenant Rollo A. de Haga Haig carried out further flights and during one of these Sholto Douglas had to make a forced landing at Henbury with sparking-plug problems. The aircraft was easily folded and pushed through four gateways to a suitably large field, from which a successful take-off was made and the Pixie was flown to Filton. Thus the Pixie III had successfully demonstrated its transport ability in advance of the transport tests shortly to be held at Lympne. The only modifications made to the Pixie before delivery to Lympne were to increase the area of the rudder and elevators.

Parnall originally planned to enter Pixie *G-EBJG* as two aircraft; in biplane configuration as Number

Above *With the top wing added the total wing area of the Pixie IIIA was increased from 140 ft² to 243 ft². (Flight photograph)* **Below** *Pixie Number 19 flying in biplane configuration at the 1924 Lympne trials. Both Pixies were plagued by engine trouble. (Flight photograph)* **Bottom** *Pixie III Number 18 photographed at Lympne in October 1924. (Via Terry Heffernan)*

Top *The Pixie III's wing folding arrangement received official praise though for Service use the building of wings in quantity would have been problematical because not two wing ribs were alike.* **Above** *Pixie III G-EBKK in monoplane form. The original 35 hp Blackburne Thrush engine was later exchanged for a 1,000 cc Anzani.* (*Flight* photograph) **Below** *Pixie III G-EBJG was flown as Number 18 in the 1924 Lympne trials, powered by an ungeared Bristol Cherub engine.*

18 and as a monoplane numbered 17. The pilot was to be de Haga Haig. Sholto Douglas was to fly the Thrust-engined *G-EBKK*, numbered 19 for the trials. When the first aircraft was presented for scrutiny by the officials they demanded to see it present in both configurations at once! Bolas decided to dispense with the monoplane, Number 17, and both Pixies were entered as biplanes.

In the event both aircraft were dogged with engine trouble. De Haga Haig's aircraft had to forced-land at one point when the Cherub threw a con-rod through the engine crankcase, while Bolas was flying

as passenger; and *G-EBKK*'s Thrush engine seized. Nevertheless Sholto Douglas flew 450 miles in 10 hrs 5 mins flying time and also won the slow speed test with an average of 37 mph. Both Pixies competed in the Grosvenor Cup Race held after the trials on 4 October, but neither was successful. Sholto Douglas in aircraft Number 19 withdrew with engine trouble and de Haga Haig came in fifth.

The official report on the Pixie III was generally favourable. The detail design was considered excellent, particularly the wing folding arrangement and the engine cowling. The type was considered suitable for mass production though for Service use the building of wings in quantity was regarded as problematical as no two ribs were alike. A Service machine would be damaged frequently and a considerable stock of spares would be required for the Pixie. The basic design was also considered to be too complicated for cheap upkeep as a dual trainer. The cockpits were considered satisfactory and the view from the pilot's seat was favoured in both versions. The flying qualities were considered to be excellent though it was noted that the monoplane was probably more suitable for general work.

Later, Pixie *G-EBJG* was sent to the Aeroplane & Armament Experimental Establishment at RAF Martlesham Heath where it was flown by Service pilots in order to determine its suitability as a Service trainer. Apart from the poor downward view over the wing they thought the Pixie an excellent aeroplane. In August 1925 *G-EBJG* was returned to Yate and in the following year took part in the Air Ministry trials at Lympne in September. Numbered 14, the Pixie was flown in the capable hands of Frank Courtney. He encountered a number of problems and at one point rain in the carburettor forced him to put the Pixie down on the Brighton racecourse. During the trials the Pixie covered the requisite 1,994 miles at an average speed of 59 mph and used 440 lb of fuel, coming fourth overall.

After passing through various hands *G-EBJG* spent the war in store at Kirklington and after several more post-war owners the aircraft is now in the care of the Midland Aircraft Preservation Society.

Parnall Pixie *G-EBKK* was used as an engine test-

bed and flew with a 1,100 cc British Anzani and the Bristol Cherub III engine. In 1926 '*KK* was modified permanently to a monoplane and in 1930 was sold to the Bristol & Wessex Aeroplane Club. In February that year it crashed and the registration marks were cancelled that September.

Parnall Pixie III data	
Span	32 ft 4 in
Length	21 ft 3 in
Height	not available
Wing area	140 ft^2
Empty weight	522 lb
All-up weight	925 lb
Maximum speed	not available
Cruising speed	not available
Stalling/landing speed	not available

Parnall Pixie IIIA data	
Span	25 ft 8 in
	(upper wing)
	32 ft 4 in
	(lower wing)
Length	21 ft 3 in
Height	not available
Wing area	243 ft^2
Empty weight	540 lb
All-up weight	891 lb
Maximum speed	not available
Cruising speed	not available
Stalling/landing speed	not available

Short Satellite

Looking at the different types entered for the Air Ministry's two-seater lightplane trials held at Lympne in 1924 it is hard to believe that they were all designed at more or less the same time. One has only to compare Flight Lieutenant Comper's boxy CLA 2 with the sleek futuristic metal Short Satellite monoplane to illustrate the point. Both were designed for the same tasks but one would be forgiven for thinking that they were years apart. The CLA 2, of course, was built by an impecunious group of enthusiasts whereas the Satellite was turned out by a long-standing, money-almost-no-object aircraft company. Interestingly enough the CLA 2 was, as far as the trials were concerned, far more successful than its shining contemporary, though the Short aircraft was an interesting experiment in miniaturising construction methods pioneered with that company's Silver Streak and Springbok aircraft.

In layout the Satellite was conventional enough. It

was a cantilever, mid-wing mounted tandem-seat monoplane powered by a 32 hp Bristol Cherub flat-twin air-cooled engine. The unusual feature was its method of construction, which, for a lightplane, was unique.

The Satellite's fuselage was a Duralumin monocoque of circular section. The Duralumin sheeting was riveted to the elliptical rings of L-section which formed the frames of the structure; short longitudinal stiffening strips ran between and were cleated to each frame. The fact that it was impossible to bend sheet metal around a sphere without beating meant that the Satellite's fuselage could not be shaped in the form of a smooth curve longitudinally. Instead it was fashioned in a series of straight lines. Where a sharp change in curve direction occurred, the sheets were made narrower, as can be seen in the accompanying drawing. A gentler curve allowed the use of larger metal sheets. The resulting structure was somewhat heavier than it would have been if made in wood.

The original plan was to construct a corrugated high-tensile steel wing spar but the design was uncompleted by July 1924 and, with the Lympne trials only two months away, there was insufficient time to design and construct such a spar. Instead the Satellite's wing had wooden box spars, with three-ply webs and laminated mahogany flanges. The ribs were of Duralumin Warren-girder construction. The aerofoil section used for the Satellite's wing was RAF 15 over the outer half of the span, thickening to a deeper section toward the root. Since the spar tapered uniformly, it was necessary to attach the ribs to the spar with brackets from the web members instead of directly from the flanges. The full-span ailerons were operated by torsion tubes and rods and, as on many of the other aircraft competing at Lympne, a variable camber device was fitted. This allowed both ailerons to be depressed together, the differential action being retained. The two wings were bolted to strong fuselage frames by fishplates and large diameter hingepins, in order to facilitate dismantling. When the wings were removed for transporting by road they

The Satellite is pushed out for the folding and transport tests at Lympne in October 1924. (Via Terry Heffernan)

The Satellite looked very advanced for 1924; its aerodynamic cleanliness was praised by Air Ministry officials.

were placed with their leading edges resting on the overhang of the undercarriage axle and on the tailplane leading edge.

The Satellite's undercarriage was of the divided type, each axle being pivoted about a point just below the bottom of the fuselage. The main leg incorporated compression rubber shock absorbers. The rear undercarriage struts converged to a point on the bottom of the fuselage. Both the axle and the telescopic undercarriage legs were enclosed in a streamlined casing. The tailskid was a simple horizontal steel tube fitted with a removable shoe on its end.

The tail unit rested on top of the fuselage and was strutted to the bottom of the fuselage from a point about half-way along the tailplane's span. Steel tubing was used in the construction but the ribs were

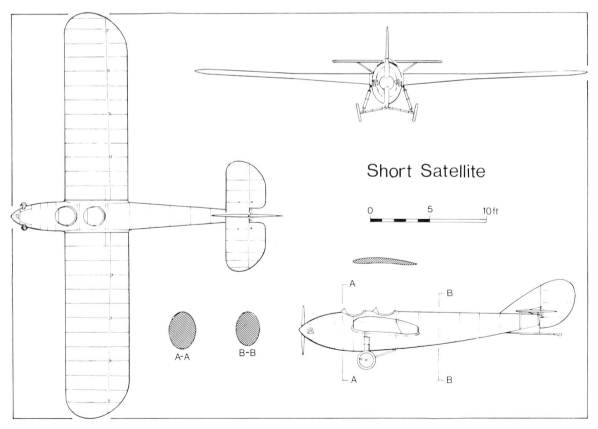

Short Satellite

0   5   10 ft

A-A   B-B

made of sheet Duralumin stiffened by a plate riveted on at the spar connection. Like the wings, the tail-plane was fabric-covered.

The Bristol Cherub engine was mounted on an aluminium casting anchored to the front fuselage bulkhead. The casting was further braced by steel tubes. The 3½ gal fuel tank and oil tanks were located behind the fireproof bulkhead. The engine was neatly faired by a conical cowling, and a spinner completed the aerodynamic lines of the Satellite.

John Lankester Parker made the first flight tests of the Satellite and, though they began on 10 September 1924 at Lympne, the Short test pilot did not take the aircraft off the ground until 16 September, after trouble with the Cherub engine had been cleared. From the onset it was obvious that the Satellite was overweight. It would fly reasonably well with one up but, like several other two-seaters designed for the 1924 Lympne trials, it refused to fly with a passenger, despite several changes of propeller. It was imposible to find a geared Cherub II with which to replace the direct-drive Cherub I. With little hope of achieving anything, the Satellite, numbered 8 for the competition, began its elimination tests with Parker at the controls. Still it stubbornly refused to fly with two aboard and it was swiftly eliminated. Parker fared much better when he flew it in the Grosvenor Cup Race. With a specially tuned Cherub I installed and with an all-up weight of 867 lb the Satellite came sixth, reaching 72 mph.

Eventually a geared Cherub II was fitted and, with a larger propeller, the Satellite flew well, though wing flutter developed during one flight when the aircraft reached 90 mph. After the wing span had been reduced by 2 ft the trouble disappeared and even in dives to a speed of 120 mph there was no recurrence of the dreaded flutter.

The Air Ministry observers' report on the Satellite's performance at Lympne was mixed in its criticism. The machine was considered suitable for the private owner and its aerodynamic cleanliness was highly regarded. The aircraft's excessive weight was considered due to wastage of weight in both the fuselage and wings. The use of laminated mahogany in the spar construction was not understood and the report regarded the use of tapered spars in an untapered wing as wasteful of weight, both in the spar itself and in the superstructure required to support the ribs. The use of the casting in the engine mounting was frowned upon because of the undesirable effect continuous vibration must eventually have on its crystalline structure. Apart from the points already mentioned the Satellite was considered suitable for mass production, provided that sufficiently skilled labour was available. The report felt that the cockpit was cramped, though the view for the pilot

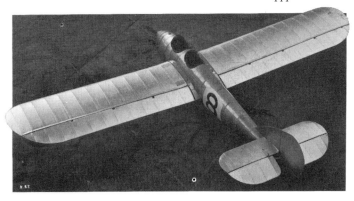

Above *This three-quarter view of the Satellite shows the full-span ailerons. The wings and tail unit were fabric-covered though the fuselage was covered with duralumin sheeting.* **Below** *John Lankester Parker flying the Satellite during the Lympne trials in October 1924.* **Bottom** *For the Lympne Bank Holiday Meeting, held at Lympne on 1 August 1925, the Satellite was flown as a single-seater.* (*Flight* photograph)

was satisfactory. The view from the rear cockpit was restricted both forwards and downwards.

The Satellite was registered *G-EBJU* and a Certificate of Airworthiness was granted on 8 September 1926. In the same year the aircraft was acquired by the Seven Aero Club, run by a group of RAF officers at RAF Eastchurch, who intended to enter the Satellite for that year's Lympne trials in September. They had also entered a Westland Woodpigeon, presented to them by the Westland company. The club re-engined the Satellite with a 40 hp ABC Scorpion II and fitted a Fairey-Reed metal propeller. Arriving at

Lympne as Number 15, flown by Flying Officer G.E.F. Boyes, the Woodpigeon and the Satellite were involved in a fracas with the competition stewards over the shared use of metal and wooden propellers. Each aircraft had earlier arrived at Lympne fitted with the other's propeller with the intention of swapping them back for the trials. The officials refused to allow the change to take place. In addition, the Satellite's undercarriage was damaged and the stewards refused permission to make repairs, so the aircraft was eliminated.

Later the Satellite was returned to Short at Rochester, where it was stored in the rafters of Number 1 Shop for a number of years.

Short Satellite data	
Span	34 ft 0 in
	(later 32 ft 0 in)
Length	23 ft 9 in
Height	not available
Wing area	168 ft²
	(later 160 ft²)
Empty weight	640 lb
	666 lb (Scorpion)
All-up weight	1,060 lb
	867 lb (Scorpion)
Maximum speed	72 mph
Cruising speed	not available
Stalling/landing speed	37 mph

Supermarine Sparrow

We have already seen how large amounts of prize money put up by the Air Ministry for the 1924 Two-Seater Light Aeroplane Trials attracted large established aircraft manufacturing companies, who would normally not have demeaned themselves for what were really aerial motor cycles. The Supermarine company — which had not built a landplane since its parent Pemberton Billing days — decided to have a go, and design was entrusted to Reginald Mitchell who, a dozen years later, was to be fully engaged on the design of that company's Spitfire fighter. While Mitchell pencilled the lines of the Lympne contestant, so Hawker's Sydney Camm was playing with the same problem, for that company too had entered a two-seat biplane for the 1924 competition. Later, of course, Camm was to design the Hawker Hurricane fighter, which, with the Spitfire, was to provide the backbone of Britain's fighter force. It is interesting, therefore, to compare the designs these two men produced for somewhat more peaceful purposes.

Like the Hawker Cygnet, Mitchell's Sparrow was a normal biplane with a sesquiplane layout — the upper wing being of greater span and chord than the lower. The interplane struts were raked. The wings were staggered such that, when the thrustline was level, the upper trailing edge was directly above the lower.

The Sparrow's fuselage was built of four longerons with vertical struts and diagonals, all of spruce. The entire fuselage was ply-covered. Both the top and bottom longerons sloped up towards the tail (relative to the thrust line) to give greater wing incidence on the ground. Though the sides and bottom of the fuselage were slab-sided the top decking was slightly cambered.

The foldable wings were of normal construction and had spruce I-section spars. The drag struts were of box section with three-ply sides and flanges, corner fillets and three-ply formers. The wing ribs had three-ply webs — suitably lightened — and spruce flanges. Interestingly the top and bottom wings had different aerofoils, the top wings having a modified RAF 15 section and the bottom pair being AD1 (Admiralty Air Department). Both sections were of the low-drag, high speed type. The Sparrow's upper ailerons were carried on false spars supported on overhung ribs on the top wing; the lower ailerons were mounted directly on to the bottom wing rear spar. All four ailerons were full span and could be used as variable camber devices — a feature that was common to many of the 1924 competing aircraft. The wing centre-section was supported on vertical struts above the top longerons and was cross-braced with streamline wires. The trailing edges of both wings were cut back from the fuselage to give the rear cockpit occupant a good view downwards.

The V-type undercarriage embodied telescopic steel tubes carrying leather-covered crutches wound with rubber cord shock absorbers. The rear radius rods were cross-braced and the wheels were carried on a slightly overhung axle which gave extra shock absorption by deflection.

The tail unit was made up of two spindled-out spruce spars, square-section drag struts and wire bracing. Steel tube struts formed bracing beneath the

Above left *The Supermarine Sparrow in its original 1924 Lympne form, with 35 hp Blackburne Thrush engine. The fuselage was doped dark blue with aluminium wings, tail unit and engine cowling.* (Via Philip Jarrett) Above *For the 1926 Lympne trials the Sparrow was entered as a monoplane with a 32 hp Bristol Cherub III engine installed.* (*Flight* photograph) Right *The Sparrow seen at Lympne during the 1926 trials. Because the wings did not fold they had to be detached and secured to the fuselage side for transporting by road.* (*Flight* photograph) Below right *The Sparrow II monoplane was heavier and slower than its biplane configuration. After the 1926 Lympne trials it was used by the Air Ministry for testing wings of different sections and aerofoils.* (Via Philip Jarrett) Bottom right *A rare photograph of the Sparrow II wearing its civil registration letters G-EBJP, taken possibly at the time it was owned by the Halton Aero Club* (A.J. Jackson Collection)

tailplane and wire bracing ran from the same anchorage points to the fin post. Originally the rudder came to a point at the top, but was rounded off during construction.

The 1,096 cc three-cylinder Blackburne Thrush engine was bolted direct to a steel plate which formed the front fuselage bulkhead and which was attached to each longeron by three bolts. The engine was very neatly cowled, except for the tops of the cylinders and the oil sump, which was built integral with the crank case. The petrol tank was housed in the fuselage deck fairing in order to provide direct gravity feed to the engine.

The dark blue and aluminium Supermarine Sparrow was completed early in September 1924 and the company's test pilot, Henri Biard, took it into the air for the first time on 11 September, from Hamble. Right from the beginning there was trouble with the Thrush engine, which was both temperamental and unpredictable. It would work perfectly one day and then run for barely seconds the next. Much of the problem lay with the wooden propeller, which had been fitted in an attempt to coax the maximum engine revs recommended by the manufacturers, ie 3,500, which was rather on the high side. Even with a change of propeller, fitted on 27 September, things did not look very promising. The Sparrow arrived at Lympne for the trials on the same day.

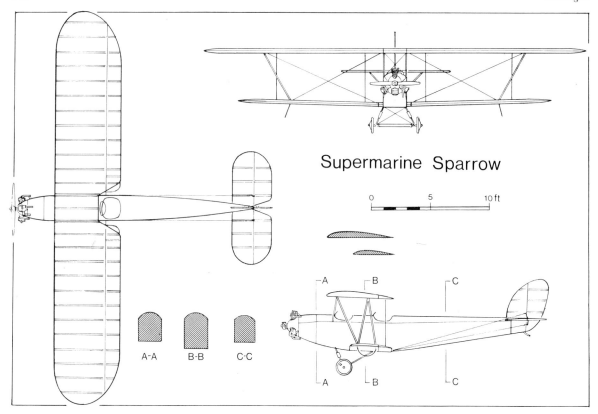

Supermarine Sparrow

Numbered 9 for the competitions, the Sparrow failed to pass the elimination tests, but only just, when a connecting rod through the crankcase necessitated changing the engine. This could not be achieved in sufficient time and so the Sparrow was knocked out of the trials before they had begun. This was a bitter blow to the Supermarine team because when it did behave the new engine performed extremely well — though it did seize up the day after it was installed, causing Biard to pull off a very skilled forced landing among the other competing aircraft. The engine was repaired in time for the Sparrow to take part in the Grosvenor Challenge Cup race, though it could only be run at full bore. It came fourth with an average speed of 62 mph.

The official Air Ministry report on the Sparrow was generally favourable, though some adverse comments were made. The wing bracing was criticized, mainly because it was felt that the wing bays were too wide. The cockpits were judged to be too far apart and the Sparrow's exterior was criticized for being cluttered with external control rods and cables. Lack of power gave the biplane little power reserve and the centre-section bracing wires were considered to be too close to the pilot's face. There was no upward view at all from the front cockpit.

After Lympne the Sparrow was rarely flown and, after a period of inactivity, it was converted into a high wing monoplane for the 1926 *Daily Mail* Two-Seater Light Aeroplane Competition. Mitchell also re-engined the Sparrow with the well-proven Bristol Cherub III engine.

Numbered 7 for the 1926 competitions and again flown by Biard, the Sparrow suffered misfortune once more. When the time came for Biard to take off, the wind changed and he elected to take off into it. By so doing he failed to cross the starting line. Unaware of this, he battled out over the course but soon lost his way. By the time he had found his position and began heading for the Brighton turning point, he was becoming concerned about his fuel state, so he turned back for Lympne. Though he was disqualified for not crossing the starting line, Biard decided to press on regardless but his luck was still out and he was forced to land near Beachy Head after one of the pins securing one of the wing struts began working itself loose. As the Sparrow landed it blew over in the wind. By the time the securing pin was replaced it was too late to fly back and Biard spent the night with his machine. He returned to Lympne the following day, but not before further adventures.

During the following year the Sparrow embarked

on a series of Air Ministry trials testing wings of different sections and aerofoils. Those tested included Clark Y, T64, RAF 30 and SA12. The Sparrow was ideal for this kind of flying because its wing was located high up and out of disturbed air. Much of the work was carried out at RAF Worthy Down.

On completion of this experimental flying the Sparrow was kept in a Hythe shed until it was given to the Halton Aero Club in May 1929. The Certificate of Airworthiness expired in January 1930 and was not renewed, though the aircraft was still in existence at Wilstead during 1933.

Supermarine Sparrow data	
Span	33 ft 4 in (I)
	34 ft 0 in (II)
Length	23 ft 6 in (I)
	23 ft 0 in (II)
Height	7 ft 5 in
Wing area	256 ft² (I)
	193 ft² (II)
Empty weight	475 lb (I)
	605 lb (II)
All-up weight	860 lb (I)
	1,000 lb (II)
Maximum speed	72 mph
	65 mph with RAF 30 wing
Cruising speed	not available
Stalling/landing speed	27 mph

Vickers Type 98 Vagabond

Having entered the Viget for the 1923 *Daily Mail* lightplane trials, the Vickers company entered a larger and heavier biplane for the following year's two-seater competitions. Called the Vagabond, the new aeroplane utilized some of the Viget's fuselage fittings but was otherwise an entirely new design.

The Vickers Vagabond was a conventional single-bay biplane, having a fuselage of girder construction, braced with tie rods, with longerons and struts of spruce. The longerons were of square section and the struts were spindled out to cruciform section where the loads permitted. The top and bottom of the fuselage were faired with three-ply formers and spruce stringers. The fuselage from behind the rear cockpit to the sternpost was a separate structure which was hinged at the bottom longerons — the joins at the top longerons being in the form of worm gears. These gears could be operated from either cockpit to raise the entire tail in order to increase the wing incidence when the aircraft was on the ground, which aided the braking effect when landing. The mechanism required to move the entire rear fuselage up and down in this manner was a somewhat formidable assembly of pulley fittings.

The wings were of normal construction and made of spruce. N-type spruce ribs were attached to the I-section spars, and the compression ribs were of box-type with three-ply webs. Ailerons were fitted to both upper and lower wings and extended to about half the span. The lower wing trailing edges, between the fuselage and the ailerons, could be hinged down to facilitate wing folding. The spars of the bottom wings passed through the fuselage and were secured to the bottom fuselage longerons. The centre-section was of normal construction and had the trailing edge cut away for access to the rear cockpit and to improve the view. The interplane struts were made of solid streamline-section spruce.

The undercarriage was the standard V-type and embodied streamlined steel tube struts and rubber cord shock absorbers. The wooden wheels had a hardwood core connected to a laminated elm rim by dished two-ply mahogany discs supported by formers.

The tailplane was of normal construction, the spars being strutted to the bottom fuselage longerons. An extension of the sternpost formed the finpost, to which was attached the unbalanced rudder.

The engine mounting was built up of steel plate

The Vagabond was built by A. V. Roe at Hamble and the completed airframe was sent to Weybridge for covering and finishing by Vickers.

The Vagabond was plagued with engine trouble during the 1924 Lympne trials and severe vibration from the geared Cherub engine put it out of the competitions. (A.J. Jackson Collection)

The folded width of the Vagabond was exactly 10 ft and it passed the transport tests at the 1924 Lympne trials by the skin of its fabric! (Via Terry Heffernan)

and bolted direct to the longerons. In order to damp the vibration of the Bristol Cherub engine, heavy washers were inserted under these anchorages.

So as to achieve a good finish to the fuselage, the top and bottom fairings projected some way past the vertical sides, so that when the fabric was applied it did not touch the fuselage side frames. Though this provided an excellently smooth surface, care needed to be taken when handling the aircraft on the ground.

In 1924 the Vickers Weybridge factory was busy churning out Virginia bombers for the RAF and the workforce was too busy to attend to the construction of the Vagabond. The job was given to A.V. Roe at Hamble, though the completed airframe was sent to Weybridge for covering and finishing.

The first flight of the Vagabond was carried out at Brooklands, probably by chief pilot H.J. Payn, late in September 1924. Though the Vagabond had been designed to take either the Bristol Cherub or the Blackburne Thrush engines the final choice was left almost until the eve of the trials, which began on 27 September. The geared Cherub was fitted and the aircraft was delivered to Lympne for the elimination events.

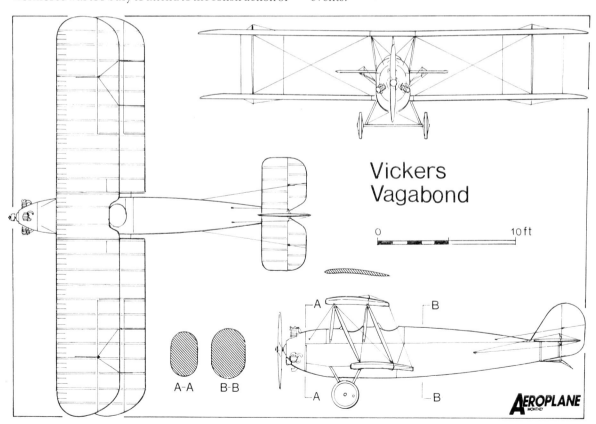

Vickers Vagabond

0   10 ft

A-A   B-B

Aeroplane MONTHLY

Numbered 16, the Vagabond was in trouble even before it got off the ground. The transport tests required all aircraft to pass through a 10 ft gateway, which in reality was a wooden rectangular frame. So fine was the Vagabond's clearance that officials had to check that the sides of the gateway frame were exactly vertical! Passage could only be achieved after removal of the pitot tube, which was then bent and re-fastened. The Vagabond's designed folded width was *exactly* 10 ft.

On arrival at Lympne the Vagabond's engine mounting was causing great concern. After the official inspection the engine shook the mounting almost to pieces. It had to be removed, and repairs and modifications were made at a local workshop. A separate mounting for the carburettor was designed on the spot with the aid of a ruler and a piece of paper, and then knocked up by the same workshop. But it was all in vain, for it was too late and the Vagabond was eliminated. Frustratingly, the problem was solved later during the week and Squadron Leader Payn was able to demonstrate the Vagabond's excellent flying qualities.

The official Air Ministry report on the Vagabond considered it to be well designed but too complicated for mass production as a club machine. There was too much welding and because many of the metal fittings had to be slid along the longerons during construction the fuselage had to be dismantled before such fittings could be replaced in the event of damage. Great interest was shown in the novel form of tail adjustment, though it was considered that the standard type of variable incidence tailplane would have been more desirable. The front cockpit was considered cramped and the upward view from both cockpits somewhat restricted.

The Vagabond was registered *G-EBJF* in May 1925 and was subsequently fitted with a 35 hp Blackburne Thrush engine. In 1927 the aircraft was scrapped and it is doubted whether the registration letters were ever carried.

Vickers Type 98 Vagabond data	
Span	28 ft 0 in
Length	22 ft 0 in
Height	9 ft 5 in
Wing area	224 ft²
Empty weight	527 lb
All-up weight	887 lb
Maximum speed	77 mph (Cherub)
Cruising speed	not available
Stalling/landing speed	33 mph (Cherub)

Westland Widgeon I

For the 1924 Lympne two-seater aeroplane trials the Westland Aircraft Works entered both a biplane and a monoplane, with equal wing area and wing loading in order to compare the performance of the two configurations. While the Woodpigeon biplane was of normal design, the Widgeon parasol monoplane was distinctly unorthodox. The work of Westland's designer Arthur Davenport, the Widgeon had the distinctive feature of a thick, lozenge-shape wing.

Models of both the Woodpigeon and Widgeon had been tested in Westland's wind tunnel at Yeovil. The results of these tests predicted that, with the same type of engine, at the same weight and carrying the same loads, the two aircraft would have identical performance. It was thus with considerable interest that the company looked forward to the trials, when both aircraft could be evaluated and direct comparisons be made between the biplane and monoplane configurations. It would be an interesting exercise too to compare the wind tunnel forecast with the performance of the full-size aircraft.

The fuselage construction of the Widgeon was almost identical to that of the Woodpigeon, described in the next chapter. The rectangular structure was girder-braced by piano wire tightened by turnbuckles. The fuselage sides and bottom were flat but

The wind-tunnel model of the Westland Widgeon. Note there is no engine fitted.

the top decking was cambered. The longerons were spruce, as were the struts.

The wings were of propeller section derived from R & M 322 and tapered in plan and thickness outwards and inwards from the point of support for the struts, at slightly less than half span. This resulted in quite a small chord and depth in front of the rear seat, which gave minimum obstruction for the occupant. The struts to both spars were attached to the fuselage at a point on the bottom longeron vertically below the rear spar. The rear spar was supported above the top longeron by two struts which sloped backwards to form an acute angle at the spar. The front spar was supported at the centre-section by a strut from the anchorage of the main wing struts. The wing spars were mainly of H-section, the flanges consisting of spruce glued and screwed to each side of a three-ply web, the ribs being of normal spruce N-girder construction. The undersurface of the wing was straight, the variation in thickness kinking the upper surfaces only. In order to accomplish this with full-span ailerons, a superstructure was built on the Duralumin tube aileron spar.

The wings folded about the centre-section support to the rear spar, the centre-section arrangement being similar to that of the Woodpigeon. The tail-

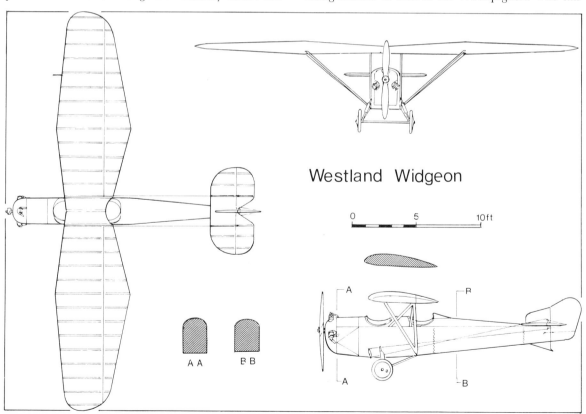

Westland Widgeon

0   5   10 ft

A A   B B

plane too was of similar construction to that of the biplane, embodying a front spindled wooden spar and steel tubular rear spar with compression ribs and piano wire bracing. The undercarriage was of the friction-damped spring-type. The three-cylinder 35 hp Blackburne Thrush engine was mounted on a triangulated steel structure, similar to that of the Woodpigeon.

The Widgeon was completed at Yeovil in September 1924. It came out heavier than the Woodpigeon and consequently the wing loading was also higher. The first flight was made on 22 September from Yeovil and was uneventful.

Numbered 6 for the Lympne trials, the Widgeon arrived there amid great interest, no photographs of the aircraft having been published before the event, save one of the wind tunnel model. With Captain Winstanley as pilot the Widgeon began its full load tests at Lympne on Saturday 27 September, ballast being carried in place of a passenger. There was half a gale blowing and, as Winstanley reached the first turning point, the Widgeon was blown to the ground by a downdraught caused by a nearby ridge. A wingtip caught the ground and the aircraft cartwheeled and broke up. Though the pilot escaped injury the Widgeon was clearly out of the trials. Winstanley later flew the second Woodpigeon for the remainder of the meeting.

During the short period that the Widgeon had flown it was obvious that it was underpowered and

overweight. The wing structure was particularly heavy, especially where the ailerons had been contoured to follow the unusual wing shape. The Air Ministry report on the aircraft regarded it as superior to its biplane sister, particularly in regard to aerodynamic cleanliness. The pilot's view was regarded as good, as was the method of wing folding. The flying characteristics could not be assessed to any great extent because the aircraft was written off before the Air Ministry's observers could get their hands on it.

The damaged aircraft was taken back to Yeovil and rebuilt as the Widgeon Mk II. It was re-engined with a 60 hp Armstrong Siddeley Genet I radial engine and the rudder area was reduced. Registered *G-EBJT* and doped green and silver, the Widgeon II was some 335 lb heavier at its all-up weight of 1,150 lb. The maximum speed of 110 mph was better by 40 mph. The Mk II handled well, but was very sensitive and had a vicious stall.

In September 1926 the Widgeon II competed in the Grosvenor Cup race at Lympne and achieved the fastest time with an average speed of 105 mph in the hands of L.P. Openshaw.

In January 1928 *G-EBJT* was sold to private owner Dr E.D. Whitehead Reid and was delivered to his Bekesbourne base in Kent by Westland test pilot Harald Penrose. Thereafter the Widgeon was a familiar sight at events around the country but, on 10 October 1930, the owner lost his life in the Widgeon when he was caught in bad weather at East Sutton Park near Detling and crashed into a field.

The Widgeon story does not end there, although with an all-up weight of 1,400 lb the production version of the type, the Widgeon Mk III, falls outside the scope of this book. With an empty weight greater than the all-up weight of the original Widgeon the Mk III and IIIA Widgeon was a virtual redesign that went into production during 1927-29.

Westland Woodpigeon

For the Air Ministry's two-seater lightplane trials held at Lympne in 1924 the Yeovil-based Westland Aircraft Works produced both a biplane and a monoplane, with the object of determining the relative merits of the two configurations, with identical wing areas and power loadings. The unlucky Widgeon monoplane is described in the previous chapter. Despite its initial setback the type eventually went into production in much-modified form.

The idea of entering a biplane was that of Robert Bruce, Westland's managing director. The Woodpigeon biplane was a normal single-bay aircraft with equal span wings. Like the Gloucestershire Gannet it was a miniature aeroplane, scaled down by about thirty per cent. Despite its normal appearance the Woodpigeon incorporated a number of novel features.

The forward portion of the fuselage was of Warren-girder type, in spruce, but aft of the rear cockpit it changed to normal construction with vertical struts and piano wire bracing, the final bay being plywood-covered. In the front fuselage the top longerons sloped downwards to accommodate the steel tube engine mounting. Access to the two cockpits was easy and was facilitated partly by the special struts which were part of the wing-folding system and partly by a hinged centre-section trailing edge which folded upwards. The controls were of the orthodox joystick type and the elevators were operated by cables from external cranks.

The wing spars were of box section, the spindled spruce flanges being recessed to take three-ply webs. The ribs were of normal lattice girder construction in spruce. The aerofoil section was Number 64. Drag bracing was by spruce struts braced with piano wire and the streamlined interplane struts were made of solid spruce. Full-span ailerons were fitted to both top

Westland Widgeon I data

Span	30 ft 8 in
Length	21 ft 0 in
Height	7 ft 3 in
Wing area	145 ft²
Empty weight	475 lb
All-up weight	815 lb
	1,150 lb (Genet I)
Maximum speed	72 mph
	110 mph (Genet I)
Cruising speed	not available
Stalling/landing speed	40 mph

The Cherub-powered Woodpigeon photographed shortly after completion. Numbered 5 for the 1926 trials it was flown by Flying Officer Gaskell.

and bottom wings and acted as flaps or camber-changing devices, the flaps functioning either automatically or manually and capable of being locked in any position. The ailerons were hinged direct to the rear spars, the bottom aileron spars being of steel tube while those on the top wings had box spars of spruce with corner fillets. Aileron return was effected by means of rubber cord on the top aileron surfaces. There was no separate centre-section: the front spars met over the fuselage centreline. The rear spars stopped short and were hinged to the equivalent of a centre-section rear spar, carried on inverted V-struts from the top longerons. These two inverted vees, of steel tubing, were laterally braced by wires across the top of the fuselage. The two front wing spars were not supported direct from the fuselage and in place of the usual front cabane struts were longer struts running down the exterior of the fuselage. These struts were fitted in the position normally occupied by jury struts and were a permanent part of the structure.

The undercarriage was of the normal V-type, with cross bracing on the rear radius rods. An oleo-pneumatic shock-absorber was incorporated in the front legs, though on the second Woodpigeon the leg had a coil spring in a steel tube, sleeve-damping being effected by a Ferodo lining.

The tailplane was of normal construction and embodied a front spindled wooden spar and a tubular steel rear spar with compression ribs and piano wire drag bracing. The front spar was attached to the top longerons and braced to the finpost. The rear spar was supported on the sternpost and braced to the rear finpost and to the bottom longerons.

The 32 hp Bristol Cherub II engine was mounted on a wire-braced steel tubular structure. The petrol and oil tanks were on a steel structure behind this mounting.

Above *The second Woodpigeon, powered by a three-cylinder Blackburne engine, was flown in the 1924 trials by Winstanley and took the place of the withdrawn Widgeon following its crash. (Flight photograph)* **Below** *Woodpigeon G-EBJV was later acquired by the Seven Aero Club and re-engined with a 30 hp ABC Scorpion engine. This was later replaced with a 60 hp Anzani. (Flight photograph)* **Bottom** *Woodpigeon G-EBJV seen with the 60 hp Anzani engine installed and with wingspan increased to 27 ft. (Leonard Bridman photograph)*

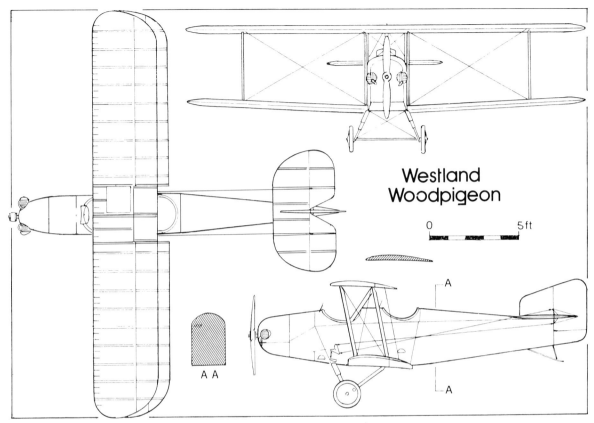

Westland
Woodpigeon

0   5 ft

A A

Though only one Woodpigeon was originally entered for the 1924 Lympne trials, two examples were built. With the withdrawal of the Widgeon following its crash the second Woodpigeon, powered by a three-cylinder Blackburne engine, took its place. The Cherub-powered Woodpigeon, registered *G-EBIY*, was first flown on 17 September 1924, by L.P. Openshaw. It was numbered 5 for the trials and was flown by Flying Officer Gaskell. The second aircraft, numbered 6, was taken to Lympne on 2 October and was flown by Winstanley the following day. Number 5, like the Widgeon, fell foul of the stiff wind and on an early flight was blown to the ground at almost the same point at which the Woodpigeon had succumbed. It refused to be flown back to the aerodrome and had to be transported by road. Even so, it was one of eight out of sixteen machines to qualify for the trials. The stiff wind persisted and Gaskell's Woodpigeon refused to give full power. Winstanley's machine appeared to have more reserve of power and fared better, though the results were disappointing for the Westland team. Gaskell managed to clock up only 125 miles in a little over 2½ hrs and came second in the Grosvenor Challenge Cup race held after the trials had finished.

The Air Ministry's evaluation of the Woodpigeon suggested that there was something seriously wrong with the aircraft's design. The all-up weight had been gravely underestimated and consequently the wing loading had come out higher than had been intended, resulting in loss of performance. In addition the Woodpigeon was unclean aerodynamically, with many fittings unfaired. There was a large gap between the fuselage and tailplane and all the tailplane controls were carried outside the fuselage aft of the cockpit. However, praise was bestowed on the wing-folding mechanism and the aircraft's general robustness. The rubber cord tension return on the ailerons was adversely criticized and it was considered that for a training aircraft the two cockpits were too widely separated for adequate communication. The report concluded with the recommendation that the handling and performance could probably be improved by increasing the wing area and the engine power.

Later, both Woodpigeons were modified to Mk II standard. *G-EBJV* was first re-engined with a 30 hp ABC Scorpion for the Seven Aero Club and subsequently entered for the 1926 Lympne trials. The club, consisting of RAF officers, also entered the

Right *Woodpigeon* G-EBIY, *fitted with an Anzani engine, reposing on a scrap dump in the 1940s.*

Short Satellite. For the flight to Lympne the Woodpigeon was fitted with a metal propeller, though the intention was to use the Satellites's wooden propeller during the trials. Though the Lympne officials were aware of the club's intentions they refused to allow the Woodpigeon to fly with the different propeller; the rules of the competition stated that parts could not be replaced, even though the trials proper had not yet begun. The club decided to carry on but a seized rocker arm presented a further problem. Though this was repaired the officials argued at length as to whether the repair was a major one — if it had been, the aircraft would have been disqualified. By the time it had been decided that the repair was a minor job, it was too late for the Woodpigeon to continue the course and there were some ugly scenes between the disappointed Seven Club members and the trials officials. In the event the Woodpigeon covered 1,080 miles using 334 lb of fuel.

By the following year both Woodpigeons had been modified to Mk II standard. Both were fitted with the 60 hp Anzani radial engine and the wingspan was increased to 27 ft. Adjustable tailplanes were also fitted. Aircraft *G-EBJV* was sold to L. Taylor in June 1927 and passed through several owners before being withdrawn from the civil register in 1933. The other Woodpigeon, *G-EBIY*, was sold to Flying Officer A.F. Scroggs of RAF Henlow and its last owner was Miss Cicele O'Brien, who purchased the aircraft in 1930. The airframe survived the war and is believed to have ended its days on a Ferrybridge scrap dump, where it was seen as late as 1949.

Westland Woodpigeon data	
Span	22 ft 9 in
	27 ft 0 in (Mk II)
Length	19 ft 6 in
	20 ft 9 in (Mk II)
Height	7 ft 0 in
	7 ft 1 in (Mk II)
Wing area	155 ft²
	200 ft²
Empty weight	450 lb
	545 lb (Mk II)
All-up weight	800 lb
	885 lb (Mk II)
Maximum speed	72 mph
	70 mph (Mk II)
Cruising speed	not available
Stalling/landing speed	32 mph
	35 mph (Mk II)

Short S 1 Cockle

The Short Cockle was regarded by many as one of the more remarkable lightplanes of its day. Powered by two 32 hp Bristol Cherub engines, the all-metal Cockle was one of the first light seaplanes to be built in Britain.

Short Bros at Rochester had over the years amassed a great deal of experience in metal construction, in both airships and aircraft. In 1920 the company exhibited the all-metal Silver Streak at Olympia; it was the first all-metal aeroplane to be designed and built in Britain. Many of the Streak's constructional features were retained and developed in the Short Springbok, and soon Oswald Short began thinking of all-metal flying boats. The great advantage of such construction was that metal hulls and floats eliminated water soakage and attendant deterioration, particularly in the tropics. Successful hydraulic pressure tests were carried out on a specimen fuselage for the Silver Streak and a small twin-engined floatplane was subsequently planned with a view to studying the hydrodynamic behaviour and the corrosion resistance of metal floats and hulls.

During a visit to America in the early part of 1924

This photograph of the Duralumin hull of the Short Cockle, taken shortly after construction, shows clearly the two steps.

Above *This view of the Short Cockle shows clearly the arrangement of the two Blackburne Vee-twin engines. Note the fullspan ailerons.* **Below** *The Blackburne engines of the Short Cockle were very underpowered and developed roughly half their available power at a maximum useable 2,400 rpm (A.J. Jackson Collection)* **Bottom** *In order to persuade the Cockle to leave the water the wings had the incidence increased to 7°. The pilot has to make sure that he was lightly dressed and wore plimsolls! (A.J. Jackson Collection)* **Above right** *The Short Cockle after delivery to the Air Ministry for evaluation by MAEE. It is fitted with a taller fin and rudder and was later re-engined with two Bristol Cherub II engines.* (Imperial War Museum photograph)

Short tried to interest American manufacturers in licence-building a twin-engined floatplane. Although he returned home unsuccessful, a wealthy Australian by the name of Lebbaeus Hordern approached the company asking for a small sporting aeroplane for cruising. He had already purchased a converted F 5 Rolls-Royce Eagle-powered flying boat from Shorts and it was not too difficult for Oswald Short to interest the Australian in purchasing a small single-seat flying boat suitable for messing about in and around Botany Bay.

Oswald Short and Francis Webber designed the little seaplane shortly afterwards. Originally named the Stellite, the seaplane was the first Short aeroplane to receive a company index number — S 1. Soon after it was built the Air Ministry asked that the name be changed and so Cockle was chosen to avoid confusion with the similar-sounding Satellite.

The Cockle's Duralumin monocoque hull was similar in construction to that of the Streak. The frame and 'timbers' were rings of Duralumin, of L-section to which were riveted the plates that formed the covering. As with the Satellite the longitudinal stringers did not run the full length of the hull but merely served as stiffeners between the rings. The hull had a flared V-bottom and the main step occurred just aft of the centre of gravity. A second step was located about two-thirds along the length of the hull. The space inside the hull was entirely unobstructed and the formers projected no more than a couple of inches inward from the skin. The exterior of the hull was simple and extremely clean. The steps were built separately on to the primary hull and their rear frames were open at the rear to enable water that had collected to run out once the boat was airborne.

The Cockle's thin wing was braced by short struts to the hull. The wing section was RAF 15 and the wing was built on two spars of corrugated high-tensile steel, with Duralumin ribs. The full-span ailerons were of wide chord and were operated by cranks that

ran vertically down inside the hull. Small floats were carried under the wingtops. The tail unit was built of metal tube spars with channel section sheet ribs and, as with the wings, was fabric covered.

In order to facilitate handling ashore, a pair of large-diameter wheels was supplied. These could be fitted to a tube which passed through the Cockle's hull, positioned in line with and slightly above the forward step. There was provision to carry the wheels within the hull and the Cockle could be manhandled without difficulty by one person.

The pilot sat in the extreme nose, from where he commanded an excellent, unobstructed view. In addition to the normal controls, two starting levers were carried, one for each engine.

Though the Cockle was originally designed to fly with two 32 hp Bristol Cherub engines these were found to vibrate excessively at full power. In their place a couple of 697 cc Blackburne V-twins were fitted, with subsequent loss of power. The Blackburnes were coupled directly to the long propeller shafts and they developed only 32 hp between them.

When the hull was completed it was loaded with 800 lb of ballast and then left on the water for 24 hours to measure water leakage. Only an eggcupful was collected and of course there was no water soakage which, on a large wooden flying boat, could amount to 600 lb added weight.

The Cockle was registered *G-EBKA* and launched on 18 September 1924. It refused to fly. By increasing the wing incidence to 7° the seaplane took to the air for the first time on 7 November, with test pilot John Lankester Parker at the controls. During the 10 min flight it became only too clear that the aircraft was grossly underpowered. Amusingly, Parker could only coax the Cockle into the air by wearing plimsolls and very light clothing. Not surprisingly the Australian customer declined to take delivery of the aircraft and it was returned to its shed for modification. The fin and rudder were enlarged and in this form it

was evaluated by the Air Ministry as *N193* in July 1925. The MAEE (Marine Aircraft Experimental Establishment) pilots at Felixstowe found the Cockle difficult to get off the water and it was returned to Rochester and re-engined with two Bristol Cherub IIs, fitted with reduction gearing, and was sold to the Air Ministry. It was used for carrying out exposure tests to determine the hull's resistance to corrosion.

Short S 1 Cockle data	
Span	36 ft 0 in
Length	24 ft 8 ½ in
Height	not available
Wing area	196 ft²
Empty weight	814 lb
All-up weight	1,062 lb
Maximum speed	68 mph
Cruising speed	not available
Stalling/landing speed	not available

Cranwell CLA 3

Comper decided to enter a racing aeroplane for the Lympne 1925 trials, but was rather restricted by the limited facilities at his disposal. The resulting design was a minute, single-seat high wing monoplane powered by a 32 hp Bristol Cherub. Much attention was paid to streamlining, and it was reckoned that the new machine would be capable of 100 mph. Comper would no doubt have favoured a tapered wing for the CLA 3 but the limited resources necessitated a constant chord wing of simple structural design. This was not a cantilever structure but was strut-braced, and Comper kept the wings light to offset the drag of the metal struts.

The fuselage was well streamlined forward of the cockpit with only the Cherub cylinder heads

Above *The completed but uncovered CLA3 fuselage photographed in mid-1925 with the Bristol Cherub installed.* **Below** *The CLA3 photographed shortly after completion, probably at RAF Cranwell in the summer of 1925.* **Bottom** *Flight Lieutenant Nicholas Comper seated in the CLA3 after fitment of a spinner and 36 hp Bristol Cherub engine.*

protruding from the metal cowlings, the precise curvature of which were determined by wood stringers attached to the main fuselage structure. Aft of the cockpit, the fuselage was slab-sided, with a curved top deck running from the cockpit to the tail.

The model club of the Boys' Wing built a half-scale model of the CLA 3, Philip (later Sir Philip) Sassoon and Frank (later Sir Frank) Whittle apparently helping in its construction. The engine for the model was designed and built by Mr Westbury, a laboratory technician. This model was later presented to the Science Museum after serving its purpose at Cranwell. Tests indicated that the Eiffel No 371 wing section was suitable, being fairly deep with flat bottom camber and having a slight rise to the leading edge. Flight Lieutenant G.T.H. Pack was responsible for the woodwork of the full-size aeroplane, and Flying Officer F.H. Cashmore masterminded the engine installation and associated cowling work.

First photographs of the CLA 3 showed the aircraft in an uncovered state, and further details of its construction can be gleaned from the accompanying photograph. The Warren-girder structure of the rear fuselage is evident, as it is the conventional wire-braced construction used forward of the cockpit. The Bristol Cherub was mounted on overhung bearers and attached to the engine plate, and a fireproof bulkhead extended right out to the cowling. The 4½ gal fuel tank was located just forward of the pilot, inside the fuselage decking, positioned to give direct gravity feed to the engine. The conventional undercarriage consisted of V-struts with rubber shock absorbers.

The tiny cockpit was almost tailor-made for Comper although Flight Lieutenant E.P. Mackay was to act as reserve pilot for the trials. In order to reduce frontal area the pilot sat on the fuselage floor, which necessitated an unusual arrangement of the

control column. Like so many aircraft of the same class, access to the cockpit was an acquired art, but a removable hatch eased the problem.

The wings were made up of the two I-sectioned spruce spars with simple lattice ribs covered with fabric, although the wing leading edge was covered in aluminium. The wing had no dihedral and was carried above the fuselage on four steel struts, braced at either side with two steel tube wing struts. The tailplane was of normal structure and the incidence could be varied on the ground.

The 1925 Lympne trials were scheduled to start on 31 July, and the CLA 3 was completed just in time. It was finished in silver overall and looked very racy for the period. Its wing span was 21 ft, just a foot more than the Pitts Special, and it was extremely light, weighing only 325 lb empty. Even fully-loaded it weighed only 525 lb. With a wing area of 70 ft^2 the wing loading was in the region of 7.6 ft^2. The Cherub engine developed about 30 bhp which gave a power loading of 17.5 lb/hp. Coupled with the clean aerodynamic lines, this suggested that the CLA 3 would have a fair turn of speed.

The first flight was performed by Comper before the staff and students of Number 4 Wing from the Cranwell south aerodrome. The take-off was normal, but before the aircraft had flown one mile the engine cut dead and Comper was forced to put down in a hurry. The problem was simply in the petrol feed and was soon remedied. There was little time for Comper to familiarize himself with the aircraft before it was crated up for the rail journey to Lympne, where it arrived during the last days of July, wearing the registration *G-EBMC*.

The first day of the trials was marred by low cloud and rain, and it was not until the afternoon that the Cranwell aircraft made its public debut. As the only amateur-built aircraft competing it had received

Above *The CLA 3 at the 1925 Lympne trials. It achieved the best speed over a 3 km course — 87 mph, but this was far short of the 100 mph expected.*

much attention all day. Following the afternoon's flying, Comper removed the thin rubber strips used to seal the gaps between the ailerons and elevators and reduce drag, as they made the controls too stiff for comfort.

The 1925 trials were open to aircraft with engines weighing 170 lb or less, which broadened the scope of the competition. The Cranwell machine was the only new aircraft taking part. In addition to those that had taken part the previous year, de Havilland had entered two DH 60 Moths and a DH 53; the Royal Aircraft Establishment entered their 1923 Hurricane and Austin flew the Whippet. There was also one foreign entry, a Pander monoplane from Holland.

The first events were races, and Comper, still unfamiliar with his mount, retired in his heat with an overheating engine. He fared better in the Single-Seater Light 'Plane Scratch Speed Race in which only four aircraft competed, maintaining an early lead and winning the £50 first prize. In the competition to determine the greatest speed over a 3 km course the CLA 3 again came out top with a speed of 87 mph (140 km/hr) although this was far short of the 100 mph expected.

Throughout the trials Comper became more familiar with the CLA 3, and towards the end he was flying nearly vertical banked turns. Although he only just missed a place in the International Handicap Race, held over a 100 mile course, he managed a third place in the Grosvenor Challenge Cup Handicap out of a field of twelve.

The CLA 3 was flown regularly during the next year and even turned up at the following year's Lympne trials, as a visitor. By this time it had

128

Ultralights

exchanged its original engine for a 36 hp Bristol
Cherub driving a metal propeller, and it was in this
configuration that it was entered by Squadron
Leader W. Thomas for the 1926 King's Cup Air
Race. The race was split into four separate cross
country circuits, starting and finishing at Hendon
and totalling 732 miles. Comper flew the machine
and covered the first circuit without incident at an
average speed of 86.6 mph. During the early part of
the next lap the aircraft developed severe vibration
and Comper was forced down in a cornfield near
Duxford. It was damaged when it was turned over
and had to be retired from the race.

The CLA 3 was scrapped in 1929, the year that
Comper founded the aircraft company that bore his
name.

Above *The Missel Thrush photographed shortly after completion,
fitted with the 35 hp Blackburne Thrush engine.* **Below** *Aptly bearing
the competition number 13, the repaired Missel Thrush flying during one
of its rare trouble-free moments at Lympne in September 1926. (Flight
photograph)*

Cranwell CLA 3 data	
Span	21 ft 0 in
Length	18 ft 6½ in
Height	not available
Wing area	70 ft²
Empty weight	325 lb
All-up weight	530 lb
Maximum speed	100 mph
Cruising speed	not available
Stalling/landing speed	not available

ANEC IV Missel Thrush

In 1923 W.S. Shackleton left ANEC for William
Beardmore and Co Ltd, where he was to design the
Beardmore WB XXIV Wee Bee for the 1924
Lympne competitions. His place was taken by John
Bewsher, an ex-Sopwith man who had been respons-
ible for the crescent-winged Airdisco glider *Phi-Phi*,
which competed in the 1922 Itford gliding compe-
tition. This parasol glider had a wing section similar
to that of a bird's, and had a very good glide angle.
Bewsher's first product for ANEC was the ANEC
III, a hideous 60 ft span seven-seat commercial
biplane powered by a single 350 hp Rolls-Royce
Eagle VIII engine. Three of these aircraft were supplied to the Larkin Aircraft Supply Company Ltd of
Melbourne, Australia, and were subsequently modified to carry eleven passengers.

In 1926 the aviation-minded and ever publicity-
conscious *Daily Mail* put up £5,000 prize money for a
competition for two-seat light aircraft to be held at
Lympne. The rules specified that aircraft must have
dual controls, foldable wings and an engine of not
more than 170 lb in weight. John Bewsher produced
drawings of a very neat streamlined biplane which
not only embodied the mandatory requirements, but

was a serious attempt at producing a practical two-
seat touring aircraft for the private pilot. For this
purpose the ANEC IV had to be cheap to produce
and fly and, above all, be reliable and safe. Pilot
comfort was also considered.

Although aesthetically pleasing, the ANEC IV was
of orthodox construction. The semi-monocoque fuselage was a light but strong wooden framework
covered with ply, and consisted of four main
longerons and a series of transverse bulkheads
comprising vertical, cross and diagonal struts
reinforced with plywood. The cross-section of the
fuselage varied. At the nose it was triangular, with the
base at the bottom so as to neatly accommodate the
inverted Y shape of the engine. The cross-section
became rectangular in the vicinity of the cockpits,

providing maximum space for their occupants and for a large luggage locker located between them. Towards the tail the fuselage reverted to triangular section, but with the base uppermost, thus providing a solid base for the tailplane mounting. The 35 hp Blackburne Thrush air-cooled, three-cylinder radial engine, weighing only 132 lb and built by the Blackburne Aeroplane and Motor Company Ltd at Olympia in Leeds, was attached to the engine bulkhead by means of a system of triangulated tie-rods radiating out from the bulkhead to the engine crankcase. Behind the fireproof bulkhead was the 6 gal fuel tank. A neat metal cowling enclosed the engine, except for the three cylinders, closely following the fuselage contours.

The wings were of thin section, built on spruce and plywood box spars with spruce and three-ply ribs, and were fabric covered. The wing leading edges were of aluminium tubing, except for the lower wing tips, which were of steel tubing. Both upper and lower sets of wings had pronounced dihedral and were well staggered, the lower wings being of shorter span and of smaller chord. The stagger gave the pilot, who normally occupied the front seat, excellent forward vision, especially downwards and ahead of the lower wing. The wing folding mechanism was simple, and folding could easily be carried out by one person without disconnecting control cables or any wing bracing. The wings were hinged at the rear spars and folded snugly against the sides of the fuselage. Like the CLA 4, the lower wings were attached to short wing roots built into the fuselage. The top wings were attached to the centre-section, which was mounted above the fuselage on two half-I-struts braced by cables running from the top of each strut to fore and aft points on the fuselage. Thus the entire centre-section was remarkably clean and uncluttered. The wing struttery was

similarly simple and clean; the single I-struts being made of laminated wood with a streamlined section. They were attached to the wings by simple U-plates at each fore and aft extremity of the strut, and passed around the wing compression point.

The tail surfaces were of simple wood construction, similar to the wings, and were fabric covered, the vertical and horizontal surfaces being similar in planform and of ample proportions. The rudder hinge line was raked forward, an unusual feature at the time, presumably because, for structural reasons, the designer wanted the rudder's centre of pressure further forward than it otherwise would have been. The horizontal tail was firmly attached to the flat fuselage top with four bolts.

Above *The Missel Thrush fitted with 80 hp Genet II and featuring faired cockpit and wing centre-section fuel tank, taking off from Hendon on 20 July during the start of the 1928 King's Cup air race. (Flight* photograph) **Below** *Another view of the Missel Thrush leaving Hendon at the start of the 1928 King's Cup race. Hours later the aircraft was destroyed and the pilot dead after the ANEC IV flew into Broad Law, Peebles in poor weather.*

Perhaps the only feature which dates the Missel Thrush was its undercarriage, which was the V-type and rather unusual. The undercarriage legs consisted of a pair of steel tubes bent to form a narrow, curved V. The lower ends were joined by a metal axle box, the axle itself passing out between the tubes of the legs and being secured in place by the inevitable rubber cord. The lower extremities of the undercarriage forks were pegged and projected below the axles, clearing the ground by a mere 4 in. This curious design feature was to be the undoing of the Missel Thrush as far as the Lympne competitions were concerned.

After successful test flying at Brooklands the Missel Thrush, in an attractive dark red and white trim colour scheme, was flown down to Lympne a day or two before the event by Colonel G. L. P. Henderson, later of Henderson-Glenny Gadfly fame. During tests the aircraft looked promising, but then disaster struck. Whilst making a normal landing the Missel Thrush came down on rough ground, taking the rubber shock absorbers beyond their limit. The undercarriage forks dug into the ground and the aircraft flipped smartly over onto its back. Henderson stepped out unhurt, but the aircraft was badly damaged. The fuselage was buckled up to the front cockpit, the undercarriage was wrecked, and there was damage to the lower starboard wing. The Missel Thrush was knocked out of the competitions before they had even begun. However, it was immediately transported by road back to Brooklands, where it was repaired. Five days later it was returned to Lympne, in time to compete in a race for aircraft eliminated in the competitions. After only one lap, plug trouble forced Henderson to retire. Nor was he any luckier the next day, whilst competing in the Grosvenor Cup Race. Engine trouble again robbed the ANEC team of any chance to show the Missel Thrush's capabilities.

Shortly afterwards, the Air Navigation and Engineering Co faded from the aviation scene and the Missel Thrush, now registered *G-EBPI*, was sold to Guy Nevile Warwick of Harpenden in Hertfordshire. Warwick also possessed a couple of 45 hp Anzani six-cylinder engines, and with John Bewsher's supervision installed one in the Missel Thrush. Bewsher was at this time working for Colonel Henderson at Brooklands on the ugly HSF 1. With modified engine cowlings and a fuel tank installed in the wing centre-section, the Missel Thrush was towed to a convenient field and test flown. A later flight ended prematurely when engine failure forced Warwick to put down on the Polytechnic Sports Ground at Chiswick.

The second Anzani was installed, and this, in turn, was replaced by an 80 hp Armstrong Siddeley Genet II. It was in this form that *G-EBPI* faced the starter's flag at the 1928 King's Cup Race at Hendon on 20 July. In trouble from the start, Warwick took 2 hrs 21 mins to complete the first 99 mile leg to Norwich and was well down the field when he arrived at Newcastle. So many pilots failed to arrive at the next check point, at Renfrew, that no-one worried about the non-arrival of the Missel Thrush. However, by the following day there was considerable concern, and despite air and land searches it was not until three days later that a shepherd came across Warwick's body and the wrecked aircraft on Broad Law, near Peebles. Pieces of the aircraft still mark the spot. There is little doubt that Warwick encountered low cloud and rain in the area, and that he flew into Broad Law in poor visibility.

Had fate been kinder, perhaps the Missel Thrush would have been put into production.

ANEC IV Missel Thrush data (Thrush)	
Span	28 ft 0 in
Length	21 ft 6 in
Height	8 ft 0 in
Wing area	210 ft²
Empty weight	500 lb
All-up weight	1,150 lb
Maximum speed	80 mph
Cruising speed	60 mph
Stalling/landing speed	not available

Cranwell CLA 4

Encouraged by the success of the CLA 2 at the 1924 Air Ministry trials for two-seaters, and with funds boosted by the prize money and compensation for the loss of their first aeroplane, the Cranwell Light Aeroplane Club followed up the CLA 2 with the 100 mph CLA 3 high-wing monoplane, described earlier.

For the CLA 4, designed for the 1926 Lympne trials, Comper chose an unusual inverted sesquiplane layout, the top wing being shorter and narrower of chord than the lower wing. The competition rules stipulated that all entries should be two-seaters, fitted with dual controls, and should carry a load of not less than 170 lb. The engine weight was restricted to less than 170 lb and, in common with previous trials, the wings had to fold. Comper had chosen the inverted sesquiplane layout for various reasons, and reckoned that the advantages outweighed the slight losses in aerodynamic efficiency. The two cockpits were arranged in tandem, with the front cockpit forward of the top wing and the rear cockpit behind its trailing edge, resulting in excellent all-round vision, particularly upwards, for both occupants.

The CLA4's designer, Flight Lieutenant Nick Comper, winning the Steward's Handicap at the Lympne Trials, September 1926. (*Flight* photograph)

The fuselage comprised a rectangular spruce frame, with wire cross-bracing from the engine mountings to the back of the rear cockpit and rigid diagonal-bracing behind that. Over the front section the inner frame was faired out to an oval cross-section. The wings had spruce I-section spars and were of a modified RAF 31 section. They were hinged at the rear spar for folding, in compliance with the competition rules. The top wing was supported by four vertical steel struts at the centre-section (which contained the fuel tank) and a single I-strut, raked inwards and upwards towards the wing tips, with streamline wire bracing. The fixed tailplane and the rudder were made of steel tubing, and the flying surfaces were of conventional wooden construction. The vee undercarriage was formed from small diameter light gauge steel tubing, with a through axle and the usual rubber chord shock absorbers. The undercarriage struts were attached to the roots of the lower mainplane.

The Club decided to build two CLA 4s, and both were entered for the Lympe trials. One, later to be registered *G-EBPB*, was powered by the well-proven Bristol Cherub III and the other, later *G-EBPC*, was to have been powered by a revolutionary new engine designed by another Cranwell officer, Captain Douglas Rudolph Pobjoy, who was Education Officer of the Apprentices Wing. He had designed and built a small seven-cylinder engine which he called the Pobjoy P. The principle behind his engine

was that all parts subjected to heavy load should be substantially built and that there should be no parts that did not contribute to the working of the engine. The resulting engine was capable of 65 bhp, but weighed only 100 lb. Fuel consumption was very low and, coupled with the fact that only one P engine existed, the Cranwell team had a valuable card up its sleeve.

It came as a sharp blow, therefore, when weeks before the race the Pobjoy P suffered a breakdown during preliminary type-testing trials at Farnborough. A screw worked loose in a connecting rod attachment — if it had been a left-hand thread instead of a right-hand one it would have worked itself tight. The breakage could have been repaired, but it would have been necessary to retest the engine and there was insufficient time to do this before the trials. The Club, robbed of an excellent chance of winning most of the competitions, was forced to pin its hopes on the much lower-powered Cherub CLA 4. Although the Pobjoy P bows out of this story, its development into the Pobjoy R is one of the many success stories in British engine technology. Coupled with the CLA 7, alias the Comper Swift, the Pobjoy R became a record breaker in no uncertain fashion.

The 1926 Lympne trials were held from 10-18 September, and apart from the Cranwell machine there were entries from Blackburn, de Havilland, Bristol, Hawker, Avro, Supermarine, Short and Westland. The Halton Aeroplane Club, formed by

The inverted sesquiplane layout of the CLA4A, G-EBPB, is well shown in this photograph. (*Flight* photograph)

Top *Another photograph of the CLA4 being put through its paces by its designer at the 1926 Lympne Trials. (Flight photograph)* **Above** *The CLA4 being manoeuvred throught the 10 ft gateway during transport tests at Association Francaise Aerienne light aeroplane trials at Orly, France in September 1928. (Flight photograph)*

Halton Apprentices and no doubt inspired by the Cranwell Club's earlier efforts, had entered the Halton HAC 1, powered by a Bristol Cherub III. All other entries came from commercial aircraft manufacturers.

When the Cranwell team arrived at Lympne they were aware that one of the metal tube undercarriage legs had a flaw. Comper immediately sent off for a replacement, presumably from the other CLA 4 grounded at Cranwell, and notified the trials officials during their initial inspection of the aircraft. The rules regarding the replacement of parts during the competition were stringent, and the officials appeared happy that a replacement undercarriage

would be fitted during the course of the trials. During the early part of the competitions the CLA 4, bearing the trials number 12, showed great promise. Predictably the defective undercarriage leg failed, although it was only bent and was not broken, allowing the aircraft to be taxied under its own power. The replacement undercarriage was fitted, but the stewards would not allow the aircraft to continue, claiming that it was different to its original condition. Despite protests the officials stuck rigidly to their decision. The efforts of the Cranwell team were dashed by paper rules and the aircraft was forced to retire. Other aircraft suffered similar fates and the competition organisers and its officials were severely criticized by the aviation press.

Comper had to content himself with demonstrations and passenger flights, one of his passengers being the Commandant of the RAF Cadet College at Cranwell, Air Commodore Borton. All was not lost for the Cranwell team, for on 17 September the CLA 4 won a race held for those aircraft that were eliminated from the trials. Even this nearly ended in failure. As Comper circled, awaiting the other contestants to finish the race, the Cherub III cut out and he was forced to make a dead-stick landing in a field outside the aerodrome. Even the ambulance despatched to his assistance managed to travel only halfway before it, too, suffered engine failure. Luckily the CLA 4 landed without damage and the cause of the failure was found to be a bluebottle fly which had entered by the air intake. Had it done so earlier it would have cost the Cranwell team £50 in prize money. During the latter part of the Lympne meeting the CLA 3 *G-EBMC* flew in and took part in the Grosvenor Cup flown by Comper, competing with the CLA 4 flown by Flight Lieutenant Walmsley. Neither aircraft was placed.

The CLA 4A, *G-EBPC*, was later re-engined with a Bristol Cherub III but was lost in a crash on 4 March 1927. The following month Comper took *G-EBPB* down to the Bournemouth Easter Meeting and raced with limited success. He came second in the twenty mile Winton Handicap Race with a speed of 64.5 mph and was third in the ten mile Ensbury Park Stakes with 60.5 mph. By this time Comper had been transferred to Felixstowe, where he formed the Felixstowe Light Aeroplane Club. He had taken 'PC with him, and attended the Bournemouth Whitsun Meeting a month later and came second in the Low Power Handicap for machines with engines of less than 1,500 cc. Comper also entered *G-EBPB* for the 1927 King's Cup, held at Hucknall on 30 July, but yet again was dogged by bad luck when a leaking oil pipe forced him to withdraw. Other apperances followed at the Hampshire Air Pageant at Hamble and the Blackpool Air Pageant at Squires Gate, both

CLA4, G-EBPC, *was to have been fitted with the Pobjoy P engine for the 1926 Lympne Trials. It was not ready in time and a 36 hp Cherub III was installed in its place.*

in the following year.

In September 1928 the Association Francaise Aerienne held a Competition for Light Aeroplanes, the French equivalent of the Lympne trials. It was an international meeting, and was held at Orly. The Felixstowe Light Aeroplane Club entered *G-EBPB* and Comper flew it to Orly with an overnight stop at Abbeville. Alas, the Orly meeting was another chapter of disaster for Comper, which began with a forced landing before the trials had even begun. The CLA 4's unhappy incidents are ably summed up by F.D. Bradbrooke, reporting at the time for *The Aeroplane*:

'One's special, private award of one million points goes to Flight Lieutenant Comper for abiding good humour in the face of the most crushing ill-luck. With generous French help and the stout efforts of the Bristol mechanic he repaired his undercarriage after Sunday's forced landing. He completed his folding test on Monday only to be forced down after a few seconds of the qualifying five minute flight. Examination revealed a fly in the carburettor jet. The fly was long since dead, of course, but deserved something lingering and humorous with boiling water in it. A tyre gave way just before the start of the altitude test, but at last Comper was seen mounting merrily and appeared — as he afterwards confessed — to have come to the end of his troubles. Two hours later anxiety began to be felt, but it was not until the next morning that the news of his third landing came through. The oil pipe had broken at 3,000 ft and being intent on airspeed and climb, the pilot failed to notice it until his engine was effectually *hors de combat*. At no time did his machine have a chance to show

what it could do, probably through entering the contest with too little preparation after a season's hard work.'

In May 1930 *'PB* was sold to J.T.H. Baldwin at Catterick, by which time Comper had resigned his RAF commission and had formed the Comper Aircraft Company at Hooton Park in Cheshire. In 1933 *'PB* was scrapped at Heston.

Cranwell CLA 4 data	
Span	22 ft 0 in (upper wing) 27 ft 4 in (lower wing)
Length	22 ft 3½ in
Height	6 ft 7½ in
Wing area	164 ft²
Empty weight	450 lb
All-up weight	860 lb
Maximum speed	not available
Cruising speed	not available
Stalling/landing speed	not available

Halton HAC 1 Mayfly and HAC 2 Minus

In addition to the established aircraft firms and the odd individuals who entered aircraft for the *Daily Mail* and Air Ministry lightplane trials of the 1920s, it is interesting to note the number of Service groups

An early photograph of the HACI Mayfly. Note the unconventional X interplane struts. (Flight photograph)

and clubs that showed active interest in the quest for a very light single/two-seat sporting aeroplane. In addition to the Cranwell Light Aeroplane Club, formed by apprentices and staff of Number 4 Apprentices Wing at the RAF College at Cranwell, and the Royal Aircraft Establishment Aero Club consisting of RAE personnel there was also the Halton Aero club, made up of aircraft apprentices and others, totalling 1,000 members in all, from the RAF School of Technical Training at RAF Halton.

The Halton club had as its designer C.H. Latimer-Needham, a name which will crop up frequently within the pages of this book. In 1924 he was an education officer at Halton and had developed early a fascination for small aeroplanes. He had watched with interest the performance of competitors in the 1923-24 Lympne trials and was spurred on by what he saw to design something for the trials planned for 1925. When these were deferred until the following year Latimer-Needham decided that there was ample time to produce an aircraft that, even if it could not compete with the products of the aircraft industry, would at least have an average performance.

Armed with all the data, performance and specification of the 1923-24 trials aircraft, Latimer-Needham subjected the better types to his own system of averaging such items as span, weight, wing loading and so forth. In addition he analyzed control surface volumes in order to obtain a set of formulae and con-

stants for both monoplanes and biplanes. Eventually he came up with a compromise, both dimensionally and with regard to the wing arrangement, settling for a one-and-a-half wing or sesquiplane layout, hoping to achieve the advantages of both the monoplane and biplane concepts. In every other way the Halton design was normal, the designer shrewdly regarding any design innovation as a risky business for amateurs to indulge in.

Design work took more than a year and the final drawings were approved by the Halton Aero Club in December 1925. Latimer-Needham had wisely consulted Captain Geoffrey de Havilland and his colleague and adviser C.C. Walker for advice. As a result of this consultation the wing gap was increased and work on building the Mayfly began in February 1926. Completion was planned for August, in good time for the *Daily Mail* two-seater trials at Lympne. While the apprentice members worked on production of wing ribs and other smaller items, skilled instructors undertook the task of constructing major components. Work proceeded at a leisurely pace but as time progressed the pace increased rapidly in an effort to get the Mayfly completed on schedule.

Disappointingly, though the structure was complete, there were small items to be finished and the Mayfly was not ready in time for the trials. Thereafter the pace at Halton slackened and work continued at a leisurely pace until the machine was

The Mayfly was first flown on 31 January 1927 by Flight Lieutenant C.F. le Poer Trench, from RAF Bicester. (Flight photograph)

Above left *The Mayfly competing at the Bournemouth meeting during June 1927, with the forward cockpit faired over.* (*Flight* photograph)
Above *The HAC2 Minus during its appearance with the RAF 'new types' at the 1928 RAF Pageant at Hendon.* (*Flight* photograph)
Below *The HAC2 Minus with streamlined struts and a spinner added.* (*Flight* photograph) **Bottom** *Flight Lieutenant le Poer Trench taking part in the Cambridge Aero Club's display in the Minus in June 1929.* (*Flight* photograph)

finished around Christmas.

The Halton Mayfly's fuselage was of the flat-sided box type and was built up of a light skeleton of spruce covered with plywood. There were no metal fittings in the fuselage structure, struts being simply butted on to the longerons. The fuselage decking had a slight double curvature and applying the plywood panels presented some difficulty.

The heavily staggered single bay wings were of RAF 15 section and, shortly after they were made, it was discovered that there had been a serious error in the stressing. Evidently the load factors for the drag bracing were inadequate and, as there was insufficient time to build another set of wings, the existing pair had to be braced by adding external drag wires to the nose and tail. The wings had a couple of interesting features. The wing struts were in the form of an asymmetrical X, necessitated by the position of the bottom wing spar, which was located a little less than halfway from the leading edge along the chord of the heavily staggered wing. This position was chosen in order to bring the top and bottom spars into vertical alignment. It would otherwise have been difficult to design hinges for the folding wings. Full-span ailerons were fitted to the top wings only and they acted as flaps or variable camber devices.

The tailplane was of orthodox design concept except that the fin was well forward and the horn-balanced rudder was placed entirely above the undivided elevator. All tail control cables were concealed inside the fuselage.

The simple V-type undercarriage of steel tubing with built-on fairings was fitted with rubber cord shock absorbers and located forward of the lower wing.

The 32 hp Bristol Cherub III engine was mounted on light steel brackets which were built up to form four pyramids, one at each corner of the fuselage bulkhead. A Fairey-Reed propeller was fitted and fuel was gravity-fed from a tank located in the top wing centre-section.

On completion the Mayfly was taken to nearby RAF Bicester for its first flight. This was carried out by Flight Lieutenant C.F. le Poer Trench on 31

January 1927 after just one preliminary ground run. After official Air Ministry testing in February the Mayfly was registered *G-EBOO*.

That season's first flying meeting was the Hamble Air Pageant. The Mayfly competed in and won the Wakefield Cup Race. Unfortunately the rules specified that each aircraft must carry a passenger and, as the Mayfly had flown only with ballast under the faired-over front cockpit, it was disqualified. Better luck came when Trench won the President's Cup and £150 in prize money in front of an appreciative audience of old and new Halton aircraft apprentices, many of whom had worked on the Mayfly. Further successes followed at Bristol and Liverpool but during that year's King's Cup air race the Mayfly ran out of fuel only five miles from the finishing post.

In 1927 there was no longer a competition need for a two-seater tourer. The de Havilland DH 60 Moth was already in full production and other types were emerging from other manufacturers. There appeared, though, to be some future in air racing and the Mayfly was groomed for this sport. By streamlining nuts and bolts and generally cleaning up the airframe the Mayfly's top speed had been progressively increased from 67 mph to 83 mph. The only way to increase the speed further was to remove the lower wing and modify the Mayfly into a parasol monoplane. At the end of the 1927 season such a conversion was made. This involved replacing the lift wires with lift struts, shortening the full-span ailerons to two-thirds span and removing the bottom wing. In its monoplane form and now called the Minus, the maximum weight of the aircraft was reduced by 125 lb to 655 lb and there was a reduction in wing area of nearly 32 per cent.

The 1928 flying season opened for the Minus with a return visit to Hamble for another crack at the Wakefield Cup race. This it won with an average speed of 95 mph. In that year's King's Cup air race the Minus was forced to retire with a broken rocker arm in the magneto; but shortly afterwards it really made the big time when it was flown in the New Types flypast at that year's RAF Display at Hendon where, numbered 9, it looked rather out of place among all the service aircraft.

The Minus continued to attend all manner of meetings around the country, including participation in the 1929 King's Cup where it fared no better than before. In the hands of Flight Lieutenant G.R. Ashton the aircraft hit a boundary fence at Newcastle and though the pilot was unhurt the Minus was unable to continue.

After the Certificate of Airworthiness expired in September that year the Halton Minus was dismantled at RAF Halton and the registration marks were cancelled in 1931.

Halton HAC 1 Mayfly data	
Span	28 ft 6 in
Length	22 ft 0 in
Height	not available
Wing area	200 ft²
Empty weight	480 lb
All-up weight	920 lb
Maximum speed	83 mph
Cruising speed	75 mph
Stalling/landing speed	28 mph

Halton HAC 2 Minus data	
Span	28 ft 6 in
Length	22 ft 10 in
Height	not available
Wing area	135 ft²
Empty weight	450 lb
All-up weight	665 lb
Maximum speed	95 mph
Cruising speed	85 mph
Stalling/landing speed	30 mph

De Havilland DH 71 Tiger Moth

When Captain Geoffrey de Havilland landed the prototype DH 60 Moth *G-EBKT* at Stag Lane after its first flight on 22 February 1925, a new era in light aviation had dawned. For many years aircraft designers had dreamed of producing a motor cycle-of-the-air, assuming that low-powered engines and light structures would produce the answer. As it happened, the only engines available were converted motor cycle engines, and they were unreliable. Producing light but sufficiently strong airframes was very costly and the end results during those pioneering days were small, costly and unreliable aircraft that had no appeal to anyone but a well-off adventurer. The DH 60, on the other hand, was a far more logical approach to the problem of producing a light touring aircraft for the private owner and the flying clubs. It was virtually a half-scale version of the well-proven DH 51 and its Cirrus engine was more or less one half of the DH 51's V-8 Airdisco engine, designed by Major Halford and manufactured by the Aircraft Disposal Company. The new Cirrus engine kept the Airdisco cylinders and pistons but used a new crankcase. By using motor car engine components including magnetos and carburettors, the price of the engine could be kept very competitive. The engine/airframe combination was an immediate success. The price was right and the Moth was economical to run and maintain — and above all, it was reliable.

By 1926, though, the cost of producing the Cirrus began to rise as the supply of Airdisco engines began to dwindle. Rather than rely on an outside engine manufacturer, Geoffrey de Havilland decided to set up the company's own engine manufacturing department and he asked Major Halford to design a Cirrus replacement for successive Moth models. What he wanted was a four-cylinder light engine with a low thrustline capable of producing 100 hp. In addition to the Moth he envisaged an important market for such an engine with other aircraft manufacturers.

While work began on the new engine de Havilland decided to produce a clean, low-wing sporting aeroplane as a private venture in which he could test the new engine. In addition he was anxious to prove to the Air Ministry the distinct advantages the monoplane layout had over existing biplanes which, in the main, were powered by big radial engines of large frontal area. He hoped too that the new aircraft would shatter a few world records in the lower power categories, which would result in much-needed publicity.

The decision was taken to build the new racer to fit the company's test pilot. Fortunately Hubert Broad was then of slight stature and the story goes that he was sat on the floor against a wall and his outline was drawn in chalk in order to determine the minimum cockpit dimensions and the width of the fuselage. The aircraft was then literally tailor-made for its pilot.

Work on constructing two aircraft began during 1927. The intention was to enter both for that year's King's Cup race, due to be held at Hucknall on 30 July. Named Tiger Moth, the DH 71s were constructed in strict secrecy at Stag Lane. Two different sets of wings were built. The smaller set, of 19 ft span, was to be used for speed work and the 22 ft 6 in span wings would be used for touring and for participation in the King's Cup race.

The construction of the DH 71 Tiger Moth followed normal de Havilland methods of the time. The fuselage was plywood-covered and generally similar in construction to the DH 60 Moth, though the cross-section was quite different. The fuselage sides of the '71 had a pronounced outward slope towards the top longerons and the section conformed roughly to the shape of a man seated with his legs outstretched, the greatest width occurring at the point of the pilot's shoulders. Where the pilot's head protruded, a neat fairing ran aft from the back of his head to a point at the tail. Similarly, a fairing ran from the engine to the pilot's windscreen. Doors each side of the cockpit hinged down and, once the pilot was inside, they

Three views of DH 71 Tiger Moth prototype G-EBQU, fitted with the 130 hp Gipsy Experimental engine. This aircraft was fitted with an 85 hp Cirrus II for its initial test flights. (Flight photograph)

closed around his shoulders. The fuselage bottom was rounded and all the surfaces and corners merged smoothly, the joints being quite invisible.

Where the wing spars were attached, substantial transverse bulkheads occurred. The wings were of normal construction, with I-section spruce spars and normal wooden ribs. The wing was built in two halves, the spars forming a butt joint at the centreline. They were secured with steel plates and bolts after being passed through holes in the fuselage sides. Streamline wires formed the wing bracing above and below the wings, the lower set running in a vee to the wheel discs. The wings had no dihedral.

Above *Hubert Broad brings the first DH 71 in to land at Stag Lane during mid-summer 1927. Note the wire-braced undercarriage. (Flight* photograph) **Below** *Hubert Broad sitting in the tailor-made cockpit of the DH 71. Celluloid vision panels enabled the pilot to see forward either side of the engine. (Flight* photograph) **Bottom** *The second DH 71, G-EBRV was entered for the 1927 King's Cup air race but withdrawn. Hubert Broad is seen running up the Cirrus II of the all-black racer. (Flight* photograph)

The undercarriage was unusual for the time in that the shock absorbers were enclosed within the wheels, there being no axle. Bracing was by two streamline wires that ran across from one wheel centre to the other.

The engine was beautifully cowled, there being no excrescences from the engine accessories. The engine crankcase was ribbed at the bottom, the ribs projecting through at the bottom of the fuselage in order to assist oil cooling. The overhead valve gear was enclosed in the cowling and, though the starboard side of the engine was covered, the port sides of the cylinders were left uncovered. The 16.75 gal fuel tank was located in the deck fairing behind the engine and in front of the pilot.

The cockpit was necessarily small but in spite of being designed around Hubert Broad it could accommodate a larger pilot without difficulty. The pilot's view forward was not brilliant but celluloid vision panels made in two halves in the fairing in front of him were quite adequate and he was able to see forward on either side of the engine. Because of the lack of space in the cockpit the controls were somewhat unusual. The stick was universally mounted as usual but lateral control was via a crank on the stick operating a T-shaped piece which in turn actuated the ailerons via pushrods and torque tubes.

The first DH 71 Tiger Moth, registered *G-EBQU*, was completed in June 1927. In order to check its handling characteristics it was fitted first with an 85 hp ADC Cirrus for its first flights, which Hubert Broad carried out from Stag Lane on 24 June. The aircraft was then returned to the factory where the new, untried 135 hp Gipsy engine was installed. Time, though, was running short. The second DH 71, *G-EBRV*, powered by an 85 hp Cirrus II, made its maiden flight on 28 July, just two days before the King's Cup race. It was entered for the event by Lord Wakefield and was flown by Hubert Broad. The aircraft was numbered 17 and painted black overall. Although 'RV arrived at Hucknall for the start of the race the Gipsy-engined racer was withdrawn and tweaked up for a series of record attempts.

One of the problems with the Tiger Moth was that it was very sensitive to control movements, despite damping in the form of strips of sponge rubber inserted between the main rear spars and the aileron leading edges. Similar strips were used in sealing gaps between the elevator and tailplane. The weather for the 1927 King's Cup was appalling and, though Broad managed to beat the handicap formula by almost 4 mph, he was forced to retire at Spitalgate in Lincolnshire because of severe bumps, which either banged his head against the cockpit fairing or caused him to alter the throttle settings involuntarily. Indeed his take-off run across the poor Hucknall surface was doubled because the throttle slipped closed. Despite this the DH 71 average 166 mph up to the point of its retirement.

Meanwhile the first prototype was readied for an attempt on the Class II Light Aeroplane Category 100 km closed-circuit speed record. At a loaded weight of 905 lb Broad broke the existing record on 24 August with an average speed of 186.47 mph. Following this, on 29 August, an attempt was made on the Class III height record, which stood at 22,251 ft. At 19,191 ft Broad was unable to climb any further due to oxygen starvation. At the time the DH 71 was still climbing at 1,000 ft/min and seemed good for a further 9,000 ft before reaching its ceiling.

The first prototype DH 71 appeared at the RAF Display at Hendon on 30 June 1928, numbered 8 in the New Types park, but the grass surface was too rough for the aircraft to take off. Thus a rare chance of showing off its capabilities before an RAF audience was lost. It was in fact faster than any of the fighters present, except for the Westland Wizard. The yellow and black racer was next exhibited at the Olympia Aero Show in London during July of the following year. In 1930 it was shipped to F.K. Bardsley as *VH-UNH* but was still bearing its British registration when it was test flown by Major Hereward de Havilland at Point Cook after reassembly. On 17 September 1930 the aircraft was destroyed in a crash following engine failure on take-off from Mascot aerodrome. David Smith, the pilot, was killed.

G-EBRV, the second Tiger Moth, carried on flying with its Cirrus II engine until 1928, when it was withdrawn from further experimental work. Its engineless airframe was hung from the rafters of the Stag Lane flight shed and was only brought down for the 1933 King's Cup race, though it was only displayed above a notice board outside the new de Havilland factory at Hatfield to promote the race. The racer remained at Hatfield and for a while rested in the roof, above where the Comet racers were being built for participation in the England-Australia race. And there it stayed until 3 October 1940 when a German Junkers Ju 88 dropped its lethal load on the factory, killing a number of people and destroying one of British light aviation's truly remarkable aircraft.

The first DH 71 Tiger Moth, G-EBQU, *was completed with an 85 hp Cirrus II engine during type handling tests.* (British Aerospace photograph)

de Havilland DH 71 Tiger Moth data	
Span	22 ft 6 in
	19 ft 0 in
	(short wing)
Length	18 ft 7 in
Height	7 ft 0 in
Wing area	76½ ft²
	62½ ft²
	(short wing)
Empty weight	618 lb
All-up weight	905 lb
Maximum speed	166 mph
	193 mph
	(short wing)
Cruising speed	not available
Stalling/landing speed	60 mph

ABC Robin

ABC Motors Ltd (All British Engine Co Ltd) was formed at Redbridge, Hampshire in 1910. The company's first aircraft engines were produced in 1911, and in 1912 a 40 hp ABC engine was fitted in a Sopwell-Wright biplane. On 24 October 1912, Harry Hawker flew this combination for 8 hrs 23 mins to set a new British duration record. During the First World war ABC produced several types of engine for the British Government, namely the 40 hp Gnat, 120 hp Mosquito, 170 hp Wasp and the 320 hp Dragonfly, the last-named being perhaps the best known.

After the war the company turned its attention to the car and motor cycle industry, and even produced an attractive light car with an air-cooled engine. ABC's interest in aviation was revived at the time of the first Light Aeroplane Trials at Lympne in 1924. Two of the aircraft taking part were Hawker Cygnets, Sydney Camm's first design for the Hawker company. The Cygnet I was powered by a 1,100 cc Anzani, but the Cygnet II, *G-EBJH*, was fitted with a

Above and left *Two photographs of the uncovered Robin taken at Walton-on-Thames early in 1929 before installation of the Scorpion engine.* (*Flight* photograph) **Below left** *The completed Robin with original windscreen photographed at Walton-on-Thames. Registered G-AAID the Robin was doped in the orange and black colour scheme of National Flying Services.* (*Flight* photograph) **Bottom left** *The Robin takes to the air in its original form, in June 1929. The aircraft's top speed was about 105 mph* (*Flight* photograph)

30 hp ABC Scorpion, a modified version of the company's car engine. The Cygnet II did not distinguish itself in the trials, but the engine was developed into the Scorpion II and was fitted into two aircraft competing in the 1926 Lympne trials, the Short Satellite and the Westland Woodpigeon.

The ABC Scorpion II was a two-cylinder, horizontally-opposed air-cooled engine which normally developed 35 bhp at 2,300 rpm and had a maximum output of 40 hp at 2,750 rpm. It was certified in July 1926, and soon proved to be very popular in Germany, Poland, France and America. In Britain, however, there was little in the way of suitable airframes despite the popularity of the Lympne meetings, which did much to stimulate interest in ultra-light aircraft.

The managing director of ABC Motors in 1928 was T.A. Dennis, and it was he who bravely decided that ABC should provide such an aircraft to complement the Scorpion II. He chose as his designer A.A. Fletcher, a man who brought a wealth of design experience with him. 'Tony' Fletcher's career dated back to 1915, when he was chief assistant at Martinsydes. He subsequently became chief designer with the Central Aircraft Company at Kilburn, and was responsible for the Centaur II aircraft, amongst others. He then went to Japan and became chief designer of the Kawanishi company, but returned to Britain and joined Westland at Yeovil, where he worked on the Wizard fighter in 1926.

Fletcher set to work to design a single-seat cabin monoplane around the 40 hp Scorpion. He had pilot comfort very much in mind, the enclosed cabin being unique for a British single-seater at that time and enabling the pilot to fly all the year round without the inconvenience of wearing heavy protective clothing. Provision was made for stowage of two suitcases, the wings were foldable and the aircraft was to be cheap and economical to run.

Construction of the Robin began at the company works at Walton on Thames in the winter of 1928. The first photographs released in May the following year revealed a structurally complete but uncovered Robin, minus engine.

The photographs show the simplicity of the design. The Robin was constructed of wood except for metal fittings and a few highly stressed parts. The fuselage was of the wooden box type, based upon four spruce longerons, the top, bottom and sides covered with a thin plywood veneer. Light formers were placed at intervals to retain the rectangular cross-section, and consisted of panels with very light spruce frames and thin plywood walls lightened by large cut-outs.

Aft of the cabin the fuselage was deep, and the top-decking formed the roof, incorporating a hinged skylight which could be raised to facilitate entry via a door in the starboard side of the fuselage. As well as aiding upward visibility, the skylight was intended to be used as an emergency exit. Behind the skylight was a hatch which gave access to the luggage. In front of the cabin the decking dropped considerably to allow for the windscreen. The lower longerons extended up to the engine bulkhead, but due to the sudden drop in the deck in front of the cabin, the top longerons from the engine mounting were short separate lengths, terminating at the front wall of the cabin.

The engine bulkhead was a multi-plywood former, attached to the longerons by fittings of short lengths of square-section steel tube. Steel tubing also formed the diagonal bracing of the forward fuselage, from the cabin to the bulkhead. The 8 gallon, gravity-fed petrol tank was located above the pilot's legs in the forward deck fairing. The wings were built in two halves, hinged to the fuselage top corners and braced by a pair of V-struts. The upper ends of the struts were attached to the wing spars by steel straps, while at the fuselage end the two tubular struts had fork ends fastened over a steel fitting bolted to the fuselage. A steel strap ran from each side of this fitting, across the bottom of the fuselage, and, together with a tie rod, helped transmit tension.

The wing spars were of solid spruce spindled to an I-section, this method of construction being cheaper than a box-section spar. The ribs were light girders of square section spruce attached to the spars by corner strips. An RAF 34 bi-convex section was used, as it had an almost stationary centre of pressure. The tail surfaces were of wood, with the exception of the trailing edges of the rudder and elevators, which were of streamlined steel tube. The tailplane incidence could

*The Robin pictured at Brooklands after the windscreen was moved back to bring the fuel filler caps outside the cockpit. The fuselage has been modified and the fin and rudder enlarged. (*Flight* photograph)*

be adjusted on the ground. A split undercarriage was provided, the wheels being supported by a bent axle which was held in a fore and aft direction by a radius tube and in the vertical plane by a telescopic leg, the upper end of which was bolted to the side of the fuselage. Endless rubber rings formed the shock absorbers, and were slipped over crutches and enclosed in streamlined fairings. There was no damping device to check bouncing. The wheels could easily be removed without the use of special tools by means of a quick release pin.

The Robin was completed in June 1929, and was doped in Cellon in the orange and black markings of National Flying Services aircraft. This colour scheme caused *The Aeroplane*'s editor to comment, 'it is an exceedingly attractive little vehicle but one volunteers the suggestion that the colour scheme of black and orange is not well chosen. Black is too funereal and in some peculiar way the square fuselage painted black looks like a railway sleeper.'

But Fletcher was well pleased with his new aeroplane. His weight estimates had come out just right, and after the first flight, made at Brooklands in June, he found his estimated performance figures were comfortably exceeded. In July the Robin was exhibited on the minute ABC stand at the Olympia Aero Show, in company with examples of the Hornet and Scorpion engines. The Robin was advertised at £375, the £80 engine being included in the price. C.G. Grey was doubtful if a market for the Robin existed, although he was full of praise for the aircraft, it being designed by an old friend of his. *Flight* described the Robin as one of the prettiest machines it had ever seen, and considered it ideally suitable for the lady pilot.

Initial test flights led to the conclusion that the Robin was too light on the controls, and soon after the Olympia Show it returned to Brooklands for modification. When it re-emerged in November it had an enlarged fin and rudder, which improved control, and the windscreen had been moved back so that the fuel and filler caps were located in front of it.

The Robin had an empty weight of 415 lb, of which the engine accounted for 109 lb, and the gross weight, which included a fairly beefy pilot, a reasonable amount of baggage and four hours fuel at cruising speed, amounted to 680 lb. At the 85 mph recommended cruising speed the fuel consumption was very low, working out at about 40 mpg. In 1929 petrol cost about 1s 7d per gallon; thus the Robin could cruise around the sky for about a halfpenny a mile! Even the total running costs were estimated to be less than 1½ d per mile. The top speed of the Robin was about 105 mph and the landing speed was 40 mph. The initial climb rate was 750 ft/min and its service ceiling was 17,000 ft.

Hopes for Robin production were high, and whole page advertisements appeared in *Flight* and *The Aeroplane* on behalf of the Cellon company, stating that large orders for the Robin had been placed by National Flying Services, and that production aircraft would be built by S.E. Saunders Ltd of Cowes. It was not the policy of ABC to construct aircraft, but rather to design types to suit their own engines and sub-contract their manufacture to approved aircraft constructors, but these plans came to nil, and Robin *G-AAID* was to remain the sole example.

A Certificate of Airworthiness was not granted until 27 June, 1930, just in time for the Robin to participate in that year's King's Cup Air Race. It was entered by H.A.G. Howard, an ABC director, and flown by A.G. Mortimer. The 750 mile race, flown on 5 July, started from Hanworth and ran the length and breadth of the country. The Robin, racing as Number 95, was the fourth of 88 aircraft to take off, and its 3 hr 4 min handicap meant that it had departed before many of the spectators had arrived. Its take-off was long, engine revs were well down, and things were obviously not well. *G-AAID* later forced-landed at Old Sarum, near Salisbury, and retired from the race, which was won by Miss Winifred Brown on Avro Avian III *G-EBVZ* at a speed of 102.7 mph.

A quarter of the competing aircraft dropped out, and it is interesting to note that another ABC-engined competitor, the prototype Comper Swift *G-AARX*, was also dogged by engine trouble. Big-end bearing problems forced it out before the race began.

By this time a small number of British aircraft were sporting Scorpion IIs. These included the Hendy Hobo, the HFS II Gadfly *G-AAEY* and the Boulton Paul P 41 Phoenix *G-AAIT*. The last-named was also displayed at the 1929 Olympia Aero Show. All these aircraft outlived the Robin, which was scrapped at Brooklands in 1932 after its Certificate of Airworthiness expired in June 1931.

ABC Robin data	
Span	25 ft 4 in
	11 ft 8 in
	(wings folded)
Length	17 ft 7 in
Height	5 ft 9 in
Wing area	110 ft²
Empty weight	415 lb
All-up weight	680 lb
Maximum speed	105 mph
Cruising speed	85 mph
Stalling/landing speed	40 mph

Boulton and Paul P 41 Phoenix I and II

The aircraft company Boulton and Paul Ltd is better known for the design and production of military aircraft and armament. But as early as 1918 the company embarked on a design for a light two-seat biplane of 25 ft span, powered by a 90 hp RAF 1A engine. It was designed by 25 year-old John North who, before the Great War, had designed five aircraft for the Grahame-White company at Hendon. For the major part of the war North was superintendent of the Austin Motor Co's aircraft works and in 1918 he joined Boulton and Paul in charge of aircraft design. The P 6, of which only one example was built, was followed by the slightly larger P 9, eight of these civil biplanes being constructed at the Riverside Works at Norwich.

In 1928 North completed designs for a small, two-seat parasol monoplane of 30 ft wing span, powered by a 40 hp ABC Scorpion. Some reports state that the P 41 Phoenix was built as an aerodynamic test aircraft; others say that it was a development prototype of an

intended private owner's machine. Whatever the original intention, the P 41 was completed early in 1929 and registered to the company on 11 June. In July it was exhibited at the Olympia Aero Show in London. Later that year it was flown for the first time, from Mousehold aerodrome in Norwich, whither the company's design and drawing office had moved. The pilot for that first flight was Captain J. Dawson Paul, chairman of the firm's board.

Registered *G-AAIT*, the Phoenix, in its original form, looked strangely dated for 1929. The square-tipped wings had no dihedral and the slab-sided fuselage was flat-topped and tapered to a wedge at the tail. The angular appearance was relieved by the

Below left *Boulton and Paul P 41 Phoenix, G-AAIT, in its original form with a 35 hp ABC Scorpion, pictured at Mousehold Heath, Norwich with Captain J. Dawson Paul in the cockpit. (Via A. J. Jackson Collection)* **Above** *This view of the P 41 Phoenix in its early form shows well the flat-topped fuselage and the identically shaped vertical and horizontal tail surfaces. (Via A.J. Jackson Collection)* **Right and below** *Two views of the P 41 Phoenix in its later form, with 50 hp Salmson radial engine, strengthened undercarriage, additional wing struttery and revised tail skid. (Flight photographs)*

curves of the tailplane and one unusual feature was that the rudder was identical and interchangeable with each half of the all-moving tailplane. This was in order to reduce the number of spares. The rudder, which had a thin, square-shaped fin, was set well forward of the tailplane and, like the rest of the aircraft, was of wooden construction and fabric covered.

In 1930 the Phoenix was completely redesigned and rebuilt. It was re-engined with a 40 hp Salmson nine-cylinder radial engine and took on a distinctively Italian appearance. Intended as a production model, the Phoenix II, still bearing the original

registration, was of welded steel construction, resulting in a very effective and cheap method of manufacture, later widely used by Blackburn on its B-2 trainer. The Phoenix still retained the slab-sided appearance though the forward fuselage decking was cambered to take the radial engine. The wings were braced by steel tubes at the centre-section and by single lift struts which ran from the bottom fuselage longerons to the wings, where additional struts made a very secure bracing. The undercarriage was strengthened and the type of bracing was changed more than once in the revised form.

In its modified form the Phoenix II was used extensively for aerodynamic research. It was pleasant to fly and was flown by a number of pilots, but was too underpowered for a real two-seater aircraft.

In 1935 the Phoenix II was withdrawn from the civil register and scrapped.

Boulton and Paul P 41 Phoenix II* data	
Span	30 ft 0 in
Length	not available
Height	not available
Wing area	not available
Empty weight	not available
All-up weight	1,000 lb
Maximum speed	not available
Cruising speed	not available
Stalling/landing speed	not available

*No dimensions or data for Phoenix I released.

Clarke Cheetah

The Clarke Cheetah, built in 1929, was unusual in that though the fuselage was of original design, everything else was cannibalized from other ultralight aircraft. It is not surprising therefore, that the Cheetah bears more than a passing resemblance to the DH 53 and the Halton HAC 1 Mayfly.

Flying Officer John Clarke joined the Royal Air Force as an aircraft apprentice at RAF Halton in 1923. After gaining a cadetship to RAF Cranwell he eventually passed out as the best all-round pilot in the senior term. He also won the Abdy Gerrard Memorial Prize for gaining the highest marks in Mathematics and Science and in addition won the Air Ministry Prize for aeronautical engineering. In December 1926 he was posted as a pilot to 29 Squadron and in June 1927 was promoted to the rank of Flying Officer. He became an accomplished display pilot and took part in the 1929 RAF Pageant at Hendon.

That same year he completed the construction of the Cheetah, a single-engined sesquiplane powered by a three-cylinder Blackburne Thrush radial engine. The wooden, wire-braced fuselage was of orthodox construction. The parasol top wing came from an unidentified DH 53 and the smaller lower wing came from the Halton HAC 1 Mayfly *G-EBOO*. C. H. Latimer-Needham, the Mayfly's designer, had modified the Mayfly into the Minus parasol monoplane and Clarke had used the redundant wing, complete with the Mayfly's X struts. By removing the X struts the Cheetah could be flown as a parasol and was thus reminiscent of both the Mayfly and the Parnall Pixie III. Other DH 53 components probably included the tailplane, fin and rudder.

The Clarke Cheetah was registered *G-AAJK* and a

Registered in September 1929, the Clarke Cheetah was flown by its designer on only a few occasions before he was tragically killed in an RAF Siskin the following month. (Flight photograph)

Certificate of Airworthiness was issued on 17 September 1929. On 11 October, the talented and promising Clarke was killed at Brough after hitting a shed while taking off in an RAF Siskin. The aircraft crashed and burst into flames, ending the life of a brilliant young man.

Following Clarke's death the Cheetah was purchased by Lord Malcolm Douglas Hamilton in March 1930. Six months later the Cheetah was sold to four RAF airmen, headed by A.C. Thomas, all members of 600 Squadron based at RAF Tangmere. All four learnt to fly, at their own expense, at Stag Lane and then formed a group to run the Cheetah. It was flown from RAF Tangmere and Hendon, often in parasol form, for several years before being sold to Miles Aircraft designer F.G. Miles in 1935. In May the following year the Cheetah was acquired by Cambridge undergraduate Richard Hopkinson. It was his intention to rebuild the Cheetah but lack of known-how led him to approach C.H. Latimer-Needham's Luton Aircraft Ltd, designers and builders of the Buzzard, Minor and Major ultra-light aircraft, described elsewhere in this book.

Latimer-Needham redesigned the aircraft and the task of rebuilding the Cheetah was entrusted to the late Harold Best-Devereux. A decision was taken to convert the aircraft into a low-wing monoplane; thus it was transformed into a completely different animal and named the Martin Monoplane, after Hopkinson's uncle Martin, who had provided the cash for the rebuild. The Martin Monoplane is described later in this book.

Clarke Cheetah data	
Span	29 ft 0 in
Length	not available
Height	not available
Wing area	not available
Empty weight	450 lb (monoplane)
All-up weight	678 lb (monoplane)
Maximum speed	not available
Cruising speed	not available
Stalling/landing speed	not available

Granger Archaeopteryx

Shortly after the First World War, two Nottinghamshire brothers yearned to fly as cheaply as possible in an aircraft to their own design. The Granger brothers were lace manufacturers. They had no experience of engineering and had only flown as passengers. What little knowledge of aviation they possessed had been gleaned from the aviation press.

In 1921, with a few shillings and boundless enthusiasm, they set about building a glider. Their lack of know-how brought the project to a halt, although the unfinished glider, of substantial construction, was later cannibalized to provide material for the heavier parts of successive aircraft. A second glider was begun in 1914, again to their own design, but incorporating the wings of an old Avro, possibly a 504. After completion the glider was flown only once,

The uncovered but complete Archaeopteryx airframe in late 1930.

Top *The Archaeopteryx covered and completed in October 1930.* **Middle** *The Archaeopteryx photographed at the RAF Flying Club Display at Hatfield on 15 June 1935.* **Above** *A pre-war air-to-air photograph of the Archaeopteryx taken shortly before it was put into storage for thirty years.*

during which J. Granger was more or less in control. Further flights could not be made because of the difficulty of recruiting suitable helpers to transport the glider the many miles to a remote hillside.

Undaunted, the brothers began a third glider, light enough for them to handle on their own. Design work began at Christmas 1924, and the aircraft was completed, except for the covering, twelve months later. It was at about this time that C. Newham, an ex-RAF pilot, became involved, and suggested that they fit an engine into the glider. This proposal was enthusiastically received, and the old fuselage was scrapped and a new one built to accommodate an old 400 cc ABC engine. Completed in July 1926, the biplane was christened the Linnet.

The nearest aerodrome was Hucknall, some ten miles away, and after prior permission had been received for its use the Grangers, Newham and a band of doubters and scoffers prepared the Linnet for its first flight. Results were very disappointing. The Linnet would make only the most reluctant attempt of hops into the air despite the use of various propellers of different size and pitch. It became obvious that the aircraft was underpowered and the wing section unsuitable. The aircraft weighed only 242 lb, but the undercarriage accounted for seventeen per cent of the total weight. It was the cheapest that could be found, and although the group had planned to make their own wheels of wood, the 35 lb undercarriage had the advantage of pneumatic tyres. Many Sunday mornings were spent taxiing the Linnet up and down Hucknall but, apart from one flight of 100 yds made at a height of 20 ft, the Grangers had to content themselves with being towed behind a car and gaining air experience from the resulting glides.

In the Autumn of 1926, the group was joined by B. Howard, and from this nucleus the Experimental Light 'Plane Club was formed. The Club decided to embark upon a really ambitious project, and the choice lay between building an autogyro or a tailless aeroplane based on the Pterodactyl concept of Captain G.T.R. Hill and the earlier Dunne aircraft. They opted for an autogyro, and constructed a six foot model. Tests proved that the club had bitten off more than it could chew, and that much time-consuming research was required. Plans therefore went ahead to design a tailless aircraft. The original drawings showed a tailless aircraft with swept wings, nacelle and wing tip rudders, à la Pterodactyl. The group was then fortunate enough to acquire the services of Captain C.H. Latimer-Needham, who had recently designed the Halton Mayfly *G-EBOO* for the Halton Aero Club and who later was to design the Luton series of aircraft.

Latimer-Needham carried out a stress analysis of the club's design and suggested various changes. He advised that they dispensed with the wing tip rudders and used a normal fuselage with fin and rudder. This would not only give a more effective rudder action, because it would be in the direct line of the propeller slip-stream, but the stressing of the wing structure was greatly simplified without the wing tip rudders and their attendant stresses. Longitudinal and lateral control was achieved with elevons, combined elevators and ailerons, on the wing tips. Such was Latimer-Needham's interest in the tailless concept that he designed such an aircraft for the Halton Aero Club. Designated HAC 3 Meteor, construction was ninety per cent completed in 1929, when the project was abandoned.

The Experimental Light 'Plane Club's tailless aircraft design was finalized and named Archaeopteryx,

In June 1971 the Archaeopteryx was flown from Old Warden on its first flight for 35 years following restoration by the Shuttleworth Trust. (Air Portraits photograph)

a name of similar antiquity to Pterodactyl. The swept-back parasol wing was mounted on the conventional fuselage by way of metal struts from the wing centre-section to the forward fuselage and two large metal spars running from mid-span of the wings to the bottom fuselage longerons. The bungee type undercarriage had no brakes, the tail skid being sufficient to brake and hold the aircraft straight on the ground. The 32 hp Bristol Cherub I engine drove a small two-bladed propeller, and fuel was gravity-fed from a 5 gal tank located in the wing centre-section. The cockpit was small and sparsely instrumented. Engine rev counter, ASI and oil pressure gauge were located on the panel, but the altimeter was positioned on the cockpit floor between the pilot's legs. The throttle was located outside the cockpit on the port side, and the pilot sat in a hammock-type canvas seat.

The basic wing structure of the Archaeopteryx was finished in September 1927, but the aircraft was not completed until October 1930. The first flight and initial test flights proved trouble-free, and because the aircraft was not going to be flown outside the immediate vicinity of the aerodrome it required no Certificate of Airworthiness. For two years the brothers flew free of red tape, but in 1932 the regulations governing such aircraft were tightened and in June the Archaeopteryx succumbed to officialdom and was registered *G-ABXL*, thus enabling the group to make flights further afield.

By the end of 1934, the Archaeopteryx had been flown 50 hrs and had ventured as far from its Tollerton base as Castle Bromwich, Sywell and Waltham. Its longest flight was to the RAF Flying Club Display held at Hatfield on 15 June, 1935, where it intrigued Lord Trenchard and the then new Secretary of State for Air, Sir Philip Cunliffe-Lister. Its performance in 1934 on its ten-year old Cherub I was quite lively. Its maximum speed was 95 mph, cruise 75 mph and it could be maintained in a 45° bank, nose-up, at 35 mph — just 5 mph less than its normal landing speed.

After six years of sporadic flying the Archaeopteryx was put into storage in Chilwell, near Nottingham, where it slumbered until 1968. In that year it was removed to Old Warden and the safekeeping of the Shuttleworth Trust, who stripped the aircraft to its component parts and restored it to pristine condition. Its first flight for 35 years took place in June 1971, with Squadron Leader John Lewis at the controls.

A good account of the aircraft's flying characteristics can be found in the excellent Airlife Publications book *From Bleriot to Spitfire*. In the relevant chapter Lewis regards the Archaeopteryx as a handful to fly from Old Warden and, in keeping with most tailless aircraft, it had some bad habits. Much of the trouble stems from the undercarriage and short moment of the fuselage. Combine this with Old Warden's rough grass surface, and you have the aircraft kangarooing at the low end of the speed range during landing and take-off. This problem has been partially cured by lengthening and moving the undercarriage further aft and by reducing tyre pressures.

The controls are very light and responsive, but the elevons need a little time to take effect during take-off. The low-powered and aged engine produces more noise than power, and at 60 ft/min the climb is a lengthy, ear-splitting affair. Even this rate of climb can only be achieved provided the pilot keeps his head low and his throttle arm inside the cockpit and away from the slip-stream. Lewis stresses that flying from a smooth hard runway in calm conditions is a different kettle of fish, much of the horror of take-off and landing being eliminated. Shuttleworth have pushed the Archaeopteryx to 105 mph in a shallow dive, but have kept a wary eye on the lower end of the speed scale and have not ventured below 50 mph.

What became of the Granger brothers? R.J.T. Granger, in company with his son, was invited to Old Warden to see his aeroplane fly shortly after its restoration. It is still flying fifty years after work was begun, a fitting tribute to two ambitious brothers who were determined to take to the air.

Granger Archaeopteryx data	
Span	27 ft 6 in
Length	15 ft 0 in
Height	not available
Wing area	not available
Empty weight	not available
All-up weight	not available
Maximum speed	95 mph
Cruising speed	75 mph
Stalling/landing speed	40 mph

Henderson-Glenny HSF II Gadfly

Throughout the history of British ultra-light aviation, designer after designer has striven to produce a cheap-to-build and cheap-to-fly runabout for the man in the street. More often than not the aircraft have failed dismally, either because of their unreliable converted motor cycle engines or because they were single-seaters produced for a market that possibly never existed.

In 1929 new regulations demanded that anyone requiring a 'B' flying licence had to have at least 100 hrs solo flying before it could be granted. This meant that prospective candidates had to fork out a great deal more cash than most could afford. One man who was particularly aware of this new situation was Colonel G.L.P. Henderson who, having run a successful flying school at Brooklands for many years, had set up a new establishment at Croydon at the end of 1928. Henderson was not the kind of person to take such new regulations lightly, and he immediately hit upon the idea of producing a really cheap, no-frills single-seater which would be both cheap to build and fly by those impecunious students who needed to build up the necessary hours relatively cheaply.

One of Henderson's pupils had been the wealthy A.P. Glenny, who had made his fortune in the family wool business at Hawick in Scotland. He agreed to finance Henderson's aeroplane and the Glenny & Henderson Co was set up with an office and works at York Road in Byfleet, Surrey, not far from Brooklands Aerodrome. The design of the aircraft was entrusted to ex-RFC pilot Captain K.N. Pearson who had worked for Hawker and who had been involved with that company's Horsley in its early development.

Pearson's design was simplicity itself. Named the Gadfly, the all-wood, low-wing monoplane was to be powered by a 40 hp ABC Scorpion two-cylinder air-cooled engine.

The Gadfly's fuselage was a rectangular structure built up on four ⅝ in square spruce longerons divided into nine bays by vertical and horizontal struts of the same material. The four sides of the rectangular box were braced by spruce diagonals, the three centre bays having two diagonals each to provide cross-bracing. All the fuselage joints were reinforced with plywood gussets or 'biscuits'. The fuselage decking

The first Gadfly, G-AAEY, in its original form with conventional ailerons. It was first flown in April 1929 from Brooklands. (Flight photograph)

was curved and, like the rest of the fuselage, was plywood-covered.

The one-piece wing was built up from two box spars and former ribs and was plywood covered. In order to keep cost to a minimum the wing was rectangular in planform and had square-cut tips. The wing was bolted to the fuselage with four locking pins, two on the front spar and two on the rear. Because the undercarriage was fitted forward of the wing, the latter could be easily dropped clear of the fuselage for dismantling and transporting by road. The leading and trailing edges of the wing centre-section were cut back to the two spars and so fitted snugly up into a recess in the underside of the fuselage. When the wing was released from the fuselage the pilot's seat and controls came with it, provided that the controls had first been disconnected. The dismantling operation took a couple of men a few minutes.

The Gadfly's undercarriage was of the ordinary V-type and consisted of two vees of steel tube interconnected at their lower ends by a rigid cross-tube. Springing was by rubber cord on the axle and the entire unit was cross-braced with cable in the plane of the rear legs. The ash tail-skid was hinged at its centre, had a steel shoe and was sprung by rubber cord anchored to the top fuselage longerons.

The one-piece cantilever tailplane had divided elevators and was of wooden construction, except for the steel tubular elevator spar. As with the fin and rudder, it was unbalanced and fabric covered.

The uncowled ABC Scorpion engine was attached to a steel bearer plate on the nose of the fuselage and secured with four bolts. The 9 gal gravity tank was mounted behind the engine, above the fuselage longerons, and was separated from the engine by a fireproof bulkhead. A double curvature metal cowling fitted over the front fuselage between the engine and the cockpit; under it were located the fuel and oil tanks.

The Gadfly was first flown during April 1929, from Brooklands, by Hawker test pilot Edward 'Tiny' Scholefield, who reported that the 25 ft span aircraft performed well. The finished Gadfly had actually come out some 25 lb lighter than its designed 458 lb tare weight. Tragically, Scholefield was killed on 16 May while flying Vickers 62 Vanguard *G-EBCP* when it crashed and burned out at Shepperton in Middlesex. The following day Henderson took the Gadfly up and established an altitude record for single-seaters of less than 200 kg weight, climbing to 9,915 ft. This first Gadfly was registered *G-AAEY* and a Certificate of Airworthiness was granted on 16 September 1929.

For some time now Pearson had been experimenting with a rotary aileron control system, which he hoped would replace conventional ailerons. These

Top *The Gadfly* G-AAEY *after fitment of the Pearson rotary ailerons. The device had first flown on a Renault-engined Avro 548.* (*Flight* photograph) **Below** *Another view of the first Gadfly fitted with Pearson rotary ailerons. The A&AEE found the novel controls 'not very effective'.* (*Flight* photograph) **Bottom** *The one-piece wing of the Gadfly could be detached from the fuselage by undoing four bolts thus making it easy to transport by trailer.* (*Flight* photograph)

Top *The HSFII Gadfly* G-AARK *was powered by a 40 hp Salmson AD9 radial engine and is seen here flying beneath a bridge over the Brooklands motor racing track.* **Above** *Gadfly* G-AARJ, *built in late 1929, was sold in Canada and registered* CF-AMG *the following year.*

rotary ailerons looked like a couple of oysters and were mounted on skewed pivots on shafts located midway between the front and rear wing spars. Each aileron was connected to the control column, which was so arranged with a differential device that when the stick was moved for a turn the inside aileron assumed a negative angle of around 40°, whereas the outside aileron remained almost at its original small positive angle. This system had been successfully tested on the Henderson school's Avro 548 *G-EBAJ* and it was incorporated into the second Gadfly. As the Gadfly Mk II, this aircraft was registered *G-AARJ* and awarded a Certificate of Airworthiness on 3 October 1929, by which time the prototype had also been fitted with Pearson oysters and sent to the Aeroplane & Armament Experimental Establishment at RAF Martlesham Heath for evaluation. The subsequent report, issued in September, was very critical of the aileron control. Though the Pearson ailerons eliminated the twisting effect on the wing applied by conventional ailerons, the 'scallops' necessitated coarse

stick movements in order for them to take effect in the event of a wing dropping. Thus they could catch unawares a pilot who was used to normal aileron control movements. In addition, the rotary ailerons were vulnerable to damage on the ground. The report also criticized the general construction of the Gadfly — part of the plywood decking around the cockpit was so thin that it had begun to split.

The third Gadfly, registered *G-AARK*, was fitted with a 40 hp nine-cylinder Salmson AD 9 radial engine in place of the Scorpion, which vibrated badly and more than likely contributed to the breaking up of the Gadfly's structure. In this form the Gadfly was demonstrated at Heston on 20 July 1929. It is doubtful whether the Salmson-powered Gadfly was ever issued with a Certificate of Airworthiness because the French engine had not been certified at the time by the Bureau Veritas — that country's certification authority.

Initially, there were plans to produce about a dozen Gadflies and to offer them at £370 apiece, ex-works. But after only three aircraft had been completed things started to go wrong at Glenny & Henderson. First, a crisis in the woollen industry sent Glenny back to Scotland to salvage a diminishing business. Then Henderson himself became involved with his school and after he backed out the Gadfly project folded in 1930.

The prototype Gadfly, *G-AAEY*, was sold to Oscar Grieg at Brooklands and, after changing hands again, ended up with Edmund Bradley at Wolverhampton in February 1933, though the Certificate of Airworthiness had expired back in September 1930. This aircraft was finally scrapped in 1934.

The second Gadfly, *G-AARJ*, was flown by Jock Anderson, Henderson's engineer, though it was registered to the parent company. In June 1930 the Gadfly was sold in Canada to R. Foley and registered *CF-AMG*, only to be destroyed by fire at Kitchener, Ontario on 25 August the following year. It is thought that before it left for Canada, *G-AARJ* had a bad crash when Glenny experienced engine trouble and had to put down hurriedly in a field at Wargrave-on-Thames. A photograph shows the wings, tailplane and undercarriage quite intact and it is possible that one of two uncompleted fuselages was used to rebuild the aircraft before it left for Canada.

The third and final Gadfly, *G-AARK*, actually owned by Colonel Henderson, continued to be flown by him until July 1930. On 22 July 1930 Henderson was flying aboard the Junkers F 13 *G-AAZK* when it suffered structural failure and crashed at Meopham, Kent. He and five others were killed. Gadfly *G-AARK* was withdrawn from use after its owner's death and was stored at Brooklands until 1933, when it was scrapped.

Henderson-Glenny HSF II Gadfly data	
Span	25 ft 0 in
Length	17 ft 0 in
Height	5 ft 0 in
Wing area	108 ft²
Empty weight	455 lb
All-up weight	750 lb
Maximum speed	92 mph
Cruising speed	72 mph
Stalling/landing speed	45 mph

Hendy 281 Hobo

When wealthy Lionel Bellairs approached F.G. Miles and asked for a more powerful version of the Avro Baby, the task of redesigning Avro 534 Baby *G-EAUM* — which the Miles brothers had acquired at a Hamble sale in 1927 — was given to Horace Miles (no relation), who worked with Basil B.

Four views of the Hobo in its original form, with 35 hp ABC Scorpion and large Palmer aero wheels.

Top *The Hobo after extensive modification, painted in the colours of Aircraft Exchange & Mart, at Hanworth.* **Above** *A. L. T. Naish landing the Pobjoy-engined Hobo at Hatfield during the 1934 King's Cup race. (Flight photograph)* **Below** *Lord Patrick Crichton-Stuart flying his Hobo at Lympne. The aircraft is fitted with a 90 hp Pobjoy Cataract. (Flight photograph)*

Henderson at the Hendy Aircraft Corporation. This company, like Miles' Southern Aircraft Ltd, was based at Shoreham and shortly after Horace Miles had redesigned the Baby into the Southern Martlet he and Henderson set out to produce a low-cost aircraft which would provide a cheap means of flying and yet have a reasonable performance.

The single-seat, open cockpit low-wing monoplane was to embody a patented form of wing construction that Basil Henderson had designed, which, apart from its novel construction method, had an aerofoil section with a practically stationary centre of pressure through most usable angles of incidence. Powered by a 35 hp ABC Scorpion II, the Hendy Hobo was completed during the summer of 1929 and first flown in October by aircraft designer Edgar Percival.

Of conventional appearance, the Hobo was built entirely of wood. The fuselage consisted of four spruce longerons and spruce struts and was plywood covered. The Scorpion was carried on a steel tube structure mounted on a fireproof bulkhead, with the fuel tank carried in the fairing forward of the roomy cockpit. Behind the cockpit a large suitcase could be accommodated in a locker below the faired headrest.

The fully cantilevered wings were built in three sections. The outer panels tapered in thickness and chord from root to tip, the wing section used being a modified bi-convex RAF 34. The centre-section was built integral with the fuselage. The Henderson wing embodied an entirely new form of construction. The two spars were built-up I-sections with spruce flanges glued and bradded to the three-ply webs. They were positioned close together well forward in the wing and were identical in dimensions. The spars formed one large box-girder by the attachment of diagonal cross-bracing at both top and bottom, eliminating all metal fittings. Torsional, bending and drag loads were shared equally throughout the truss complex.

Subsequent tests on the Henderson wing carried out by RAE Farnborough showed that it possessed a safety factor far beyond anything required in flying. The same method of construction was later used in the wing of Hinkler's twin-engined Ibis, described elsewhere in this book.

The Hobo's wings folded around the rear spar joints to the centre-section. To provide space for the outer wing trailing edges when folded, the trailing edges of the centre-section hinged forward. The aileron cables ran along the rear face of the rear spar. No disconnection of the pitot head was necessary as it was mounted on the centre-section. The undercarriage was of the divided axle type, each unit consisting of a hinged vee with a bent axle, fitted with large-size Palmer Aero wheels. Unusually for such a small aircraft, all the undercarriage joints and control levers were lubricated with Tecalemit greasers.

The tailskid consisted of two laminations of steel supported beneath the sternpost by a steel packing block, which insured against damage should the skid shear. The flying controls were operated by cables and differential cranks and were run inside the fuselage to the tail unit.

Early testflights of the Hobo revealed its excellent handling characteristics. The maximum speed was the magic (and marketable) 100 mph. The stall occurred at 38 mph and the little aircraft had a realistic endurance of 6 hrs. Though it was originally hoped to put the Hobo into production, no market for such an aircraft existed. In addition, the Scorpion was unreliable and vibrated badly. The Hobo was little-used and was not much seen until 1934, when it was revived for a different use to that which its designer had originally intended: Wealthy Lord Patrick Crichton-Stuart, the Marquis of Bute, had acquired a taste for air-racing and saw in the Hobo the makings of a suitable racer. The Scorpion was removed and in its place a 90 hp Pobjoy Cataract was installed. Dunlop aero wheels replaced the thin, large-diameter Palmer wheels and mass balances were fitted to the ailerons and rudder. Finally, the undercarriage was modified and lengthened. A new Certificate of Airworthiness was issued on 9 July 1934 and the Hobo was based at Hanworth.

In its modified form the Hobo was entered for the 1934 King's Cup race, held that year at Hatfield on 13-14 July. The weather was appalling, though the Hobo flew well in the hands of A.L.T. Nash. Unfortunately, the aircraft had to force-land at Reading after running out of fuel and it was almost certainly robbed of a place. It had been prohibited by airworthiness requirements to carry more than 14 gals of fuel.

The owner entered the promising Hobo for the Hatfield to Cardiff race, held on 6 October 1934. In the hands of Flight Lieutenant Robert Duncanson the Hobo won with an average speed of 125.4 mph. The Hobo won its next three races too: the Broxbourne Visitor's Handicap, the Hanworth Trophy and the Midland Challenge Trophy.

During the following season the Hobo was generally up with the front runners though it did not maintain its earlier racing form. After coming second in the Folkestone Aero Trophy race, flown by A.J.S. Morris, with an average speed of 126 mph, the Hobo came last in the 1936 event, held on 30 July. During the following month the Hobo was put into storage at Lympne on expiry of its Certificate of Airworthiness, after being sold to Lieutenant William Garthwaite. On 30 August 1940 the Hobo was destroyed in a hangar fire, the victim of a German air raid.

Hendy 281 Hobo data (ABC Scoprion)	
Span	32 ft 0 in
	14 ft 0 in
	(wings folded)
Length	19 ft 6 in
Height	7 ft 1 in
Empty weight	435 lb
All-up weight	650 lb
Maximum speed	100 mph
	130 mph
	(Pobjoy Cataract)
Cruising speed	not available
Stalling/landing speed	38 mph

Southern Martlet and Metal Martlet

In 1927 a sale was held at the former Avro factory at Hamble in Hampshire. Attending the sale was F.G. Miles, director of Southern Aircraft Ltd, a flying club and joyriding concern based at Shoreham in Sussex. Amongst his purchases was the two-seat Avro 534 Baby *G-EAUM,* mentioned in the previous chapter. This was a standard Baby but with the fuselage lengthened by 2 ft 6 in in order to accommodate a passenger in the enlarged single cockpit. After the Baby was taken to Shoreham F.G. Miles removed the 35 hp Green engine and fitted a 60 hp Cirrus I. The improved performance was so good that wealthy L.E.R. Bellairs, the co-owner of the Baby, asked Miles to design him something along similar lines but with even more power. Although Miles' burning ambition at that time was to be an aircraft designer he had no experience and the design work was entrusted to Horace Miles. Horace Miles was an ex-Avro man

The prototype Martlet taking off from Shoreham in August 1929, powered by the 85 hp ABC Hornet engine. (Flight photograph)

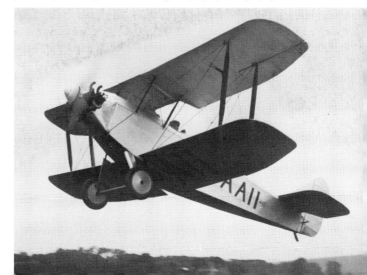

Top G-AAVD *the first production Martlet, powered by an 80 hp Genet II.* (Leonard Bridgman photograph) **Above** *Martlet G-AAYZ was built for the Rt Hon F.E. Guest and was originally powered by a 120 hp DH Gipsy II.* (Flight photograph) **Below** *Built for the Marquess of Douglas and Clydesdale, Martlet G-ABBN was best known for its displays with Cobham's National Aviation Day airshows. The aircraft was scrapped in 1935.* (Flight photograph)

who was then working with Basil Henderson, the designer of the Hendy Hobo. His brief was to base his new design on the Baby and the new aeroplane virtually retained the Baby's fuselage and wings but, instead of the Cirrus, an 85 hp ABC Hornet horizontally-opposed four-cylinder engine was used. Though of the same weight as the old Green engine the Hornet gave approximately twice the power. The tail unit was redesigned and an entirely different spring and oleo undercarriage replaced the former V-strut and bungee-sprung unit of the Baby.

The new aircraft, originally known as the Hornet Baby, was built during 1928 and the early part of 1929. Design work and construction proceeded together and quite often the drawings and calculations lagged behind the building work, such was Miles' enthusiasm to get on with the job — a trait that was to remain almost a hallmark with him throughout his later years with the Miles Aircraft company.

By August 1929 the prototype was completed and it was renamed Martlet — the bird of the same name was featured on the heraldic crest of the county of Sussex. That same month F.G. Miles conducted the first test flight and it was immediately apparent that the Martlet had an exceptional performance. The take-off was particularly impressive and the flying controls were light, powerful and effective. The Martlet was registered *G-AAII* and flown to RAF Martlesham Heath during August for acceptance trials. These were carried out in time for the aircraft to make its public debut, at Hanworth on 30 August.

The Martlet's fuselage was of wire-braced spruce construction with four ash longerons. The wings had box spars and were plywood-covered up to the front spar, the rest of the wings and the tailplane being fabric covered. The top wing centre-section carried a 15 gal gravity-fed fuel tank which gave the Martlet an endurance of 3 hrs.

The Martlet was a natural for aerobatics, and during its first year of existence it was frequently displayed by Flying Officer H.H. Leach, a 43 Squadron pilot based at RAF Tangmere, where he flew Siskins. Later *G-AAII* was re-engined with an 85 hp Genet II five-cylinder radial engine. Initially owned by Lionel Bellairs, the aircraft passed to the parent company in April 1933 and was owned by the firm's secretary, Miss Nancy Birkett. Two years later it was sold in Ireland as *EI-ABG*.

Meanwhile a further five wooden Martlets had been constructed. *G-AAVD*, the second aircraft, also powered by an 85 hp Genet II engine, was registered on 23 June 1930 and passed through several ownerships before ending its days derelict at Turnhouse towards the end of the war. In 1930 F.G. Miles raced it in the King's Cup air race but the Genet objected to being thrashed at full throttle and Miles was forced to retire.

The Rt Hon F.E. Guest ordered the third Martlet, registered *G-AAYZ* on 27 June 1930 and this too was flown in the 1930 King's Cup event. Fitted with a 120 hp DH Gipsy II four-cylinder in-line engine and raced by Miss Winifred Brown it fare better than *G-AAVD*, coming fourteenth with an average speed of 125.5 mph. The Martlet was raced in the 1932 event by Flying Officer E.C.T. Edwards but the machine was damaged after a forced landing at Runcorn. In 1934 '*YZ* was fitted with a 100 hp Gipsy I engine and Edwards had another crack at the King's Cup. This time he managed sixth place with an average speed of 120 mph. Three years later the Martlet was scrapped.

The fourth Martlet was an aerobatic aircraft ordered by Flight Lieutenant Richard Atcherley. Fitted with a 105 hp Genet Major five-cylinder radial engine, it had an inverted fuel system with an additional tank. In addition the wings had parallel chord ailerons. The inverted fuel tank was never fitted because the order was cancelled owing to the length of time taken to build the special aircraft. Once more Lionel Bellairs came to the Miles' rescue and he purchased the aircraft. It was first flown in September 1930, though its Certificate of Airworthiness was not issued until 14 July 1931. During 1934 the Martlet was flown by the Reading Aero Club. Later it appeared at Gatwick where it had been rebuilt following a crash, after which it passed to motor racing personality M.N. Mavrogordato, who kept it at Witney near Oxford. During the war the Martlet lay dismantled in a barn until Billy Butlin purchased it in June 1947, it having been advertised for £150. After refurbishment by Miles Aircraft at Woodley, '*YX* was used to entertain holidaymakers with aerobatic displays over various holiday camps. In 1949 the Martlet returned to Shoreham under the care of the newly-formed Ultra-Light Aircraft Association. In 1955 '*YX* was acquired by the Shuttleworth Trust at Old Warden and for the next thirty years remained in store pending restoration to flying condition.

The fifth Martlet, fitted with an 85 hp Genet II engine, was registered *G-ABBN* on 8 August 1930 to the Marquess of Douglas and Clydesdale and kept at Hamble. It was raced in the 1931 King's Cup race by M.L. Bramson, once an SE 5a pilot with the Savage Skywriting company and post-war owner of the Spitfire II *G-AHZI*. The following year '*BN* toured England with Sir Alan Cobham's National Aviation Day Displays Ltd and in 1935 it was scrapped.

The sixth and final wooden Martlet was registered *G-ABIF* on 30 May 1931 to Mrs Maxine Freeman-Thomas, who later became F.G. Miles' wife. Powered by an 85 hp Genet II, '*IF* took part in the 1931 King's Cup race flown by H.H. Leach. It also

Top *Martlet* G-ABIF *was the last built and is seen here as a competitor in the 1933 King's Cup air race.* (*Flight* photograph) **Above** *Martlet* G-AAYX *survived the war and is seen here in 1947 after restoration by Miles for Billy Butlin.* **Below** *The sole Metal Martlet bearing two different civil registrations, both incorrect. The wings were from the Martlet prototype* G-AAII, *and the fuselage was marked* G-AAJW. *The correct lettering,* G-ABJW, *was later applied.* (*Flight* photograph)

The Metal martlet was first flown towards the end of 1930 and bore little resemblance to the original Martlet.

took part in the 1933 event but its pilot, T.C. Sanders, was forced to retire. After a succession of owners '*IF* was finally given to the Air Training Corps in 1940.

By the time the last two Martlets were flying, a metal version was airborne at Shoreham. This had been financed by Lional Bellairs and designed by Horace Miles in conjunction with Basil Henderson. Though called the Metal Martlet, the new aircraft bore little resemblance to the wooden Martlet and only its fuselage was constructed of metal — the wings were of wood. The entire aircraft was fabric-covered and powered by a 110 hp Cirrus Hermes.

The Metal Martlet's fuselage was constructed of square-section metal tubes joined by flitch plates and rivets and the fabric covering was laid over wooden formers. There was no internal wire bracing. The undercarriage consisted of a split axle fitted with low-pressure tyres. Complete, the aircraft looked akin to a miniature, single-seat Avro Avian.

The first flight of the Metal Martlet was made towards the end of 1930, though it was not registered until 19 March the following year. Oddly enough the wrong registration letters were twice applied; at first the Martlet was marked *G-AAJW* and *G-AAII* instead of *G-ABJW*. The one and only Metal Martlet was sold to Viscountess Ratendone but was scrapped in November the following year, never having had a Certificate of Airworthiness. A second aircraft was registered *G-ABMM* in the name of W.R. Westhead of Heston but this Martlet was not completed and the registration was cancelled in December 1932.

Southern Martlet data (Genet II)	
Span	25 ft 0 in
Length	20 ft 3 in
Height	7 ft 6 in
Wing area	180 ft²
Empty weight	630 lb
All-up weight	1,040 lb
Maximum speed	112 mph
Cruising speed	85 mph
Stalling/landing speed	40 mph

Southern Metal Martlet data	
Span	23 ft 6 in
Length	20 ft 6 in
Height	8 ft 3 in
Wing area	156 ft²
Empty weight	not available
All-up weight	not available
Maximum speed	130 mph
Cruising speed	115 mph
Stalling/landing speed	not available

Hinkler Ibis

Strictly speaking, H.J. 'Bert' Hinkler's twin-engined Ibis has no place in this book. Like the Carden-Baynes Bee, described later in this book, the Ibis' all-up weight was probably half that of standard light twins of the day and can thus be classed as an ultra-light twin.

Hinkler of course is recalled for some remarkable long distance flights. In 1920, for example, he left Croydon for an attempted flight to his native Australia in his own Avro Baby, *G-EACQ*. His most notable flight, though, was a successful record flight from England to Australia in Avro Avian *G-EBOV*. The 11,000 miles were flown in 15½ days and the flight earned Hinkler the Air Force Cross.

During the Australia flight, much of it made over water and inhospitable terrain, Hinkler became very aware of the vulnerability of the single-engined touring aeroplane. By the end of the marathon flight he had formed definite ideas of what form the ideal tourer should take. On returning to England, Hinkler tried to find an existing British aircraft that would fulfill his exacting requirements. There were none. After preparing rough drawings of an aircraft to his own design, he then tried to interest a number of manufacturers in building and marketing it. No-one wanted to know. Whatever the reasons, Hinkler was certainly no businessman and throughout his life had failed to capitalize on many novel ideas. He had patented a design that allowed the undercarriage on the Avro Avian to fold back with the wings for hangarage, but a camera that he designed to take standard cine film of the time, pre-empting the Leica, and which he took on the 1920 attempted flight to Australia, undoubtedly would have made him a fortune had he marketed it.

Using some of his new-found wealth, Hinkler formed Ibis Aircraft in partnership with the designer R.H. Bound. Detailed drawings of a small amphibian were prepared and work on building a prototype began in 1929.

The resulting design was a small, all-wood shoulder-wing monoplane with a boat-like hull powered by two engines mounted back-to-back above the wing centre-section. The two occupants sat side-by-side in a large comfortable cockpit forward of the wing, affording excellent all-round visibility for both. The engine layout, in addition to giving twin-engined reliability, also gave good single-engined handling characteristics and eliminated the asymmetric problems associated with conventional twin-engined layout. In the event of a forced landing on water, the boat-like hull afforded some measure of protection.

In recognition of Hinkler's association with that bird, Ibis was the name chosen for the aircraft. Detailed design and construction of the Ibis wing was entrusted to Basil Henderson, using his patented type of wing construction, later used in the Hendy 302, Parnall Heck and in many other aircraft. The wing was built at Shoreham by Hendy Aircraft Ltd, but the rest of the Ibis was built by Hinkler himself in a tiny shed at Hamble. Work continued during 1929 and 1930. The Ibis was registered on 11 June 1929 and allocated the civil registration letters *G-AAIS*, though the letters were never actually carried.

Top *The Hinkler Ibis photographed at Hamble shortly after completion. Note the saddle-type fuel tanks between the engines, the high position of the horizontal tail surfaces and the strutless wings.* (*Flight* photograph) **Above** *No data or dimensions of the Ibis have come to light, though some idea of its size can be gauged from this photograph. Bert Hinkler, on the right, was 5 ft 4 in tall.* (*Flight* photograph) **Below** *Designed initially as an amphibian the Ibis was not built as such, though the hull was made water resistant.* (*Flight* photograph)

For financial or technical reasons, the Ibis was not built as an amphibian though its hull was made water resistant. It was claimed that in the event of a production order, a true amphibian could be built, complete with steps in the hull, without much difficulty. Similarly it was considered a minor task to convert the fixed undercarriage to a retractable unit.

The tandem engine layout was the most noteworthy feature of the Ibis. Two 40 hp Salmson AD 9 engines were mounted back to back above the wing with two saddle-type fuel tanks located between them. Though such an arrangement had distinct advantages, cooling of the rear engine must have caused problems. Also the location of the front engine so close to the cockpit would have made the Ibis lethal as a true amphibian, with crews trying to pick up buoys and keeping their heads at the same time!

Hinkler took the Ibis into the air for the first time in May 1930 from Hamble. Handling was reported as being satisfactory though there appear to be no

records of the Ibis having gone to A&AEE for official testing. Attempts to find a manufacturer for the Ibis came to nothing and Hinkler, thoroughly disillusioned, dismantled the aircraft and put it into storage in his garden at Sholing, near Southampton.

In 1931 Hinkler decided to try his luck in Canada, taking with him a British-built DH 80 Puss Moth in an effort to run a taxi and charter business. This came to nothing and Hinkler embarked on an ambitious round flight from New York to Jamaica, across the South Atlantic and on to London, breaking several records en route.

There followed a grim year of unemployment for Hinkler, but by the end of 1932 he had planned another attempt on the England-Australia record, then held by C.W.A. Scott. As with all Hinkler's flights there was little pre-flight publicity and on the early morning of 7 January 1933, only a handful of helpers witnessed Hinkler's departure from Harmondsworth in Puss Moth *CF-APK*. They were the last people to see Hinkler alive.

On 28 April 1933 Hinkler's body was found by Italian peasants close to the wrecked Puss Moth up in the Italian Alps, north west of Arezzo, where presumably he had fallen victim to the weather.

After Hinkler's death the Ibis lay forgotten in its shed until discovered in September 1952. It was saved from being scrapped by Henry Sisted, managing director of the Hampshire Aeroplane Club who had it removed to Eastleigh. Sisted intended to restore the Ibis to airworthy condition with a view to putting a modified version into production. During examination of the airframe an amazing discovery

Above *The Ibis was powered by two 40 hp Salmson AD9 radials mounted back to back in tandem above the wing. Cooling of the rear engine must have presented a problem. (Flight photograph)* **Below** *Though the Ibis survived until the 1950s its structure was too deteriorated to warrant restoration and it was scrapped in 1959. (Flight photograph)*

was made. Sewn into one of the wings was Hinkler's original log of the 1928 England-Australia flight; it is now preserved in Australia. The Ibis was exhibited, minus engines, at the Royal Aeronautical Society's Hatfield Garden party on 14 June 1953.

Nothing came of plans to put the Ibis into production and after interest had waned, the airframe was moved from one place to another until it finally turned up at Lee-on-Solent. By 1959 the Ibis had deteriorated beyond repair and after examination by the Royal Aeronautical Society was scrapped the following year.

Data on the Ibis is not available.

Comper CLA 7 Swift

During its five years of existence the Comper Aircraft Co produced five different aircraft types. All but one of them were commercial failures, although they were all fine designs in their own right. The exception was the CLA 7 Swift, which remained in continuous production from 1930 until the company failed in 1934, after 41 aircraft had been built for customers all over the world.

As we have already seen, Flight Lieutenant Nicholas Comper was no stranger to aviation. His aerial baptism occurred in 1912, at the age of fifteen, when he and his brother Adrian had a three-guinea flight in a Farman biplane at Hendon. Both became apprentices with the technical department of the Aircraft Manufacturing Company at Hendon, under Captain Geoffrey de Havilland, and in 1915 Nick

Comper joined the Royal Flying Corps. He underwent pilot training on DH 2s at Castle Bromwich, and after a short period with 57 Squadron was posted to France with 9 Squadron in 1916. There he flew BE 2cs, and it was during this period as a Second Lieutenant that his potential as a designer showed itself. He completely re-rigged his aircraft and successfully squeezed a few extra knots out of it, resulting in the Commanding Officer pinching the faster aircraft for his own use.

Comper remained with the RAF after the Great War and in 1920 he spent a year at Jesus College, Cambridge, reading aerodynamics. Subsequently he served at RAF Upavon, Farnborough and Cranwell, and in 1927 was posted to Felixstowe. While a lecturer in charge of the engineering laboratory at Cranwell, he and some of the staff and pupils formed the Cranwell Light Aeroplane Club in 1923. The four aircraft which this industrious band produced are described in earlier chapters under their own headings, but it is worth mentioning that the CLA 3 was the true forerunner of the CLA 7 Swift. It will be recalled that this parasol monoplane, powered by a 32 hp Bristol Cherub engine, was entered for the 1925 light aeroplane trials and later won the International Speed Race on 1 August with an average speed of 87 mph.

With three fairly successful designs under his belt, Comper resigned his RAF commission in 1929 and with friends, relatives and a local businessman raised £15,800 capital and formed Comper Aircraft Ltd in March the same year. The directors included brother Adrian, who had useful contacts in America, G.A.

The prototype Swift, G-AARX, being flown by Sydney St Barbe at Brooklands on 17 April 1930. Powered by a 40 hp ABC Scorpion the aircraft has the original fin and rudder shape and narrow chord solid wheels. (Flight photograph)

Above *Swift* G-AAZD *with Salmson engine and curved fin. This aircraft was later modified to Pobjoy standard, with taller fin and rudder and fitted with doughnut wheels.* (*Flight* photograph) **Left** *Nick Comper flying Swift* G-AAZF. *This aircraft was first fitted with the Pobjoy P and later flew with the prototype Pobjoy R. Though flying with a Pobjoy the Swift still retains the old-style undercarriage and tail unit.* (*Flight* photograph) **Below left** *Swift* G-ABUA *was later sold in the East Indies and modified with a longer nose to 'improve' its flying characteristics.* **Bottom left** *Pobjoy-powered Swift* G-ABPE *with wings folded. This aircraft was written off in April 1947 after crashing in a field at St Albans.* (*Flight* photograph)

Dawson, a local businessman and owner of Hooton Park aerodrome, Flight Lieutenant J.B. Allen, who had served with Comper at RAF Cranwell and who was shortly to become CFI of the Liverpool & District Aero Club, and A. Moulsdale. The company was set up at Hooton Park aerodrome and work on the prototype Swift began immediately in the far-from-ideal conditions.

The first Swift emerged from the Hooton works in December 1929. At first glance it resembled a well-fed CLA 3, although the wing was mounted directly on the top of the fuselage, in front of the cockpit and in line with the pilot's eyes. The airframe was much cleaner and power was provided by the more powerful 40 hp ABC Scorpion two-cylinder opposed air-cooled engine.

The Comper Swift's fuselage was built in three portions bolted together in order to minimize repair, replacement and transport costs. The front portion was a rigidly-braced wooden structure which would be changed to take different engines of higher power and then be bolted directly onto the middle portion. The central portion of the fuselage extended from the face of the front-spar bulkhead to the rear of the pilot's seat. This portion was also of wood and was rigidly braced. The longerons and struts were of spindled spruce with plywood gussets. The wing centre-section was supported by extending two of the fuselage bulkheads upwards via inwardly-sloping struts, with plywood attached on both sides as bracing. The decking was curved and covered with plywood. The tail section was similarly constructed, except that the decking was completely separate and detachable.

The entire fuselage was fabric-covered and the bolted joints between the section were covered with a strip of doped fabric. By tearing off the fabric and removing the four bolts the entire fuselage could easily be inspected.

The cantilever fin and rudder were built of welded steel tube. The wooden fabric-covered tailplane had a symmetrical aerofoil section and was adjustable on the ground. A short stabilizing strut was located on each side of the fuselage, though the tailplane was virtually a cantilever structure. The control surfaces were unbalanced.

The undercarriage was of the divided type and had a novel, for the time, form of shock absorption. The radius rods and axles were hinged to the centreline. The near vertical struts from the wheels on each side were attached to radius arms hinged at the centre of the fuselage and inside it, so arranged that they could travel only in the vertical plane. When horizontal they rested on stops. At their extremities inside the fuselage they were attached to fixed tubes by rubber cord in tension.

The 40 hp ABC Scorpion was bolted to the ingenious Comper Vibration Absorbing Unit. The engine bearer bolts each passed through and compressed a rubber block which was mounted in such a way that the bolts did not come into contact with the casing of the device. Four of these units were strapped to the fuselage, two at the lower longerons and two on top of two ash bearers. The engine was attached to these units and thus much of the Scorpion's vibration was damped out. A fireproof bulkhead was located between the engine mounting and the fuselage and a 9 gal fuel tank was located behind and above the engine, which was gravity-fed.

The pilot's cockpit was located immediately behind the rear spar. The two most important instruments, the altimeter and the airspeed indicator, were

Above *Non-standard engine cowlings and strut streamlining on Pobjoy Swift G-ABWE for competing in the 1937 King's Cup race.* **Below** *C.A. Butler arriving over Sydney on 9 November 1932 after taking nine days, 2 hr 20 mins to fly from Lympne, Kent to Darwin, Australia, beating the previous record by 1 hr 42 mins.*

mounted on the rear spar in line with the pilot's eyes. Underneath the main panel was a tray for gloves and maps etc. The seat could be adjusted to suit most pilot shapes and in later models a large luggage locker was located behind the cockpit in the top decking for carrying golf clubs and tennis rackets, while another locker, set at an angle just behind the engine, could take a custom-built suitcase.

There were no control wires running externally on the Swift and there were few parts exposed to the slipstream. Part of the engine had to be exposed for cooling purposes, but the entire undercarriage shock-absorbing gear was enclosed within the fuselage. The unladen weight of the prototype Comper Swift was 331 lb, and fully laden it tipped the scales at only 600 lb.

The exact date of the Swift's first flight in January 1930 is not known. The first, trouble-free flight was carried out by the designer and, after the Swift received a clean bill of health from RAF Martlesham Heath, a Certificate of Airworthiness was issued on 16

Top *Gipsy-Swift* G-ABWW, *powered by a 130 hp DH Gipsy Major, was one of three Gipsy-engined Swifts built by Compers for racing. (Flight photograph)* **Above** *The Spanish aircraft designer J. Rein Loring took delivery of the last 1932 built Swift,* EC-AAT, *ferried out to Spain as* EC-W12. **Below** *Post-war Swift survivor* G-ABUS *photographed near Elstree in August 1948. (E.J. Riding photograph)*

April 1930. The prototype Swift was registered *G-AARX*. Eleven days previously the Swift had been demonstrated at Hooton Park on the occasion of the opening of the Liverpool & District Aero Club. Its official debut, though, was on 17 April, when it gave a polished display in the hands of Sydney St Barbe at Brooklands.

A production line was immediately laid down and the Scorpion-powered Swift was offered at £400, ex-works. However, most of the initial production batch of Swifts were fitted with the Salmson AD 9 nine-cylinder engine installed and these were sold for £475. Fitted with the Salmson, the Swift had a cruising speed of 100 mph; the maximum speed was raised to 115 mph, although the tare weight was increased by 80 lb and the range reduced by 85 miles. All other figure remained the same. The operating costs of the Salmson Swift, taking into account airframe and engine maintenance, amounted to 6s 8d for every 100 miles flown. Brian Lewis and C.D. Barnard were appointed United Kingdom dealers and the first production Swift, *G-AAZB*, was sold by them to G.N. Stringer, though the aircraft was probably not delivered to him.

The first export Swift was the eighth built and the last of the 1930 batch. H.L.L. West, a New Zealand architect, took delivery of the Scorpion powered *ZK-ACG*, and it was re-erected and test-flown at Aukland prior to being registered on 10 January 1931. This aeroplane was later re-engined with a Salmson AD 9 and, after having various owners and suffering two bad crashes, *'ACG* finally came to grief in a swamp.

Also serving at Cranwell with Comper in his service days was Captain Douglas Pobjoy, an education officer with one of the Apprentices' Wings. While Comper spent all his spare time designing and supervising the building of the Cranwell Light Aeroplane Club's aircraft, Pobjoy and another team were working on a remarkable seven-cylinder geared radial engine which had an excellent power-to-weight ratio. The first engine, designated P, weighed 100 lb and produced 50 hp at 3,000 rpm.

Comper was so impressed with the P that he designed the CLA 4 biplane around it, with the intention of entering two for the Lympne Trials of 1926. The second CLA 4 was fitted with a Bristol Cherub III. Unfortunately, the Pobjoy P engine suffered a small breakage while under test at Farnborough and only the Cherub CLA 4 competed in the trials.

Pobjoy then built a second P engine designated P 1, weighing 115 lb and producing 60 bhp. The propeller was again driven via a simple reduction gear. This engine passed its tests in 1928 and a limited number was produced by George Parnall and Co.

When Comper designed the Swift he had Pobjoy's engine very much in mind and it was a very simple matter to bolt one of the first P engines into the sixth production Swift, *G-AAZF*, in time for the 1930 King's Cup race. The Scorpion-engine prototype, *G-AARX*, was also entered but neither reached Hanworth's starting line. *'ZF* developed oil frothing trouble during the flight down from Hooton and was withdrawn.

Meanwhile Pobjoy had developed and perfected the Pobjoy R, a far far superior engine weighing 130 lb and developing 75 bhp, which was to change the fortunes of both Comper and himself. In August 1930 Pobjoy Air Motors was formed, with works conveniently close to the Comper works at Hooton Park. Nick Comper's brother, Adrian, became one of the directors. For the following year's King's Cup race a Pobjoy R was fitted into *G-AAZF*. With Squadron Leader J.M. Robb as pilot, it took sixth place at an average speed of 118 mph and was favourite on the tote. Shortly after the race, Comper confidently took *'ZF* on an Italian tour covering 2,600 miles in a total flying time of 26 hrs. The bill for petrol amounted to £10.

With the marriage of the Pobjoy R engine to the Swift airframe, Comper had a much improved aeroplane with a maximum speed not far short of the RAF fighters of the day. The Pobjoy Swift took on a more sturdy appearance with enlarged fin and rudder and the characteristic doughnut-type airwheels replaced the narrow solid wheels of the Salmson Swift. The Pobjoy gave the Swift a maximum speed of 145 mph, a cruising speed of 120 mph and a more than doubled original climb rate of 1,400 ft/min, yet the all-up weight remained the same at 780 lb. Most of the original batch of Salmson Swifts were later modified to Pobjoy standard and from 1931 the R became the standard powerplant. The Pobjoy Swift was offered at £525 ex-works.

The year 1931 was to be noted for long-distance flights by Swifts. During the course of the year a further eight Swifts were built, all with Pobjoy engines. The first, *G-ABJR*, received its C of A in June 1931 and was delivered to H.C. Mayers, who raced it in the following year's King's Cup race. In 1933 *'JR* passed to Air Taxis based at Stag Lane, Edgware, and ten months later it was sold to Charles Shillingford.

On 28 January 1934, the owner attempted a low-level slow roll over Brooklands. While inverted the pilot lost control and the aircraft dived into the ground, killing him. This was not the first fatality involving a Comper Swift. That dubious honour befell the Irish-registered *EI-AAL*, and was almost predictable. Manco Scally, an official of Irish Sweepstakes in Dublin, had some business matters to settle in Ceylon and the Cape. He decided to fly there — rather ambitious for a pilot with only 40 hrs in his logbook — and, after a few brief familiarization flights in *G-ABPR*, arranged to set off for Ceylon. He began his flight by taxiing down Sackville Street, Dublin and, during his crossing of the Irish Sea, which rarely took him above 20 ft, he narrowly missed a passing ship. His intention was to clear customs at Heston, but by the time he arrived in the general area it was dark and misty and Scally settled for a field near Slough, flying on to Heston the following day. From there he managed to make Lyon

Charles Bell photographed in front of the two Argentinian Swifts, R222 and R232, at Mendoza. R222 was delivered to Comper agent Cyril Taylor in January 1932 and later it became LV-FBA. It still survives. R232 was re-registered LV-YEA. (Cyril Taylor photograph)

in two days but, shortly after leaving Lyon on 21 February 1932, he crashed near the aerodrome at Marseille and was killed.

The first long distance flight by a Swift began on 22 August 1931, when Lieutenant 'Boozy' Byas, FAA, left Heston in *G-ABNH* for a holiday in Johannesburg, in the Orange Free State. His otherwise standard Swift was fitted with an additional 10 gal fuel tank and although the journey was supposed to have been a fairly leisurely affair, the 7,320 miles were covered in ten days, which was almost a record. *'NH* never returned to England, but was sold in South Africa at the end of the year to become *ZS-AEU*. Six months later another Swift, *VR-TAF*, was sold in Tanganyika and was never heard of again.

Three months after Byas departed for South Africa, C.A. Butler set off from Lympne, Kent, on a flight which was to capture the imagination of the aviation world. At Butler's request, Comper produced a special long-range Swift with a total fuel capacity of 42 gals. It also carried a water tank, navigation lights and various other extras which pushed the all-up weight to 1,160 lb — nearly double the empty weight, or the equivalent of three men and 40 lb of baggage. It says much for the Pobjoy engine that, despite the extra weight, the take-off was only marginally longer — 120 yds in 8 secs. Butler's destination was Darwin, Australia, and he landed there on 9 November 1931, taking nine days, 2 hrs and 20 mins, beating C.W.A. Scott's record by 1 hr 42 mins.

Butler then completed a 23,000-mile tour of Australia before the Swift was shipped back to England and sold to Victor Smith, who made three unsuccessful attempts on the England-Cape record held by Amy Mollison. The first attempt ended at St Malo, the second at Oran and the last ended 160 miles from Cape Town when Smith ran out of fuel. The subsequent delay, for refuelling and a patch of bad weather, robbed Smith of a much-deserved record.

Shortly after Butler's Australian flight, Comper seriously considered using the Swift in the mail-carrying role. They reckoned that it could carry a payload of 255 lb or 8,000 letters at ½ oz each. The load distribution of the Swift was so arranged that any or all three of its luggage compartments could be full or empty without shifting the cg beyond the limits. The total space available for mail was 7½ ft³ and operating costs, with a full load at cruising speed of 112 mph, worked out at 0.824d per mile, or 7.25d in terms of ton miles. However, the scheme was not adopted and the vision of hundreds of little aerial postmen never materialized.

Of the remaining 1931 Swifts, *G-ABPY* flew for a while with National Aviation Day Displays and performed manoeuvres in response to radio messages

transmitted by air show spectators on the ground. *G-ABPR* passed through various owners and survived the war, only to be destroyed in the disastrous hangar fire at Broxbourne on 30 June 1947. *G-ABPE* spent a year in Kuala Lumpur, where it was flown by Dr Enid Robertson as *Vital Spark*. In 1936 it was bought by Flight Lieutenant D.W. Atcherley and remained with him until 1943. During his period as Commanding Officer of Number 23 Squadron, Atcherley painted *'PE* night-fighter black, added RAF roundels and the squadron code letters *ZK* and fitted long-range tanks. Thus disguised, the Swift was often used for nocturnal cross-country flights. The Swift also survived the war but, after C of A renewal, in pristine condition, it was crashed in a field near St Albans on 26 April 1947. The wings, undercarriage and various other fittings survived in the author's garage for seventeen years before rotting away.

The final 1931 production aircraft was shipped to Cyril Taylor, the newly appointed Comper agent of Aerofotos, Buenos Aires, registered *R222*. This Swift made world headlines on 9 March 1932. The story goes that Taylor's friend, Charles Bell, was very interested in the Swift but did not believe in the published performance figures. Taylor offered to fly *R222* over the 18,000 ft Andes if Bell would order a Swift on successful completion of the flight. Bell readily agreed and on 9 March Taylor took off from Mendoza bound for Santiago, with the Andes range across his route.

Both Taylor and the Swift made light of the crossing, which was made without oxygen but the flight was marred after a forced landing at Nogales, when Santiago became fogbound. While taxiing after landing at Nogales, Taylor inadvertently crossed a covered ditch which gave way under the Swift's weight, damaging the propeller in the process. A cut-down DH Moth propeller was substituted, enabling Taylor to continue to Santiago.

On 25 March he made the return crossing of the Andes and, in spite of blacking-out, reached Mendoza safely. Bell was as good as his word and ordered a Swift which was duly shipped out from Hooton and registered *R232*. During the summer of 1936 *R222* was shipped to Sweden by its owner, Miss Inga Ahlstrom, but only flew about ten hours in the Stockholm area before returning to Argentina. Some years later it was discovered by Cyril Taylor, re-purchased by him and donated to the Aeroparque Museum at Buenos Aires. While in storage there it was severely damaged by vandals, but was subsequently restored by the military and is currently on display at the Aeroparque Museum.

Swift *R232*, which later changed its registration to *LV-YEA*, was sold soon after Bell's death in a flying accident and its fate is unknown. Taylor told the author recently that no further Swifts were sold in Argentina, despite information to the contrary published elsewhere.

The Comper Swift reached peak production rate during 1931-32, with one aircraft a month emerging from the Hooton Park Works. With the Pobjoy R as the standard powerplant, the type had great potential as a racer. Many of the racing fraternity obviously had the same idea, because no fewer than eight Swifts were entered for the 1932 King's Cup Race.

Earlier that year, in March, the Comper company announced its intention of producing a Gipsy-engined Swift, provided there was sufficient interest. Two orders resulted, one from the British Air Navigation Company at Heston and the other from Flight Lieutenant E.H. Fielden, equerry to the Prince of Wales. The Gipsy Swift did not differ from the Pobjoy Swift other than by its engine installation. The gross weight was increased to 1,130 lb, which gave a higher wing loading, and the tare weight was 730 lb, giving a disposable weight of 400 lb. With the normal weight of fuel totalling 180 lb there was a useful margin for luggage and Comper was quick to stress the Gipsy Swift's suitability as a tourer.

Comper removed the wraps from the two new Swifts only a couple of weeks before the King's Cup, for which both machines had been entered. The Prince of Wales' machine, painted in Guards colours and registered *G-ABWW*, was fitted with a 130 hp DH Gipsy Major, while the other, *G-ABWH*, was powered by the less powerful 120 hp DH Gipsy III. The Prince of Wales' entry in the King's Cup that year promoted particular interest. Comper badly needed a win and the attendant publicity — and if it was a Royal win. . .

The eight Comper Swifts that faced the starter's flag at Brooklands on 7 July were *G-AAZC*, *G-AAZD*, *G-AAZF*, *G-ABJR*, *G-ABTC*, *G-ABUU*, *G-ABWH* and *G-ABWW*. Comper himself flew 'ZD into sixth place, the highest position for the Pobjoy Swifts. The race was won by W.L. Hope in Fox Moth *G-ABUT*, his third King's Cup win, and an easy one. A right royal battle raged for second place and although *G-ABWW* managed to beat the handicapper's calculations by 14 mph, Fielden nearly threw the race away when he failed to cross the finishing line at Brooklands. After he realised his mistake, amidst near hysteria from the crowd and officials, he took off, made a lightning circuit of the aerodrome and crossed the line to clinch second place at an average speed of 156 mph. It was the closest any of Nick Comper's aircraft came to winning this premier air race.

Other Swifts from the 1932 production batch included Miss Fidelia Crossley's *G-ABUA*, delivered

Alex Henshaw taking off from Brooklands in his Swift G-ACGL. (*Flight* photograph)

in March. She was injured in her Swift in July that year and the aircraft was offered for sale in the columns of *Flight* a few months later. It so happened that J.C. Meeuwenoord, one of the first private pilots in the Dutch East Indies, was looking for an aerobatic aircraft with a bit more zip than his DH 60G III, *PK-SAQ*. He purchased 'UA and had it shipped to Java. When re-erected by the Army Air Services at Andir, near Bandung, the Commander of Luchtvaartafdelnig refused to risk any of his pilots to air-test what was to them a very hot little aeroplane, and the owner had to fly it himself. He found the Swift difficult to handle because it persisted in climbing.

The head of the Air Service drawing office felt that the cg was too far aft and suggested that all would be resolved if the Pobjoy engine was moved forward 20 cm. Correspondence with Hooton produced noises of disapproval from Comper, who intimated that if any such modification was made the British Certificate of Airworthiness would become invalid. However, the Dutch authorities gave the go-ahead and the engine was moved forward. This apparently improved the handling qualities and moved the owner to remark that the Swift 'flew like a razor'. When the Dutch East Indies was invaded by the Japanese, Meeuwenoord fled, leaving *PK-SAQ* behind. The Swift was either destroyed on order of the Dutch authorities or taken by the Japanese, for, when the owner returned in 1945, there was no trace of the aircraft.

The Indian Comper agents, the French Motor Car Company of Bombay, Calcutta and Delhi, ordered two Swifts in 1932. There are no records of the first, *VT-ADF*, but the second, *VT-ADO*, was perhaps the most famous Swift of all and was the subject of an entire book.

Alban Ali, a tea planter from Assam who had learnt to fly with the Newcastle Aero Club, had seen articles on the Swift in the aviation press and ordered one on the spot. It was duly shipped out from Hooton and the owner flew it from local polo grounds with

Manco Scally standing by his Irish-registered Swift shortly before his ill-fated attempted flight to Ceylon. (Via John Carroll)

varying degrees of success. He named his Swift *Scarlet Angel* and it returns to our story a little later on.

The Swift demonstrator in 1932 was *G-ABUU* and on 21 April Marc Lacayo left Heston in it for a European tour. He visited Belgium, Holland, Germany, Denmark, Sweden and Norway and allowed several pilots to fly it. This practice led to *'UU* being damaged. A Swedish military pilot attempted to start the Swift without chocks, with no-one in the cockpit and with the throttle half open. Predictably, the Swift leapt forward and turned over on its back. The damage was repaired in time for *'UU* to compete in that year's King's Cup. She still survives, has been lovingly cared for by John Pothecary for many years and is a regular visitor to air shows.

Another survivor is *G-ABUS,* which was originally purchased by Shell Mex. In later years, in common with other Swifts, *'US* was re-engined with the more powerful Pobjoy Niagara and was particularly active in post-war air racing circles. Today, she has just passed into the hands of Captain Roger Bailey, who will strip her down and give her a new lease of life. Yet another survivor from the 1932 batch is *G-ABTC*, which was originally owned by I.C. Maxwell, a director of Pobjoy Airmotors. After years of storage after the war *'TC* was rebuilt in 1956 and is currently owned by Peter Channon.

Another Swift enthusiast was Richard Shuttleworth, whose memory is today perpetuated by the Shuttleworth Trust at his home at Old Warden. He took delivery of *G-ABWE* in 1932, not long after he had learnt to fly on his DH 60 *G-EBWD*, which still lives at Old Warden. In November 1932 he decided to enter the Swift for the Viceroy Challenge Trophy Race, the Indian equivalent of the King's Cup. He managed to persuade George Stead, a close friend

who had given him some instruction in the Moth, to accompany him. Together they visited Hooton, where Shuttleworth placed an order for the third Gipsy Swift, powered by a 120 hp DH Gipsy III. In January 1933, *G-ACBY* and *G-ABWE,* which had been overhauled for the flight to India, were ready for collection. Stead and Shuttleworth flew back to Old Warden in formation, but Shuttleworth had an unfortunate engine failure in *'WE* and the Swift nosed over during the ensuing forced landing. As there was little time before the departure for India, Shuttleworth returned to Comper and bought or borrowed *G-ABPY* for the flight.

On Wednesday 25 January, Stead and Shuttleworth, in *G-ACBY* and *G-ABPY* respectively, left Old Warden for Lympne. They arrived in Delhi just three days before the Viceroy Trophy Race. The 690 mile event was held on 10 February, and amongst the thirteen starters was Alban Ali in *Scarlet Angel*. He was in the course of flying from India to Heston, and had stopped off at Delhi to compete in the race — a rash decision, as it later transpired. The race was won by a local pilot flying a DH Moth, but Stead made fastest time with an average speed of 153 mph. Alban Ali was second fastest at 124 mph but Shuttleworth failed to finish. He was forced to land down the main street of the village when an oil feed broke, covering him and the aircraft with a liberal coating of oil. After some hasty repairs he was able to return to Delhi in time for the post-race celebrations.

Stead was anxious to return to England as he was on very extended leave from the RAF, and he and Ali left Delhi for home in loose formation on 3 March. However, they parted company near Cairo when the *Scarlet Angel* finally quit, the engine's diet of oil and sand finally taking its toll. Stead pushed on while *VT-ADO* was crated and shipped to England. On arrival the Swift was sold to George Errington, who rebuilt it, and it then acquired the British marks *G-ACTF*. In 1950 *'TF* was given a new lease of life when it was prepared for the *Daily Express* race. Generally cleaned up and with streamlined hood and high speed spats, it captured an FAI Class record with a speed of 141 mph. *Scarlet Angel* has recently been restored to prime condition by Alan Chalkley and is now in residence in North Wales.

Shortly after *G-ACBY* returned home it was entered for the 1933 King's Cup race, in which it was flown by F.R. Waller. During the course of the race the pilot forgot to pump fuel to the engine. He side-slipped steeply to lose speed but lost a wing in collision with a tree at Moulton in Northants. Waller recovered from his injuries but the Swift was a write-off.

A few months earlier, in March, the Comper company moved from Hooton to new premises at Heston, which at that time was the hub of light-aviation activity. Comper was hoping for better business with the change of location and, in addition to the Swift, the company was working on three new designs. The Streak and the Kite were specifically designed for racing purposes. The Comper Mouse, however, was a three-seat low-wing cabin monoplane with a retractable undercarriage, which Comper hoped would attract orders from the market dominated by de Havilland and Miles.

Meanwhile, Swifts were being produced at a steady if slow rate, and on 16 March, just before the move to Heston, Comper himself delivered the first Swiss Swift, *CH-351*, to Dr Kurt Tschudi in Zurich. Apparently this aircraft had been specifically modified to accommodate the owner's dog, which had a special compartment to itself. With the change of the Swiss registration system this Swift later became *HB-EXO*, and at some time, probably in 1936, flew out to Addis Ababa where it was captured by the invading Italians. A second Swiss Swift, *CH-352*, was later sold in France and became *F-ANHO*.

Two months later, after flying *CH-351* across the Channel, Comper took Gipsy Swift *G-ABWW* across to France to compete in the Coupe Deutsch de la Meurthe Race, held at Mondesir Aerodrome, Etampes. The Swift had been entered by G. Averseng and had been cleaned up for the event. It was powered by a DH Gipsy Major Special with increased compression ratio, rated to produce 146 bhp. During this flight to France Comper opened up to full throttle for 30 mins, the engine behaving perfectly. As he throttled back to cross the French coast the oil pressure went off the clock and the problem could not be diagnosed before the start of the race on 29 May. Comper was the only British competitor and his was the only high-wing aircraft in the competition. Because of the oil problem he was forced to fly a leisurely course and was one of only three pilots to finish, but at the disappointingly low speed of 149 mph. The aircraft was supposedly capable of 185 mph but, in any case, Comper was outclassed as the winner's speed was 200 mph. After the race it was found that the oil problem could easily have been rectified by simply changing the position of the breather pipe.

About two-thirds of the Swifts produced eventually took up foreign registrations, though some like *SU-AAJ*, were only temporary. *SU-AAJ* was originally *G-AAZD* from the first production batch. Mohamed Hassek Effendi entered it for the Aero Club of Egypt's Oases Rally, a two-day circuit linking scattered oases, which began and finished at Cairo. The race was held on 21-22 December 1933 and Effendi managed to run out of oil half-way round. He made a downwind forced landing in the middle of the desert some 80 miles from the nearest oasis, and had to spend one night sleeping rough until he was rescued by an Avro 626 of the Egyptian Air Force.

One of the most-travelled Swifts and the only example to appear in the USA, was Gipsy Swift *G-ABWH*. This was shipped to America in December 1933, supposedly as *NC27K* and raced at Roosevelt Field. Swift *'WH* returned to Britain in 1935 and in July 1939 was sold in Australia, where it became *VH-ACG*. It was rebuilt by the owner E.R. Burnett-Read at Adelaide in 1963 and is still airworthy today.

Final production Swifts went to Italy (*I-RASN* and *I-REBO*) and *VP-KAV* went to Kenya. The last Swift built for a British customer was *G-ACML*, first owned and successfully raced by Flight Lieutenant Pope of Air Service Training at Hamble. Swift *'ML* was later sold in Belgium as *OO-OML* but crashed on 5 June 1935. The final 1934 Swift went to India as *VT-AEY* and the last Swift built, the 41st, went to France as *F-ANEY*. This Swift survived until that country was occupied by the Germans, when it was stacked on end and burnt in company with many French light aircraft.

By June 1934 the Comper company was in financial distress. No orders for the Mouse were forthcoming, although it is understood that a number of airframes had been started. Despite urgent and frequent reshuffles of the Comper board, the company ceased trading in August 1934. The resignation of the directors, including Comper's own, were accepted and with new management and design staff Heston Aircraft was set up, producing the Heston Phoenix the following year.

Why did the Comper Aircraft Co fail? Nick Comper left the RAF in 1928 to seek his fortune in the stormy sea of commercial aircraft manufacture and in the wake of a world depression. Unfortunately, none of his aircraft were commercial. It was always his boast that he never produced a bad aeroplane. This was undoubtedly true; his aircraft were original and well made but at that time there was hardly a market for single-seat high performance aeroplanes. Secondly, Comper was solely cut out as an aircraft designer. C.G. Grey, *The Aeroplane*'s editor, said, 'he should never have attempted to enter the commercial sphere for which he was temperamentally unsuited. So long as he confined himself to the technical aspect he did very well. But in the managing director's chair he never seemed to fit happily'. Grey knew Comper well, for the designer and his family used to holiday with the Greys.

Comper retained his independence to the end. The only design to materialize after the downfall of his company was the CF 1 which he was looking forward to test-flying shortly before his tragic death in a Hythe street in June 1939, at the age of 42.

Comper CLA 7 Swift data (Scorpion)	
Span	24 ft 0 in
Length	17 ft 8½ in
Height	5 ft 3½ in
Wing area	90 ft²
Empty weight	470 lb
All-up weight	730 lb
Maximum speed	100 mph
Cruising speed	85 mph
Stalling/landing speed	35 mph

Comper CLA 7 Swift data (Salmson)	
Span	24 ft 0 in
Length	17 ft 8½ in
Height	5 ft 3½ in
Wing area	90 ft²
Empty weight	515 lb
All-up weight	780 lb
Maximum speed	115 mph
Cruising speed	100 mph
Stalling/landing speed	35 mph

Comper CLA 7 Swift data (Pobjoy R)	
Span	24 ft 0 in
Length	17 ft 8½ in
Height	5 ft 3½ in
Wing area	90 ft²
Empty weight	540 lb
All-up weight	985 lb
Maximum speed	140 mph
Cruising speed	120 mph
Stalling/landing speed	40 mph

Comper CLA 7 Swift data (Gipsy)	
Span	24 ft 0 in
Length	18 ft 4 in
Height	5 ft 3½ in
Wing area	90 ft²
Empty weight	610 lb
All-up weight	1,130 lb
Maximum speed	165 mph
Cruising speed	140 mph
Stalling/landing speed	50 mph

Comper C-25 Autogiro

In 1931 the Cierva Autogiro Co Ltd, formed in March 1926, commissioned the Hooton-based Comper Aircraft company to build a single-seat sporting Autogiro. At the time the Comper firm was

busy producing the successful Swift single-seat sporting monoplane and a standard Swift airframe was probably taken off the production line and modified to incorporate a large streamlined rotor mast to which was fitted a three-bladed rotor with flapping and drag hinges equipped with mechanical drive starting. Short, high aspect ratio stub wings were fitted and braced to the top fuselage longerons. The tailplane, which began as a fairly simple affair, underwent frequent changes after flight trials began. The Comper C-25 was powered by a 75 hp Pobjoy R radial engine.

Flight testing of the C-25 was carried out at Hooton Park aerodrome by A.H. Rawson during the winter of 1931-32 and it was soon apparent that the Autogiro had insufficient lateral control. After fitting several different tail units of varying area, Comper finally settled for a triple fin arrangement and it was in this configuration that it was flown from Heston, to where

Above left *The Comper C-25 Autogiro photographed on 20 February 1932 after a mishap at Hooton Park aerodrome. The rotors and port winglet are badly damaged.* (P.T. Capon photograph) **Below left** *Unique flight photograph of the Comper C-25 Autogiro in early form flying over Hooton Park in April 1932. A larger temporary fin has been added but more area still was required.* (P.T. Capon photograph) **Above** *Nick Comper flying the Comper C-25 Autogiro in its later form, with triple fin tail unit. The C-25 was the fastest Autogiro of its day.* (*Flight* photograph) **Right** *This photograph of the Comper C-25 shows the very tall rotor mast, the wide-track undercarriage and the short-span stub wings.* (*Flight* photograph)

the company had moved in March 1933, to Hanworth for a press demonstration on 27 April in company with the Cierva C 30 *G-ACFI*. Though the C-25 was on view it was not demonstrated and later in the afternoon Comper flew it back to Heston.

The Comper firm had no intention of putting the C-25 into production though it would have built examples to order had they materialized. The sole example built was registered *G-ABTO*, though it probably never carried these marks. During the latter part of its life the C-25 was painted with an attractive bird motif along the length of the fuselage, designed by P.T. Capon. The C-25 was probably scrapped at Heston after the parent company was absorbed by Heston Aircraft in 1934.

No data available.

Angus Aquila

'To any experienced eye the machine was obviously all wrong. The great humped fuselage behind the tiny airscrew, and the arched back over the flat-bottomed fuselage, were bound to make the controls very bad. Old as well as young designers still refuse to learn that the back of a fuselage should be straight and the belly curved...'

The above, written in January 1931, is not a quote from an official accident report, but the kind of ill-informed comment readers of *The Aeroplane* came to expect from its editor, C.G. Grey, writing about small aeroplanes. His surmise concerning humped-back aircraft with flat bottoms is, of course, nonsense; one has only to recall such craft as the Short Seamew, the Westland Wyvern and today's BAe Hawk to appreciate this.

The aircraft to which Grey was referring was the unusual creation designed and built during 1930 by wealthy young A.L. Angus of Sutton Benger, Chippenham. The Angus Aquila low-wing single-seater had a fuselage of mixed constuction. The forward section was contructed of square steel tubing to which was attached the 40 hp Salmson AD9 radial engine. A wooden box structure ran aft and formed a kind of keel upon which the rest of the fuselage was built on light formers. To this structure sheets of 20-gauge aluminium were screwed which, the designer claimed, were non-structural. The tail unit was a fabric covered welded steel tube frame, the tail-plane being braced to the fin by two small struts.

The wooden wings were of RAF 34 section and were fabric covered with plywood-covered leading

Above The Angus Aquila taking off from Hanworth early in 1931 with designer A.L. Angus at the controls. (The Aeroplane photograph) **Below** *A.L. Angus stands in front of his Aquila at Hanworth in 1931. He was to die in the aircraft on 21 March that year. (The Aeroplane photograph)* **Bottom** *Another view of the Angus Aquila being flown by its designer at Hanworth in early 1931. Note the low thrust line of the 40 hp Salmson radial engine. (The Aeroplane photograph)*

edges. They were braced with wide-chord inverted V-struts and could be folded back alongside the fuselage for road transport or for hangaring. Folding was via rear-spar hinge-points; the ailerons folded upward to clear the fuselage and the inboard wing trailing edges folded downwards.

The substantial-looking undercarriage consisted of two divided legs braced from a central inverted cabane truss. Goodyear doughnut-type wheels provided the only springing.

The Aquila owed much of its odd fuselage profile to the installation of the uncowled Salmson radial. This was mounted on a steel tube framework and flanged plate just inches above the wing chord-line and well below the fuselage centreline. Fuel was gravity-fed from a 5½ gal tank installed forward of the cockpit.

Registered *G-ABIK*, the Aquila was completed around Christmas 1930. In January it was taken to Hanworth where Angus began taxiing trials. The first flight probably took place in February and there is little doubt that its designer, who had only about fifty flying hours, found his aeroplane difficult to handle. It was probably very difficult to control longitudinally, as the elevators were very small. It also appears to have had a high stalling speed.

On 21 March 1931 Angus made a particularly bad take-off from Hanworth and, at a height of around 150 ft, side slipped and then dived into the ground from a left-hand turn. Whether this was the first stage of a spin is not clear, but Angus was killed and the Aquila was destroyed.

After the official enquiry C.G. Grey continued speculation about the cause of the accident: 'This may have been due to Mr Angus' lack of experience in the somewhat intricate business of designing low-wing monoplanes; adequate elevator control at low speeds is difficult to get with these types. Mr Angus was a most amiable young man, and there are so few young men of his type who want to build experimental machines and have the money with which to do so, that his neglect to take advice from people who could have saved him from wasting his life is the more to be regretted.'

Angus Aquila data	
Span	not available
Length	not available
Height	not available
Wing area	not available
Empty weight	488 lb
All-up weight	700 lb
Maximum speed	not available
Cruising speed	not available
Stalling/landing speed	not available

RAE PB Scarab

Formed in 1922, the Royal Aircraft Establishment Aero Club at Farnborough had produced the Zephyr and Hurricane in 1922-23, both described elsewhere in this book. Further enterprise was shown by the club during 1930-31 when it produced the PB Scarab. Designed by P.G.N. Peters and C.R. Brewer, from whose names the initials derived, the Scarab looked very much like a single-seat Widgeon and also had a marked de Havilland look about it, which was hardly surprising because the mainplanes and tailplane came from an unidentified DH 53.

P.N.G. Peters was the RAE Aero Club's Honorary Secretary and C.R. Brewer was responsible for the design and stress calculations for the Scarab. Other members directly concerned with the aircraft were Manning Harris, J. Young and W. Baker. After all eight RAF DH 53s were struck off RAF charge in 1927 the RAE Aero Club, under the leadership of Peters, had converted several of the aircraft for private use. Doubtless the wings and tail unit of the club's Scarab came from the club's spares stock or were cannibalized from an unconverted aircraft.

The Scarab's fuselage, though, was of original design, being of wooden construction and covered with plywood. The designers concentrated on providing the pilot with an excellent field of view. In addition they were looking for a low landing speed and good short take-off and landing performance. Thus a high wing position was chosen and, with a thin centre-section placed in line with the pilot's eyes, the Scarab afforded excellent forward vision.

The DH 53 wings were shortened to 30 ft span and were rigged with 5° sweepback. A cut out in the wing gave the pilot good upward vision and the view directly downwards each side was unimpaired. The wings were of wooden construction and were fabric covered. All control surfaces were designed as large as possible in order to give good control at low speeds and for ease of storage the wings were foldable.

The Scarab was fitted with a 1,228 cc Bristol Cherub III engine, rated at 32 hp at 3,200 rpm. Registered *G-ABOH* the Scarab was first flown in February 1932 by Flying Officer H.H. Leach, probably from RAE Farnborough.

Above *Looking rather similar to the Westland Widgeon II the Scarab utilized DH 53 wings and tailplane.* **Below** *The Scarab with wings folded. When rigged for flight wing sweepback was somewhat less, at 5 degrees!* (Via A.J. Jackson) **Bottom** *The Scarab survived the war but tragically it was scrapped soon afterwards.* (Via A.J. Jackson Collection).

From 1938 until the end of World War Two the Scarab was stored at Farnborough and in 1945 it was scrapped.

RAE PB Scarab data	
Span	30 ft 0 in
Length	21 ft 0 in
Height	6 ft 9 in
Wing area	127 ft²
Empty weight	not available
All-up weight	650 lb
Maximum speed	78 mph
Cruising speed	not available
Stalling/landing speed	32 mph

Miles M1 Satyr

There cannot have been many aircraft that were conceived by a husband and wife team in a room above a shop, yet that is how the Miles M1 Satyr was evolved in 1931. F.G. Miles, aged 28, had recently married, and his wife Maxine contributed greatly to the draughting and stressing of this pretty aeroplane. The Satyr owed much to the earlier Miles-designed Southern Martlet of 1929 and Miles' first aircraft, the uncompleted Gnat, built in 1926. One question that immediately springs to mind is the curious name chosen for this almost fighter-like biplane. The dictionary defines 'Satyr' as a class of Greek woodland deity in human form with horse's ears and tail, which seems hardly applicable. Don Brown, for so long a stalwart of the Miles company, suggests that some friendly critics referred to the Miles design as a satire on contemporary service aircraft, and this may well have led Miles and his wife to name their aircraft thus.

After completion of the design work in the makeshift drawing office over the Sevenoaks shop, the job of building the Satyr was entrusted to Parnall Aircraft at Yate, in Gloucestershire. Miles had earlier carried out some test-flying for this company, and at that

moment in time George Parnall had no aircraft of their own under construction.' Both Miles and his wife supervised each stage of construction, and the diminutive biplane was ready for testing in August 1932.

Described by *Jane's* as a single-seater high performance light aeroplane, the Satyr was of all-wood construction and powered by the popular and successful seven-cylinder 75 hp Pobjoy R radial engine. The fabric-covered unequal-span wings (21 ft upper and 18 ft lower), were of normal construction with plywood stiffened leading edges. Frise ailerons were fitted to the top wings only. The wings were attached to the steel tube centre-section, which was supported by two N-struts wire-braced inwards to the fuselage. The interplane I-struts consisted of two plywood-covered verticals of spruce. The forward fuselage was a ply-covered box structure with wooden girder construction aft of the cockpit. Fabric covered the light stringers and formers. The cantilever tailplane was adjustable in flight by means of a lever that moved over a notched quadrant in the cockpit, and had unbalanced elevators. The cross-axle undercarriage utilized Dowty shock absorbers and the tail skid comprised a steel leaf spring. The Satyr weighed only 594 lb empty, and had an all-up weight of 900 lb.

Shortly after the uneventful first flight in August, *Flight* published a brief but highly compli-

Above and below *Two photographs of the Miles M1 Satyr taken at Yate in 1932 before covering. Note the plywood-covered wing leading edges, forward fuselage and fuselage underside.*

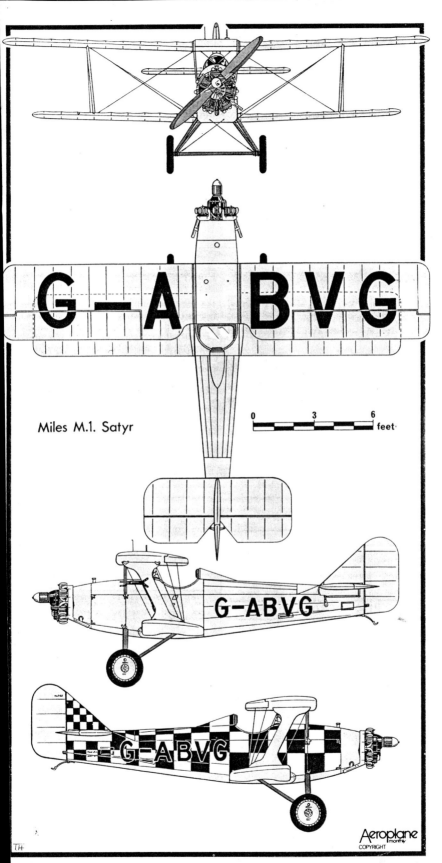

Miles M.1. Satyr

G—A BVG

0   3   6 feet

G-ABVG

G-ABVG

mentary handling report. The Satyr's 1,400 ft/min climb rate and pilot visibility during the climb were praised, as well as the general lack of blind spots. *Flight* considered that the controls were well harmonized, even in steep turns at speeds as low as 50 mph. No vicious tendencies were noticed in spins, and the report concluded; 'the Satyr is joyous to fly and had unusually reassuring factors of safety. We hope that the next time we take it up the petrol tank breather will be arranged so as not to ruin our complexion during inverted flight, because on this aeroplane it is positively wicked to stay wheels downwards for more than a few seconds at a time'. F.D. Bradbrooke of *The Aeroplane* was similarly enthused when he flew the machine.

One of the few modifications made to Satyr was the moving of the fuel tank from the centre-section to a location just behind the engine. The Satyr was allotted the civil registration *G-ABVG*, and a Certificate of Airworthiness was issued on 1 February 1933, shortly after Air Ministry trials at Martlesham Heath.

By this time Miles had moved on to greater things. The previous year, not long after the Satyr's first flight, he was flying from Yate to Shoreham in order to show the aircraft to his parents when he dropped in to Woodley, near Reading, for lunch. During this visit he met Charles Powis, of Phillips and Powis, owners of Woodley, and the two of them discussed Miles' plans for a new two seat monoplane he envisaged. The outcome of this meeting was that Miles joined the Phillips and Powis Company in October 1932 and the prototype Miles M2 Hawk was built using their facilities. The first Hawk, *G-ACGH*, made its maiden flight on 29 March 1933, flown by Miles, and the rest is history.

Miles had little time by this stage to play with the Satyr, which he had designed purely for his own pleasure. For some while the Hon Mrs Victor Bruce had been pleading with Miles to sell her the aircraft, and by April 1933 it had passed to her company, Luxury Air Tours. A month or two earlier she had joined forces with the British Hospitals Air Pageants,

Top *The Satyr photographed at Yate in 1932, where it was constructed by George Parnall. Note the over-sized wheels, which may have been taken from another aircraft.* (Via A.J. Jackson Collection). **Above** *The Satyr shortly after completion, with the fuel tank located in the wing centre-section.* **Below** *John Pugh about to take off for an aerobatic demonstration in the Satyr in 1933.*

a flying circus, not unlike Cobham's outfit, run by J. McEwan King and led by C.W.A. Scott, which was to tour the length and breadth of Britain throughout 1933. Mrs Bruce had undertaken to provide two aircraft. One was the Miles Satyr and the other was a time-expired Fairey Fox bomber she had picked up for £12 10s, including its Curtiss D-12 engine, from Coley's scrap yard. She then spent £1,000 on smartening up and certificating the Fox, which was registered *G-ACAS*, and in company with the Satyr, which had been repainted in a smart red and white

chequer-board scheme, it was ready for the first Hospitals Pageant at Hayes on 8 April 1933.

Flight Lieutenant Pugh AFC, already well known for his display flying at the RAF Pageants at Hendon, had been selected to fly the Satyr, whilst Mrs Bruce flew the Fox on pleasure flips.

Mrs Bruce's event in the Pageant was billed as the 'Fox Dive' in the programme. The procedure was to give two passengers at a time the thrill of their lives by diving at 250 mph to within 50 ft of the ground, the flight terminating with a beat-up of the crowd. John Pugh usually carried out a highly polished pro-gramme of aerobatics and then indulged in 'bombing a bucking Ford Car', which always went down well with the crowd.

The Satyr and the Fairey Fox performed together for a few months until 14 July, when disaster overtook the Fox. Pugh was flying in the vicinity of Little-hampton when the aircraft caught fire. He managed to land at Ford, Sussex, and escaped with an injured ankle, but the Fox was a write-off. Its place was taken by a Moth, probably *G-EBWI*, and the show went on, until disaster struck again a month or two later. The Hospitals Pageant had arrived at a small field just outside Stafford and Mrs Bruce wagered with Pugh that she could land the Satyr in a smaller place than he could land the Moth. Already quite a crowd had assembled to watch the day's proceedings, and they had their money's worth. Mrs Bruce approached the field low and slow, and was about to pass over the boundary of the field, which was lined with houses, when there was a loud crash and everything suddenly came to a halt. She thought she had hit one of the houses, but in fact she had flown into a bank of telephone wires. These wires arrested the Satyr very effectively, and for a while the aircraft hung in its cradle. Then there was a sudden and not entirely unexpected twang and the wires gave way, depositing the aircraft and pilot in a heap 15 ft below and four yards within the field's boundary.

Mrs Bruce won her bet and escaped unscathed, except for a lump on the head and an £80 bill from the telephone company. The Satyr came off worst, and was not insured at the time of the accident. Because of this its existence was not acknowledged by Lloyds, and consequently its subsequent history is shrouded in conjecture. According to Mrs Bruce's book, *Nine Lives Plus,* the Satyr was repaired. She told the author that the Satyr was 'half sold' to a 19 year-old Japanese who took it to Belgium. During a flight in that country it is alleged that he inadvertently entered a spin from which he failed to recover. The pilot was killed and the aircraft was written off. Certainly the Satyr was removed from the civil register in Sep-tember 1936, but its ultimate fate needs confirma-tion.

Miles M1 Satyr data	
Span	21 ft 0 in (upper wing) 19 ft 0 in (lower wing)
Length	approx 17 ft 0 in
Height	not available
Wing area	117 ft²
Empty weight	594 lb
All-up weight	900 lb
Maximum speed	125 mph
Cruising speed	110 mph
Stalling/landing speed	44 mph

Wee Mite

During the summer of 1933, holidaymakers in the Channel Islands would have had their peace shattered by the irritating whine of a high-revving ABC Scorpion engine. Anyone loitering in the vicin-ity of Vazon Bay on the island of Guernsey would have known that the noise came from a light aircraft — the locals would have known the aircraft as Mr Noël's Wee Mite.

The Wee Mite was the brainchild of Cecil Noël, a well-known figure in local circles. During the First World War Noël had flown as an NCO pilot with the Royal Flying Corps and afterwards had set up the Guernsey Aero club at a field at L'Erée, where he was chief flying instructor. Later on, in 1929, Noël began experimenting with aerofoil sections with a view to building a glider of his own design. The glider was built and its success inspired its designer to build a powered light aircraft around the glider wing, which had an aerofoil section with a sharp leading edge, a flat underside as far as the rear spar and a downturn toward the trailing edge.

Thus work began on the Wee Mite in April 1932 with the assistance of local motor engineer, Harold le Parmentier, whose name is often mistakenly used to prefix the Wee Mite. Other local helpers were garage owner Harold Duquemin, Eddie Edmunds and Harry Kaines.

The Wee Mite was a tandem two-seat high-wing braced monoplane powered by a 30 hp ABC Scorpion engine. The aircraft's structure was quite advanced for the time. The welded steel fuselage was fabric covered. The wings folded back, Moth-fashion, about a fixed centre-section. Each wing was braced with a vee lift strut and a cutout in the centre-section trailing edge allowed easy access and good visibility for the rear cockpit occupant. The Wee Mite's fuse-lage was exceptionally deep, which allowed plenty of clearance for the propeller. Louvred engine cowlings were probably engineered by the motor mechanics of

the team. The Wee Mite had distinctly de Havilland-ish wire-braced fin and rudder.

Cecil Noël made the first flight from the sands of Vazon Bay, but severe engine vibration prevented anything more ambitious than a few hops. The mounting for the Scorpion was lengthy and this undoubtedly amplified the excessive vibration which the flat-twin produced. Surprisingly, Noël thought that the problem could be cured by fitting a large-diameter home-made propeller. On the first attempted flight the propeller tore itself assunder just as the Wee Mite was leaving the ground. The decision was made to replace the dubious Scorpion with a 40 hp nine-cylinder Salmson radial. Contemporary reports say that the nose was lengthened for this installation but in fact the reverse took place and it was shortened by 12 in. Though this maintained the stiffness of the forward fuselage, the centre of gravity was now too far aft. This was remedied by modifying the front spar root end fittings to provide 18 in of sweepback.

It was a proud moment for both Noël and Parmentier when, in September 1933, they success-fully flew a round trip of the island, staying aloft for 50 mins. On 24 April 1934 the Wee Mite was registered *G-ACRL*, though it is uncertain as to whether the registration letters were ever worn by the aircraft. No pictures survive showing the Wee Mite so marked.

According to Noël, test flights revealed that the Wee Mite flew perfectly and could even be flown hands off. It was reputedly dived to 230 mph, though this seems extremely doubtful. The big rudder made the Wee Mite 'a bit fierce' laterally but the aircraft could be flown under full control down to speeds of 30 mph without stalling. Though there were plans to put the Wee Mite into production 'at a price within the means of an average car-owner', the economic climate of the early 1930s was hardly conducive to

Above *The Wee Mite complete but with the wings yet to be covered. Standing from left to right are, Harry Kaines, Harold le Parmentier, Cecil Noël and Eddie Edmonds.* (Via John Pothecary) **Below** *Another view of the Wee Mite nearing completion, fitted with the 30 hp Scorpion engine.* (Via John Pothecary) **Bottom** *A rare photograph showing the Wee Mite airborne. On 15 September 1933, C.W. Noël made a 50 min flight around Guernsey.* (Via John Pothecary)

Three photographs of the Wee Mite showing it before and after modification. The picture at top left shows it in revised form, with 40 hp Salmson, lengthened nose and with sweepback on the wings.

such plans and the machine was dismantled. It was not rebuilt and its exact fate is still a mystery.

Wee Mite data	
Span	31 ft 0 in
Length	21 ft 0 in
	20 ft 0 in
	(Salmson)
Wing area	not available
Empty weight	650 lb (Salmson)
All-up weight	970 lb (Salmson)
Maximum speed	92 mph
Cruising speed	75 mph
Stalling/landing speed	not available

Pickering Pearson KP 2

The name of Captain K. N. Pearson has already cropped up in a previous entry and he is primarily remembered as the designer of the Henderson-Glenny HSF II Gadfly, designed during the winter of 1928-29. Pearson's involvement with aviation stretched back to World War One, when he was a pilot with the Royal Flying Corps, and it continued with employment with Hawker where he became involved with the Kingston torpedo bomber, later to become the Horsley.

Some time before designing the HSF II Gadfly, Pearson had been working on a revolutionary kind of aileron control known as the Pearson Rotary, though commonly known at Brooklands as the oyster aileron. Each oyster was mounted on a skewed pivot on a shaft located midway between the front and rear wing spars and was connected to the control column, which was so arranged with a differential device that, when making a turn, the inside oyster assumed a negative angle of 40°, while the outside oyster remained almost stationary.

The Pearson Rotary aileron was first fitted to

The Pickering-Pearson KP 2 photographed at Hanworth in late 1933, before the fin was fitted. There was no rudder, directional and lateral control being effected by the wingtip Pearson rotary ailerons. (The Aeroplane *photograph)*

Top *A 40 hp Aeronca E117 engine driving a pusher propeller powered the KP2.* **Above** *The KP2 was registered* G-ACMR *and construction was completed in October 1933. It is doubtful if this wooden experimental single seater ever flew. (The Aeroplane photograph)*

G.L.P. Henderson's Renault-engined Avro 548, *G-EBAJ*, a three seater more often than not used for banner towing. Fitted with the new ailerons the Avro performed well and Pearson fitted a pair to the second Gadfly, *G-AARJ*, thus upgrading the aircraft to Mk II status. During September 1929 *G-AARJ* was appraised by the Aeroplane & Armament Experimental Establishment at RAF Martlesham Heath. Apart from adverse criticism of the Gadfly's weak structure the A&AEE did not particularly like the rotary ailerons. The pilot's report ran: 'Not very effective. . . in the event of a wing dropping while taking off opposite stick must be applied coarsely. Even then the lag is considerable and the reaction is violent. . . Nothing much happens until full control is given and then the reaction is fairly violent. . . There is nothing dangerous about the flying and manoeuvring of the aircraft once the action of the controls is appreciated but they are strange to a pilot used to standard aircraft'.

Undeterred by this report Pearson persisted with his rotary aileron and, after the Henderson-Glenny concern fizzled out shortly before Henderson's death in an air crash in July 1930, he collaborated with G.L. Pickering to design and build an ultra-light aircraft featuring his novel form of aileron control.

The new aircraft, designated the Pickering-Pearson KP 2, was built in great secrecy at Hanworth during 1933 by Pickering. The experimental, single-seat monoplane pusher was fitted with a 40 hp Aeronca E 117 engine, mounted above the fuselage behind the open cockpit on a steel tube pylon structure, the wooden two-blade propeller barely clearing the top of the fuselage. In fact, judging by the accompanying photographs, the propeller fitted would *not* rotate without striking the top decking! The crude-looking fuselage was plywood covered except for the forward fuselage decking, which was stringered and fabric covered. The wings and tail surfaces were fabric covered. Small doughnut-type wheels were fitted to a simple axle-type undercarriage and a metal tailskid was fitted.

The fuselage was angular with slab sides, top and bottom, becoming wedge-shaped at the tail, the tail-plane being bolted to the flat-topped surface. Directional control was via the rotary ailerons, which were now discus-shaped and somewhat more refined than the scallops fitted to the Gadfly. There was no rudder, though it was intended to fit a fin; however, there is no evidence for fittings for this on the photographs.

The open cockpit was fitted with a large control wheel rather than a control column. Though the aileron controls ran through the wing the elevator cables were carried externally.

The KP 2 was registered *G-ACMR* and was completed in October 1933. The author has seen no evidence to suggest that it flew and the curious little aeroplane was scrapped in 1935.

Kay Gyroplane

Among the several private individuals who experimented with light autogyros during the 1930s were David Kay and his associate John Grieve. For some years they had experimented with rotary-winged craft in the wilds of Scotland until they had developed an ingenious method of varying the incidence on rotor blades. The system was first installed in a light, single-seat autogyro, the Type 32/1, built at Perth and extensively tested at RAF Leuchars during 1932. The autogyro was flown by its inventor and by an Air Ministry pilot. The performance proved very promising and a second machine followed.

The Kay Type 33/1 was a single-seat autogyro powered by a 75 hp Pobjoy R radial engine. Construction was undertaken by Oddie, Bradbury and Cull Ltd at Eastleigh aerodrome near Southampton during 1934-35.

The all-metal fuselage of the Kay Gyroplane was a rectangular structure embodying four straight lengths of steel tube, spaced by struts of the same material, and welded at all joints. There was only one bulkhead; this acted as an engine mounting and as the anchorage for the oleo undercarriage legs and front members of the cabane structure.

The undercarriage was of the divided type. The longstroke oleo legs were attached at their upper ends to the upper fuselage longerons, and were hinged at the lower ends to the bottom longerons by steel tube

Above *The unregistered Kay Type 32/1 Gyroplane was built at Perth and tested at RAF Leuchars during 1932.* **Below** *The sole Kay 33/1 Gyroplane was built at Eastleigh and first flown on 18 February 1935* (Flight *photograph*)

axles and radius rods. Dunlop airwheels were fitted, with Dunlop-Bendix brakes. The tailskid was of the leafspring type.

The adjustable tailplane was made of Duralumin tubing with pressed ribs. The fin and rudder were of similar construction and the entire empennage was fabric covered.

The geared seven-cylinder Pobjoy R engine drove a four-bladed propeller. The fuel and oil tanks were located in the fuselage. The four rotor blades were of parallel chord and were built of swaged steel tube and Duralumin former ribs, covered with plywood and fabric, with built-up wooden tips. They had aluminium fairings over the root ends which extended to the hub knuckles and the rotor hub was carried on a steel pylon which consisted of four steel vees anchored to the top fuselage longerons. The rotor was driven via an extension of the engine crankshaft through the rear engine cover to a dog clutch, and by a short shaft to a friction cone clutch and thence by a bevel box to the vertical drive shaft. Drive was through a 7:1 reduction gear — a throwout mechanism disconnected the rotor if this overran the drive. The rotor blades could be altered through 8° incidence in the air and the rotor head could be tilted for lateral control. For hangaring, the rotor blades could be folded, two forward and two aft.

The cockpit was located immediately behind the rotor pylon. The autogyro had spectacle-type hand controls, with push-pull action for fore and aft control and rocking action for lateral control. The rudder pedals had toe brakes.

The Kay Gyroplane was completed in the winter of 1934-35 and was first flown on 18 February 1935, from Eastleigh. A second aircraft, registered G-ACVB, was not completed. The Kay Gyroplane was not put into production and the sole example, G-ACVA survives today and is exhibited at the Glasgow Museum of Transport. During the war it was stored and during the immediate post-war years was made airworthy and flown once more. Its last known flight took place in August 1947. It was later stored at Scone until moved to Glasgow.

Top *The Kay Gyroplane was powered by a 75 hp Pobjoy R radial engine. Note the position of the pitot tube, near the starboard wheel.* (*Flight* photograph) *The Kay Gyroplane spent many post-war years stored at Scone but in later years has been on exhibition at the Glasgow Museum of Transport.*

Weir Autogiros

Several companies and individuals worked towards producing a marketable ultra-light rotorplane during the 1930s, taking the Cierva Autogiro as their starting point. The Kay Gyroplane and the Hafner AR III concentrated on variable incidence rotor blades and are described elsewhere. The Weir series of Autogiros was based entirely on Cierva principles and featured jump start rotor systems where, by speeding up the rotors before starting and then suddenly releasing the drive and increasing the rotor incidence, the Autogiro would leap vertically a few feet into the air.

The Scottish firm of G. & J. Weir Ltd was founded in 1871 by George and James Weir. James Weir had two sons, William Douglas (later Lord Weir of Eastwood), and James George (later Air Commodore). While William Douglas Weir served on various aviation boards and councils, his brother took a more

Kay Gyroplane Type 33/1 data	
Rotor diameter	22 ft 0 in
Width	7 ft 6 in
	(rotors folded)
Length	7 ft 11 in
Height	7 ft 8 in
Empty weight	624 lb
All-up weight	850 lb
Maximum speed	not available
Cruising speed	not available
Stalling/landing speed	not available

Above *The unregistered Weir W 2 was built at the Weir company's Cathcart Glasgow works in 1933 and first flown in March 1934 by Alan Marsh. (Flight photograph)* **Below** *The unregistered Weir W 2 was powered by a Weir 50 hp flat-twin engine designed by C. G. Pullin. It is currently displayed at the Museum of Flight in Edinburgh. (Flight photograph)* **Bottom** *Built during 1936 the unregistered Weir W 3 was powered by a Pullin-engined 50 hp Weir engine. (Flight photograph)*

practical interest in aviation. He learned to fly in 1910 and during World War One became Controller of the Technical Department of the Air Ministry. He was instrumental in setting up the Cierva Autogiro Company Ltd in England in March 1926, when he became one of its directors. Later, in 1939, G. & J. Weir Ltd was to acquire a controlling interest in the Cierva concern several years after Cierva was killed in an air crash.

Though the Cierva company did not manufacture Autogiros itself, it granted licences to companies such as Avro, de Havilland, Comper and Parnall. G. & J. Weir received Cierva licence number C 28 in 1932, and with designer C.G. Pullin produced four small Autogiros between 1933 and 1936, after which the company turned its attention to developing a practical helicopter.

The Weir company's first Autogiro, the single-seat W 1, was completed at the Cathcart Glasgow works in mid-1933. It had a two-bladed rotor and was fitted with flapping and drag hinges and a direct-control rotor head. The W 1 was strenuously tested and during the following year a modified version, the W 2, was built. This second aircraft was built primarily to test the Autodynamic head which allowed jump take-offs.

The W 2's fuselage was a wooden monocoque structure of circular section. The empennage was similar to that of that of the Cierva C 19, with a cranked tailplane and large stabilizing fins above and below the rear fuselage. The streamlined pylon was braced with two faired tubular struts and the two rotor blades were hinged to the rotor hub. The rotor hub controls were connected to a short control column which hung down into the cockpit and the rotor could be started by means of engaging the Borg & Beck car-type clutch on the engine flywheel; this was done by pushing the control column forward. The rotor brake, engine clutch and wheel brakes were all grouped conveniently on the control column. It

was impossible to start the rotor with the brakes applied, nor could the brakes be left on when the rotor was speeded up for take-off. Both rotor blades could be folded back for storage.

The undercarriage was of the divided type, with two long-stroke oleo-pneumatic shock-absorber legs fitted with small-diameter low-pressure wheels. The tailwheel was steered by the rudder bar.

The Weir W 2 was powered by a Weir 50 hp flat-twin horizontally-opposed air-cooled geared engine which developed 45 hp at 3,300 rpm and 50 hp at 3,500 rpm.

The unregistered W 2 was first flown by Alan Marsh at Abbotsinch in March 1934. In 1936 the Autogiro was fitted with new tail surfaces and rotor pylon, later incorporated into the W 3. After another rigorous test programme the W 2 was acquired for the Science Museum in London and stored. It is currently on exhibition at the Museum of Flight in Edinburgh, doped blue with silver tail and pylon.

The Weir W 3 emerged during the summer of 1936, having been built at the Weir works at Cathcart, Glasgow. In July that year it was taken to Abbotsinch and demonstrated to *Flight* magazine. Developed with the close co-operation of Cierva, the W 3 was powered by a special 50 hp four-cylinder air-cooled inverted engine designed by C.G. Pullin and built by G. & J. Weir.

The W 3 had a wooden fuselage of simple box-type construction. The wide-track undercarriage had a long travel to absorb near vertical landings. The two-bladed rotor and rotor head were carried on an unfaired steel tube pyramid situated immediately forward of the cockpit. The rotors were not foldable but could easily be detached for transport by road. The tailplane consisted of three large vertical fins, the centre unit being fitted with a rudder.

Testing of the W 3 was entrusted to Alan Marsh and, after initial tests, the Autogiro was first publicly demonstrated at Hounslow Heath on 23 July 1936, together with the Cierva C 30 *G-ACWF*, which was also fitted with the Autodynamic rotor head. Though the W 3 had earlier shown itself capable of jumping 20 ft into the air before continuing in more or less forward flight, misbehaviour on the part of the engine prevented Marsh from demonstrating the Weir's full potential.

It was the intention to put the W 3 into production for around £500, but this did not materialize.

The final Weir Autogiro was the W 4, which followed in December 1937. Similar in appearance to

Above right *The Weir W 3 was first publicly demonstrated at Hounslow Heath on 23 July 1936 and could be jumped 20 ft vertically into the air on take off.* (*Flight* photograph) **Right** *Close-up view of the Weir W 3 cockpit. Note the hanging rotor hub control.* (*Flight* photograph)

The Weir W 4 photographed at the Weir works at Cathcart, Glasgow, in December 1937. (J. & G. Weir Ltd)

the W 3, this aircraft had a taller, faired pylon, smaller triple tail unit and a more orthodox undercarriage. During early trials the W 4 refused to take-off. Alan Marsh recalled for *Flight* that the boffins were called in and, 'they just climbed the pylon, altered two screws and, taking straight off, I turned on my back without any effort.'

The W 4 never came to anything and soon afterwards the Weir company turned its attention to producing a practical helicopter. There were plans to convert the W 4 into the W 5 helicopter but designer Pullin decided to use twin rotors on outriggers, in the manner of the Focke-Achgelis Fa 61, and only parts of the W 4 were used in the helicopter. This first flew in June 1938, piloted by the chief designer's son, R.A. Pullin. The much larger W 6 followed, making its maiden flight in October 1939. The two machines made history as the first practical British helicopters. In mid-1940 Weir ceased its aviation interests, which were taken over by Cierva. At that time Pullin took over as managing director.

Weir W 2 data	
Rotor diameter	28 ft 0 in
Width	not available
Rotor area	not available
Length	15 ft 0 in
Empty weight	not available
All-up weight	not available
Maximum speed	not available
Cruising speed	not available
Stalling/landing speed	not available

Weir W 3 data	
Rotor diameter	18 ft 7 in
Width	not available
Rotor area	not available
Length	14 ft 4 in
Empty weight	not available
All-up weight	650 lb
Maximum speed	not available
Cruising speed	80 mph
Stalling/landing speed	not available

BAC Planette/Drone and Super Drone/Kronfeld Monoplane

In a previous chapter it was mentioned that the Itford gliding trials of 1922 did not herald a widespread interest in gliding in Britain as had been hoped. Though the sport flourished in France and Germany it was to be another eight years before it was to begin to take a hold in this country. When it did, the exponents had to go to Germany for their gliders. One of the leading lights of the embryonic British gliding fraternity was Charles Lowe-Wylde, a Newcastle man in his late twenties. He was convinced that there was no need to import gliders from Germany, and set to work to design his own. His first design resembled the German SG 38 primary glider. It was named the Columbus and it was built in a few weeks by members of the Kent Gliding Club. It was first flown in February 1930, thus earning a place in

Above *A BAC IV fitted with wheels for auto-towing launching. Without wheels the glider was known as the BAC IV. It had a 40 ft 9 in wingspan and weighed around 200 lb empty.* **Below** *Lowe-Wylde's performing Planettes during a demonstration at Hanworth on 27 December 1932.*

aviation history as the first primary glider to be designed and built in Britain.

In the meantime Lowe-Wylde formed the British Aircraft Co Ltd and set up works at an old brewery in Maidstone, Kent for the purpose of building gliders. A second glider the BAC II followed in the summer of 1930. Along similar lines to the first craft, the new glider had a box-spar fuselage instead of an open girder type. A month later the wings and tailplane of the BAC II were used in the construction of the BAC III, a single-seat secondary glider with an enclosed fuselage, which was first flown in October 1930. Later, the BAC III was fitted with wheels for aero-towing behind a car, Lowe-Wylde realising that Britain had precious few slope-soaring sites to keep

pace with the growing sport.

Another single-seat secondary sailplane emerged from the Maidstone works in 1930, a version of the BAC III with longer, tapered wings of 40 ft 9 in span, and which weighed just 200 lb empty. This too was fitted with mainwheels for towed launches from behind a car and in this form it was known as the BAC VI. In a little over a year Lowe-Wylde had built several gliders to his own design and, incidentally, his FAI Gliding Certificate was the first to be issued by the Royal Aero Club.

In April 1931 Lowe-Wylde brought out a tandem-seat glider, virtually a two-seat version of the BAC VI but with a much-modified fuselage and fitted with standard aircraft-type undercarriage. The 40 ft 10 in

Above *BAC VII gliders during construction at the Maidstone works, circa 1931-32.* **Below** *Colonel the Master of Sempill flew Drone G-ADJP from Berlin to Croydon and back on 2 April 1936. The flight took 11 hr and used 25s worth of petrol.* (*Flight* photograph)

wings were interchangeable with both the BAC VI and IV, and following standard practice was car-launched, a system which allowed instruction to be carried out on flat terrain. Then, in 1932, history repeated itself, exactly ten years after Itford. It will be recalled that several Itford gliders were developed into motor gliders and if ever there was a glider crying out for an engine it was the BAC VII. By deleting the rear cockpit of the VII and mounting a 600 cc Douglas engine driving a pusher propeller on a pylon above the wings, the BAC VII Planette was born.

Before the Planette took to the air Lowe-Wylde had taken three BAC VII gliders to perform at the 13th RAF Pageant, held at Hendon in June 1932. There, three 24 Squadron DH 60 Moths towed the trio to 1,000 ft and released pilots Flight Lieutenant Edward Mole, Squadron Leader J.J. Williamson and Flight Lieutenant L.T. Keens. The three gliders glided in vee formation in a wide sweep around the aerodrome and then landed to enthusiastic applause. Lowe-Wylde and his gliders had arrived — in style. The gliders also toured with Alan Cobham's National Aviation Day Tours introducing many hundreds of

people to gliding. In 1931, 1,300 people had been towed up into the air behind L-W's Bentley on the end of a 500 ft steel cable to a height of 300 ft. Even Barbara Cartland had been towed around the country in a BAC VII bearing her name, with Edward Mole as pilot.

The first Planette, Number 1, was first flown during the autumn of 1932 and by November several others had been built. On 27 November 1932, Numbers 1 and 2 were demonstrated at Hanworth before an impressive gathering. The two Planettes were expertly flown by Lowe-Wylde and Captain E.D. Ayre. The Douglas engines were still mounted on crude tubular steel pylons but their impressively low flying speeds of between 15 and 40 mph in far from ideal conditions created intense interest, so much so that Lowe-Wylde staged another demonstration with four Planettes at the same venue on 27 December.

On 13 May 1933 Lowe-Wylde took Planette Number 1 up from West Malling to demonstrate it before members of the Maidstone Aero Club. After flying for some 20 mins the aircraft suddenly began to dive at full power. At an alarmingly low altitude the aircraft recovered but began a steep turn, still with power, and then spiralled into the ground. Lowe-Wylde was killed instantly. He had been overworking for some time and he had complained of feeling unwell while driving by car to Maidstone. At the subsequent inquest a verdict of accidental death was recorded. Lowe-Wylde contributed enormously to British gliding and his death occurred at the very time when his basic Planette design was to bring a new interest to the motor-glider movement.

Living in Britain at the time of Lowe-Wylde's death was Robert Kronfeld, a young Austrian who, during the 1928 Wasserküppe gliding meeting in Germany, had discovered that by flying a glider into currents of rising warm air it was possible to gain height. When gliding was revived in Britain a couple of years later, the British Gliding Association in con-

junction with the *Daily Express* asked Kronfeld over to Britain to demonstrate the skills of thermal and slope soaring. On Lowe-Wylde's death Kronfeld took over the BAC company and set to work to modify the Planette Number 2 into a more practical aeroplane. In its new form with the rear cockpit faired over and with a streamlined engine pylon it appeared at the opening of Speke Airport, Liverpool in July 1933.

In 1935 Kronfeld reorganised the BAC company and, after moving into larger premises at the London Air Park at Hanworth, formed the British Aircraft Company (1935) Ltd, with himself as Managing Director. The existing Planettes, Numbers 2, 3 and 4, were modified and in their new guise were called Drones. The third and fourth aircraft were registered *G-ADSB* and *G-AENZ* and the first pure Drone was aircraft Number 5, registered *G-ADMU* in August 1935.

With the arrival of aircraft Number 7, registered *G-ADPJ* in the same month, the Drone became a little more sophisticated. The 600 cc Douglas engine gave way to the 750 cc Douglas Sprite which produced 25 bhp at 4,000 rpm and 19 bhp at 3,000 rpm, driving a two-bladed wooden propeller. Folding wings gave the Drone a folded width of 10 ft and longer ailerons gave better lateral stability. The Drone's centre of gravity was moved forward 2 in in the lengthened fuselage and all the control surfaces were mass-balanced. The fuel capacity was increased to 6 gal giving the Drone a still-air range of 300 miles. A locker was located behind the forward-folding pilot's seat.

Constructionally the Super Drone, as the improved aircraft became known, was basically similar to the Planette. The wooden wing was in two sections joined on the centreline and carried above the fuselage on two wooden pylons built up from the fuselage deck. The fuel tank was located in the centre-section.

The wings were braced with parallel struts on either side of the fuselage. They were made to fold by

Above *This early production Drone was fitted with a cockpit canopy and is seen flying from Hanworth early in 1936. (The Aeroplane* photograph) **Below** *The Kronfeld Trainer being demonstrated hands-off at Hanworth in 1936, in company with Drone* G-AEDC. (*Flight* photograph)

means of an auxiliary spar which carried the rear spar root hinges out some distance from the centre-section. When the wings were folded back they were supported by a jury strut and stays were fitted to brace the wingtips from the tailplane spar. The fabric-covered wings had plywood leading edges and long, narrow-chord ailerons.

The ply-covered fuselage was a wooden rect-angular structure with a domed decking. The pilot's cockpit was located forward of the wing, thus affording him excellent all-round visibility. The cross-axle undercarriage consisted of two small steel-tube vees and a steel-tube axle. The only springing was provided by the low-pressure wheels.

The Super Drone was immediately popular with novices and experienced pilots alike. Because of its low cruising speed (60 mph) it could be flown in poor visibility quite safely. Fuel consumption was in the region of 1¾ gal per hour, and with a landing speed of 22 mph in still air, the Super Drone certainly had great potential. The selling price in November 1935 was a mere £275.

The Drone proved too that it was reliable. This was

Two views of the Kronfeld Monoplane G-AESG, powered by a 30 hp Carden Ford. It first flew on 7 May 1937 from Hanworth, flown by Robert Kronfeld. (Flight photographs)

demonstrated in sensational fashion on 2 April 1936 when *G-ADPJ* was flown from Croydon to Berlin and back in eleven hours; the cost of petrol amounted to £1 5s. The pilot was BAC Chairman Lord Sempill. The man in the street, the potential customer, was able to see the same aircraft displayed at Selfridges a week later. Robert Kronfeld had already flown the Drone to Paris and back on 6s worth of fuel and oil and 1936 was to prove to be the year of the Drone, twenty being built at Hanworth. In addition the type was licence-built in France by the Société Française des Avions Nouvelles of Issy-les-Moulineaux, of which Kronfeld was technical director. In Belgium the Drone was licence-built by the Société Gantoise des Avions sans Moteur for school use at Ghent. One

or two Drones found their way further afield, a couple apparently ending up in India.

During 1936 Kronfeld produced a complete family of three trainers starting with a non-flying ground-trainer from which a pupil could graduate to a simple primary-glider-type trainer. Finally, at the top of the range, there was the two-seater, the Super Drone, which looked very similar to the Shackleton-Lee Murray SM-1 and was designed as a Drone replacement. These three new designs came into being after Kronfeld renamed BAC as Kronfeld Ltd.

The ground-trainer was a simple stick-and-string apparatus consisting of a single spruce-beam fuselage upon which sat the fledgling pilot. A Ford engine was carried on an intricate steel tube structure which also carried the undercarriage. The wings and tail were of steel tube, though the ailerons were wooden; the whole was fabric covered. The flightless trainer had an adjustable throttle which could be progressively altered as the pupil's proficiency increased and, though the trainer could taxi at speeds of up to 50 mph, it had no inclination to take off. To lessen the chance of damage from ground looping, pram-like wheels were fitted to the wingtips. The first ground trainer was demonstrated in August 1936 and about half a dozen were sold.

By fitting the ground-trainer with Drone wings the flying trainer was produced to take the fledgling birdman on to the next stage of his training. It had an incredibly low landing speed of 14 mph and, like the ground trainer, cost £195 to buy.

Shortly after the Kronfeld company was formed an improved aircraft named the Kronfeld Drone de Luxe was introduced. This was powered by the 30 hp Carden-Ford water-cooled four-cylinder engine, Sir John Carden's conversion of the Ford car engine. In order to take a large-diameter propeller, the Drone's pointed top decking had to be removed and a flat top substituted. In addition, a bungee-braced undercarriage replaced the earlier design.

The first conversion was carried out on *G-AEEN*, which was distinctively painted in red and adorned with Dragon's teeth and eyes on the aircraft's nose by the great Heath Robinson. Because the propeller tips turned so close to the Drone's structure the engine noise was totally unacceptable. Kronfeld cured the problem by fitting slightly swept-back wings. In addition he moved the propeller 6 in aft and introduced slotted ailerons. The Drone de Luxe's performance was only marginally better than that of the Super Drone: there was an increase of only 3 mph to a maximum speed of 73 mph and an improvement of 5 mph to the cruising speed. The rate of climb, however, was improved from 380 ft/min to 480 ft/min and the range was increased to 340 miles.

Though 1936 had been an excellent year for the

Kronfeld company the following year was to prove disappointing. A number of orders were lost through late delivery and the company was a little shaky financially. The final Drone built was *G-AFBZ*, registered to Lord Sempill in September 1937 and powered by a 35 hp flat-four Ava 4A-02 engine.

As sales of the Super Drone and de Luxe dropped during 1937, Kronfeld was working on a replacement two-seater. Known as the Kronfeld Monoplane, it is doubtful whether the aircraft flew other than as a single seater. Though broadly similar in appearance to the Drone family the Monoplane was a totally different animal. Gone were the straight utility lines and square-cut features of the Drone. The wings and tail unit were rounded and widely-faired V-struts had replaced the Drone's parallel lift struts. In addition, the parallel-chord wings had dihedral and there was a wider gap between wings and fuselage. The fuselage too was wider and, whereas the Drone's pylon-mounted engine had been integral with the fuselage, the Monoplane's 30 hp Carden-Ford was mounted on a wire-braced steel-tube structure together with the wing. The tailplane was attached to the fin at about a foot above the fuselage and had larger control surfaces than those of the Drone. The undercarriage was of the divided leg type with rubber in compression shock absorbers mounted on struts which ran to the wing centre-section.

The Kronfeld Monoplane was built by the Hanworth-based General Aircraft Co. After obtaining an Authorisation to Fly on 7 May 1937, the aircraft, registered *G-AESG*, made its first flight from there on the same day. The pilot of the Monoplane was Kronfeld. On 9 May *G-AESG* was flown to the Royal Aeronautical Society's Garden Party at Heathrow.

Plans to power the Monoplane with a 55 hp Weir engine do not appear to have materialized. Though work started on a second aircraft, registered *G-AESH*, it was not completed when Kronfeld Ltd went into receivership on 24 September 1937. Both *G-AESG* and the uncompleted airframe were acquired by C.H. Latimer-Needham, and they remained at his Gerrards Cross Phoenix Works until destroyed in a fire in 1943.

A number of Drones survived the war, though of the fourteen survivors only seven were to fly again — and not all of those with official blessing. Three airframes survive at the time of writing. Drone *G-AEDB,* first registered in March 1936 to G. Scott-Pearce of Perth, is currently flying at Duxford after restoration by Captain Mike Russell. Drone *G-AEJR* is stored at Thetford by Gerry Eastell, having originally been registered to L.A. Clarke of Doncaster in July 1936. And finally, *G-EAKV*, first owned by E. Crossley in January 1937, is currently owned by Mike Beach and kept at Brooklands.

BAC Super Drone data (Douglas)	
Span	39 ft 8 in
	10 ft 0 in
	(wings folded)
Length	21 ft 2 in
Height	7 ft 0 in
Wing area	172 ft²
Empty weight	390 lb
All-up weight	640 lb
Maximum speed	73 mph
Cruising speed	65 mph
Stalling/landing speed	22 mph

Kronfeld De Luxe Drone data (Carden-Ford)	
Span	39 ft 8 in
	10 ft 0 in
	(wings folded)
Length	27 ft 10 in
Height	not available
Wing area	172 ft²
Empty weight	460 lb
All-up weight	720 lb
Maximum speed	75 mph
Cruising speed	62 mph
Stalling/landing speed	28 mph

Kronfeld Monoplane data	
Span	39 ft 8 in
Length	21 ft 2 in
Height	7 ft 0 in
Wing area	172 ft²
Empty weight	390 lb
All-up weight	640 lb
Maximum speed	73 mph
Cruising speed	65 mph
Stalling/landing speed	28 mph

Aeronca 100

America was late in entering the ultra-light aeroplane field, due largely to the ready availability of large numbers of cheap Curtiss OX-5 engines. During the late 1920s, though, the Aeronautical Corporation of America, Aeronca for short, built 112 single-seat, open-cockpit, high-wing Aeronca C-2 monoplanes. Powered by the 26 hp Aeronca E-107A two-cylinder, horizontally-opposed, air-cooled engine, these little aircraft could cover 100 miles at a cost of one US dollar. When they went into production at the Cincinnati factory, Aeronca became the first American company to build and market a truly light

Above *Bill Thorn flying the imported Aeronca C-2 G-ABHE in 1931. The open cockpit single-seater was powered by a 26 hp Aeronca E-107A engine. In its later years it was converted to a glider.* **Below and bottom** *Aeronca C-3 G-ADSP was one of sixteen C-3s imported to Britain and erected at Hanworth. It flew initially as a demonstrator before joining other C-3s at the Hanworth-based London Air Park Flying Club. (*Flight *photograph)*

aeroplane. Credit for the C-2's design originated with the Roche-Dohie monoplane of 1926. Aeronca acquired the design and then re-engined the aircraft before modifying it slightly for ease of production. As the C-2 it enjoyed limited success in America.

Following close on its heels came a two-seater version which, with a 36 hp E-113 engine and retaining the open cockpit, became the C-3. As a two-seater it found a ready market and around 200 were built. In 1935 the design was taken a stage further when the cockpit was enclosed, the razor-back fuselage was made rounded, the tail unit changed to a rounded shape, and refinements such as brakes were offered.

Shortly after the C-2 took to the air in America in October 1929, an example was imported into Britain by Colonel Ormande Darby and registered *G-ABHE* in December 1930. After it was erected at Croydon the aircraft was airtested and subsequently demonstrated by S.A. 'Bill' Thorn. The little aircraft attracted a great deal of interest and Colonel Darby was prompted to import a batch of sixteen C-3s from America. The first two to arrive came via the Aeronca company's Canadian subsidiary. Aircraft *CF-AYC* became *G-ADSO* and *CF-AYB* was registered *G-ADSP*; both became UK demonstrators. Earlier, one other C-2 had been imported and registered *G-ABKX* by Colonel Darby, but it was sold abroad in May 1931.

In 1935 Light Aircraft Ltd acquired a licence to build the Aeronca C-3 in Britain and J.A. Prestwich Ltd began licence-building the Aeronca C-113C engine as the JAP J-99. In April 1936 the Aeronautical Corporation of Great Britain Ltd was formed to acquire the assets and goodwill of Light Aircraft Ltd, and the Walton Works at Peterborough were acquired from Frederick Sage and Co Ltd — a firm that had built aircraft during World War One. A production line of Aeronca C-3s was laid down and the first aircraft emerged toward the end of that year.

Peterborough-built Aeroncas differed from the American C-3 in a number of minor points. Known as the Aeronca 100, the first example was registered *G-AENW* in November 1936.

The Aeronca 100 had a welded steel fuselage consisting of five nearly parallel longerons forward and three which ran from the back of the seat aft to the tail-post. The forward section of the fuselage was rectangular and it faired to a smooth curve towards the tail. The wings were anchored to the single top longeron which formed the apex of the triangular-sectioned aft fuselage.

The wings were built in two sections and consisted of two solid spruce spars. The wing section was Clark Y. On American-built C-3s the fabric-covered wings had interchangeable Duralumin ailerons and double wire drag-bracing. British-built Aeroncas were fitted with wooden ailerons because flutter had been experienced with the metal units. The tailplane was a welded steel framework covered with fabric, with interchangeable elevators. The fin was built integral with the fuselage.

The divided-type undercarriage consisted of two steel axles, hinged at their inner ends to two short oleo shock absorbers inside the fuselage, and fitted with standard airwheels. The JAP engine was suspended on three points on a welded steel tube mounting that was built integral with the fuselage.

The pilot and passenger were accommodated side-by-side in a closed cockpit below the wings in somewhat intimate conditions. Upward vision was via transparent panels in the wingroots. Luggage could be carried in a compartment behind the seat and entry to the cabin was via a single door on the passenger's side.

British-built Aeroncas were constructed with fuselage tubing of greater gauge than those built in America, and the materials used were of higher specification. In addition, static mass-balance weights were fitted to the ailerons and rudder. These changes added a further 34 lb to the empty weight, increasing it to 569 lb. The first Aeronca 100s were offered for sale at £395 ready to fly.

Unfortunately, production at Peterborough exceeded demand and, sadly, production ceased after six months, when 24 airframes had been completed. Aircraft were test flown and then stored subject to sale. Most were eventually disposed of to Aircraft Exchange & Mart Ltd and resold.

In addition to the standard Aeronca 100 model, two further versions were produced by the Peterborough firm. The Peterborough Ely 300 and 700 had 10 in wider fuselages and were built with two doors. Two Peterborough 700s were built; *G-AFLT* and *G-AFLU* both flew with the local Peterborough Flying Club during 1939. *G-AFLT* was scrapped in 1941, its registration letters later being used by *Flight* magazine's Miles Gemini after the war. The second Peterborough 700 survived the war to fly first with the Blackpool Flying Club and then with the Denham-based Speedbird Flying Club before being cannibalized at Farnborough in November 1952.

The sole Peterborough 300 was built in 1938 and registered *G-AEVE*. It was evaluated by the Aeroplane & Armament Experimental Establishment at RAF Martlesham Heath during the winter of 1938-39. The flying and handling qualities were regarded as good though the ailerons were considered heavy and it was thought that the aileron control system had excessive friction. As with many JAP engines, a dead spot was encountered between 1,400 and 1,600 rpm. After the A&AEE had done its work *G-AEVE* joined other Aeroncas at the Peterborough

Flying Club until the outbreak of war. After the war *G-AEVE* donated its wings to Aeronca 100 *G-AEVT*, rebuilt by Arthur Ord-Hume and Paul Simpson during 1948-49.

Aeronca 100s were mainly operated by the Peterborough Flying Club, the London Air Park Flying Club (which had six) and by a number of private owners. Three were sold in Australia and when civil flying ceased in the autumn of 1939 most of the twenty or so survivors were put into mothballs for the duration of the war. Some mouldered away, while others served as instructional airframes with Air Training Corps units. With the return of peace, eleven Aeroncas flew again and, at the time of writing, two survive in airworthy condition.

Below *Post-war photograph of Aeronca 100* G-AEVS *flying near Denham in March 1950.* (E.J. Riding photograph) **Bottom** *The sole Peterborough 300, built in 1938 and registered* G-AEVE *and pictured here during evaluation by the Aeroplane & Armament Experimental Establishment at RAF Martlesham Heath during the winter of 1938-39.* (Via Terry Heffernan)

Aeronca C-2 data	
Span	36 ft 0 in
Length	20 ft 0 in
Height	7 ft 10 in
Wing area	142.2 ft²
Empty weight	426 lb
All up weight	700 lb
Maximum speed	80 mph
Cruising speed	65 mph
Stalling/landing speed	32 mph

Aeronca C-3/100 data	
Span	36 ft 0 in
Length	20 ft 0 in
Height	7 ft 10 in
Wing area	142.2 ft²
Empty weight	569 lb
All-up weight	1,005 lb
Maximum speed	95 mph
Cruising speed	87 mph
Stalling/landing speed	35 mph

Carden-Baynes Scud III Auxiliary

Anyone passing Woodley aerodrome by car just before dusk on the evening of 8 August 1935 would have seen what appeared to be a glider taking off without the assistance of a cable or tow-line, and would then have watched it climb to 5,000 ft in about 15 mins. If they had pulled up by the roadside, switched their engine off and watched the glider return, they would probably have been mystified. For without an engine visible the glider would have passed silently overhead to land back at Woodley.

Dr J.P. Dewsbery had just landed after taking the Carden-Baynes Auxiliary up on its first powered flight. The noisy 250 cc Villiers two-stroke engine had automatically retracted into the wing pylon after the engine had stopped, thus allowing the Auxiliary to perform as a normal glider, without the extra drag of the engine and propeller.

This ingenious idea was the brainchild of L.E. Jeffrey Baynes, whose series of Scud sailplanes were in full production at the Abbott-Baynes Sailplane Works at Farnham in Surrey. Baynes' Scud I became the first British sailplane to soar for one hour, in the hands of Flight Lieutenant Edward Mole. In 1935 a Scud II had been taken to a record altitude for a glider of 8,750 ft, with Mungo Buxton as pilot. In 1934 Baynes had been approached by Sir John Carden, a distinguished engineer and technical director of Vickers-Armstrong Ltd who was then in charge of the company's tank designs for the Army. Sir John wanted a self-launching glider in order to be independent of other people for launching on soaring flights. L.E. Baynes took up the challenge and, after estimating the weight and power required, discovered that the sailplane would require a far greater wing span than the Scuds and that the power required to lift such an aircraft off the ground could be obtained from a small engine of 250 cc. A single-cylinder two-stroke Villiers of around 9 hp driving a pusher propeller would, he reckoned, do the job nicely.

The fuselage of the Auxiliary was designed with a low pylon to take a cantilever wing, and the pylon had to be large enough to accommodate the engine and

propeller during gliding or soaring flight. In order that the propeller would be clear of the fuselage when running, the engine had to be inverted to raise its thrustline. The engine was mounted on a tubular steel structure hinged at its base and extended or retracted by a worm gear. For retraction the propeller needed to be aligned by the hand starter so that it would lie within the pylon.

Work on constructing the Auxiliary began at Farnham during the winter of 1934-35. The aircraft was of all-wood construction, the fuselage being built of plywood and planed spruce, the wings having plywood leading edges and fabric-covered control surfaces. The tapered wing had a pronounced camber but it was flat on the underside at the root where it joined the fuselage. With this arrangement the wing spar was quite deep and consequently very strong. Towards the wingtips the aerofoil section changed to one of small chord and thickness, with reflex curvature. This progressive change of section and angle of incidence ensured that the central portion of the wing stalled first. A gentle dropping of the nose during the stall was further assured by the trailing edge of the wing being nearly straight, though the leading edge swept back, adding the certain measure of stability inherent in tail-less aeroplanes. The ailerons were differentially operated, in order to avoid adverse yawing moments. The wings were removable and the entire aircraft could be dismantled in a few minutes for transport by trailer. The Auxiliary was finished in natural varnish on the woodwork with wings and tail surfaces clear doped, the engine cowling and the petrol tank above the crankcase being painted gold.

When construction was completed, the Auxiliary was taken by trailer to suitable fields near Farnham where free flights as a pure glider were undertaken. It was necessary to check stability and control before powered flight could be attempted. The Auxiliary was launched in time-honoured fashion, by means of a rubber bungee. The first glide was absolutely perfect: in the still air the Auxiliary glided silently and straight with Baynes and Sir John bounding after it as it floated seemingly for ever across the slightly inclined field.

And so to the first powered flight on the August evening in 1935. Dr Dewsbery was an experienced pilot who had flown many hours on Scuds. Unfor-

Left *The Carden-Baynes Auxiliary, with Dr Dewsbery in attendance. On 8 August 1935 he made the first powered flight in the Auxiliary, from Woodley aerodrome. (The Aeroplane photograph)* **Above right** *The Carden-Baynes Auxiliary was powered by a Villiers two-stroke engine which gave 9 hp at 3,450 rpm. (The Aeroplane photograph)* **Right** *Showing how the Villiers engine retracted into the neck of the Auxiliary's wing pylon.*

Dr Dewsbery standing by an Auxiliary, which has the Villiers engine in the running position. **Below** *The Carden-Baynes Auxiliary, later called the Scud III, reverted to sailplane status in the 1950s, having taken up British registry in March 1949.*

tunately Sir John Carden was away on business and was unable to witness the first powered flight. Under power the Auxiliary climbed to 5,000 ft before the engine was shut off and retracted. Several silent circuits were made before it landed, securing a record all of its own. The Auxiliary became the lowest powered aircraft to have flown at the time.

Two Auxiliary Scud IIIs were built, priced at £250. In addition to Sir John's machine, the Duke of Grafton ordered one in September 1935. But a double tragedy left Abbott-Baynes Sailplanes with two ownerless Auxiliaries. On 10 December 1935 Sir John was killed in a Belgian Savoia-Marchetti S.73 while returning on a Sabena flight from Belgium to Croydon, and the Duke of Grafton lost his life in a racing car accident in Ireland. In addition, the gliding fraternity showed little enthusiasm for powered gliding, and so the two Auxiliaries were deprived of their engines and sold as sailplanes. The Duke of Grafton's machine, completed in December 1935, was sold a year later to L.H. Barber at Norton-on-Tees in Durham. It survived the war and was re-fitted with a Villiers engine and registered *G-ALJR*, a Certificate of Airworthiness being granted in April

1949. In 1953 it was converted back to a sailplane but by the end of the 1950s it had started to deteriorate. It was rescued in 1961 and a syndicate began a leisurely rebuild that was completed in 1976, the Scud taking to the air once more on 20 June. The Scud still flies at the time of writing and is based at Duxford.

Incredibly, after more than half a century, Sir John's Scud is also still airworthy and is flown every so often from its base at Dunstable.

Carden-Baynes Scud III Auxiliary data	
Span	45 ft 6 in
Length	22 ft 6 in
Height	not available
Wing area	120 ft²
Empty weight	310 lb
All-up weight	500 lb
Maximum speed	not available
Cruising speed	35 mph
Stalling/landing speed	not available
	(25 mph as Scud III)

Mignet HM 14 Pou du Ciel

Tucked away in a corner at the 1935 Paris Salon, a diminutive French aircraft, of very odd appearance, attracted considerable attention and comment. Its bereted creator was invariably to be seen and heard enthusing to a continuous stream of intrigued onlookers who somehow identified themselves with the tiny, toylike aeroplane. Little did anyone present, except perhaps its designer, realise the impact that the tandem-winged craft would have on light aviation. Its importance and influence on British light-plane development alone was to have a lasting effect.

The centre of attraction at Paris in 1935 was Henri Mignet's HM 14 Pou du Ciel. To the French it was known as the Sky Louse, named after a popular car, extant in France, which the French had dubbed the Pou-de-la-route. Sky Louse was just a little too earthy for the English, and on the other side of the Channel it was called the Flea. Hoping that his creation would become the cheap airborne vehicle for the layman, Mignet borrowed the soubriquet for the HM 14.

The HM 14 exhibited at Paris was the culmination of more than a dozen years of persistent experimentation punctuated with constant heartbreaking frustrations. Never has the saying, 'If at first you don't succeed...' been more applicable than in the case of Mignet. Before looking at the HM 14 in more detail it is worth mentioning some of Mignet's earlier efforts to produce a simple-to-build, easy-to-fly cheap aircraft for the masses.

Like others before and since, Mignet was fascinated by birdflight. After much study he came to the conclusion that the apparently complicated movement of the birds' wings and tails could be reduced to a few comparatively simple principles and then translated into structures of more or less conventional form, without creating insurmountable engineering problems. Mignet's first aircraft thus attempted to imitate birdflight, though without using flapping wings. What Mignet was trying to achieve was complete controllability in a stallproof aeroplane.

One of Mignet's first aeroplanes was a parasol monoplane devoid of fin and rudder. In place of vertical tail surfaces he substituted a large tailplane with pronounced dihedral. Though not adjustable for incidence it could be rocked around its longitudinal axis. By using this control method Mignet attempted to translate the bird's method of using its tail as a rudder rather than as an elevator. In order to turn to the left, the left hand side of the tailplane was raised by swivelling, thus depressing the right hand side. By adopting this method Mignet hoped that his aeroplane would be spinproof.

Top *Stephen Appleby flying* G-ADMH, *the first British-built Pou to fly. It was flown for the first time on 14 July 1935, from Heston.* (*Flight* photograph) **Above** *Stephen Appleby's Pou after its accident on 29 July 1935 shortly after take-off from Heston.* (*Flight* photograph) **Below** *Appleby's Pou after modification by L.E. Baynes. The wing was rebuilt with thicker spars and given 5 ft extra span; the pivot point of the wing was moved further forward relative to the chord, and the front of the fuselage was redesigned to accommodate most of the Carden engine.* (*Flight* photograph)

The wing, with very large ailerons taking up almost half the span, was of Göttingen 426 section. With the control column held central and moved fore and aft, both ailerons could be raised and lowered together. Lateral movements of the stick

The master himself; Henri Mignet, complete with beret, pictured in one of his own HM14s. (Flight photograph)

produced lateral control. The aircraft was powered by a 10 hp Anzani two-cylinder car engine. The undercarriage consisted of two wheels mounted beneath the extreme nose of the machine, whilst a third wheel was located forward of the tailplane. With the cockpit set very far aft the aircraft had very little prospect of flight and the HM 4 was hopelessly directionally unstable.

Mignet perservered and further designs included a helicopter, the HM 7, and the orthodox-looking — for

Below *This Flea, G-ADSC, powered by a 25 hp Poinsard engine, was built by Mignet in France for Alan Cobham's National Aviation Day Displays Ltd for the 1935 season.* **Bottom** *This Perman-Ford powered Pou was built by E.G. Perman Ltd for F.W. Broughton.* (*Flight* photograph)

Mignet at least — HM 8. This 26 ft span high-wing monoplane was a success and Mignet produced a handwritten book entitled *Le sport de l'air,* which was a complete instruction book on how to build one's own 'Avionette' for around £50, less engine. The HM 8 was equipped with conventional ailerons, elevator and rudder. But Mignet could not cope with conventional ailerons and shortly after it was built he lost control in gusty conditions and the HM 8 crashed.

Convinced that his reflexes were too slow to cope with normal three-axis controls, Mignet concentrated on designing and building an aeroplane with 'natural' controls. There followed the HM 9, with pivoting wings operated differentially, which also crashed, and this was succeeded by the HM 10, which featured a rear-mounted engine and a shaft-driven propeller.

The HM 11, regarded as the first Pou, had a Junkers-type trailing flap to control pitch. The HM 13, resembling the HM 14, had the wing and tail in close proximity, the tail having grown to the same size as the wing. In order to prevent the rear wing from stalling, the front wing had a reflex trailing edge. Elevators had been dispensed with and lateral control was achieved by pivoting the wing, so that instead of pushing down the tail in order to climb one merely pivoted the wing in the direction in which one wanted to go — rather akin to today's weightshift microlight aircraft. Thus, while the fuselage remained level in the climb, the wing angle corresponded with the direction of flight.

Having more or less perfected his unorthodox yet to him logical method of control, Mignet arrived at the HM 14, which was built and flown in 1933. With this aircraft Mignet felt that he had achieved all his objectives; a cheap, easy-to-build aeroplane which could be flown with just the hands, there being no rudder pedals. The HM 14 had reduced the number of flying surfaces to just three; the movable front wing, a fixed rear wing and a big rudder. Having achieved his aims, Mignet wanted to share them with the world. He published another book in which he detailed his early experiments leading up to the HM 14. The book was also an instruction manual and such was its appeal that it soon went out of print. Mignet's adage was that anyone who could put together a packing case could also build a Pou.

Mignet demonstrated the HM 14 wherever he could. During the winter of 1934 he proved beyond doubt that his little machine was not just a fair weather toy. He demonstrated the HM 14 at Orly in a wind gusting to 40 mph and even landed safely with a dead engine. As amateur aviators were frowned upon in France at the time, Mignet must have had a great kick out of landing at Orly, for neither he nor his machine were licenced by the French authorities.

The HM 14 exhibited at Paris in 1935 was powered by a 17 hp Aubier et Dunne inverted two-cylinder, two-stroke in-line engine. Structurally the all-wood Pou was simplicity itself. The wings were constructed of normal spruce box-spars with plywood ribs, covered with fabric. The fuselage was a box frame covered throughout with plywood and the large rudder was a wooden frame covered with fabric. The undercarriage consisted of a metal tube which passed through a slot in the bottom of the fuselage, rubber cord in tension acting as shock absorbers. Two small wheels beneath the rudder were interconnected for steering on the ground. The 4.6 gal fuel tank was located in the wing.

By the time the HM 14 was appearing at Paris a number of Poux were already flying in France and the type was also taking a hold in England. The *Daily Express* had given the Pou many column inches and by so doing had captured the imagination of the man in the street, Mignet's prime target.

One of the first people in England to begin building a Pou was Stephen Appleby. Work began on what was to be the first British-built HM 14 to fly during the winter of 1934-35. Appleby had earlier built a Harley-Davidson-powered HM 8 whilst living in Nice, France, its maiden flight taking place there in December 1931. His HM 14 was built in a small shed owned by Airwork at Heston and it was completed in July 1935. During construction Appleby had the good fortune to be contacted by Sir John Carden who told him that he was working on a conversion of a standard 10 hp Ford car engine to a 30 hp unit suitable for use in a small aeroplane. A Carden engine was duly installed in Appleby's Flea and on the evening of 14 July 1935 he made his first tentative circuits around Heston. Registered *G-ADMH*, the Flea not only made history by becoming the first British Flea to hop into the air but was also issued with Permit to Fly No 1. The permit system was a timely waiving by the Air Ministry, then responsible for

both civil and military aircraft, of many of the expensive restrictions on design and construction. Under the new legislation ultra-light aircraft were allowed to fly without a full Certificate of Airworthiness, providing that they were flown only for sporting purposes and insured against third party risk. This relaxation of the regulations paved the way for a trickle of new ultra-light types and Flea fever was greatly encouraged as a result. On 29 July 1935 *'MH* was publicly demonstrated at Heston for the benefit of the aviation press. Mignet had advised Appleby to put a 5m wing on his machine, unaware that it was

Above *Pou G-AEDN was built at Southend and was originally powered by an ABC Scorpion.* **Below** *The Abbott-built Pou G-AEJD covered with wool tufts and flown by Stephen Appleby. Most of the port half of the front wing is stalled due probably to a certain amount of sideslip.*

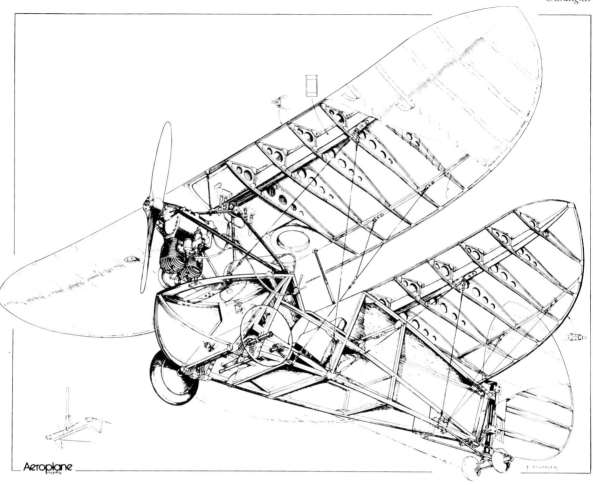

Above *Mignet HM14 Pou du Ciel.* **Below** *The first Cantilever Pou, G-AEGD, built by Abbott-Baynes, with revised bracing and new control system.* (*Flight* photograph)

going to be powered by the much heavier Carden engine. The weather on 29 July was hot and humid and there was little wind. After Appleby took off he was unable to maintain height and was forced to crash land in an adjacent ploughed field, the Flea turning over on its back.

The Flea was rebuilt by L.E. Baynes of Abbott-Baynes Aircraft, a firm which built sailplanes. The work was paid for by the *Daily Express*, which had been keeping its readers fed with progress reports on the Flea throughout its construction. Baynes increased the wingspan to 6m and also thickened the main spar. In addition the front wing pivot point was moved further forward relative to the chord line and the engine was mostly enclosed. In this form '*MH* was flown across the English Channel, at the suggestion of Sir John Carden, on 5 December 1935. The flight from Lympne to St Inglevert, Calais, took 35 mins and Appleby became the first and only pilot to fly a Flea from England to the land of its birth. The journey in the other direction had already been made by Henri Mignet, on 13 August 1935, taking nearly 50 mins in a stiff headwind to complete the crossing. On his arrival the *Daily Express* sponsored a tour of seaside resorts and the die was cast. The first British Pou club was formed that October at Leicester.

The Leicestershire Flying Pou Club had fifty members. The Air League of the British Empire translated Mignet's book into English as *The Flying Flea* and it sold out immediately. The League even built its own Flea and within a year of Appleby's first flight nearly 100 Fleas were registered, with many others being furtively built without official sanction. Not only was the man in the street building Fleas but many small companies mushroomed for the express purpose of building Fleas in small numbers. In addition, sailplane and small aircraft companies turned out Fleas, and by the middle of 1936 it really looked as though the motor cycle of the air had finally materialized. Most prolific of Flea builders was E.G. Perman and Co, which built eleven; and E.D. Abbott Ltd which built three so-called Cantilever Poux designed by L.E. Baynes. These were strut-braced and were pushrod controlled.

Though Mignet claimed that none of his Fleas cost him more than £10 to build, they were to cost more in Britain during the height of the craze. In addition to forming a Pou Club the Air League also provided kits containing all the necessary wood, bolts, fabric, tubing and so on required to make the Pou, for about £25. In addition the most costly item, the engine, could be acquired for as little as £60 and the total cost of building a Flea was reckoned to be anything from £90 to £150. The engines, though, were a problem. There were a number of motor cycle engines available but generally they were under-powered. The British Scott Flying Squirrel two-cylinder inverted in-line and the French Aubier et Dunne were suitable but expensive. The Carden Ford was too heavy for Fleas of minimum span (the wing could be 4, 5 or 6m span) and many large span Fleas were underpowered when fitted with the lower-powered cycled engines.

In April 1936 there were sufficient numbers of completed Fleas to warrant a Flea meeting and the first of several took place at Ashington on 6 April. It developed into a grand free-for-all and though there was not a great deal of flying there was plenty of fun and no shortage of enthusiasm.

On 20 April 1936 a Renfrew-based Flea, *G-ADVL*, dived inexplicably into the ground soon after take-off, killing R.H. Paterson, its pilot. On 5 May another Flea killed its pilot in identical circumstances. Ironically the pilot was Flight Lieutenant A.M. Cowell, who, on behalf of the Air League, was sent out to check rigging and make test flights of amateur-built Fleas. Later that month a third Flea, *G-AEBS*, crashed in Lincolnshire, killing Squadron Leader C.R. Davidson. In each case the three Fleas had entered an involuntary dive which steepened despite the efforts of the pilots to recover. These three fatalities, though, did little to reverse the ever-rising tide of enthusiasm and more Fleas took to the air that summer. Another Flea meeting was held, this time at Ramsgate, on 3 August. This was a highly successful event which included a race for Fleas in which two teams of four French and British Fleas took part. The meeting was all the more popular because Mignet attended with a cabin version of the Pou, the HM 18. Appleby too was there and he put up the fastest time in the Flea race, averaging 60 mph.

In September a fourth Flea fatality prompted the Air League into sending its own Flea, *G-AEFV*, to the RAE at Farnborough, where it was small enough to be mounted in the Establishment's wind tunnel for testing during September. Similar tests were carried out in France. The tests revealed that when the negative angle of wing incidence exceeded $-15°$ there was insufficient pitching moment to raise the nose. No matter how hard the pilot tried to raise the nose, the dive only steepened until the Flea hit the ground. The Flea was banned immediately. The Swiss had banned the type six months earlier and four French Fleas had killed their pilots in similar circumstances. More than eighty British Fleas had received Permits to Fly and 123 were registered; countless others were hopping around the country unlicenced.

Though Mignet was to soldier on with the basic Flea concept, the Flea was dead in Britain and in most other countries. It was to be another forty years before another Mignet design took up British registry, by which time Henri Mignet had died, in 1965, at the age of 71.

Mignet HM 14 Pou du Ciel data (Aubier-Dunne)	
Span	18 ft 6 in (front wing) 13 ft 1 in (rear wing)
Length	11 ft 6 in
Height	not available
Wing area	not available
Empty weight	220 lb
All-up weight	not available
Maximum speed	62 mph
Cruising speed	50 mph
Stalling/landing speed	not available

Abbott-Baynes Cantilever HM 14 Pou data (Carden-Ford)	
Span	22 ft 0 in (front wing) 13 ft 0 in (rear wing)
Length	12 ft 3 ½ in
Height	5 ft 6 in
Wing area	137 ft²
Empty weight	327 lb
All-up weight	550 lb
Maximum speed	70 mph
Cruising speed	60 mph
Stalling/landing speed	not available

Perman Parasol

When Flea fever was at its highest pitch in Britain in 1935 a number of British companies joined the bandwagon in an attempt to cash in on the craze while it lasted. While most of the attraction of the Flea was the thrill of building and flying one's own handiwork, there were many other people who would rather buy one off the shelf — the comparatively low price being within the reach of many who perhaps did not have the time or patience to do it themselves. Among the companies and individuals who produced small numbers of Fleas were F. Hills and Sons, licence-builders of the Praga, E.D. Abbott Ltd, builders of the Baynes-designed Cantilever Poux, Puttnam Aircraft Ltd, and the largest producer of the breed — E.G. Perman and Co Ltd of 24 Brownlow Mews, Guildford Street in Gray's Inn Road, London, who built a dozen Fleas before the type was banned from flying in Britain. Many of the Perman-built Fleas were powered by Perman conversions of the standard 10 hp Ford car engine. Though it was cheaper than Sir John Carden's conversion the Perman Ford's large, vertically-mounted Scintilla magneto increased the engine's already large frontal area.

It was around this engine that F.W. Broughton, a foreman of a printing business, designed a Pou replacement. Apart from the fact that the wing section was the same Clark Y section and that its aspect ratio was 5:1, it bore little resemblance to Mignet's HM 14 Pou. Broughton's goal was to produce a single-seater with a reasonably good performance for less than £200.

Called the Perman Parasol, the Broughton design was a small parasol-winged ultra-light built entirely of wood. The short fuselage was simply constructed of four spruce longerons spaced by bulkheads aft of the cockpit and with an engine bulkhead forward. The longerons terminated forward in a hardwood mounting which carried the engine bearers and the large engine radiator. At its rear end the Perman engine was carried on standard Ford bearers bolted to the

The Perman Parasol G-ADZX photographed at Gravesend aerodrome in May 1936, shortly after its first flight. (Flight photograph)

hardwood blocks on the top longerons. The wooden fuselage framework was stiffened by a double skin of plywood, 3 mm thick on the inside and 1.5 mm on the outside. The fuselage had a turtledeck of bent ply which was neatly faired into the fin and tailplane. A small luggage locker was located behind the cockpit.

The one-piece wing consisted of two box-spars that tapered towards the tips, the wingtips embodying handgrips. There were 24 spruce and plywood ribs of orthodox construction but the most unusual feature of the 25 ft 6 in span wing was the method by which it was mounted to the fuselage. In addition to the normal centre-section pylons and a pair of metal V-struts that were attached some distance forward of the undercarriage, a pair of bracing wires ran from the lift strut rear spar attachments to a wiring lug at the tailskid — a strange idea that must have caught many pilots and onlookers on the hop. The lift struts were of narrow diameter circular-section steel tubing and were probably not strong enough to resist bending. The undercarriage was of the split-axle type, and oil-damped coil springs provided adequate suspension.

The Perman's cockpit was surprisingly roomy, though production models would have had even more legroom. The view from the cockpit was good and would have been better still had it not been for the vertical magneto and downdraught carburettor. As with the Pou, the emphasis was on simplicity of control. No rudder bar was fitted, its place being taken with two footplates hinged to the floor at their lower ends which pulled direct on cables. Most of the cabling for the rudder and elevator controls was carried externally for ease of servicing. The instrument panel carried the usual dials and gauges except that the makers must have deemed the engine's lubrication system infallible, because no oil gauge was fitted.

The Perman-Ford engine developed 32 hp at cruising rpm and ran at 3,300 rpm for take-off. The engine drove a Perman-made laminated mahogany propeller of 4.1 ft diameter. Fuel was supplied from a 6 gal tank located in the wing centre-section.

The Perman Parasol was built at Brownlow Mews and actually begin life as one of the Perman Fleas, *G-ADZG*. The incomplete airframe was finished as Perman Parasol *G-ADZX*. In May 1936 the aircraft was taken by road to Gravesend aerodrome and on 23 May Arthur Clouston made the first flight. Clouston had previously tested some of the Perman-built Fleas and was later to make his name as a test pilot with the RAE and as an accomplished record breaker.

In October 1936 the Perman Parasol was purchased by Air Worthiness Ltd at Gravesend, by which time it was called the Perman Grasshopper. The aircraft survived only a few months before it was

Above *E. G. Perman and Co Ltd hoped to market the Perman Parasol for £175. Instead it was burnt during a fire-fighting demonstration a little over a year after it first flew. (Flight photograph)* **Below** *The Perman Parasol was first flown on 23 May 1936 by Arthur Clouston from Gravesend aerodrome. G-ADZX was the only example built. (Flight photograph)* **Bottom** *Close-up of the Perman Parasol's Perman-converted Ford car engine. At 3,200 rpm the engine produced about 32 hp (Flight photograph)*

allegedly destroyed in a fire-fighting display in July the following year.

Perman Parasol data	
Span	25 ft 6 in
Length	15 ft 6 in
Height	not available
Wing area	not available
Empty weight	425 lb
All-up weight	600 lb
Maximum speed	76 mph
Cruising speed	68 mph
Stalling/landing speed	35 mph

Hillson Praga

In 1934 the Czechoslovakian company Ceskomoro-avska-Kolben-Danek Co Ltd of Prague built the Praga Air Baby for the Czechoslovak National Flying Competition. The all-wooden, high-wing monoplane, registered *OK-PGA*, was powered by a 36 hp Aeronca engine and, in the course of a year, flew around Europe to notch up about 200 hours' flying. Seating two people side-by-side, the Air Baby cruised at 80 mph and was put on the market for about £280.

Designer M. Slechta built a second prototype, registered *OK-PGB* and installed a 36 hp Praga B engine. Designated Praga 114, the new Air Baby was flown to Heston on 15 August 1935 by M. Kostalek and its designer, and was demonstrated publicly the following day.

The Praga 114 was built mostly of wood and had a single-piece cantilever wing which tapered in chord and thickness from the rectangular middle portion.

Hillson Praga, G-AEEU, became the Hillson company's demonstrator. It was powered by a licence-built Praga B engine. (Flight photograph)

The wings and ailerons were ply-covered, and had no internal bracing. Four easily-removable bolts secured the wing to the fuselage.

The Praga's fuselage was a hexagonal box structure, covered with plywood. The tailplane and elevator were made of welded steel tube and were fabric covered. The plywood-covered fin was built integrally with the fuselage and the aerodynamically-balanced rudder was likewise covered with ply.

The divided steel-tube undercarriage carried semi-doughnut tyres on cast magnesium wheels. The two faired-in vees were hinged to the lower edges of the fuselage and were anchored to the centre line of the fuselage underside. Rubber-in-compression springing was located inside the enlarged wheel hubs.

The enclosed cockpit was located immediately forward of the wing and the occupants sat side-by-side with their heads beneath the wing leading edge. The side windows and roof were hinged at the front wing spar and folded back as one piece on to the wing to allow easy access to the roomy cockpit, using the wheels as steps. In addition to large folding luggage lockers behind each seat — almost large enough to take a third person — the seats could accommodate back-type parachute packs. The Praga was fitted with dual controls and the right-hand set could be removed if required. The rudder and elevators were cable-operated, while aileron control was via vertical shafts and chain wheels.

On arrival at Heston, sceptics were surprised by both the performance and the amount of room in the Praga. With two people aboard, *OK-PGB* took off in 120 yds in still air and climbed to 1,000 ft in less than 3 mins. At cruising speed the Praga used only 1.7 gal/hr and had a range of 4 hrs at 70 mph. With full load and full tanks the all-up weight was a little over 1,000 lb. The Czech price for the production version was £385, which was subject to a 30 per cent tax on importation to Britain.

The woodworking company F. Hills & Sons Ltd of Trafford Park in Manchester was so impressed with the Praga that a licence was acquired to put it into production, the first aircraft appearing in mid-1936. In the meantime Flight Lieutenant Nicholas Comper, of Swift fame, and a partner imported a Praga E 114. After registration as *G-ADXL* it flew with C.W.A. Scott's circus before flying to South Africa in a bid to attract further orders. Though the flight to the Cape was achieved in just over sixteen days, no orders were forthcoming.

Hills laid down a batch of 35 Hillson Pragas, all initially powered by the Praga B engine, licence-built by Jowett Cars Ltd, though most were later fitted with the 40 hp JAP J-99. The first Praga was exported to Australia, and the first UK registered example was *G-AEEU*.

Above *This early Czech production aircraft, G-ADXL, was imported by Comper and Walker Ltd and flown by C.W.A. Scott's Flying Display in 1936. (Flight photograph)* **Right** *Like many other Hillson Pragas, G-AEPJ was flown by the Northern Aviation School and Club Ltd at Barton during the last months of peace. (Flight photograph)* **Below right** *Hillson Praga G-AEUU flew with the Ipswich Aero Club before being scrapped during World War Two.* **Bottom** *This Hillson Praga was written off in a crash in June 1939 and was one of the NSA fleet based at Barton.*

The largest operator of the Hillson Praga was the local Barton-based Northern Aviation School and Club Ltd, formed specifically to operate the type. Others were flown by the Ipswich Aero Club and an assortment of private owners. Some were sold abroad and several remained unsold. Some were allocated registrations but were never completed. Though appealing to the impecunious, the Hillson Praga was too underpowered to be any use as a practical touring aeroplane and in Britain it was short-lived.

Its low power made the Hillson Praga unsuitable for impressment into the RAF on the outbreak of war as a hack or communications aircraft and most examples were put into long-term storage. Only five survived to reappear after the war, but only two were to take to the air again. *G-AEUP* was eventually lost in Turkey while being flown by Flight Lieutenant F. Bosworth in July 1946. Praga *G-AEEU* survived a further eleven years until it was destroyed after

forced-landing in Italy in 1957. The remaining three were not flown post-war.

Hillsons did not abandon aircraft production after the Praga and the Hillson Pennine and Hellvellyn were built in 1937 and 1939. The Pennine, registered *G-AFBX*, was a side-by-side wooden cabin monoplane superficially similar to the Praga but designed by Norman Sykes and built by the parent company at Trafford Park. The Pennine was fitted with a normal-type elevator but lateral control was by means of spoilers located on the wing leading edges.

In 1939 the parent Czech company produced a much improved version of the Air Baby powered by a 60/80 hp Praga D flat-four which gave a vastly improved take-off and climb performance, though the stalling speed was kept below 40 mph. The price had increased to £450 but war was imminent and none was imported into Britain.

Hillson Praga data	
Span	36 ft 0 in
Length	21 ft 1 in
Height	7 ft 2½ in
Wing area	164 ft²
Empty weight	625 lb
All-up weight	1,050 lb
Maximum speed	92 mph
Cruising speed	81 mph
Stalling/landing speed	37 mph

Luton LA 1 Buzzard

One name that recurs in the annals of British light aviation is that of C.H. Latimer-Needham. In an earlier chapter his Halton HAC 1 Mayfly and HAC 2 Minus are described and his name is also linked with that of the Martin Monoplane, described later, which he created from the remains of the Clarke Cheetah.

The Luton LA1 Buzzard under construction during the winter of 1935 at Barton-in-the-Clay aerodrome in Bedfordshire.

The Mayfly was designed for the Halton Aero Club while Latimer-Needham was serving as an education officer at RAF Halton. Apart from designing powered aircraft he became interested in gliding when the sport reached popularity in Britain during 1930. In that same year he designed a 42 ft span glider which he called the Albatross, destined to become the first British designed and built sailplane. It was built by the RFD company at Guildford. In January 1935 Latimer-Needham resigned from the Service and formed the Dunstable Sailplane Co in company with glider designer W.L. Manuel. Several months later the company moved to the now defunct Barton-in-the-Clay aerodrome at Luton in Bedfordshire where Latimer-Needham formed Luton Aircraft Ltd and set himself up as managing director and chief designer. Springing as it did from the glider company, the first powered aircraft he designed was naturally enough glider-like.

The Luton LA 1 Buzzard was a single-seat, low-wing semi-cantilever monoplane built entirely of wood with the engine mounted above and behind the pilot's cockpit, driving a wooden pusher propeller. The 7 ft 6 in centre-section was built integral with the fuselage and was braced above by single struts connected to the engine bulkhead. The detachable 16 ft 3 in wing panels were attached to the centre-section by three bolts and butterfly nuts, giving a total span of 40 ft and the high aspect ratio of 11:1. The controls of the tapering ailerons were connected by a pin that engaged in a slot on a differential lever fitting. The outer wing panels tapered in chord and thickness and consisted of single box-spars and a light secondary spar to which the ailerons were connected. The wings had torsion-resisting plywood-covered leading edges, the rest of the wing surfaces being fabric covered.

The Buzzard's fuselage was a spruce and plywood monocoque structure of squared-off section which decreased in depth aft of the cockpit to a slender boom in order to give sufficient clearance for the two-bladed propeller. The pilot sat in a roomy cockpit in the fuselage nose, forward of the slipstream, which gave an unrestricted view in every direction except immediately behind. The tailplane was the all-moving type and there was a finless rudder. The tail was a spruce structure covered with plywood and fabric.

The undercarriage consisted of two short canti-lever legs which each carried balloon wheels, trousered-in fairings being fixed to the underside of the centre-section. In order to steepen the Buzzard's fine gliding angle, small split flaps were fitted to the centre-section. They could be activated by a cockpit lever and allowed a maximum glide angle of 1 in 8.

The 28 hp Scott Flying Squirrel engine was originally installed in the completed Buzzard but when it

refused to start it was replaced with a 35 hp Anzani inverted-V air-cooled motor. The 5 gal fuel tank was carried in the fuselage.

The Luton Buzzard's first flight took place from Barton during the early summer of 1936. It received the registration *G-ADYX* and required no modification after initial testing. The Buzzard's streamlined glider-like form gave it good speed range, in the region of 25-80 mph, unlike the BAC Drone which though basically a converted glider was somewhat less aerodynamically efficient than Latimer-Needham's design. The Buzzard was pleasant to fly and could be turned on rudder alone. The controls were light and effective and the landing run was short. The Buzzard's relatively high cruising speed of 75 mph made it a practical cross-country tourer.

Following a landing accident at Christchurch in Hampshire on 16 November 1936 the Buzzard was taken to the company's new Phoenix works premises at Gerrards Cross in Buckinghamshire to be rebuilt. It emerged during the following summer in much modified form. The wingspan had been shortened by 6 ft, the open cockpit was now enclosed with a hinged Perspex canopy and the engine was now enclosed, apart from the cylinder heads, in a streamlined fairing. The engine was the Luton Anzani, modified by the company to incorporate dual magneto ignition and an impulse starter. The tailplane reverted to the conventional type, becoming a fixed unit with ele-

Above *The Buzzard was first flown during the early summer of 1936. Though it was designed with the Scott Flying Squirrel engine in mind, a 34 hp Anzani engine took its place when the Squirrel proved impossible to start.* (*Flight* photograph) **Below** *Close up of the Buzzard with its designer, C.H. Latimer-Needham, in the cockpit; summer 1936.* (*Flight* photograph) **Bottom** *The Buzzard's top speed of 90 mph was three times that of the landing speed.* (*Flight* photograph)

Top The Buzzard II coupe had shorter wings, the engine was totally enclosed and the undercarriage trouser fairings were better streamlined.
Above The Buzzard II photographed after a bad landing by Robert Kronfeld during a demonstration at the Heathrow Garden Party of the Royal Aeronautical Society on 8 May 1938.

Luton LA 1 Buzzard II data	
Span	35 ft 6 in
Length	21 ft 6 in
Height	6 ft 6 in
Wing area	137 ft^2
Empty weight	400 lb
All-up weight	600 lb
Maximum speed	95 mph
Cruising speed	80 mph
Stalling/landing speed	30 mph

Broughton-Blayney Brawney

The story of the tongue-twistingly named Broughton-Blayney Brawney is really the continuation of the development of the Perman Parasol, described earlier. By the time that the Perman was flying at Gravesend, F.W. Broughton was working on an improvement — though it bore only a passing

vators and the undercarriage trousers were improved aerodynamically.

The Buzzard II was first flown in 1938. Fully laden it weighed 180 lb less than the Mk I, so the performance was appreciably increased. The maximum speed was improved by 10 mph and the cruise speed was increased by 6 mph. Interestingly, the top speed came out at three times the landing speed.

The Buzzard, priced at £320, was a direct competitor with the Kronfeld Drone family and it is rather ironic that the Buzzard II met its end in the hands of Robert Kronfeld himself. On 8 May 1938 the Buzzard was being demonstrated at the annual Royal Aeronautical Society Garden Party at Heathrow when Kronfeld crashed after its landing was baulked by another aircraft. The aircraft was damaged beyond repair and it was taken back to Gerrards Cross, where it remained until consumed by the disastrous Phoenix Works fire of 1943.

Luton LA 1 Buzzard data	
Span	40 ft 0 in
Length	20 ft 0 in
Height	not available
Wing area	not available
Empty weight	600 lb
All-up weight	800 lb
Maximum speed	85 mph
Cruising speed	75 mph
Stalling/landing speed	29 mph

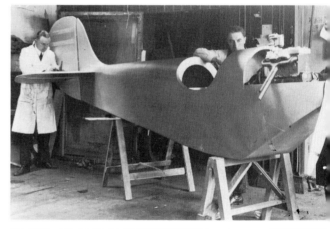

Below left *The prototype Brawney under construction with the Carden-converted Ford car engine already installed. (Flight photograph)* **Bottom left** *The completed Brawney prototype photographed at the Hanworth Garden Party in 1936, complete with price tag for the benefit of the Press. (Flight photograph)* **Above** *An early flying shot of the prototype Brawney, G-AENM, shortly before its crash of 21 March 1937.* **Below right** *The second Brawney, G-AERF, crashed in Bromley Hill Cemetery, Kent, on 6 June 1937, as the result of engine trouble.* **Bottom right** *Miss Jennie Broad was test pilot with the Broughton and Blayney Aircraft company and is seen here with the prototype Brawney. (Flight photograph)*

resemblance to its predecessor, being Flea-like though without the tandem wing.

The Brawney was designed around the Carden-Ford car engine conversion and, with financial help from partner A.J. Blayney, Broughton had a batch of three Brawneys built by T.H. Gill & Son of 75 Kilburn Lane London W10 — a company of which Blayney was a director.

The all-wood Brawney was similar in layout to the Perman, retaining the large area Aeronca-like rudder and the parasol configuration. However, the straight dihedral-less wing was mounted far closer to the fuselage top longerons and had very little incidence, a factor that may have had some bearing on its unfortunate safety record. The wing bracing was substantially increased, the V lift strut giving way to an N-strut arrangement. The I-sectioned Duralumin struts were faired with balsa wood into a streamlined shape. The main characteristic of the Brawney was the shape of the nose, produced by the slipper-type cooling radiator.

The first flight of the prototype Brawney was carried out by H.J. Wilson, later to become a respected RAE test pilot. The maiden flight was flown from Hanworth on 19 September 1936 — the day of the Hanworth Garden Party. After the first flight the Brawney's price tag of £195 was daubed on its nose and the aviation press was told that the aircraft would be put into production within the following week or so. In fact only two other Brawneys were to materialize.

The prototype was registered *G-AENM* and was granted an Authorisation to Fly on 8 October 1936. The other two aircraft, *G-AERF* and *G-AERG*, received their Authorisations on 23 December 1936 and all three machines were initially registered to Broughton-Blayney Aircraft Ltd at Hanworth.

The first aircraft was sold in March 1937 to Alexander Scaife. On arrival at Hanworth on 11 March the new owner wisely decided to familiarize himself with his new acquisition before flying it back to his home at Keighley in Yorkshire. Alas, he was never to embark on that particular journey. During his first flight in the Brawney he stalled in a turn and the aircraft crashed into the RASC Depot at Feltham; the pilot was killed.

The second Brawney, *G-AERF*, differed from the prototype in that though the large pair of tubular struts was retained, the third unfaired strut running from the bottom longeron at the rear of the cockpit to the front spar attachment was deleted. Its place was taken by a bracing wire. This aircraft was sold to Alfred Bacon, a tobacconist from Canterbury. On 6 June he collected his aircraft from Hanworth and, during his trip home to Canterbury, experienced engine trouble over Bromley Hill in Kent. This resulted in a crash in the local cemetry, where the pilot died instantly.

Shortly before *G-AERF* had been sold to Bacon, the Broughton-Blayney company had employed the services of Miss Jennie Broad as test pilot and demonstration pilot. Miss Broad regarded the Brawney as a strong aircraft and easy to fly. Despite Miss Broad's confidence, after the crash of the first two aircraft the type failed to attract further orders. The third and final aircraft remained at Hanworth, unsold. After its Authorisation to Fly expired in December 1937, *G-AERG* was withdrawn from use, by which time there was a general mistrust of ultra-light aeroplanes, partly fired by a number of fatal

accidents with the Flea. Thus another brave attempt to provide a motor cycle of the air came to nought.

Broughton-Blayney Brawney data	
Span	25 ft 6 in
Length	15 ft 6 in
Height	6 ft 0 in
Wing area	125 ft^2
Empty weight	425 lb
All-up weight	600 lb
Maximum speed	80 mph
Cruising speed	70 mph
Stalling/landing speed	30 mph

Dart Pup

In 1934 two Germans formed a company to build gliders and light aircraft at premises in Luton Road, Dunstable, Bedfordshire, a stone's throw from the headquarters of the London Gliding Club at the base of Dunstable Downs. Alfred R. Weyl, an experienced designer, had recently arrived in England from Germany where, in 1922, his first successful glider had been the Udet I. On arrival in England, Weyl teamed up with Eric P. Zander, and as Zander & Weyl they first built several Zogling-type gliders based on the Dagling. They also built Pou-du-Ciel *G-ADSE* for C.F.R. Griffin of Gerrards Cross. The HM 14 Pou was registered in October 1935 and was named *Winnie the Pou*. It was the first powered aircraft built by the partnership. Also in 1935 Zander and Weyl built a number of replica gliders for Alexander

The sole Dunstable Dart, later named Dart Pup, photographed by its designer, A.R. Weyl. The Dart Pup was based very loosely on the Slingsby Type 4 Falcon 3 glider and was first flown in July 1936.

Korda's film, *The Conquest of the Air*. These included a 1902 Wright glider, two Lilienthal types and a Cayley glider.

Hardly surprisingly, the company's first powered aircraft design owed much to the Zogling-type glider. However, it was based more on the 58 ft span Slingsby Type Falcon 3, first flown at Sutton Bank in April 1935. Named the Dart and designed by Weyl, the new aircraft had a span exactly half that of the Falcon 3 and, though generally similar in layout, having pronounced wing sweepback and no dihedral, it was a completely different design.

On 11 May 1936 Zander and Weyl changed the name of their company to Dart Aircraft Ltd and moved into larger premises at 29 High Street North in Dunstable. The Dart was renamed Dart Pup and it was completed by July that year.

The Dart Pup was a single-seat, high-wing pusher monoplane powered by a 27 hp Ava 4A-00 four-cylinder opposed air-cooled two-stroke engine mounted immediately behind the rear spar of the centre-section. The fuselage had wooden longerons and built-up bulkheads, and was plywood covered. The metal nose was detachable to facilitate adjustment of the rudder controls and a skid under the nose helped prevent the Pup from nosing over during taxiing and landing.

The wings were designed to fold and were braced with streamlined steel vee bracing struts. Built on two box spars the wings had ply-covered leading edges and were otherwise fabric covered.

The tail unit consisted of box spars and plywood-webbed ribs and was fabric covered except for the ply-covered leading edges. The tailplane was attached to the ply-covered fin and was strutted to the bottom of the fuselage. The unbalanced elevator was pushrod and cable operated and the tailplane could be adjusted in flight.

The undercarriage was of the split type with hinged

Top *The Dart Pup was powered by a 27 hp Ava four-cylinder two-stroke engine but was later re-engined with a 36 hp Bristol Cherub III.* **Above** *A rare photograph of the Pup in flight, flown by A. R. Weyl its creator. In September 1937 the Pup was sold to A. E. Green and was destroyed in a take-off crash in August the following year. (Squadron Leader Alan Curtis photograph)* **Below** *The wrecked Dart Pup after stalling on take-off from a field near Solihull in August 1938.* **Bottom** *The pronounced sweepback of the Dart Pup's wings are well shown in this photograph of* G-AELR. *(Via A.J. Jackson Collection)*

axles, shock absorber legs and radius rods. Braking was by a novel expanding axle-wheel brake, recently devised by Gurney Grice. A swivelling Palmer tail-wheel of solid rubber was spring controlled and had rubber-disc suspension.

The pilot sat well forward of the engine and wing, and had excellent all-round vision. The tail trim could be operated by a ratchet lever in the cockpit and the brakes were actuated by triggers on the control column. Both rudder pedals and seat could be adjusted.

The Ava engine was mounted on four Silentbloc bearings and the thrustline could be altered. Fuel was gravity-fed from three tanks positioned in the wing centre-section and gave sufficient range for almost 4 hrs at full throttle.

The Dart Pup was registered *G-AELR* and was first flown in July 1936. A number of problems were encountered. The section Weyl chose for the Pup was NACA 23012 which, though fine for fast flight, was unsuitable for a low-powered engine such as the Ava. Though rated at 34 hp the Ava developed only 27 hp which made the Pup quite underpowered. Its reluctance to leave the ground was further affected by the fact that it landed in a level flight attitude. Hence, on taking off, it was easy to raise the tail too high and for the take-off to become a rather protracted affair. This problem was solved by fitting a taller undercarriage, which increased wing incidence on the ground. A horn-balanced rudder was also fitted. More power was provided with the fitting of a 36 hp Bristol Cherub III engine, thereby improving the take-off and overall performance.

In September 1937 the Pup was sold to A. E. Green of Tachbrook but in August the following year it was lost in a take-off crash.

Dart Pup data	
Span	29 ft 7 ½ in
	9 ft 8 ½ in
	(wings folded)
Length	19 ft 8 ½ in
Height	6 ft 3 in
Wing area	114 ft²
Empty weight	485 lb
All-up weight	705 lb
Maximum speed	90 mph
	(Cherub III)
Cruising speed	62 mph
Stalling/landing speed	not available

Dart Flittermouse

While work was progressing on the Dart Pup, Zander and Weyl had designed and built the Dart Cambridge glider, a 46 ft 4 in span single-seater resembling the German Grunau Baby. Two were built, the first flying in December 1935. The Cambridge was followed by the Dart Totternhoe, a slightly smaller single-seat secondary glider which took to the air for the first time in May 1936. At about this time Dr H.N. Bradbrooke, brother of *The Aeroplane*'s staff-writer F.D. Bradbrooke, asked Weyl to design and build him a

Below *The Dart Flittermouse G-AELZ photographed at RAF Abingdon in May 1937, powered by a Scott Squirrel of an alleged 28 hp* (Squadron Leader Alan Curtis photograph) **Bottom** *Another view of the Flittermouse taken at RAF Abingdon in May 1937. It was built to the order of Dr H. N. Bradbrooke, brother of* The Aeroplane's *F. D. Bradbrooke.* (Squadron Leader Alan Curtis photograph)

single-seat ultra-light powered aircraft. Once again Weyl settled for a pusher design, to be powered this time by a 25 hp Scott Squirrel engine. Called the Flittermouse (after the bat), the resulting aircraft looked more like a powered primary glider with a plywood monocoque nacelle for the pilot. Aft of the cockpit and engine was an upright rectangular box-like structure of steel tubes which supported the tail-plane. The top pair of tubes ran parallel from the rear wing spars, just inboard of the centre-section trailing edge cutout for the propeller. The lower pair ran from the bottom of the nacelle to join the upper pair at the tail, converging in a vee. In addition to wire bracing, the four longerons were braced midway along their length by four struts.

In order to keep the cost of the Flittermouse as low as possible and to save time, the aircraft was fitted with a pair of Totternhoe wings, modified with a centre-section and attached to the top of the nacelle with the engine. Below the engine the nacelle was streamlined to a point, beneath which was attached a landing skid. The wings were braced by a pair of V-struts attached to the bottom of the nacelle; they were positioned behind the undercarriage legs for backward wing-folding.

The Dart Flittermouse was completed in the summer of 1936 and registered *G-AELZ*, receiving its Authorization to Fly on 28 August that year. It was flown by the owner at Witney and then in May 1938 it was purchased by A. Carpenter of Coventry.

The new owner fitted the Flittermouse with a castoring nosewheel and moved the main under-carriage further back, dispensing with the skid. Carpenter hoped to soar the Flittermouse in suitable conditions, with the Scott Squirrel switched off, but as far as is known he only made a few short hops around Whitley aerodrome.

The Flittermouse survived the war and in 1950 was acquired by Geoff Chamberlain. It was scrapped, though, in the following year when it was discovered that the glue had deteriorated and the metal fittings had all corroded.

Dart Flittermouse data	
Span	40 ft 6 in
Length	22 ft 6 in
Height	5 ft 2 in
Wing area	not available
Empty weight	not available
All-up weight	640 lb
Maximum speed	64 mph
Cruising speed	not available
Stalling/landing speed	not available

Dart Kitten

Having designed and built the Pup and Flittermouse, the Dunstable-based Dart Aircraft company embarked on a more orthodox design during 1936. Weyl produced drawings of a neat 31 ft 9 in span low-wing single-seat monoplane, which he christened the Kitten. The all-wood cantilever aircraft was built at Dunstable and was completed by Christmas 1936.

The Dart Kitten had a fuselage of rectangular structure with a fabric-covered curved top decking. The spruce framework was otherwise covered with ply. The wings were tapered and though the aerofoil

The prototype Dart Kitten, G-AERP *photographed at Hatfield in 1937. It was first flown on 15 January that year. (*Flight *photograph)*

section was basically NACA 23012 it changed from root to tip. Each wing was made up of a single spruce-and-plywood box spar and an auxiliary rear spar interconnected with shear boxes. The former ribs were of spruce and plywood and, while the leading edges were ply-covered back to the auxiliary spars, the rest of the wing surfaces and the ailerons were fabric covered. The wings were attached to a parallel-chord centre-section which was built integral with the fuselage.

The tailplane was a cantilever structure similar in construction to the wings. The rudder and elevators had wooden frames and were fabric covered, though the balanced portion of the rudder was ply-covered.

The undercarriage was of the single-leg cantilever type and comprised a rather crude fork-mounted wheel with rubber-in-compression springing. Large angular fairings located just below the wing leading edge housed torque links.

The Kitten was initially powered by the French Ava flat-four two-stroke engine which on a good day would produce 27 hp. Weyl had planned to use a more powerful engine but the only one available was the Bristol Cherub III, which the impecunious firm found too expensive, as well as too heavy. The 10 gal fuel tank was located behind the Kitten's fireproof bulkhead.

The prototype Kitten was registered *G-AERP* and it was granted its Authorisation to Fly on 31 December 1936. On 15 January 1937 it made its first flight. From the beginning it was apparent that though the Ava engine was making a great deal of noise the Kitten was very underpowered. The

Top *The prototype Dart Kitten flying near Dunstable in January 1937, shortly after its first flight. The engine is a 27 hp Ava flat-four two-stroke, characterized by its long, straight exhaust pipes. (Squadron Leader Alan Curtis photograph)* **Above** *F.D. Bradbrooke swings the second Dart Kitten's compass at Hatfield three days before the Isle of Man air race in May 1937. The engine is an Aeronca JAP J-99 flat twin. (Squadron Leader Alan Curtis photograph)* **Below** *John Fricker airtesting Kitten II G-AEXT for The Aeroplane in 1950, following a complete rebuild by W.G.A. Harrison. (The Aeroplane photograph)*

Walrus-like straight-down exhaust stubs emitted a deafening noise and the engine vibrated badly at cruising revs. Tests revealed that the Kitten cruised at a steady 65 mph, had a maximum speed of between 75 and 80 mph and stalled at 37 mph. The layout of the wing, whereby the tips appeared to drop at the leading edge, gave effective washout and kept the wingtips free from stalling even after the centre of the wing had lost lift. The nett result was a smooth viceless stall with no wing drop but a gentle even keel sink. The Ava-powered Kitten was offered at £345.

While the Kitten was being flown by a number of pilots, a second aircraft was nearing completion at Dunstable. The Kitten Mk II incorporated several changes, the most important being a more powerful engine. A new 36 hp Aeronca-JAP J-99 two-cylinder opposed air-cooled engine, licence-built by J.A. Prestwich Ltd, was installed, effectively increasing the Kitten's cruising speed by 20 mph — and it was much quieter. Other modifications included a remodelled top decking and the fitting of an L-type undercarriage axle. The pitot head was repositioned from the leading edge of the port wing to beneath the wing and out of harm's way. Registered *G-AEXT*, the Kitten Mk II was first flown during May 1937, its Authorisation to Fly having been issued on 30 April.

During May *G-AEXT* was fitted with a detachable canopy and wheel spats and entered for the 1937 London-Isle of Man air race, held on 29 May. The Kitten set off from Hanworth flown by that champion of British light aviation, F.D. Bradbrooke, whose brother had earler commissioned Dart Aircraft to build him the Flittermouse. Engine trouble prevented Bradbrooke from reaching the Isle of Man but the aircraft competed in further air races until the outbreak of war, in the hands of C.G.M. Alington and others.

After changing hands several times *G-AERP* spent the war in a Surrey shed, while its sister craft spent the duration in the company of Taylorcraft and Auster at Rearsby. After the war the prototype Kitten was re-engined with an Aeronca JAP J-99 and soldiered on until it crashed at Broxbourne in Herts on 23 November 1952, killing its pilot.

The Kitten II flew on for a further twelve years before it too came to grief at Willingdale on 29 November 1964, again with fatal consequences for its pilot. A long restoration programme began during the late Seventies and after various changes of ownership 'XT was completed in September 1985. After a break of nearly 21 years the Kitten took to the air again on 28 September, piloted by owner Clive Stubbings.

After the second Kitten was completed back in April 1937, the Dart company underwent some major changes. Eric Zander became progressively

The sole Kitten III, G-AMJP, fitted with wheel brakes, crashed at Hillington, King's Lynn, on 5 June 1966.

more involved with the lucrative production of sailplanes, being ideally placed on the doorstep of the London Gliding Club. Weyl meanwhile was struggling with his powered-aircraft designs and in August 1937 the two men parted company. Shortly after the formation of Dart, a young glider designer by the name of W.R. Scott had joined the company. In his spare time he built three Hutter 17 gliders, selling two and keeping one for himself. Both Scott and Zander left Dart to set up a business of their own in another part of Dunstable, initially to build more Hutter gliders. Meanwhile Weyl worked on developing the Kitten further and produced drawings for a two-seat version which he called the Weasel. This 36 ft 1 in span trainer/tourer would have been powered by a 80/90 hp Cirrus engine and used the wing design of the Kitten. With a top speed of 100 mph the side-by-side cabin aircraft was publicised in October 1938 but, though aimed primarily at the recently-formed Civil Air Guard, the Weasel was never completed.

The outbreak of the Second World War put a stop to further Dart activity, though at the time it had just completed the construction of the Handley Page HP 75 Manx tailless research aircraft. Despite this 'military' work no further contracts were awarded to the ailing Dart company, and it went to the wall.

The Dart story did not end with the war, though. Weyl built a third Kitten, the Mk III, in 1951. Registered *G-AMJP*, it was granted a Certificate of Airworthiness in January 1952. This aircraft differed from the Mk II in that it was fitted with wheel brakes. Curiously, though built to the same specification as the earlier aircraft, the Kitten III came out some 30 lb overweight. Though the intention was to put the Kitten into production the old problem of absence of a suitable engine put paid to any such ideas. Weyl continued to produce paper developments of the Kitten, including a Speed Kitten fitted with a 75 hp engine, but these came to nothing and by 1965 Weyl was a shadow of his former self. During the war he had been interned on the Isle of Man for four years as an alien. His partner Zander had wisely taken out

British nationality shortly before the war and was thus spared this indignity. The years of imprisonment and other pressures drove Weyl to take his own life. It is hoped that Dart Kitten *G-AEXT* will provide a living testimony to this gifted designer.

Dart Kitten (Ava)	
Span	31 ft 9 in
Length	21 ft 9 in
Height	7 ft 11 in
Wing area	129 ft²
Empty weight	510 lb
All-up weight	752 lb
Maximum speed	75-80 mph
	95 mph (JAP J-99)
Cruising speed	65 mph
	83 mph (JAP J-99)
Stalling/landing speed	37 mph
	38 mph (JAP J-99)

Hafner AR III Mk 2 Gyroplane

Encouraged by the work of Juan de la Cierva, several designers during the 1930s turned their attentions to providing a lightweight autogyro for the private owner. Taking the Cierva Autogiro as their starting point they turned their attention to development along slightly different lines. At least three individuals progressed to the point of producing experimental prototypes, although none reached the production stage. The Weir jump-start autogyro was based entirely on Cierva principles; the Kay Gyroplane Type 33/1, built at Eastleigh, is described in another chapter. The third, the Hafner AR III Mk 2

Gyroplane, was designed by Austrian Raoul Hafner and was the result of years of development work during the early 1930s.

The Hafner Gyroplane was remarkable for its time because it featured variable incidence rotor blades. The blades were attached to the rotor head in the normal way, with horizontal hinges which permitted the blades to flap, and with vertical hinges with friction dampers to permit the blades slight freedom to alter their spacing. The method by which the blades were attached to hinged forks gave them a third degree of freedom, allowing them to alter their pitch. The inner ends of each of the three blades carried a crank arm on a vertical hinge. The hinge was incorporated to allow the blades freedom to 'catch up' or lag behind one another. A 'spider' mounted centrally above the rotor head, carried three arms mounted on vertical hinges. The free ends of the blade cranks were connected by cup and ball joints to the free ends of the spider cranks. When the spider was raised, by means of a separate control in the cockpit, the three crank arms rose with it, carrying with them the free ends of the blade cranks. Thus the pitch angle of all three blades could be increased. When the spider was lowered, the blade pitch angles were reduced. In addition, a flying control shifted the centre of lift of the entire rotor system by causing the blades to assume an increased pitch angle at one point of their travel around the circle and a decreased pitch angle at other points. This was simply effected by tilting the spider. When the spider was tilted back the blades assumed a low angle of pitch when passing through their rearmost position, thus shifting the centre of lift ahead of the rotor pivot, causing the aircraft to climb. Similarly, when the spider was tilted to the left, the pitch angle would be great on the right-hand side and the machine would bank and turn to the left. The flying controls on the AR III also included a trim-

The Hafner AR III Mk 2 was powered by a 90 hp Pobjoy Niagara III engine and was capable of taking off in a couple of yards. (Flight photograph)

ming tailplane and a pedal-operated rudder of the orthodox type.

The rotor blades had single steel-tube spars of small diameter but heavy gauge. No attempt was made to reduce the weight of the blades — in fact it was kept deliberately high to maintain a good fly-wheel effect in order to assist take-off. The rotor blades were of aerofoil section over the outer two thirds only, the inner third of their length being of plain streamline section. Each of the three rotor blades weighed 35 lb.

The drive for starting the rotor included a clutch, gearbox unit and freewheel device. The drive incorporated a synchromesh arrangement and great trouble was taken to protect the rotor head and blades against shock loads during the revving up process. For engine-assisted take-offs the rotors were speeded up to around 240 rpm.

The AR III Gyroplane was built by the AR III Construction Co in the Martin Baker Aircraft factory at Denham in 1936. Martin Baker completed the fuselage assembly. The Gyroplane was powered by a 90 hp Pobjoy Niagara engine. On 26 July 1935 it was registered *G-ADMV* to T.V. Welsh, a director of the company.

The Gyroplane was first flown on 6 February 1937 from Hanworth, probably by Arthur Clouston. Certainly on the same day he demonstrated the autogyro before an impressed audience. In the 20 mph wind he managed to take-off in less than 2 yds and maintained a long, steep climb. The Hafner Gyroplane could be hauled around in tight circles and S-turns. In the words of *The Aeroplane*'s reporter, 'It was switch-backed up and down, over and around our heads in a manner which was frankly terrifying, though calculated by its confidence in the non-stalling propensities of the motor to have delighted the hearts of any Pobjoy people if they had been there to see.'

The Gyroplane was regarded by the makers as a flying test bench rather than a production model and it was later tested by the Royal Aircraft Establishment at Farnborough by Clouston. It was finally leased to the RAE for further research and was scrapped during the war.

Top *Much of the initial test flying of the Hafner AR III Mk 2 was carried out by Arthur Clouston, seen here flying the machine at Hanworth early in 1937.* **Above** *Another view of Arthur Clouston flying Hafner AR III Mk 2 G-ADMV at Hanworth. The fuselage was built by the Martin Baker company.* (*Flight* photograph) **Below** *The Hafner Gyroplane's rotors were made with single steel-tube spars, their weight being kept deliberately high to obtain a good flywheel effect.* (*Flight* photograph)

Hafner AR III Mk 2 Gyroplane data	
Rotor diameter	32 ft 10 in
Width	not available
Rotor area	20 ft^2
Height	not available
Empty weight	640 lb
All-up weight	900 lb
Maximum speed	120 mph
Cruising speed	110 mph
Stalling/landing speed	not available

Gordon Dove

At the height of British Flea hysteria, Mervyn Chadwick and Raymond Gordon ran an aircraft maintenance business at Ashington in Kent, trading as the Canute Air Park Co. The two men had seriously considered the idea of building Fleas when the crash came and the type was banned from British skies. This prompted Chadwick and Gordon to design and market a replacement which could be sold either complete or in kit form.

In November 1936 a new company was formed with capital of £500. Premier Aircraft Constructions Ltd was set up at Harold Wood in Essex, and S.C. Buszard came up with the design of a very pretty low-wing single-seater that looked as though it had come from the pencil of E.O. Tips, for the design looked uncannily like the Belgian Tipsy S 2, one of which came over to England on a demonstration tour earlier that year. Though Buszard's design had a slightly larger span, the empennage in particular was almost identical to that of the Tipsy.

The Premier aircraft, named the Gordon Dove,

was built during the winter of 1936-37 and in March 1937 it was taken from the Harold Wood premises to Maylands aerodrome at Romford, where it made its first flight on Sunday, 3 March, in the hands of C. Oscroft.

The Gordon Dove was a low-wing cantilever monoplane constructed of wood. The wing structure consisted of a main box spar which was transversely braced to a subsidiary rear spar. The wings were plywood covered up to this rear spar and then fabric covered to the wing trailing edge. They were detachable for storage. The fuselage was a plywood-covered rectangular framework with a curved top decking. A small faired headrest distinguished the Dove from the lookalike Tipsy.

The wooden tailplane was fabric-covered and wire-braced to the fin. The divided-type undercarriage consisted of two cantilever long-travel telescopic shock absorber legs fitted with medium pressure wheels carried in forks. The wheels were originally designed to be faired in streamlined trousers but, in the event, wheel spats similar to those used on the Tipsy were fitted.

The Dove was initially powered by a 28 hp Aero Engines Sprite two-cylinder opposed air-cooled engine mounted on rubber blocks on laterally braced steel-tube bearers. The mounting was designed to take any engine of 100 lb weight and of approximately 30 hp. The 8 gal fuel tank was carried in the fuselage and the surface-cooled oil tank was located below the engine.

The open cockpit was located over the wing and featured an adjustable pilot's seat and an optional coupe top. There was a baggage locker behind the cockpit.

The Dove was marketed at £225 complete, or for £165 in kit form for construction by homebuilders. In addition, if a Dove was bought off the shelf the purchase price included full instruction to 'A' Licence standard on a Gipsy Moth!

Shortly after the Dove's first flight the company was restructured and its capital increased to £2,500. The following month Premier Aircraft began a series of Sunday ultra-light fly-ins, held at Maylands, the primary purpose of such meetings being to demonstrate the company's new product. The Dove, now registered *G-AETU*, was sold in July to the Romford Flying Club.

A batch of seven Doves was registered in the *G-AEZA*, *'ZB* and *G-AFAC-'AG* series but sadly only two were built. *G-AEZA* was registered to the Earl of Cardigan and received its Authorisation to Fly on 1 July 1937; the second Dove, *G-AEZB*, was Authorized on 24 August and sold to J.K. Flower. Two weeks later the brand new aircraft was damaged beyond repair at Tilbury.

Below *Remarkably similar to the Tipsy S2 the pretty little Gordon Dove, designed by S.C. Buszard, was flown on 3 march 1937. (The Aeroplane photograph)* **Bottom** *The prototype Gordon Dove, G-AETU, was powered by a 750 cc Douglas Sprite and had a maximum speed of 95 mph. (Flight photograph)*

The Dove was put on the market at a fly away price of £225, including free instruction on Gipsy Moth trainers, or for £165 in kit form. (Flight photograph)

The year 1937 was also a bad year for the rival Tipsy S 2. Of the six built, two crashed and the others were withdrawn from use or scrapped, all in the space of six months. Whether this had an adverse affect on the Doves one cannot say. The Tipsy machine had a vicious stall and the Dove too dropped a wing sharply, though its mean chord made the drop less marked than that of the Tipsy. Tipsy cured the problem to some extent by fitting leading edge slats and adding washout at the wingtips.

The Dove was also underpowered. Perhaps if it had flown with a larger engine and had possessed less alarming stalling characteristics, this neat little aeroplane would have fared better than it did. In the end the company had insufficient funds to market the Dove effectively and the final batch of five Doves never materialized. Curiously, the same fate overtook Tipsy Light Aircraft over at Hanworth. The three final aircraft, allocated registration marks in the same batch as the unbuilt Doves, were never built. Further plans to produce a two-seat cabin version powered by an eight-cylinder vee engine of around 65 hp came to nothing and the Premier company went the same way as so many small firms in the immediate pre-war years.

Gordon Dove data	
Span	27 ft 3 in
Length	18 ft 3 in
Height	5 ft 8 in
Wing area	112 ft²
Empty weight	382 lb
All-up weight	600 lb
Maximum speed	95 mph
Cruising speed	85 mph
Stalling/landing speed	28 mph

Carden-Baynes Bee

The Carden-Baynes Bee twin-engined high-wing monoplane had an all-up weight in excess of 1,000 lb and strictly speaking has no place in this book. It is included because its maximum weight of 1,350 lb was almost half that of standard light twins of the day; it can thus be classed as an ultra-light twin.

L.E. Baynes' first venture from sailplane design to powered aircraft began with the Carden-Baynes Scud III Auxiliary described in an earlier chapter. The Auxiliary was built to the order of Sir John Carden, whose work on converting a Ford car engine into a useful, reliable powerplant for ultra-light aircraft was outlined in the chapter covering British-built Mignet HM 14 Poux. Before the Flea hysteria L.E. Baynes had joined up with E.D. Abbott to form Abbott-Baynes in 1931 to build Scud sailplanes. Later they built a Flea variant powered by Sir John Carden's converted Ford 10 car engine and, when Sir John was killed in December 1935, Baynes took over the Carden engine concern and set up Carden-Baynes at Heston. Shortly afterwards Baynes finalized a design for an unorthodox twin-engined ultralight which embodied a revolutionary folding wing device.

The Carden-Baynes Bee was a two-seat twin-engined high-wing cabin monoplane, built at Heston in 1937. The fuselage was a wooden rectangular section structure of spruce and plywood. The decking aft of the wing was split longitudinally and hinged along the outer edges in order that it could be folded out of the way when the wing was revolved in the manner to be described. The plywood skin was stiffened by attaching external half-rounded beaded strips, rather in the fashion that de Havilland strengthened the Dragon and Desoutter the Monoplane.

Above *The Bee photographed at Heston early in 1937 from where Hubert Broad made the aircraft's first flight on 3 April. (The Aeroplane photograph)* **Left** *The Bee's two 40 hp Carden SP1 engines were fully concealed in the wings and were arranged so that they lay horizontally behind the rear boom of the spar. (The Aeroplane photograph)* **Below left** *The most remarkable aspect of the Bee was the way in which the wing was turned through 90° for folding, giving a folded width of 9 ft. (Flight photograph)* **Bottom** *Sketch of structure showing position of fuel tanks in the wing leading edge, the accessibility of the cabin, the large doors and the fuselage's proximity to the ground.*

The one-piece wing consisted of a single broad box beam with spruce booms and plywood walls, with light spruce former-ribs. The wing leading edge was ply-covered and the remainder of the wing was fabric covered. The Bee's party piece was the way in which the wing was turned on its axis for storage. The wing was attached to the fuselage at three points. By withdrawing pins at the two front attachment points the entire wing was allowed to swivel around the third point through 90° to allow the wing to lie along the

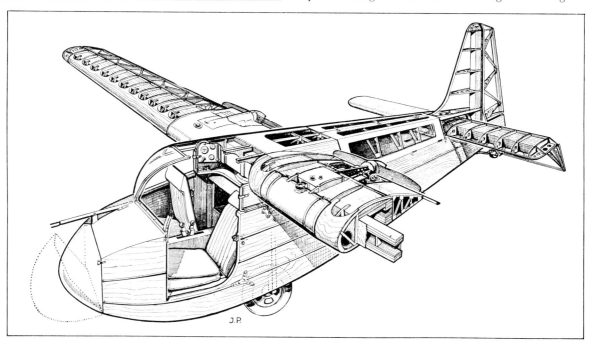

top of the fuselage. With the wing swivelled into the folded position the Bee had a width of 9 ft.

The tail unit consisted of a single plywood-covered box for the tailplane, while the fin, rudder and elevators were wooden frames covered with fabric. The two Dowty undercarriage legs were mounted vertically inside the fuselage walls and were fitted with low-pressure wheels which protruded through the fuselage floor.

The two 50 hp Carden four-cylinder inline water-cooled engines were mounted on their sides in the wing trailing edges. They drove pusher propellers via extension shafts. The engine mountings consisted of flanged steel plates sandwiched between the upper and lower halves of the crankcases and attached to the top and bottom flanges of the wing spar. The radiators lay flat in the wing in such a way that cool air was allowed to flow above and below them. Each engine had a 5 gal fuel tank installed ahead of it in the wing leading edge.

Access to the Bee's cabin was simple. Doors were located either side of the low 42 in-wide fuselage. The canopy was hinged to the top of the wing and could be laid back on the top of the wing in a similar fashion to that of the Praga. Inside the cockpit there was a single 'Y' type control column and duplicated rudder stirrups. The backs of the seats were shaped to take parachutes and they could be tilted forward for access to the baggage compartment behind.

Test pilot Hubert Broad, who had test flown many of de Havilland's aircraft, made the Bee's first flight, from Heston on 3 April 1937. Sadly, Carden-Baynes Aircraft went into receivership on 29 June and, though there were plans to modify the Bee to carry three or more seats, very little further work was carried out. Although it was allocated the registration letters *G-AEWC*, it never carried these markings. In due course Heston was acquired by the Air Ministry and companies such as Carden-Baynes were forced to move or quit. The Bee was scrapped in 1939 at about the same time that civil flying ceased on the declaration of war in September.

Carden-Baynes Bee data	
Span	29 ft 10 in
	9 ft 0 in
	(wings folded)
Length	23 ft 0 in
Height	4 ft 9 in
Wing area	141 ft^2
Empty weight	880 lb
All-up weight	1,350 lb
Maximum speed	110 mph
	(estimated)
Cruising speed	100 mph
Stalling/landing speed	40 mph

De Bruyne-Maas Ladybird

The use of plastics in aircraft construction will hardly raise an eyebrow today, but in the early 1930s, the concept was the subject of incredulity and some suspicion. One of the pioneers of the use of plastics in this field was Dr de Bruyne, Director of Aero Research Ltd. The company was formed at Duxford, Cambridgeshire in 1934 to carry out research into the

The De Bruyne Ladybird research aircraft, built by Aero Research in 1937 but completed by J. N. Maas later that year. (CIBA-GEIGY (UK) Ltd photograph)

Top *Squadron Leader Doig seated in the completed Ladybird. The aircraft was allotted the civil registration G-AFEG — the markings visible in this photograph are unidentified.* (Via A.J. Jackson Collection)
Above *Poor but unique photograph of the Ladybird during early taxi trials with Doig at the controls.* (Via Doig)

characteristics of reinforced synthetic resin materials in relation to their use in aircraft construction. In April that year Captain Geoffrey de Havilland had referred to the possible use of synthetic resin materials in aircraft construction in a paper he read before the Royal Aeronautical Society. De Bruyne received considerable assistance from de Havilland in connection with research into the use of plastics in the construction of variable-pitch propellers. Further work looked into the problems of stressed-plywood skin construction. In order to put his theories into practice, de Bruyne's Aero Research company built a four-seat low-wing cabin monoplane called the De Bruyne Snark. Built in 1934, the Snark embodied low-weight, bakelite-bonded plywood, stressed skin in the wing and fuselage structures. Powered by a 130 hp DH Gipsy Major engine, the 42 ft 6 in span research aircraft weighed 1,200 lb empty and 2,200 lb fully loaded. Registered *G-ADDL*, the Snark was first flown at Cambridge by its designer on 16 December 1934. It was granted a Certificate of Airworthiness the following April shortly before it was sent to RAE Farnborough as *L6103* for research into the aero-

dynamic characteristics of thick-wing monoplanes.

In December 1936 de Bruyne set to work on a second research aircraft on which to test two products which were to be of great significance to aircraft manufacturers. The first was a synthetic material known as Aerolite, which was Bakelite reinforced with fabric or cord. This material proved to surpass all other materials, including high-tensile steel, in stiffness/weight and strength/weight. The other product was a glue which, after approval by the Air Ministry, was quickly supplied to British manufacturers of aircraft and propellers. The de Havilland Aircraft company was one of the first companies to produce propeller blades made of cord Aerolite.

Dr de Bruyne's second research aircraft, named the Ladybird, was begun by Aero Research during 1937 but was sold before it was completed to Dutch student J.N. Maas later that year. The unorthodox-looking Ladybird was a shoulder-wing single-seater powered by a 25 hp Scott Squirrel engine. The monocoque fuselage was of oval section and was plywood covered. The wing had a rectangular centre-section to which were attached the tapered wings. The centre-section had a high-lift aerofoil which changed to a symmetrical section at the tips. Each wing was a single-spar structure with plywood-covered leading edges to retain torsional rigidity. Slotted Frise ailerons were fitted and the wing was attached to the fuselage just forward of the cockpit by simple plates. The all-wood cantilever tailplane had all the controls enclosed and the fin was built integral with the fuselage.

Unusually for the time, the Ladybird had a tricycle undercarriage with a steerable nosewheel. The two main wheels were carried in faired cantilever legs. The trailing edge of each faired leg could be rotated to act as an airbrake.

Registered *G-AFEG*, the Ladybird was first flown by R.G. Doig, of Scheldemusch fame, from Cambridge late in 1937. The Scott Squirrel was later replaced with a 30 hp Bristol Cherub two-cylinder air-cooled engine. The Ladybird survived the war and is rumoured to be in storage somewhere in the Peterborough area.

De Bruyne-Maas Ladybird data	
Span	32 ft 0 in
Length	20 ft 0 in
Height	not available
Wing area	106 ft²
Empty weight	420 lb
All-up weight	800 lb
Maximum speed	95 mph
Cruising speed	75 mph
Stalling/landing speed	not available

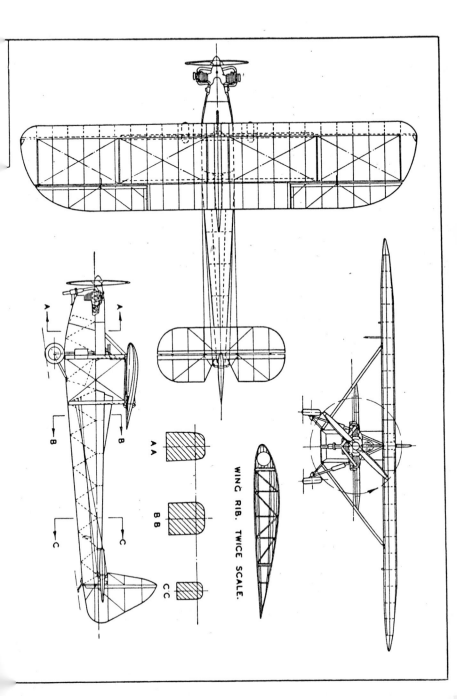

WING RIB. TWICE SCALE.

A A

B B

C C

Luton LA 2/LA 3 and LA 4 Minor

When the Flea craze had reached its peak in Britain, and soon after a number of home-built examples had crashed with fatal consequences for their pilots, one or two British aircraft designers decided to either improve the breed or produce something along similar lines but possessing better stability and more orthodox means of control. In addition to the Perman Parasol and the Broughton-Blayney Brawney there was the Luton LA 2, designed by the talented C.H. Latimer-Needham, creator of the Halton Mayfly and the LA 1 Buzzard, both described elsewhere in this book.

The Luton LA 2 was originally to be known as the Minor but in the event this name was used for the later LA 3, described later. Like Mignet's HM 14, the LA 2 was of tandem-wing configuration but differed in that it had ailerons and an orthodox tail unit. The 22 ft span forward wing was mounted 18 in above and forward of the 20 ft span rear wing on a centre-section pylon. This arrangement provided a slot-effect and made it impossible for the rear wing to stall. The wing section of both wings was Clark YH, though originally it had been the intention to use another section for the rear wing at a later date. The Clark YH section had good stalling characteristics and only a small movement of the centre of pressure. It was planned to give the rear wing variable incidence of $+1°$ to $+10°$. In the event the incidence was fixed at $+4°$, with the front wing incidence set at $+1°$.

The LA 2 was constructed of wood and the forward section of the fuselage was of plywood box-construction, while the rear portion was fabric-covered spruce Warren-girder structure. Each wing was built around large-section rectangular box spars 12 in wide and 6 in deep which took both bending and torsion loads. A pair of single lift struts supported each wing and the rear portion of the centre-section of

Above *Two views of the tandem-winged Luton LA2, powered by a 34 hp Anzani inverted V air-cooled engine, designed as a Pou replacement.*
Below *The sole Luton LA3, G-AEPD, the forerunner of the LA4 Minor was completed in February 1937.*

the front wing was Perspex-covered to give the pilot adequate view. The aircraft sat on a simple under-carriage consisting of a pair of axle tubes hinged at, and protruding from, the base of the fuselage sides. The inner extensions acted on compression rubbers. Power for the LA 2 was supplied by a 34 hp Anzani inverted V air-cooled engine.

The aircraft was built at Barton-in-the-Clay in Bedfordshire and was completed towards the end of

1936. Early flights revealed a poor climb performance. Had the wing incidence-changing mechanism been incorporated, as originally planned, perhaps further tests would have produced the estimated performance. If this had been the case the LA 2's successor — an aeroplane that was to become one of the most successful ultra-lights produced in this country — may never have materialized.

Because the small Luton Aircraft company had insufficient funds to modify the LA 2's wing for variable incidence, the decision was taken to produce a more conventional high-wing monoplane. In January 1937 work began on the Luton LA 3. This involved marrying a completely new wing to the LA 2 fuselage. The aircraft was finished in February 1937 and an Authorisation to Fly was issued on 3 March, the day it made its first flight, from Heston. Registered *G-AEPD*, the sole LA 3 was the forerunner of the LA 4 Minor. It was sold to A.J. Cook of

Anstruther in Fife and survived the war to be wrecked shortly afterwards when a car backed into it. The LA 3 had a top speed of 80 mph and cruised at 60 mph; it could cover 60 miles to the gallon.

The prototype LA 4 Minor which followed was superficially similar but differed from the LA 3 in detail. It was built at the company's new Phoenix Works at Gerrards Cross and was fitted with a 40 hp ABC Scorpion engine. Registered *G-AFBP* and priced at £200, the Minor was designed solely for home construction and was the only example built by the parent company. All subsequent Minors were built from plans supplied by Luton Aircraft.

The Luton Minor had a fuselage of rectangular structure with a cambered decking. The spruce framework was ply-covered throughout. The wings were of low aspect ratio and the aerofoil chosen was RAF 48, a section which combined good aerodynamic qualities with gentle stalling characteristics. The large-area parasol wing was supported in two sections above the fuselage on steel tube pylons, and braced on either side by a pair of parallel struts. The wings were built up on two wooden plank spars and were ply-covered at the leading edges and at the tips, the rest of the structure being fabric-covered. The wing panels were easily detachable. The tailplane was a fabric-covered structure with unbalanced elevators, but with a balanced floating rudder.

The undercarriage was of the split type and consisted of telescopic legs with rubber shock absorbers, the upper ends of which were attached to the upper fuselage longerons, with the lower ends hinged to

Above *The Luton LA 3 Minor used components from the LA 2 and was powered by the same Anzani engine and first flown from Barton-in-the-Clay in 1936.* **Below** *The prototype Luton LA 4 Minor, G-AFBP was powered by a 40 hp ABC Scorpion and was the first aircraft to be built at the Luton company's Phoenix Works premises at Gerrards Cross.*

steel tube vees which in turn were hinged to the bottom longerons.

The open cockpit was positioned immediately beneath the wing and a door on the port side gave easy access. The view from the cockpit was good except for immediately above.

The 35 hp Luton Anzani two-cylinder inverted-V air-cooled engine was fitted with dual ignition and an impulse starter. A 6 gal fuel tank was carried in the fuselage.

The first flight date of the prototype Minor is not recorded. The aircraft remained the property of Luton Aircraft for five years until it was destroyed in the works fire of 1943. Although four homebuilt Minors were registered before the war, only two were completed. The first was *G-AFIR*, built by J.S. Squires at Rearsby and completed in 1938. The other was *G-AFRC*, built at Douglas on the Isle of Man by J.E. Carine and later flown from Hall Caine's privately-owned aerodrome. On 2 September 1939 the aircraft forced-landed into trees while approaching RAF Jurby with a dead engine. Although undamaged by its arrested landing, its subsequent return to terra firma seriously damaged the machine and vandals made sure that it never flew again after it was put into storage at Andreas aerodrome. Luton Minors *G-AFIU* and *G-AFUG* were only partially built and the fuselage of the former aircraft is stored at Cheadle in Cheshire at the time of writing.

Since the war around fifty Luton Minors have been registered and in March 1958 C.H. Latimer-Needham and Arthur Ord-Hume founded Phoenix Aircraft Ltd to acquire the Luton design rights. The airframe was re-stressed to allow the use of modern, more powerful engines and the tailplane was redesigned with fin and horn-balanced rudder. With the all-up weight increased from 690 lb to 750 lb the new design was designated LA 4A. With plans sold all over the world, Minors were flown with many different types of engine. It is quite probable that the Luton Minor will enter the history books as the ultralight with the longest continuous production record.

Luton LA 4 Minor data (Luton Anzani)

Span	25 ft 0 in
Length	20 ft 0 in
Height	6 ft 3 in
Wing area	125 ft²
Empty weight	380 lb
All-up weight	600 lb
Maximum speed	85 mph
Cruising speed	75 mph
Stalling/landing speed	30 mph

The prototype Chilton DW1, G-AESZ, *photographed at Chilton Foliat shortly after completion in March 1937. (The Aeroplane photograph)*

Chilton DW 1

One of the finest British ultra-light aircraft ever built came not from an established aircraft company but from two talented ex-students of the de Havilland Technical School at Hatfield. A.R. Ward, son of the Hon Sir John Ward, and the Hon Andrew H. Dalrymple, son of Lord Stair, were educated at Eton together, though they were not to become acquainted until a school outing to one of the RAF Pageants at Hendon in the early 1930s. Both men became students at the de Havilland Technical School, where they worked on the TK 1 and TK 2 aircraft, thereby receiving a thorough grounding in aircraft construction, aerodynamics, stressing and so forth. Towards the end of their term the two men considered that they could produce an aircraft better than existing ultra-lights and the germ of the idea for the Chilton was born.

Originally to be called the Mayfly, the Chilton was committed to paper during 1935-36. Ward was more or less responsible for the Chilton's lines and his partner worked out the structure and stressing. The Chilton was an original design and had nothing to do with the TK 3, nor was it a copy of the Miles Hawk as has been recorded elsewhere. Rather than mess about with noisy unreliable two-stroke engines, the designers opted for the Carden-Ford, a 32 hp conversion of the Ford 10 car engine which was available for around £50. At a weight of 180 lb, though, it was very heavy and was to account for almost half the Chilton's tare weight. The water-cooled Carden was, however, a reliable, smooth, four-cylinder engine that had been well-tried in various aircraft. Dalrymple had his work cut out juggling with the position of the centre of gravity and, with a power-to-weight ratio of nearly 5 lb/hp, the little aeroplane was a designer's nightmare.

The task the designers had set themselves was to produce an orthodox aeroplane in miniature, capable of a decent performance, with a cruising speed of 100

Above *This photograph of the prototype Chilton shows well the split trailing edge flaps beneath the wings and centre-section.* **Below** *The Chilton's roomy cockpit was located over the centre of the wing and the semi-reclining seat was slung between the spars. Two luggage compartments were located behind the seat, capable of carrying a load of 20 lb.* (*Flight* photograph)

mph. Construction of the first Chilton began in early May 1936, in a tiny shed at the back of Ward's parents' home, Chilton's Lodge, at Chilton Foliat near Hungerford in Berkshire. Fred Luscombe, who had been lured away from his job as a junior instructor at de Havilland, was employed and by the time jigs had been made and static testing had taken place a year was to pass before the first aircraft was completed. After the prototype had flown a small work force was employed to build subsequent models. The static tests, incidentally, were carried out by simply loading bricks on to a test wing. Even before the wings had been attached Ward was taxiing the Chilton around the grounds in order to assess its ground handling.

The prototype Chilton, *G-AESZ*, was completed toward the end of March and it was taken to Witney for its first flight. This was carried out by another ex-de Havilland Technical School student Ranald Porteous, who test flew a number of ultra-light aircraft before the war and who subsequently became Auster Aircraft's test pilot during the 1940s and 1950s. The Chilton was first flown on 16 April 1937 and, though the aircraft flew faultlessly, the engine overheated and the radiator and cowling subsequently required modifications. Overheating persisted until further modification were made and then, on 3 May 1937, *G-AESZ* flew its first cross-country flight, from Witney to Brooklands. Shortly afterwards it was badly damaged during a forced landing when it ran out of fuel. It was back in the air by 11 August and there followed a great deal of flying during which nearly ninety pilots tried their hands at the Chilton. In 1938 the prototype was sold to J.A.

Talbot at Roborough, Plymouth.

The prototype Chilton had proved to be a practical, easy-to-fly aeroplane and, though there were problems with propellers and the high-revving Carden engine, there were few snags with the basic design. Interestingly, the only engine problems occurred when the Chilton was refuelled away from base and this was caused by pilots filling up with 65 octane fuel instead of 80 octane Shell which could be obtained from local garage pumps.

The Chilton DW 1 was a low-wing cantilever monoplane of orthodox construction and design. The fuselage was a rectangular wooden semi-monocoque structure built on spruce longerons and ribs, the whole frame being ply covered. The fuselage top decking had a slight double curvature.

The wings, built in three sections comprising the parallel centre-section with detachable tapered outer panels, were built up on two spruce box spars with birch plywood and spruce ribs. The wing was ply-wood covered as far back as the rear spar, aft of which they were fabric covered. The differential wooden-framed ailerons were also fabric covered. Split trailing edge flaps occupied 50 per cent of the span.

The cantilever tail unit was of wooden framework. The fin and tailplane were ply covered and the elevators and rudder were fabric covered. The wide-track undercarriage was of the divided type, each undercarriage leg being a robust cantilever structure of steel tubing with coil spring telescopic legs, giving a 4 in travel. Each unit was neatly faired in a stream-lined trouser fairing, the front of which could easily be detached for inspection purposes. The tailskid was rubber-mounted and sprung.

Above *The second Chilton DW1,* G-AFGH, *photographed near Denham in April 1949 with Squadron Leader H. R. Bilborough at the controls.* (E.J. Riding photograph) **Below** *Chilton* G-AFGI *photographed post-war after Lieutenant Commander John Sproule added an Olympus sailplane-type bubble canopy in order to add a further 5 mph to the top speed.*

The 32 hp Carden-Ford four-cylinder inline upright water-cooled engine had dual ignition and was fitted with a special crankcase incorporating a heavy-duty ball race to take the propeller thrust. In order to reduce the weight of the heavy engine a special cylinder head and many light castings were made of alloy. Because of the absence of vibration, the engine was bolted directly to the fuselage. Behind the engine was a metal fireproof bulkhead, and behind that was the 8 gal fuel tank.

The roomy open cockpit was located over the centre of the wing and the semi-reclining seat was slung between the spars — the Moseley Float-on-air upholstery. Entry was via flap doors either side of the

Above *The Train-engined Chilton DW1A G-AFSV was completed just before the war and was the fourth and last Chilton completed. (Flight photograph)* **Below** *In 1956 Chilton G-AFSV was fitted with a 62 hp Walter Mikron engine. The aircraft, named Barbara Ann III, is seen here being flown by the late Manx Kelly. (Air Portraits photograph)*

fuselage and an efficient draught-free windscreen was fitted. An optional closed cabin top was advertised at additional cost. There were two luggage compartments, one large one behind the seat with a smaller locker above it, capable of carrying a load of 20 lb.

At £315 ex-works, the Chilton was an exciting proposition for a sporting pilot. It was fully aerobatic and had a maximum speed of 112 mph. The still-air take-off run was only 80 yds and the landing run was only 50 yds. With the 6 ft undercarriage track there was little danger of groundlooping.

While the prototype Chilton was giving many pilots their first experience of flying a monoplane, two other Chiltons were nearing completion at Chilton Foliat. On 28 April 1938 Dalrymple took the blue and silver *G-AFGH* into the air for the first time and on 8 May it was demonstrated at the Royal Aeronautical Society's Garden Party at Heathrow. The third Chilton, *G-AFGI*, followed and the only difference between these aircraft and the prototype was

the shape of the engine cowlings. *G-AFGH* was the only Chilton to be fitted with fixed slats. Chilton *G-AFGI* was registered on 20 October 1938 and was sold to F.D. Paul who kept it at Broxbourne in Herts.

In August 1937 Chilton Aircraft took over the Carden-Ford engine business. The engine's designer, Sir John Carden, had died in December 1935 in an aircraft accident, and for a while the company had been run by Carden-Baynes. The Chilton concern took over the company only to satisfy its own engine requirements, though it would have sold them to anyone, and there were no plans to put the engine into production. Any engine work was later passed to a local garage, though carried out under Chilton supervision. Shortly afterwards Ward began looking around for a suitable lighter air-cooled engine and managed to track down a Train engine in France. Rated at 44 hp, this engine was fitted into the fourth and final Chilton, *G-AFSV*, which was given the designation DW 1A. This aircraft had steel tube engine bearers and was first flown in July 1939, just two months before the outbreak of war. The Train-engined Chilton had a fly-away price of £375, making it appreciably more expensive than its Carden-powered brethren. In addition, spares for the French engine would undoubtedly have proved a problem.

Shortly after its first flight, *G-AFSV* was entered and flown in the Folkestone Aero Trophy Race, held at Lympne on 5 August 1939. Andrew Dalrymple won the race averaging 126 mph but it was to be the last major air race before war stopped all civil flying. The Wakefield Challenge Cup, in which three Chiltons were entered, was cancelled.

When war was declared, Chilton Aircraft had already started work on a two-seat cabin version of the DW 1. Designated DW 2, construction of this aircraft was interrupted first by the building of *G-AFSV* and then again when *G-AFGH* required repairing after a crash at Leicester. Designed with the needs of the Civil Air Guard in mind, the DW 2 was about two-thirds completed when work stopped with the war. The DW 2 was to remain in the Chilton Lodge coach house for 45 years before being rediscovered by the author in 1984, together with a collection of Chilton DW 1 components. Everything was removed to Hamble in the hope that the DW 2 will be completed at least to static condition.

All four Chiltons spent the war in company with a spare fuselage in a small hangar on the Earl of Cardigan's strip at Savernake. Chilton Aircraft dabbled in glider design and construction towards the end of the war but from the moment that Andrew Dalrymple was killed flying a Fieseler Storch on Christmas Day 1945, the company's aeronautical activities ceased. Though the Chilton company was engaged mainly with the production of small machined parts, two uncompleted DFS Meise sail-planes were moved to Elliots of Newbury for completion and that company later put the type into production. Chilton Aircraft later became Chilton Electric Products and the company exists today as Chilton Ottermill, producing circuit breakers and shaver sockets. Following Dalrymple's death some equipment and Chilton components, plus the four Chiltons, were sold. Sadly, all the Chilton jigs were used to make benches for an expanding wartime workshop. Ward did not return to aviation. Though Chilton Aircraft disappeared, the four Chiltons survived to fly for some considerable time.

With its immediate pre-war promise as a racing machine, the type competed regularly in many post-war race meetings. The first post-war success occurred when Ranald Porteous broke the 100 km closed-circuit record at Lympne on 31 August 1947 in *G-AFSV*, still in its black and white colour scheme, with an average speed of 124.5 mph.

Chilton *G-AFGH* was bought by Ranald Porteous but it was soon sold to Dr Myles Bickerton at Denham. Unfortunately the aircraft crashed at South Chalfont on 3 July 1949 and as the aircraft was required for competing in the National Air Races, to be held at Elmdon from 29 July-1 August, the fuselage of *G-AESZ* was borrowed to replace the damaged centre-section and fuselage of 'GH. Still registered *G-AFGH*, the Chilton came thirteenth in the Grosvenor Challenge Cup Race at 95.5 mph with Squadron Leader H.R. Bilborough flying. Later a spare fuselage was used to repair 'GH; *G-AESZ* was whole once more and remained so until it was destroyed in a crash near Felixstowe on 24 May 1953, seriously injuring its owner, Dr W.L. James.

The two other Chiltons, *G-AFGI* and *G-AFSV*, were both extensively raced and variously modified for that purpose. Lieutenant Commander John Sproule's *G-AFGI* was given an Olympia sailplane-type bubble canopy which added a further 5 mph to the top speed. This aircraft was acquired in 1951 by Hugh Kendal who stripped it and generally lightened the structure before re-covering it and entering it for the *Daily Express* air race held from Shoreham in September 1951. Kendal ran away with the race with an impressive average speed of 129 mph. Fifteen years later this Chilton was flying with a 55 hp Lycoming engine installed.

Chilton *G-AFSV* had its Train engine replaced with a 62 hp Walter Mikron II. It too was fitted for a while with a bubble canopy and, in this state, with almost double the original power of the prototype Chilton, won the Kemsley Challenge Trophy race with an average speed of 148.7 mph.

At the time of writing only *G-AFGH* is airworthy, though *G-AFGI* and *G-AFSV* are under restoration.

In addition to restoring *G-AFSV* to its Train-engined configuration, owner Roy Nerou is building a new Chilton DW 1A, registered *G-BDLV*. In addition Don Giffin of Savanna, Ontario is building another, registered *C-GIFF*.

The following operating costs for the Chilton, taken over a three-year period up to the war, make interesting reading and were supplied by the co-designer of the aircraft, A.R. Ward:

Purchase price of the aircraft	£315	
Resale value after three years	£80	
Depreciation	£230	
	or 3s 1d per hr	

Comprehensive insurance at £50 per annum	2s 0d per hr

Maintenance costs:

Engine overhauls, including reboring and renewal of most working parts after each 400 hrs at £12	£12
Airframe maintenance and renewal at £10 per 400 hrs	£10
Repainting once per 1,000 hrs at £10	£4
Detail replacements, supplies, cleaning materials — £1 per 100 hrs	£4
Total maintenance costs	£30 per 400 hrs

Running costs:

Petrol 1.8 gal per hr at 1s 4½ d per gal	2s 6d
Oil ½ pint per hr at 4s per gal (including refills)	3d
Total running costs	2s 9d per hr

Operating costs:

Depreciation	3s 1d
Insurance	2s 0d
Maintenance	1s 6d
Running costs	2s 9d
Total operating costs	9s 4d per hr

Chilton DW 1 data (Carden-Ford)	
Span	24 ft 0 in
Length	18 ft 0 in
Height	4 ft 10 in
Wing area	77 ft²
Empty weight	398 lb
All-up weight	640 lb
Maximum speed	112 mph
Cruising speed	100 mph
Stalling/landing speed	35 mph

Chilton DW 1A data (Train)	
Span	24 ft 0 in
Length	18 ft 0 in
Height	4 ft 10 in
Wing area	77 ft²
Empty weight	380 lb
All-up weight	650 lb
Maximum speed	135 mph
Cruising speed	115 mph
Stalling/landing speed	35 mph

Currie Wot

It was F.D. Bradbrooke of *The Aeroplane* who said that there were two approaches to the problem of designing an ultra-light aircraft. One, he said, was to design for the performance of a real aeroplane using modern gadgets, which would result in an 'aerodrome' machine. The other course was to resign oneself to the fact that such modern gadgets as were practicable in a cheap aeroplane did not help take-off and therefore large wings and low loading were necessary — better, he said, to make something on the old, well-proved and sound lines without disguise.

John Robert Currie certainly subscribed to the latter philosophy when he designed the dated and angular-looking Currie Wot back in 1937. Currie was both a pilot and a qualified ground engineer and was also a lecturer at the College of Aeronautical Engineering at Chelsea. He designed the Wot as a simple, safe and cheap-to-run single-seater with no frills, suitable for operation by flying clubs. Sharing his ideals and enthusiasm was W.E. Davis, the managing director of the Lympne-based Cinque Ports Flying Club, where Currie worked as the club's chief ground engineer and during 1937 work began on two aircraft in the corner of the Lympne workshop.

Looking rather like a scaled down Avro Avian, the Wot had a large wing area and was of low weight. Powered by a 40 hp Aeronca JAP J-99 two-cylinder engine, it was simply-built of spruce and plywood with mild steel fittings throughout.

The Wot's fuselage consisted of spruce longerons and cross members with plywood decking and sides. There were three stiffening bulkheads and a fireproof bulkhead, to which the JAP engine was mounted on mild steel bearers, which in turn were mounted on rubber to absorb vibration. A 6 gal fuel tank was positioned between the pilot and the engine, with plenty of provision for extra tankage if required. A locker was located in the top fuselage decking behind the pilot.

Each wing was made up of two solid spars of

spruce, with three bays of wooden bracing. There was no spindling or routing. Each wing had eleven main ribs and nine nose ribs and a plywood-covered leading edge. The cabane consisted of six faired, mild-steel tubular struts braced with two pairs of wires. The interplane struts were of spruce.

The simple undercarriage consisted of two V-shaped tubular legs to which were welded two tubular crosspieces. A streamlined axle, attached with bungee cord, bore two low-pressure wheels. There were no brakes, the tailskid providing adequate braking on grass.

The prototype Wot, *G-AFCG*, was completed during the summer of 1937 and received its Authorisation to Fly on 22 November that year. It was first registered to Cinque Ports Aviation Ltd. The second Wot, registered *G-AFDS*, was granted an Authorisation to fly on 21 March 1938 and was put into service with the local Cinque Ports Flying Club. It is said that the two aircraft shared the same 40 hp Aeronca JAP motor, taken from the wrecked Aeronca C-3 *G-ADZZ*.

The two Wots differed in minor respects. The wingtips of the prototype were square-cut, the top of

Above right *The prototype Currie Wot,* G-AFCG, *photographed at Lympne in December 1937 a month after receiving its Authorisation to Fly. (The Aeroplane photograph)* **Right** *The Currie Wot was initially offered on the market at £250, less than half the price of a standard sized biplane.* G-AFCG *remained with Cinque Ports Aviation Ltd.* **Below** *The second Currie Wot,* G-AFDS, *differed from the prototype in minor ways. The rudder was taller, the diagonal centre-section struts sloped backwards and the nose was a different shape.*

Above *Currie Wot* G-APWT *was first flown on 20 October 1959, 22 years after the prototype first flew. It was initially powered by a 60 hp Walter Mikron II engine.* (*Flight* photograph) **Below** *The Currie Wot* G-APWT *powered by a 70 hp Rover axial flow gas turbine engine, installed in November 1960.* (*Flight* photograph)

the rudder was a different shape, the diagonal centre-section struts sloped forward and the underside of the nose was rounded rather than square-cut as on the second Wot.

The Wot was put on to the market at £250, which was considerably less than half the price of a Moth or Avian. It could take off in 50 yds, cruise at 72 mph and burned around 2 gal of fuel an hour. It was very pleasant to fly, had a reasonable climb performance

and was viceless. The cockpit was roomy for a 20 ft-aircraft. For all this the Wot was not put into production and, on the outbreak of war, both aircraft were put into storage at Lympne, where they remained until destroyed during a German air raid in May 1940. But that is not the end of the Wot story.

After the war John Isaacs, later of Isaacs Spitfire and Fury fame, acquired the original Wot drawings and, with financial help from Vivian Bellamy, two further Wots were built by the Hampshire Aeroplane Club at Eastleigh, where John Currie was working as chief engineer. The first new aircraft, *G-APNT*, was powered by an Aeronca JAP engine and was first flown on 11 September 1958, from Eastleigh. Six further aircraft were planned with a view to selling them for £600 each, and sets of plans were made available to home-builders at £12/10s per set.

It soon became evident that the Aeronca-engined Wot was underpowered, and a 60 hp Walter Mikron II was fitted in its stead. In addition, Wessex Ship-yard at nearby Bursledon built a set of floats for *G-APNT*; but the aircraft was purchased by Westland test pilot Harald Penrose before trials of the Wet Wot, as it was called, could be undertaken. With the

Walter Mikron the Wot's performance was improved considerably and as such '*NT* became known as the Hot Wot, though it was delivered to Penrose with the 36 hp JAP engine. In January 1960 the aircraft was re-engined with a 55 hp Lycoming and was returned to Penrose. Named *Airymouse* this aircraft was made the subject of a most delightful book by its owner.

By October 1959 the second post-war Wot, *G-APWT*, was flying. It differed from '*NT* by way of its shorter nose and a fin and rudder of increased area. The heavier Walter Mikron II engine necessitated shortening the nose to correct the centre of gravity. After successful tests on the float under-carriage '*WT* was fitted with a 60 hp Rover gas turbine engine. It was first flown in this form by Bellamy in January 1960 and not surprisingly it became known as the Jet Wot. In November that year a 90 hp TP/90.1 turboprop was fitted to the Wot. This engine had run for years in cars and was even used as an APU for the Vulcan and Argosy. Rover considered that the engine had distinct possibilities in the light aircraft market and it was hoped that it would be fitted into the aging Austers and some of the Cessna and Piper range. When fitted into the Wot it gave the aircraft a very quiet, smooth performance; even in the Wot's open cockpit there was hardly any audible engine noise and only the faintest vibration was perceptible.

During the following year the Wot reverted to its Mikron engine and in this form was sold to Roy Mills' MPM Flying Group and based at Elstree. Since then several home-built Wots have been built, powered by various engines. Six were built for film work by Slingsby Sailplanes Ltd. Built to represent World War One SE 5s, these aircraft were registered *G-AVOT-G-AVOY* and were designated Slingsby Type 56. Powered by 115 hp Lycoming engines, these 83 per cent scale replicas were featured in the films *Darlin' Lili, I Shot Down Richthofen* and *Dubious Patriot.*

Currie Wot data (prototype)	
Span	22 ft 0 in
Length	18 ft 2 in
Height	6 ft 9 in
Wing area	145 ft^2
Empty weight	405 lb
All-up weight	575 lb
Maximum speed	77 mph
Cruising speed	65 mph
Stalling/landing speed	35 mph

Howitt Monoplane

One of the many individuals to get hooked on Henri Mignet's HM 14 Pou de Ciel was R.C. Howitt of Garsington, near Cowley, Oxford. Shortly after Appleby's Flea *G-ADMH* took to the air, Howitt had his own built. Registered *G-AEEX*, the aircraft was regularly flown at RAF Abingdon, often by Flight Lieutenant H.R.A. Edwards, during 1936. When the Flea was banned from flying in England, Howitt, in company with other amateur and professional designers, decided to produce something along similar lines. The resulting aircraft was a single-seat parasol, powered initially by a 600 cc Douglas motor cycle engine, called the Howitt Monoplane.

The Howitt Monoplane was built at Manor Road, Garsington by J.B. Acres, chief ground instructor of

Poor photograph of the Howitt Monoplane. Built at Garsington during 1937 the Howitt was latterly powered by a 1,000 cc Brough Superior. (Via A.J. Jackson Collection)

the Oxford University Air Squadron. It had a plywood-covered fuselage and fabric-covered wings and tailplane. The aircraft was registered *G-AEXS* and first flown by Flight Lieutenant H.R.A. Edwards from RAF Abingdon in 1937, though other sources quote the test pilot as Adjutant Flight Lieutenant (later AVM) H.J. Kirkpatrick.

At some stage the aircraft was re-engined with a 1,000 cc Brough Superior. At the onset of war the Howitt was put into storage in the Oxford University Air Squadron's hangar at RAF Abingdon but, like so many stored civil aircraft, disappeared.

Howitt Monoplane data	
Span	37 ft 3 in
Length	21 ft 0 in
Height	not available
Wing area	not available
Empty weight	not available
All-up weight	510 lb
Maximum speed	not available
Cruising speed	not available
Stalling/landing speed	not available

Martin Monoplane

As described in an earlier chapter, the Martin Monoplane began its chequered career as the Clarke Cheetah, *G-AAJK*. It was acquired by Flying Officer Richard Hopkinson in May 1936 and was sent to Luton Aircraft at Gerrards Cross for rebuilding. The work was financed by Hopkinson's uncle, Martin Hopkinson, and in gratitude for this windfall his young nephew renamed the aircraft the Martin Monoplane.

Under C.H. Latimer-Needham's supervision, the late Harold Best-Devereux converted the aircraft to a low-wing monoplane, retaining the original fuselage and the DH 53 wings and tail unit but discarding the lower wings, which came from the old Halton HAC 1 Mayfly. The Blackburne Thrush engine was replaced with a 32 hp Bristol Cherub III. In addition, the DH 53 wings were braced by two inverted V-struts, the aircraft looking for all the world like a modified DH 53. Doped green with silver wings, the 'new' Martin Monoplane was registered *G-AEYY* to Flying Officer Hopkinson on 6 July 1937 and was first flown in October from Denham. Three days later it was accepted by its owner, who was at the time serving with the RAFVR at RAF Sealand, and he took off from Denham for his home near Barton aerodrome near Manchester. Shortly after taking off from Denham, plug trouble forced him down in a field where the Martin was damaged.

The aircraft was rebuilt at Heston with a new ply-covered fuselage. The work was completed in about a fortnight and, after test flying had been completed at Heston, the aircraft was finally delivered. During the next couple of years the Martin was flown regularly, but following another forced landing at Stoke-on-Trent the undercarriage was damaged and the aircraft was sold to J.F. Ford in June 1939. The undercarriage was repaired but the war put paid to any further flying and the Martin Monoplane was stored in a garage and forgotten. During the late 1950s the Shuttleworth Collection borrowed the tailplane of the Martin and copied it to assist in the restoration of the Collection's prototype DH 53, *G-EBHX*.

The Martin Monoplane remained in Ford's

The Martin Monoplane photographed at Heston after its rebuild during the winter of 1937-38. (Via A.J. Jackson Collection)

ownership until the mid-1970s. He had earlier planned to restore the aircraft but never did so and hung on to the airframe despite repeated offers from enthusiasts to purchase it. After the aircraft was damaged by vandals, during which someone ran over the wings and liberated the cockpit instruments, Ford parted with the remains to Captain Mike Russell of Russavia. Russell plans to produce two aircraft from the remains. One will be a new DH 53, painted in RAF markings and the other will be a new Martin Monoplane. At the time of writing the DH 53 is well on the way to completion and should be flying in 1987.

Despite much research by many people there is no positive proof of the identity of the DH 53 that donated its wings to the Cheetah/Martin Monoplane. Mike Russell would like to believe that they originated from *J7325/G-EBQP*. This aircraft's Certificate of Airworthiness expired three months after the Cheetah flew, though it was already registered in July 1929. In any case 'QP was still flying five years later until it was totally destroyed in a crash at Roborough on 21 July 1934. When the majority of RAF DH 53s were converted to civil aeroplanes by the RAE Club at Farnborough there was doubtless much swapping around of component parts, so the true identity of the donor of the Martin's wings is likely to remain a mystery.

The Martin Monoplane's resemblance to the DH 53 was due to generous cannibalization — the wings and tail came from an unidentified DH 53. (Via A.J. Jackson Collection)

Martin Monoplane data	
Span	30 ft 0 in
Length	not available
Height	not available
Wing area	not available
Empty weight	not available
All-up weight	not available
Maximum speed	80 mph
Cruising speed	not available
Stalling/landing speed	not available

Shapley Kittiwake

Nearly all of the aircraft described in this book emanated from persons or companies with some kind of aeronautical experience or background. Not so the Shapley Kittiwake. Errol Shapley, its designer, was an accountant by profession, working in the family wine, spirits and food business. He often accompanied his brother to Brooklands to watch him race cars and soon acquired an interest in flying, later learning to fly himself. While keeping his hand in at the local flying club at Roborough, Plymouth, Shapley began to formulate his own idea as to what a light aircraft should feature. Having had no formal

technical training, he read up all he could on aerodynamics, aircraft design and allied subjects; then, armed with his limited knowledge, came up with an unusual gull-wing, open-cockpit two-seater monoplane with a monocoque fuselage. The design was finalized with the help of a stress engineer and premises were acquired in a disused storeroom in a Torquay iron foundary.

The Kittiwake was built during 1937 and was of all-wood construction. The 20 ft 3 in-long fuselage was ply covered. The 31 ft 7 in span gull-wing was also ply covered, as was the gracefully shaped tail unit. The Kittiwake was powered by a 40 hp Continental A50 four-cylinder, horizontally opposed air-cooled engine and was designed to be aerobatic. The narrow track undercarriage was trousered.

The Kittiwake Mk I was completed in June 1937 and was registered *G-AEZN*. Its first flight took place during the same month and on 29 June the aircraft was granted an Authorisation to Fly. Later that summer the Kittiwake was damaged when its owner-designer made a forced landing at Roborough. The undercarriage was torn off and, though the damage was not extensive, Shapley already had plans for a larger and more powerful aircraft.

The first Kittiwake, G-AEZN, was an open cockpit monoplane powered by a 50 hp Continental A50 engine.

Above *Looking like something out of a Rupert Bear Annual the Kittiwake Mk II's odd appearance belied its useful performance. (The Aeroplane* photograph) **Below** *The Kittiwake's gull wing is very evident in this photograph of* G-AFRP, *taken shortly before the war. (The Aeroplane* photograph)

Much of *G-AEZN* was cannibalized to provide parts and materials for the Kittiwake Mk II. This emerged during the summer of 1938, only slightly larger but appreciably heavier than its predecessor. Powered by a 90 hp Pobjoy Niagara III radial engine, the 32 ft span cabin two-seater weighed in at 901 lb tare and could be loaded to an all-up weight of 1,600 lb which, strictly speaking, excludes the Mk II from these pages. However, the Shapley Kittiwake story would be incomplete without a description of the second aircraft, and so we will continue.

With almost twice the power of the prototype, the Kittiwake II's performance improvement was dramatic. Registered *G-AFRP*, it was first flown during the summer of 1938 from Roborough by F. Symonson. It was soon discovered that the Mk II would unstick in 90 yds and had an initial rate of climb of 900 ft/min. The maximum speed was 120 mph and the aircraft stalled at 56 mph.

Neither of the Shapleys was pretty by an stretch of the imagination, looking as they did like something out of a Rupert Bear annual, yet for an amateur the Kittiwake was a fine performer. On arrival at RAE Farnborough its flying characteristics were favourably criticized and, on completion of its trials, the designer planned to put the Mk II into production. However, war prevented any such plans and *G-AFRP* was put into storage at Torquay until after the war.

Whereas the stories of many promising ultra-lights ended with the onset of the war, the Kittiwake was an exception. After the war Shapley, who had served for the duration in the Air-Sea Rescue Service, teamed

up with Symonson, who had flown throughout the war as an ATA ferry pilot. Between them they got the Mk II back into the air during April 1946, from Rochester. Soon plans were prepared to put the Mk II into production, together with a single-seat version and a four-seater powered by either a DH Gipsy major or Gipsy Six engine. The three variants were the SK I, SK II and SK III. Negotiations were at an advanced stage between Shapley and an unspecified company when disaster put a halt to the enterprise.

In December 1946 Symonson was carrying out spinning trials in *G-AFRP* at Exeter when the aircraft failed to recover from its gyrations. The pilot wisely decided to make a hasty exit and the Kittiwake was left to bore a large hole in a Devonshire field. From that moment all plans for producing further aircraft evaporated and no more Kittiwakes were built.

Errol Shapley, somewhat disillusioned with the state of the British light aircraft industry, left England and aviation for South Africa, where he took up farming before finally settling in Australia.

Shapley Kittiwake Mk I data	
Span	31 ft 7 in
Length	20 ft 3 in
Height	7 ft 0 in
Wing area	130 ft²
Empty weight	630 lb
All-up weight	1,000lb
Maximum speed	116 mph
Cruising speed	99 mph
Stalling/landing speed	45 mph

Shapley Kittiwake Mk II data	
Span	32 ft 0 in
Length	20 ft 10 in
Height	not available
Wing area	not available
Empty weight	901 lb
All-up weight	1,600 lb
Maximum speed	120 mph
Cruising speed	99 mph
Stalling/landing speed	not available

Tipsy B and Tipsy Trainer

In 1935 E.O. Tips, who represented the Société Anonyme Avions Fairey, the Fairey company in Belgium, designed a very pretty little single-seater low-wing monoplane powered by a 600 cc Douglas engine. In appearance it resembled the Gordon Dove, described in a previous chapter. Built entirely

Top *The Kittiwake II airborne for the benefit of* The Aeroplane's *photographer. War put paid to any plans of putting the aircraft into production. (*The Aeroplane *photograph)* **Above** *Powered by a 90 hp Pobjoy Niagara III the Kittiwake II could take off in less than 100 yds and climb at 900 ft/min. (*The Aeroplane *photograph)*

of wood, the 24 ft 6 in span Tipsy S, registered *OO-TIP*, flew for about 1½ hrs on the day of its first flight; no modifications or adjustments were subsequently made to the aircraft.

The fuselage consisted of four spruce longerons with spruce frames, covered with a birch plywood stressed skin. The wing had a mainspar of I-section located at the deepest point of the wing section, at about 25 per cent chord and an auxiliary spar. The wing's torsional rigidity was maintained by pyramid bracing between the spars and by plywood covering over the wing leading edge. The wing section varied from RAF 48 near the root to RAF 38 and 28, becoming thinner at the tips. Aft of the main spar the wing was fabric covered.

The forward part of the fuselage was built integral with the wing and ended flush with the trailing edge. The rear portion was fixed to the forward section by four detachable nickel-steel fittings. The plywood-covered fin was integral with the rear fuselage and the rudder was fabric covered.

The adjustable tailplane was also fabric covered aft of the plywood-covered leading edges. The rudder and fin were positioned well forward of the tailplane and elevators. The undercarriage consisted of two spatted low-pressure airwheels held in forks attached to the main spar.

The Tipsy S weighed only 287 lb empty and had an all-up weight of 532 lb. The performance was quite

exceptional: it could take off in 160 yds in nil wind and cruise at 70 mph. Rather surprisingly the production S 2 did not enjoy the great success that it deserved, even though a cabin version powered by a 32 hp Sarolea engine gave a higher top speed of 108 mph.

Aero Engines Ltd of Kingsdown, Bristol, built nine Tipsy S 2s under licence. They were all initially owned by Tipsy Light Aircraft Ltd, except for *G-AESU*, which was owned by Fairey Aviation at Harmondsworth. Only three British-built Tipsy S 2s were granted Authorisations to Fly and all were scrapped or had ceased flying in 1937. Registrations were allotted to three further airframes but the marks were never taken up.

The basic Tipsy S 2 design was very promising and E.O. Tips went ahead with a two-seat version, the Tipsy B, powered initially by a 50 hp Czech Walter Mikron engine. Basically similar in construction to the S 2, the Tipsy B had staggered seating and dual controls. The wing was made in one piece and could be detached from the fuselage in four minutes. Though it was somewhat larger than the S 2 (the wingspan was 31 ft 2 in), the tare weight was kept down to just less then 500 lb. It had a normal loaded weight of 935 lb, which included two people and 55 lb of baggage.

In May 1937 the prototype Tipsy B, *OO-DON*, was brought to England and demonstrated at Heathrow on 14 May. Subsequently Brian Allen Aviation Ltd acquired the UK selling rights and it was initially advertised at £400.

Production versions were powered by the 62 hp Walter Mikron II, which gave the magic 100 mph cruise. The first two Tipsy Bs to be imported to England were *G-AFCM* and *G-AFEI*. They were originally registered in Belgium as *OO-DOS* and *OO-DOV* respectively. In addition, Tipsy Aircraft Ltd put the Tipsy B into production at the London Air Park at Hanworth, Middlesex. The first British-built model was registered *G-AFGF* and it differed from its Belgian counterpart in several ways. The wings were strengthened and given washout at the tips and the ailerons, elevators and rudder were all mass-balanced. The weights were all concealed in the leading edges of the control surfaces, though early machines had rudder bob-weights on a projecting arm. In addition, camber-changing flaps were installed and the aircraft featured a steerable tailskid.

Top left *The pretty little Tipsy S was powered by a 600 cc Douglas engine. It weighed only 287 lb empty.* (*Flight* photograph) **Middle left** *Tipsy S 2 G-AESU was built by Aero Engines ltd of Kingsdown, Bristol. It crashed in September 1937.* **Left** *The prototype Tipsy B, OO-DON, photographed during a demonstration at Heathrow in May 1937.*

The passenger sat slightly behind the pilot, on his right, and there was storage space for 22 lb of luggage behind the seats. In August 1938 the Tipsy B was advertised at £675.

With all these modifications the designation of the British aircraft was changed after the sixth aircraft to Tipsy Trainer. With the ninth aircraft the maximum weight limit was increased to 1,200 lb and subsequent aircraft were known as Tipsy Trainer Is. In all, fifteen Tipsy two-seaters were built before the war stopped further production. The type was ideal for use by the newly-formed Civil Air Guard and half were used in this role by the Yorkshire Aeroplane Club and by Airwork. Apart from one that was sold in India, the other aircraft went to private owners.

The Tipsy B was pleasant to fly. The controls were crisp and responsive, and the aircraft was simplicity itself. A central control column was positioned for the pilot's right hand, though it had provision for an extension arm towards the passenger. In addition to the dual pedals there was a folding footrest to keep the passenger's feet away from the controls when necessary. The washed-out wingtips gave good control down to the 37 mph stalling speed and the glide was fairly flat. The limited elevator travel allowed the stick to be pulled right back when near the ground, allowing the Tipsy to land in the classic three-point attitude. With two large occupants the tandem seating was necessary and the instructor's throttle was on the left of the cockpit, within easy reach of his left hand which had to be slipped behind the pilot on his left.

In addition to the fifteen Tipsy two-seaters built before the war, Tipsy Aircraft Ltd built a further three after hostilities had ceased. The three aircraft, *G-AISA-G-AISC* were built during 1947-48 at the company's new premises on the Slough Trading Estate in Buckinghamshire, whither the company had moved in 1939. Ten pre-war aircraft survived to fly after the war, though three were sold overseas.

Shortly before the war the second prototype Tipsy B, *OO-DOP*, was modified to a cabin model by raising the rear fuselage decking and by adding a Perspex canopy becoming the Tipsy BC. This aircraft turned up in Britain in 1940 and, registered *G-AGBM*, flew as a communications aircraft with Fairey Aviation Co Ltd. Three further Tipsy BCs arrived unfinished into the country in 1957. They were registered *G-AOXO, G-APIE* and *G-APOD*. Tipsy Trainer *G-AFJR* was converted to BC standard at around the same time and all four aircraft were still flying three decades later.

Above right and right *The first British-built Tipsy 1 was G-AFGF, registered in August 1938 and burned at Slough in 1952.* (*The Aeroplane* photograph)

Tipsy S 2 data (Douglas)	
Span	24 ft 6 in
Length	18 ft 8½ in
Height	4 ft 10 in
Wing area	100 ft²
Empty weight	287 lb
All-up weight	532 lb
Maximum speed	80 mph
	100 mph
	(Sarolea)
Cruising speed	70 mph
Stalling/landing speed	43.5 mph

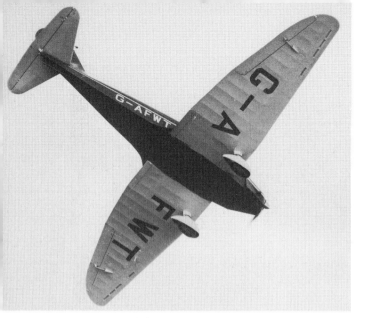

Left *Unusual view of Tipsy Trainer 1 G-AFWT, registered just weeks before the outbreak of war and still flying forty years later.* (E.J. Riding photograph) **Below left** *Tipsy Trainer 1 G-AFJR was converted to a Belfair, with enclosed cabin, in 1957.* (R.T. Riding photograph)

Barnwell BSW Mk 1

C.G. Grey, founder editor of *The Aeroplane*, paid a rare compliment when, on the death of Bristol's chief designer Captain Frank Barnwell, he referred to him as 'beyond question one of the best aeroplane designers in this country or the world. No other designer has turned out so many first-class aeroplanes which have become historic.'

Captain Frank Sowter Barnwell OBE AFC was born at Lewisham in 1880 and was educated at Fettes School in Edinburgh; later he learned engineering on the Clyde with his brother Harold. Together they built a large aeroplane in Scotland in 1908, and another followed in 1909. By 1911 they had built and flown a monoplane but shortly afterwards Barnwell joined Bristol, then known as the British & Colonial Aeroplane Co, where he became chief draughtsman. His first successful design was the pretty little Bristol Scout biplane. The Bristol M 1 Monoplane and the famous F 2B Fighter followed. After the First World War his designs included the Bulldog and the Blenheim. But in addition to designing fighting machines, Barnwell was interested in ultra-light aircraft: for the 1924 Lympne two-seater aircraft trials he designed the Bristol Brownie, described in an earlier chapter.

During the mid-1930s Barnwell designed a single-seat low-wing monoplane powered by a 28 hp Scott Squirrel engine. He had intended to build the aeroplane himself but pressure of work — it was the time of the RAF's expansion programme — meant that the construction was given to a company at Whitchurch aerodrome, Bristol. Named the Barnwell BSW Mk 1 (BSW signified Barnwell Scott Whitchurch), the monoplane was built during 1938 and was registered *G-AFID*. An Authorisation to Fly was issued on 25 June of the same year.

Apart from designing and building the BSW Mk 1 for his own amusement, Barnwell also had the recently-formed Civil Air Guard in mind, which urgently required aircraft for cheap instructional flying. In addition Barnwell was no longer permitted to fly around in company aircraft, being considered uninsurable as a pilot, so the little wooden aircraft would do nicely as a private runabout.

The Barnwell BSW Mk 1 was first flown at the end of July 1938. After making some adjustments Barnwell made a second flight on 2 August. The weather at Whitchurch that day was rather gusty. After climbing to about 100 ft the aircraft stalled and

Tipsy B data	
Span	31 ft 2 in
Length	21 ft 8 in
Height	7 ft 0 in
Wing area	129 ft^2
Empty weight	495 lb
All-up weight	990 lb
Maximum speed	124 mph
Cruising speed	106 mph
Stalling/landing speed	46 mph

Tipsy Trainer I data	
Span	31 ft 2 in
Length	21 ft 8 in
Height	7 ft 0 in
Wing area	129 ft^2
Empty weight	668 lb
All-up weight	1,073 lb
Maximum speed	110 mph
Cruising speed	100 mph
Stalling/landing speed	37 mph

crashed on to the road on the edge of the aerodrome. Barnwell was killed instantly.

C.G. Grey, who disliked little aeroplanes or 'pop-bottles' as he referred to them, commented that Barnwell regarded the BSW Mk 1 'more or less as a joke and as a youngster would regard a favourite toy. But he certainly did not regard it as a serious contribution to aeronautical science. The pity is that such a valuable man should have been killed by a plaything'.

Barnwell BSW Mk 1 data	
Span	25 ft 0 in
Length	not available
Height	not available
Wing area	not available
Empty weight	not available
All-up weight	750 lb
Maximum speed	not available
Cruising speed	not available
Stalling/landing speed	not available

Top *The Barnwell BSW Mk 1 photographed at Bristol Whitchurch, where its short life began and ended in 1938. (W.K. Kilsby photograph)* **Above** *Another photograph of the nearly-completed BSW Mk 1 at Whitchurch in 1938. The engine is a 28 hp Scott Squirrel. (Via A.J. Jackson Collection)* **Below left** *The BSW Mk 1 at Whitchurch during test running of the Scott Squirrel engine. (Via A.J. Jackson Collection)* **Below right** *Close-up of the Scott Squirrel engine installed in the BSW Mk 1 at Whitchurch in 1938. (Via A.J. Jackson Collection)*

Watkinson Dingbat

In addition to turning out some of the finest aeroplanes in the world, the de Havilland Aircraft Co at Hatfield produced some remarkable graduates from the Technical School, particularly in the field of aircraft design. We have already described the contribution made be ex-students Ward and Dalrymple in building the impressive Chilton DW 1; now we turn to two other de Havilland Technical School old-boys who teamed up to produce their own idea of a lightweight, robust and practical single-seater aircraft.

Eric Watkinson, a South African, studied aircraft design at Hatfield, while Cyril Taylor learned all there was to know about stress analysis. After Hatfield they both joined the British Aircraft Co at Hanworth where they worked on the BA Swallow and Eagle as design draughtsmen. Like others the two men kept a watchful eye on the Mignet HM 14 Pou, no doubt thinking that they could do better. In 1936 they began to formulate a design for a light single-seater modelled around the 32 hp Carden-Ford converted car engine.

Below *The newly finished Watkinson Dingbat is manhandled from its Heston hangar in 1938.* (*Flight* photograph) **Bottom** *Construction of the Dingbat cost a little under £200. It was built in a garage at Teddington, Middlesex.* (*Flight* photograph)

Named the Watkinson Dingbat, the chunky little aircraft began to take shape at Teddington in Middlesex. The wings were of Clark YH section and were built on two box spars with solid spruce flanges and ply webs. The wings were detachable and could be clipped 'Lympne fashion' to the sides of the fuselage for towing behind a car. The ply-covered wing featured full-span ailerons which moved upwards only.

The ply-covered centre-section was built integral with the fuselage and to it was secured the 7 ft track undercarriage, which was fitted with doughnut-type wheels. The water-cooled Carden-Ford engine was mounted directly to the top fuselage longerons, dispensing with expensive welded steel tubing. Two radiators kept the engine water cool; one was located in the Dingbat's nose, the other was positioned beneath the port trailing edge of the centre-section, its position revealed by the airscoop below it.

The Dingbat was not a hit-and-miss exercise. Careful and detailed drawings were prepared before construction began and the little aircraft was stressed for aerobatics. When it was completed in mid-1938, not only was its weight within the designer's calculations but very little modification was subsequently required.

Another de Havilland Technical School old-boy was roped in to test-fly the Dingbat, and so it was on one June day in 1938 that Ranald Porteous lifted the Dingbat off from Heston on its maiden flight. A little more than a year earlier Porteous had test flown the prototype Chilton, *G-AESZ*, for Messrs Ward and Dalrymple.

The Dingbat was offered at £300; the prototype registered *G-AFJA* had cost Taylor and Watkinson less than £200 to build. Interestingly the Chilton, with better all-round performance, was being offered for £315. But whereas the sleek-lined Chilton racer was received with great acclaim by the aviation press and by the pilots who flew it, the Dingbat received

from C.G. Grey the kind of caustic comment he regularly handed out on light aviation matters: 'Frankly we cannot see why anybody should want to buy such an aeroplane for any purpose. The general design reminds one of the Light Aeroplane Trials of 1923. And now that everybody is to fly at the Government's expense people expect something bigger, with more power'. Grey was referring to the Civil Air Guard, first announced in July 1938.

The Dingbat received a Permit to Fly on 29 July 1938; after a year's flying and with war imminent it was put into storage at Twickenham where it gathered dust for nine years. In May 1948 the newly-formed Ultra-Light Aircraft Association paid £50 for the Dingbat and removed it to Elstree where the Experimental Group of that organization began restoring it. Two years later the uncompleted Dingbat was moved to Redhill where it was acquired by J.H. Pickrell and D.O. Wallis and restored over a six year period.

Almost twenty years after its last flight, the Dingbat took to the air again at Hornchurch in Essex towards the end of 1959; the Authorisation to Fly was issued on 10 December that year. A succession of owners followed, and then the Dingbat was badly damaged in a crash. It has since been rebuilt and is still extant at the time of writing.

Above *E. T. Watkinson and C. W. Taylor stand next to their Dingbat at Heston in 1938. The aircraft was designed around the 30 hp water-cooled Carden-Ford engine.* (Flight *photograph*) **Below** *The Dingbat looking rather forlorn, probably at Croydon in 1953.* **Bottom** *The Dingbat currently owned by Roy Nerou and no doubt will be airworthy before too long.*

Watkinson Dingbat data	
Span	28 ft 0 in
Length	16 ft 0 in
Height	6 ft 3 in
Wing area	125 ft²
Empty weight	460 lb
All-up weight	700 lb
Maximum speed	85 mph
Cruising speed	80 mph
Stalling/landing speed	39 mph

Luton LA 5 Major

During the late 1930s the Americans practically dominated the lightweight cabin aircraft market. The well-proven strut-braced high-wing cabin layout, with either tandem or side-by-side seating, was certainly proving popular with private and touring pilots alike. One or two British designers attempted to produce aircraft to this well-tried formula.

In 1939 C.H. Latimer-Needham designed a tandem-seat high-wing monoplane of very light wooden structure, initially powered by a 54 hp Mikron I four-cylinder inline inverted air-cooled

Above *The late Harold Best Devereux lends scale to the prototype Luton LA5 Major at Denham in the spring of 1939.* (*The Aeroplane* photograph) Below *Luton Major G-AFMU was powered by a 54 hp Walter Mikron I but was designed to take the 60 hp Mikron II.* (*The Aeroplane* photograph) Bottom *The prototype Luton Major was first flown on 12 March 1939 from Denham. A small production-line was in operation when the war brought further work to a standstill.* (*Flight* photograph)

engine. Somewhat Cub-like in appearance, the Luton LA 5 Major was built at the Gerrards Cross Phoenix Works and was ready to fly in March 1939.

The Luton Major was of all-wood construction, though the engine mounting, undercarriage and stress-carrying members of the fuselage were made of tubular steel. The fuselage was of round-topped rectangular section and was plywood covered. The two wing halves were of conventional design and were attached to the top fuselage longerons. They were braced to the bottom of the fuselage with steel V-struts. By detaching two pins at the front spar joints, the wings could be folded about the rear spar hinges, giving a folded width of 11 ft 8 in. Because the wingroots were attached to fuselage members the space between them, which would normally have been occupied by a wing centre-section, was clear; a Perspex covering gave excellent upward vision.

The undercarriage was of the split type and consisted of two faired side vees hinged to the bottom fuselage longerons, and two half axles with their inner ends anchored to the apex of a steel tube pyramid.

The cantilever tail unit was a fabric-covered wooden structure; the elevators had trim tabs that were adjustable from the cockpit. For reasons of safety the elevator controls were so rigged that backward movement on the stick was limited just sufficiently to allow a three-point landing. Initially the location of the pilot's seat also limited the backward travel of the stick and later adjustments were made to allow more elevator travel. Entry to the Major's cabin was similar to that of the Piper Cub. Two horizontally hinged doors opened upwards and downwards and locked at the centreline of the fuselage.

The Major's first flight was carried out by Squadron Leader Edward Mole from Denham aerodrome on 12 March 1939, eight days after the Authorisation to Fly was issued. The first flight proved eventful for, soon after take-off, the pilot's seat broke loose from its fitting, leaving the pilot clutching wildly for the controls as he slipped backwards. Fortunately Mole managed to regain control and a safe landing was made. Further flight tests revealed that the aileron control was insufficient, particularly for manoeuvring near the ground and this was subsequently geared up. With the ailerons differentially operated, very little rudder correction was necessary. With ample rudder, sideslips could be easily performed, even at low speed. During initial testing one of the aileron cables slipped off its pulley, but the fault was discovered before the situation became dangerous.

The Major proved to be very suited for inexperienced pilots. It was docile at slow speed, there being no wing drop at the stall, the aircraft mushing gently on an even keel without even the nose dropping. The maximum speed of 105 mph was respectable and the aircraft's inherent stability was graphically, if foolishly, demonstrated by a pilot who flew the prototype from Bristol Whitchurch to Denham without any aileron control, one of the aileron horns being completely disconnected. The flight concluded with a touchdown speed of 70 mph in an attempt to avoid instability at low speed.

Registered *G-AFMU*, the prototype was demonstrated on 14 May 1939 at the Royal Aeronautical Society's Garden Party. The aircraft remained in the hands of the parent company until 1943, when it was destroyed in the fire that burnt

Above *The Luton Major had a speed range of 35-105 mph and was particularly docile in flight, especially at and near the stall. (Flight photograph)* **Below** *The provisional price of the Luton Major in 1939 was £525. Wing folding was a simple operation requiring the removal of a single pin. The wings locked automatically when folded.*

down the Phoenix Works.

Unlike the Minor, the Major was not originally intended for homebuilding by amateur constructors. When war was declared six months after the Major's first flight, any hopes of putting the aircraft into production were dashed. Another twenty years were to pass before plans were made available through Phoenix Aircraft, a company set up by the aircraft's designer and Arthur Ord-Hume to market plans of both the Minor and Major. Even then, though some builders were to embark immediately on building Majors, it was to be almost another ten years before a second example was to take to the air. At the time of writing several Majors are flying worldwide, powered by a variety of engines and flying at increased weights. The post-war story of the Luton Major is beyond the scope of this book but no doubt Majors and Minors will be appearing from the lofts and bedrooms of homebuilders for many years to come.

During the last months leading up to the war, Latimer-Needham was working on a development of the LA 4 Major. Designated LA 6 Sports Major, this aircraft had a reduced wingspan and was to be powered by the more powerful 95 hp DH Gipsy Major engine. The disposable load was increased to 520 lb, giving an all-up weight of 1,220 lb. The LA 6 would have been similar in appearance to the LA 5, but war prevented it from progressing beyond the paper stage.

Luton LA 5 Major data (62 hp Walter Mikron II)	
Span	35 ft 2 in
	11 ft 8 in
	(wings folded)
Length	23 ft 9 in
Height	not available
Wing area	163 ft^2
Empty weight	600 lb
All-up weight	1,030 lb
Maximum speed	105 mph
Cruising speed	95 mph
Stalling/landing speed	35 mph

Ultralight engines

An A-Z of principal companies that produced light engines for use in ultra-light aircraft, with brief data on 26 selected engines.

ABC

ABC Motors Ltd, Walton-on-Thames, Surrey.

The All British Engine Company was formed in 1910 at Redbridge, near Southampton. In the same year Captain Ronald Charteris, RFC, the founder of the company, was joined by Granville Bradshaw as chief designer and ABC Motors was set up early in 1912 to produce aero engines. One of the first was supplied to T.O.M. Sopwith, a close friend of Charteris. During 1913 the company began manufacturing motor cycles but returned to aero engines during the First World War. A series of largely unsuccessful aero engines included the 40 hp Gnat, 120 hp Mosquito, 170 hp Wasp and the 300 hp Dragonfly.

From 1918 to 1924 ABC concentrated on motor car and motor cycle manufacture and it was in 1923 that the company turned its attention to adapting motor cycle engines for aircraft use. An ABC 400 cc engine was so adapted for W.O. Manning's English Electric Wren, the first aeroplane to fly with this ABC engine. Following close on its heels came the ABC Scorpion, a modified car engine, which was widely used in ultra-light aircraft of the 1920s.

ABC: 8 hp, two-cylinder, horizontally-opposed, air-cooled. **Bore and stroke:** 69 mm × 54 mm. **Capacity:** 400 cc. **Normal engine speed:** 2,000 rpm to produce 3 ¾ hp. **Maximum engine speed:** 4,500 rpm to produce 7-8 hp. **Weight:** 35 lb. **Aircraft in which engine was flown:** English Electric Wren.

ABC Scorpion I: 30 hp, two-cylinder, horizontally-opposed, air-cooled. **Bore and stroke:** 87.5 mm × 91.5 mm. **Capacity:** 1,100 cc. **Normal engine speed:** not available. **Maximum engine speed:** 3,000 rpm to produce 30 hp. **Weight:** 93 lb. **Aircraft in which engine was flown:** Hawker Cygnet and Westland Woodpigeon.

ABC Scorpion II: 40 hp, two-cylinder, horizontally-opposed, air-cooled. **Bore and stroke:** 102 mm × 91.4 mm. **Capacity:** 1,500 cc. **Normal engine speed:** 2,300 rpm to produce 34 hp. **Maximum engine speed:** 2,750 rpm to produce 40 hp. **Weight:**

ABC 398cc in English Electric Wren.

ABC Scorpion.

ABC Hornet.

109 lb. **Aircraft in which engine was flown:** ABC Robin, Comper Swift, HSF II Gadfly, Hendy Hobo and Wee Mite.

ABC Hornet: 81 hp, four-cylinder, horizontally-opposed, air-cooled. **Bore and stroke:** 102 mm × 122 mm. **Capacity:** 3,990 cc. **Normal engine speed:** 1,875 rpm to produce 75 hp. **Maximum engine speed:** 2,075 rpm to produce 81 hp. **Weight:** 225 lb. **Aircraft in which engine was flown:** Southern Martlet.

Aero Engines Ltd

Aero Engines Ltd, Kingswood, Bristol

Following its formation in 1935 this company acquired a licence to manufacture and sell Hispano-Suiza engines. It also took over the V-4 and V-6 inverted air-cooled engines developed by General Aircraft. In addition Aero Engines Ltd took over the Douglas 750 cc horizontally-opposed engine and after a re-design put it into production.

Aero Engine Mk1 750cc.

In May 1938 the company announced plans to licence-build a 40 hp four-cylinder Weir engine, subsequently named Pixie.

Aero Engines Sprite: 25 hp two-cylinder, horizontally-opposed, air-cooled. **Bore and stroke:** 70 mm × 82 mm. **Capacity:** 803 cc. **Normal engine speed:** 2,850 rpm to produce 22.7 hp. **Maximum engine speed:** 3,150 rpm to produce 24.3 hp. **Weight:** 82 lb. **Aircraft in which engine was flown:** Tipsy S 2, Gordon Dove and BAC Super Drone.

Aeronca

The Aeronautical Corporation of America, Lunken Airport, Cincinnati, Ohio, USA

Formed in 1928 to manufacture Aeronca light aircraft and engines. Early engines included the very successful E-107 and E-113 series, developed to power the company's Aeronca C-2 and C-3 high-winged single/two-seat monoplanes.

In 1936 Light Aircraft Ltd acquired a licence to build Aeronca engines in Great Britain but this was soon taken over by motor cycle engine manufacturers J.A. Prestwich Ltd. The Aeronca E-113C engine was manufactured as the JAP J-99 and was used to power British-built C-3s (Aeronca 100) produced at Walton Aerodrome, Peterborough by The Aeronautical Corporation of Great Britain Ltd. JAP engines were, unlike their American counterparts, fitted with dual ignition.

Aeronca E-107A: 30 hp, two-cylinder, horizontally-opposed, air-cooled. **Bore and stroke:** 104 mm × 101.6 mm. **Capacity:** 1,725 cc. **Normal engine speed:** 2,000 rpm to produce 26 hp. **Maximum engine speed:** 2,500 rpm to produce 30 hp. **Weight:** 114 lb. **Aircraft in which engine was flown:** Aeronca C-2.

Aeronca E-113-C (JAP J-99): 40 hp, two-cylinder, horizontally-opposed, air-cooled. **Bore and stroke:** 108 mm × 101.6 mm. **Capacity:** 1,860 cc. **Normal**

Aeronca E 113-C (JAP J-99).

engine speed: 2,400 rpm to produce 36 hp. **Maximum engine speed:** 2,500 rpm to produce 40 hp. **Weight:** 121 lb. **Aircraft in which engine was flown:** Aeronca C-3 (Aeronca 100), Currie Wot, Hillson Praga and Luton LA 4 Minor.

Anzani
Anzani Moteurs d'Aviation, Courbevoie, France

This French motor cycle manufacturer produced its first aero engine in 1909. One of its first products was an air-cooled three-cylinder W (a Vee with additional vertical upright cylinder), one of which powered M. Blériot across the English Channel in July 1909. Several types of Anzani engines were still in production after the First World War, varying in size from a three-cylinder 25 hp unit to a twenty-cylinder radial weighing 1,220 lb. Anzani engines were generally similar and simple in construction.

With the announcement of the 1924 Air Ministry two-seater lightplane trials the British Anzani Engine of Scrubbs Lane in North London, produced a Vee-twin air-cooled engine which was used in one of the competing Hawker Cygnets and the ANEC II. In 1938 Luton Aircraft Ltd acquired the manufacturing rights for the Anzani Vee-twin (*qv*).

Armstrong Siddeley Motors Ltd,
Armstrong Siddeley Motors Ltd, Parkside, Coventry

Prolific producers of aero engines since the First World War, Armstrong Siddeley concentrated on static radial air-cooled engines for high performance civil and military aircraft during the inter-war years. At the lower end of their power range was the Genet series, ranging from the 150 hp Genet-Major to the 80 hp five-cylinder Genet for use in light aircraft.

Armstrong Siddeley Genet: 80 hp, five-cylinder, radial, air-cooled. **Bore and stroke:** 101.6 mm × 101.6 mm. **Capacity:** 4,116 cc. **Normal engine speed:** 1,850 rpm to produce 65 hp. **Maximum engine speed:** 2,200 rpm to produce 80 hp. **Weight:** 168 lb. **Aircraft in which engine was flown:** Southern Martlet (Genet II), Blackburn Bluebird, Westland Widgeon and ANEC IV Missel Thrush.

Ava
L'Agence Général des Moteurs 'AVA', Paris, France.

This French company licence-built a four-cylinder two-stroke engine designed by M. Voilet, a two-stroke engine specialist. The special feature of the Ava engines was the rotary inlet distributor valve. In July 1936 A.B. Gibbons of Dorset Street, London W1, acquired a licence to build Ava engines in Great Britain.

Ava 4A-00: 30 hp four cylinder, flat-twin, air-cooled. **Bore and stroke:** 70 mm × 70 mm.

Above *British Anzani.* **Below** *Armstrong Siddeley Genet 80 hp.*

Capacity: 1,077 cc. **Normal engine speed:** 2,300 rpm to produce 25 hp. **Maximum engine speed:** 2,500 rpm to produce 30 hp. **Weight:** 81 lb. **Aircraft in which engine was flown:** Dart Pup and Dart Kitten.

Blackburne Tomtit 690 cc.

Blackburne

Burney & Blackburne Ltd, Atlas Works, Bookham, Surrey

Known for the production of excellent motor cycle engines, this manufacturer became involved with aero engines at the time of the *Daily Mail* lightplane trials of 1923. Several competitors installed the Blackburne 697 cc overhead valve motor cycle engine and were rewarded with excellent results in a competition that was dogged with engine failures. There followed the Tomtit engine, a modification of the original 697 cc motor cycle engine with steel instead of cast iron cylinders and modified to run inverted.

Blackburne Tomtit: 26 hp, two-cylinder, Vee-twin, air-cooled. **Bore and stroke:** 71 mm × 88 mm. **Capacity:** 697 cc. **Normal engine speed:** 2,000 rpm

Blackburne Thrush 1500 cc.

to produce 15 hp. **Maximum engine speed:** 4,000 rpm to produce 26 hp. **Weight:** 79 lb. **Aircraft in which engine was flown:** ANEC I, DH 53 and Gloucestershire Gannet.

Blackburne Thrush: 38 hp, three-cylinder, radial, air-cooled. **Bore and stroke:** 81 mm × 97 mm. **Capacity:** 1,498 cc. **Normal engine speed:** 2,500 rpm to produce 30 hp. **Maximum engine speed:** 2,760 rpm to produce 38 hp. **Weight:** 132 lb. **Aircraft in which engine was flown:** ANEC IV Missel Thrush, Supermarine Sparrow, Westland Widgeon, Vickers Viget, Avro Avis and Parnall Pixie III.

Bristol

Bristol Aeroplane Company Ltd, Engine Department, Filton, Bristol

Following the failure of the Cosmos Engineering company in January 1920, its aero engine assets, which included the Jupiter engine and its designer Roy Fedden, were acquired by the Bristol Aeroplane Company. Whilst development of the Jupiter and other radial engines continued the company produced a small flat-twin specifically for use in ultralight aircraft. Fedden's Bristol Cherub engine was the first small engine to pass the new Air Ministry type tests and was available in direct drive or geared form. It was introduced in time for the Air Ministry's two-seater lightplane trials in 1924. With the introduction of the Cherub III the normal output of the standard Cherub was increased from 22 to 30 bhp without any increase in engine weight.

Bristol Cherub I: 34 hp, two-cylinder, horizontally-opposed, air-cooled. **Bore and stroke:** 85 mm × 96.5 mm. **Capacity:** 1,095 cc. **Normal engine speed:** 2,500 rpm to produce 24 hp. **Maximum engine speed:** 4,000 rpm to produce 34 hp. **Weight:** 81 lb (direct drive), 105 lb (geared). **Aircraft in which engine was flown:** Beardmore Wee Bee I, Bristol Brownie, CLA 2, Parnall Pixie I, Short Satellite, Supermarine Sparrow, CLA 3 and Granger Archaeopteryx.

Bristol Cherub III: 36 hp, two-cylinder, horizontally-opposed, air-cooled. **Bore and stroke:** 90 mm × 96.5 mm. **Capacity:** 1,228 cc. **Normal engine speed:** 2,900 rpm to produce 33 hp. **Maximum engine speed:** 3,200 rpm to produce 36 hp. **Weight:** 95 lb. **Aircraft in which engine was flown:** ANEC II, Parnall Pixie III/IIIA, RAE Scarab, Short Satellite, Bristol Brownie, Hawker Cygnet, Westland Woodpigeon, Halton HAC I, RAE Scarab, de Bruyne Ladybird and Martin Monoplane.

32 hp Bristol Cherub.

Carden Ford in Mignet H.M.14.

Carden

Carden Aero Engines, Heston Airport, Middlesex

As early as 1923 Sir John Carden built a 750 cc vertical two-cylinder, two-stroke engine designed specifically for the Gloucestershire Gannet biplane. Unfortunately the engine had not been tested sufficiently and the Carden suffered from overheating and oil failure. In 1935 Sir John set up a company to manufacture aero engines suitable for use in ultra-light aircraft generally but in particular the British-built Mignet HM 14 Poux that were being built in great profusion all over the country. The first Carden engine was a conversion of the standard Ford 10 car engine. Though all wearable parts were Ford components most of the engine was re-designed. New components included a modified cylinder block, a new crankshaft incorporating a thrust race, a special

Bristol Cherub.

cylinder head and inlet manifold, to mention just a few.

Following Sir John's death in an air crash in December 1935, the company was taken over by Carden-Baynes Aircraft Ltd. In 1937 the company's interests were acquired by Chilton Aircraft at Hungerford in Berkshire in order to facilitate production of the Carden-powered Chilton DW 1. Though heavy, the Carden engine was reliable and relatively free from vibration.

Carden-Ford: 31 hp, four-cylinder, in-line, water-cooled. **Bore and stroke:** 63.5 mm × 92.5 mm. **Capacity:** 1,172 cc. **Normal engine speed:** 3,000 rpm to produce 28 hp. **Maximum engine speed:** 3,600 rpm to produce 31 hp. **Weight:** 131 lb (dry and without radiator or water). **Aircraft in which engine was flown:** Broughton-Blayney Brawney, Chilton DW 1, Carden Baynes Bee, Kronfeld Monoplane, Watkinson Dingbat, and Mignet H.M.14

Continental

Continental Motors Corporation, Aircraft Engine Division, Muskegon, Michigan, USA

In 1925 Continental Motors, one of the world's largest manufacturers of car engines, acquired the patent rights to the Burt-McCollum monosleeve valve from British Argyll. The company's first sleeve-valve air-cooled radial engine was produced in 1927. The following year Continental produced the seven-cylinder A-70 radial engine, and in 1931 introduced the flat-four A40 horizontally-opposed engine. This simple, low-priced engine was ideally suitable for use in light aircraft. The improved A50 engine followed in 1938 and this in turn led to the Continental A65, one of the most successful lightplane engines ever produced.

Continental A50: 50 hp, four-cylinder, horizontally-opposed, air-cooled. **Bore and stroke:** 98.43 mm × 92.08 mm. **Capacity:** 2,800 cc. **Normal engine speed:** 1,900 rpm to produce 50 hp. **Maximum engine speed:** not available. **Weight:** 170 lb. **Aircraft in which engine was flown:** Shapley Kittiwake Mk I.

Douglas

William Douglas (Bristol) Ltd, Kingswood, Bristol

Better known for manufacturing motor cycle engines, the Douglas company produced special versions of its 500 cc, 600 cc and 750 cc flat-twin motor cycle engines for use in aircraft. A third of the 1923 *Daily Mail* lightplane entrants were powered by Douglas engines. The Douglas aero engine interests were acquired by Aero Engines Ltd in 1935 (*qv*).

Douglas: 17 hp, two-cylinder, horizontally-opposed, air-cooled. **Bore and Stroke:** Not available. **Capacity:** 500 cc. **Normal engine speed:** 2,500 rpm to produce 10 hp. **Maximum engine speed:** 4,000 rpm to produce 17 hp. **Weight:** 58 lb. **Aircraft in which engine was flown:** Parnall Pixie I, Avro 558.

Luton Anzani

Luton Aircraft Ltd, Phoenix Works, Gerrard's Cross, Bucks

Luton Aircraft Ltd, formed by C.H. Latimer-Needham in November 1935 to build aircraft of his

Luton Anzani.

own design, acquired the manufacturing rights for the Anzani V-twin. Luton produced a much-modified improvement which included redesigning the valves, the fitting of dual ignition and fitment of impulse starters.

Luton Anzani: 35 hp, two-cylinder, inverted Vee, air-cooled. **Bore and stroke:** 83 mm × 101.5 mm. **Capacity:** 1,098 cc. **Normal engine speed:** 2,700 rpm to produce 23 hp. **Maximum engine speed:** 3,000 rpm to produce 35 hp. **Weight:** 110 lb. **Aircraft in which engine was flown:** Luton Buzzard.

Pobjoy

Pobjoy Airmotors Ltd, Hooton Park Aerodrome, Wirral, Cheshire

While Captain D.R. Pobjoy was an education officer at RAF Cranwell he designed a very light seven-cylinder air-cooled radial engine. It was hoped that the first engine, designated Pobjoy P, would be fitted into the Cranwell Light Aeroplane Club's CLA 4, designed by Flight Lieutenant Nicholas Comper for the 1926 Lympne trials. In the event the engine was not ready in time but it was developed further until finally, in 1928, it passed the official Air Ministry type test. The first batch of Pobjoy engines was produced by George Parnall but on leaving the RAF in 1930 Captain Pobjoy formed Pobjoy Airmotors to put a developed Pobjoy, known as the R, into quantity production. Because the seven pistons of the Pobjoy engine ran at high revolutions the engine produced virtually no vibration and drove a geared propeller. This lightweight engine became one of the most popular light engines of the period.

Pobjoy P1: 67 hp, seven-cylinder radial, air-cooled. **Bore and stroke:** 72 mm × 87 mm. **Capacity:** 2,478 cc. **Normal engine speed:** 3,000 rpm to produce 64 hp. **Maximum engine speed:** 3,300 rpm to produce 67.5 hp. **Weight:** 115 lb. **Aircraft in which engine was flown:** Comper Swift.

Pobjoy R: 85 hp, seven-cylinder, radial, air-cooled. **Bore and stroke:** 77 mm × 87 mm. **Capacity:** 2,835 cc. **Normal engine speed:** 3,000 rpm to produce 75 hp. **Maximum engine speed:** 3,300 rpm to produce 85 hp. **Weight:** 130 lb. **Aircraft in which engine was flown:** Comper Swift, Comper C-25 Autogiro, Miles Satyr, Kay Gyroplane.

Pobjoy Niagara: 90 hp, seven-cylinder, radial, air-cooled. **Bore and stroke:** 77 mm × 87 mm. **Capacity:** 2,835 cc. **Normal engine speed:** 3,200 rpm to produce 84 hp. **Maximum engine speed:** 3,500 rpm to produce 90 hp. **Weight:** 154 lb. **Aircraft in which engine was flown:** Shapley Kittiwake Mk II, Hafner AR III Mk II Gyroplane.

Praga

Praga, Ceskomoravska-Kolben-Danek Company, Prague, Czechoslovakia

Formerly known as Breitfeld-Danek and Company, this firm began building aero engines of the Hiero type, under licence, in 1915. After the First World War the company produced engines of original design in addition to its licence-building activities. In 1937 the Praga D and DR engines first appeared. The earlier Praga B engine is described below.

Praga B: 46 hp two-cylinder, air-cooled flat-twin, opposed. **Bore and stroke:** 105 mm × 110 mm. **Capacity:** 1,904 cc. **Normal engine speed:** 2,440 rpm to produce 42 hp. **Maximum engine speed:** 2,510 rpm to produce 46 hp. **Weight:** 105.7 lb. **Aircraft in which engine was flown:** Hillson Praga.

Salmson

Société des Moteurs Salmson, Billancourt, Seine, France

The French Salmson company began manufacturing aero engines in 1912, specializing in water-cooled radial units. As early as 1913 the Dunbridge Iron Works company was licence-building the water-cooled Salmson (Canton-Unné) radial engine at its Stroud works. In 1930 another British company took out a licence to build Salmson aero engines at Raynes Park in London. The British Salmson Aero Engines company produced amongst others the AD9 radial engine, which most suited light aircraft and powered several ultra-light types during the 1930s.

Salmson AD9 and AD9R: 54 hp, nine-cylinder, radial, air-cooled. **Bore and stroke:** 70 mm × 86 mm. **Capacity:** 2,970 cc. **Normal engine speed:** 2,100 rpm to produce 48 hp. **Maximum engine speed:** 2,310 rpm to produce 54 hp. **Weight:** 160 lb. **Aircraft in which engine was flown:** Angus Aquila, Comper CLA 7 Swift, Boulton and Paul P 41 Phoenix and Hinkler Ibis.

Sarolea

Sarolea, Maison Sarolea SA, Herstal, Belgium

This company was founded in 1850 to manufacture small arms. In 1898 it began building air-cooled engines and motor cycles and a few Vee-4 engines were produced in 1908. After the First World War Sarolea became one of Europe's largest motor cycle manufacturers. The company later developed two of its motor cycle engines for use in light aircraft; the 916 cc Epervier and the larger 1,100 cc Vautour, capable of producing 32 hp.

Sarolea Epervier: 27 hp, two-cylinder, flat-twin, horizontally-opposed, air-cooled. **Bore and stroke:**

Above *Pobjoy P* **Below** *Salmson AD9 MkII.*

Scott two-stroke engine.

Walter Mikron.

80.5 mm × 90 mm. **Capacity:** 916 cc. **Normal engine speed:** 3,000 rpm to produce 25 hp. **Maximum engine speed:** 3,650 rpm to produce 27.5 hp. **Weight:** 109 lb. **Aircraft in which engine was flown:** Tipsy S2.

Scott

The Scott Motor Cycle Company (owned by Scott Motors (Saltaire) Ltd, Shipley, Yorkshire

Universally known as a producer of motor cycles and light industrial engines, the Scott Motor Cycle Company introduced a light two-stroke engine during the mid-1930s designed specifically for use in ultra-light aircraft, in particular the Mignet HM 14.

Scott Flying Squirrel: 34 hp, two-cylinder, inverted, in-line, air-cooled. **Bore and stroke:** 73 mm × 78 mm. **Capacity:** 652 cc. **Normal engine speed:** 2,800 rpm to produce 16 hp. **Maximum engine speed:** 5,200 rpm to produce 34 hp. **Weight:** 85 lb. **Aircraft in which engine was flown:** Mignet HM 14, Luton Buzzard, De Bruyne Ladybird, Barnwell BSW Mk I.

Train

Etablissements E. Train, Courbevoie, France

Founded in 1889, this company was owned by one of France's earliest aviation pioneers. The firm produced a family of four inverted, in-line engines of two, four and six cylinders which used common general components. The 40 hp Train 4T was the lowest powered of the range and was suitable for powering light aircraft.

Train 4T: 45 hp, four-cylinder, inverted, in-line, air-cooled. **Bore and stroke:** 80 mm × 100 mm. **Capacity:** 2,010 cc. **Normal engine speed:** 2,300 rpm to produce 40 hp. **Maximum engine speed:** not available. **Weight:** 101 lb. **Aircraft in which engine was flown:** Chilton DW 1A.

Walter

Walter Motor Cars and Aero-engines, Ltd, Prague, Czechoslovakia

This company was formed in 1920 and began building water-cooled engines of its own design, as well as licence-building Bristol Jupiter radial engines. In 1929 A.S. Walter introduced air-cooled in-line engines to its range, including the Walter Minor and Mikron suitable for use in light aircraft.

Walter Mikron II: 62 hp four cylinder, in-line, inverted air-cooled. **Bore and stroke:** 88 mm × 96 mm. **Capacity:** 2,334 cc. **Normal engine speed:** 2,600 rpm to produce 60 hp. **Maximum engine speed:** 2,800 rpm to produce 62 hp. **Weight:** 135.5 lb. **Aircraft in which engine was flown:** Tipsy B, Luton Major.

Index